A Tropical Fish Yearns for Snow

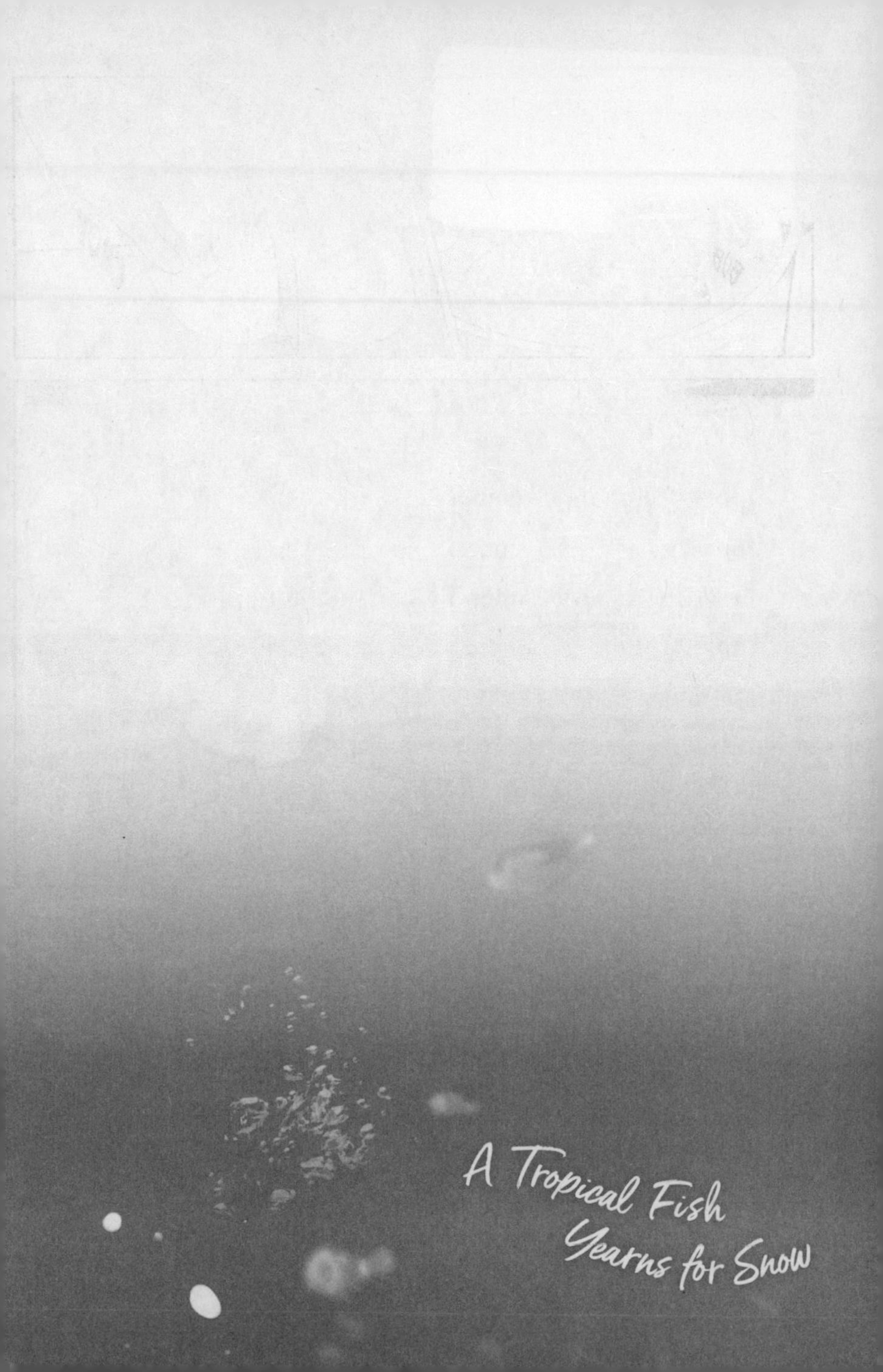
A Tropical Fish
Yearns for Snow

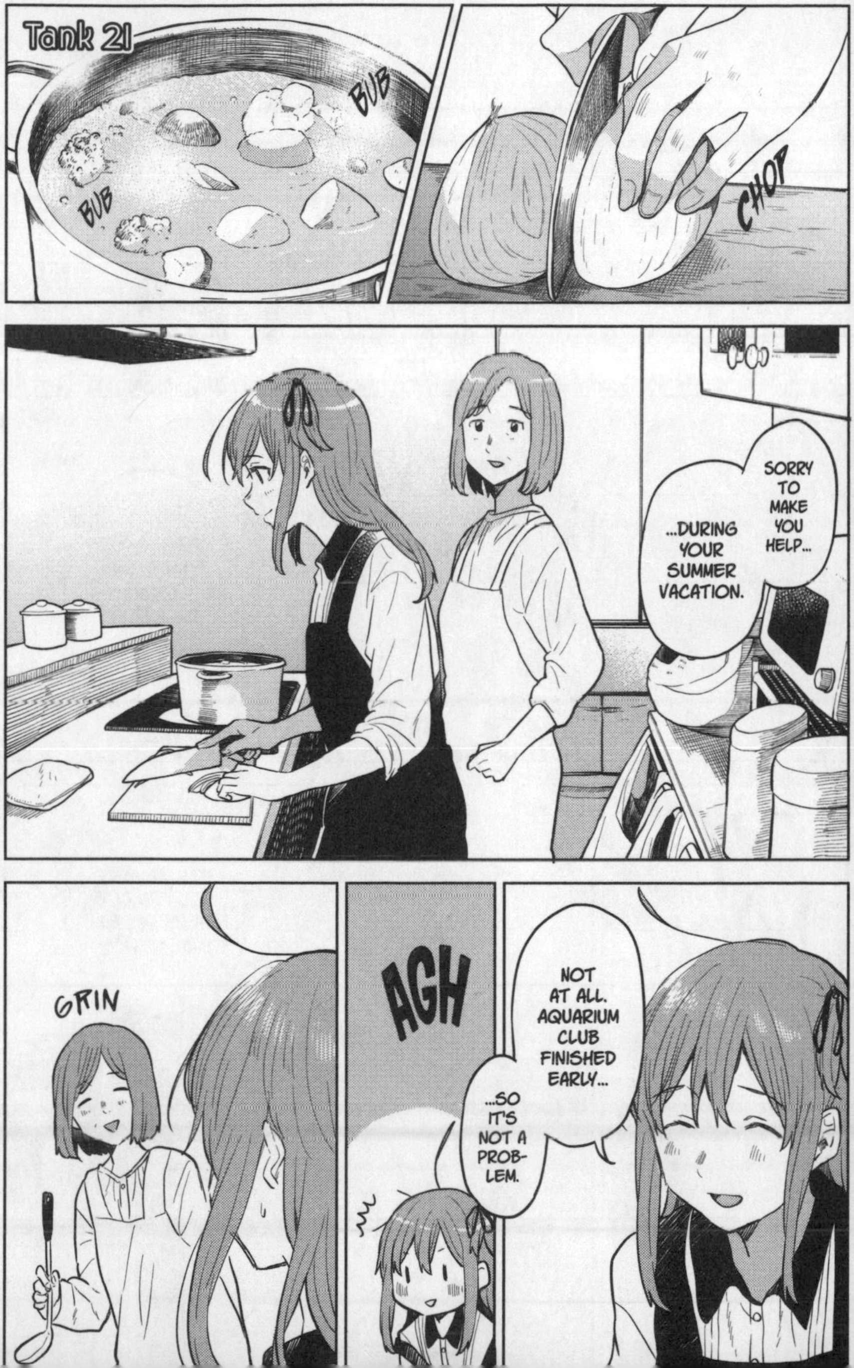
CHOP
Tank 21
BUB
BUB
SORRY TO MAKE YOU HELP...
...DURING YOUR SUMMER VACATION.
NOT AT ALL. AQUARIUM CLUB FINISHED EARLY...
...SO IT'S NOT A PROB-LEM.
AGH
GRIN

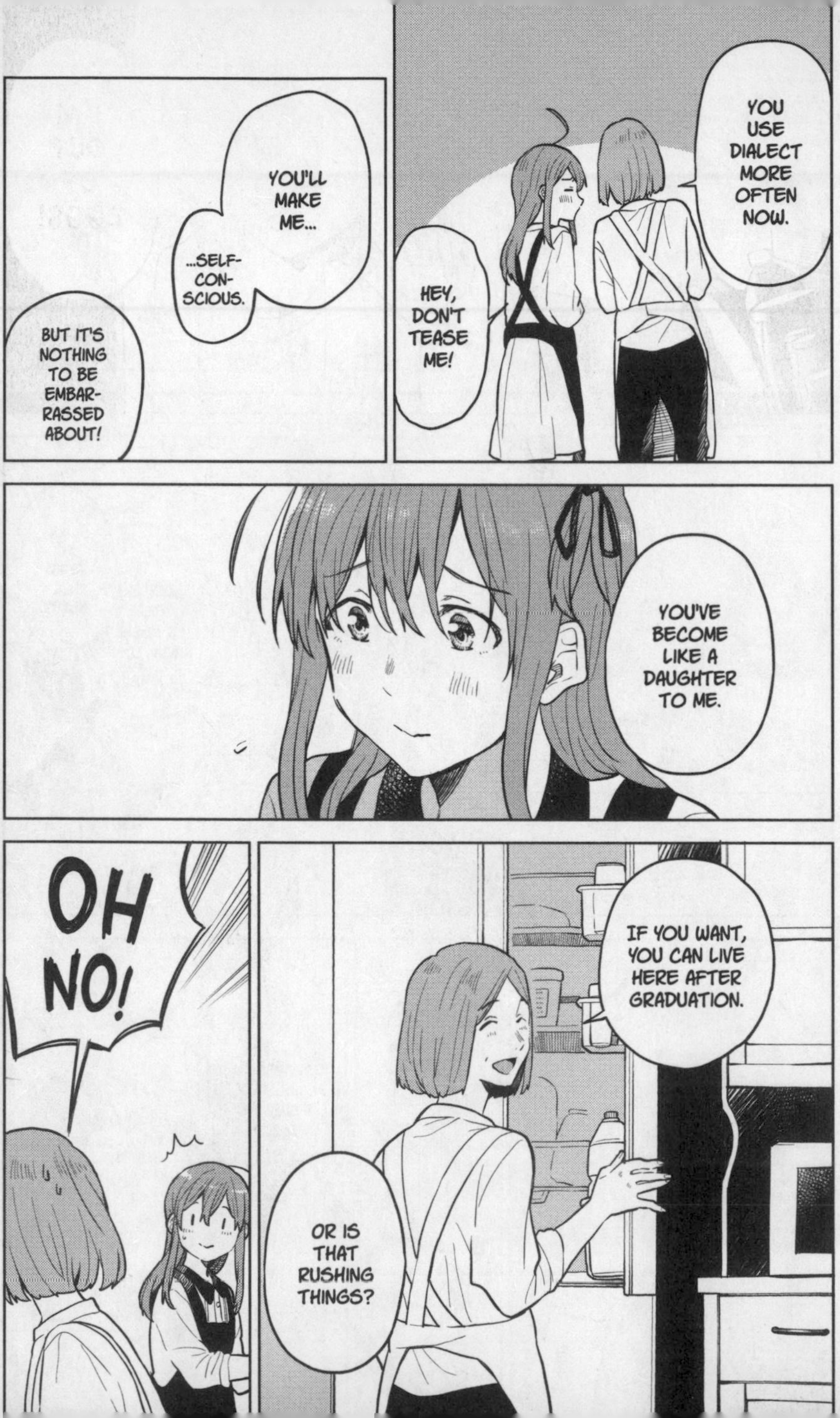
YOU USE DIALECT MORE OFTEN NOW.
HEY, DON'T TEASE ME!
YOU'LL MAKE ME...
...SELF-CONSCIOUS.
BUT IT'S NOTHING TO BE EMBARRASSED ABOUT!
YOU'VE BECOME LIKE A DAUGHTER TO ME.
IF YOU WANT, YOU CAN LIVE HERE AFTER GRADUATION.
OR IS THAT RUSHING THINGS?
OH NO!

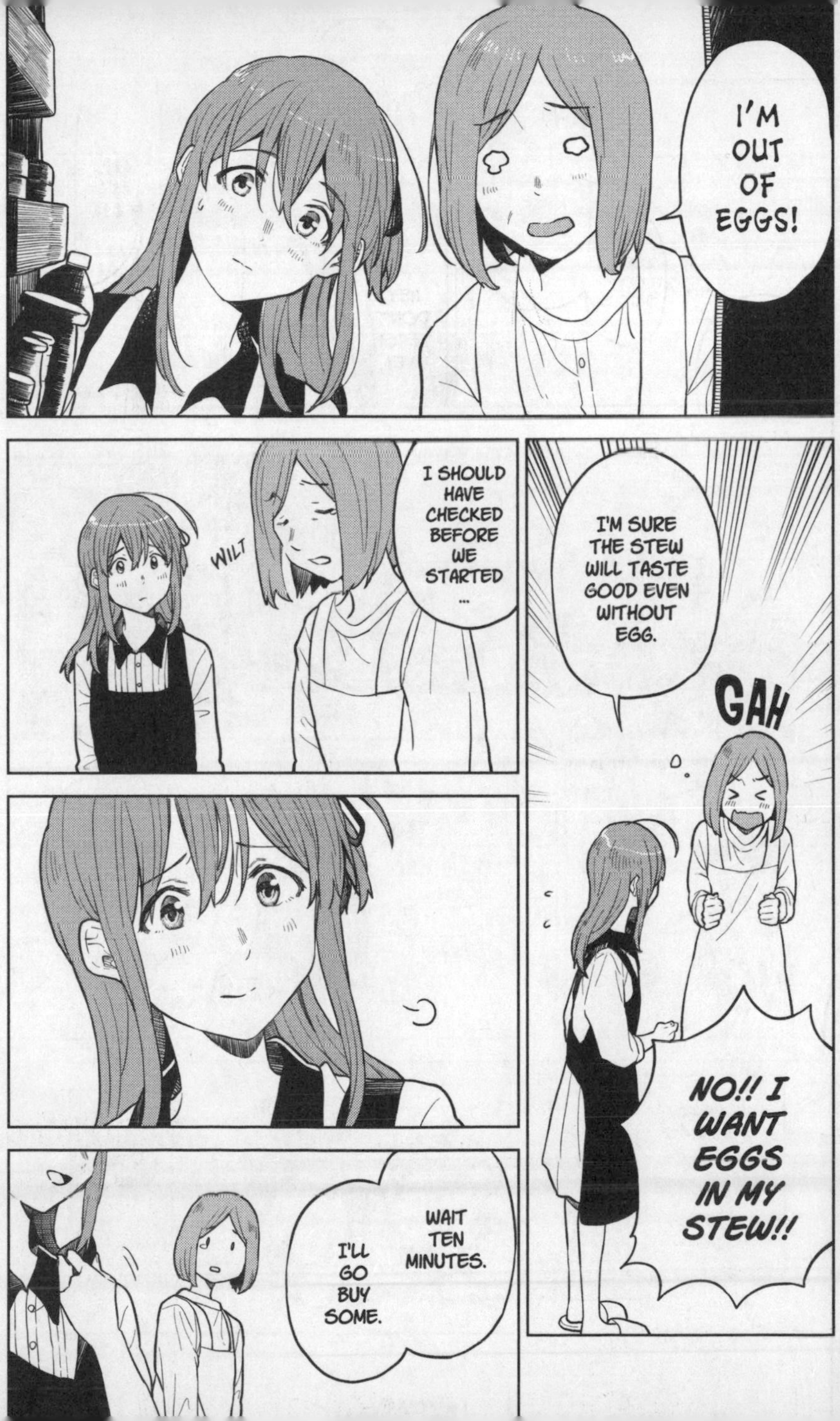
I'M OUT OF EGGS!
I'M SURE THE STEW WILL TASTE GOOD EVEN WITHOUT EGG.
GAH
NO!! I WANT EGGS IN MY STEW!!
I SHOULD HAVE CHECKED BEFORE WE STARTED ...
WILT
WAIT TEN MINUTES.
I'LL GO BUY SOME.

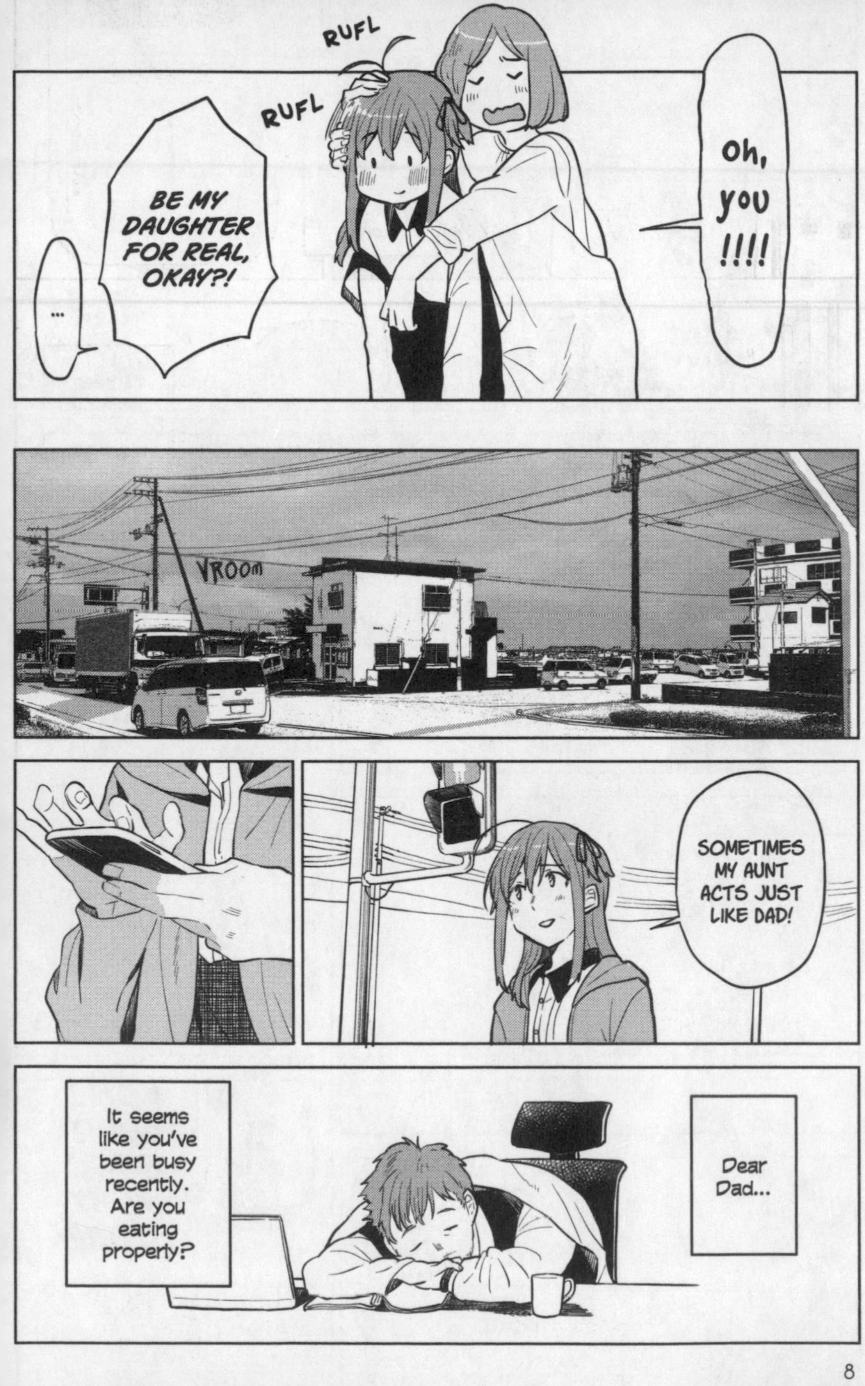
Oh, you !!!!
RUFL
RUFL
BE MY DAUGHTER FOR REAL, OKAY?!
...
VROOM
SOMETIMES MY AUNT ACTS JUST LIKE DAD!
Dear Dad...
It seems like you've been busy recently. Are you eating properly?

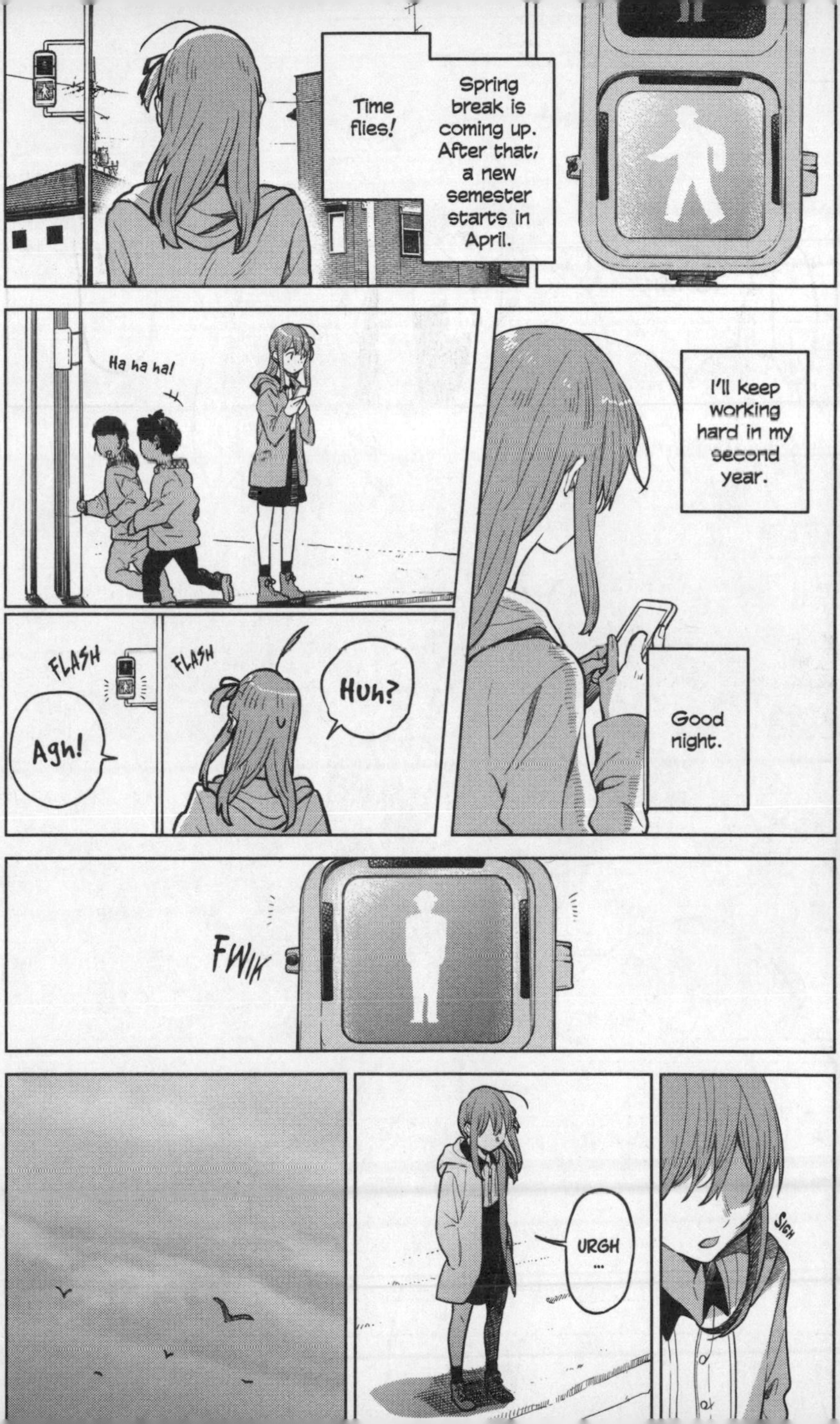
Spring break is coming up. After that, a new semester starts in April.
Time flies!
I'll keep working hard in my second year.
Good night.
Ha ha ha!
FLASH
Huh?
FLASH
Agh!
FWIK
SIGH
URGH ...

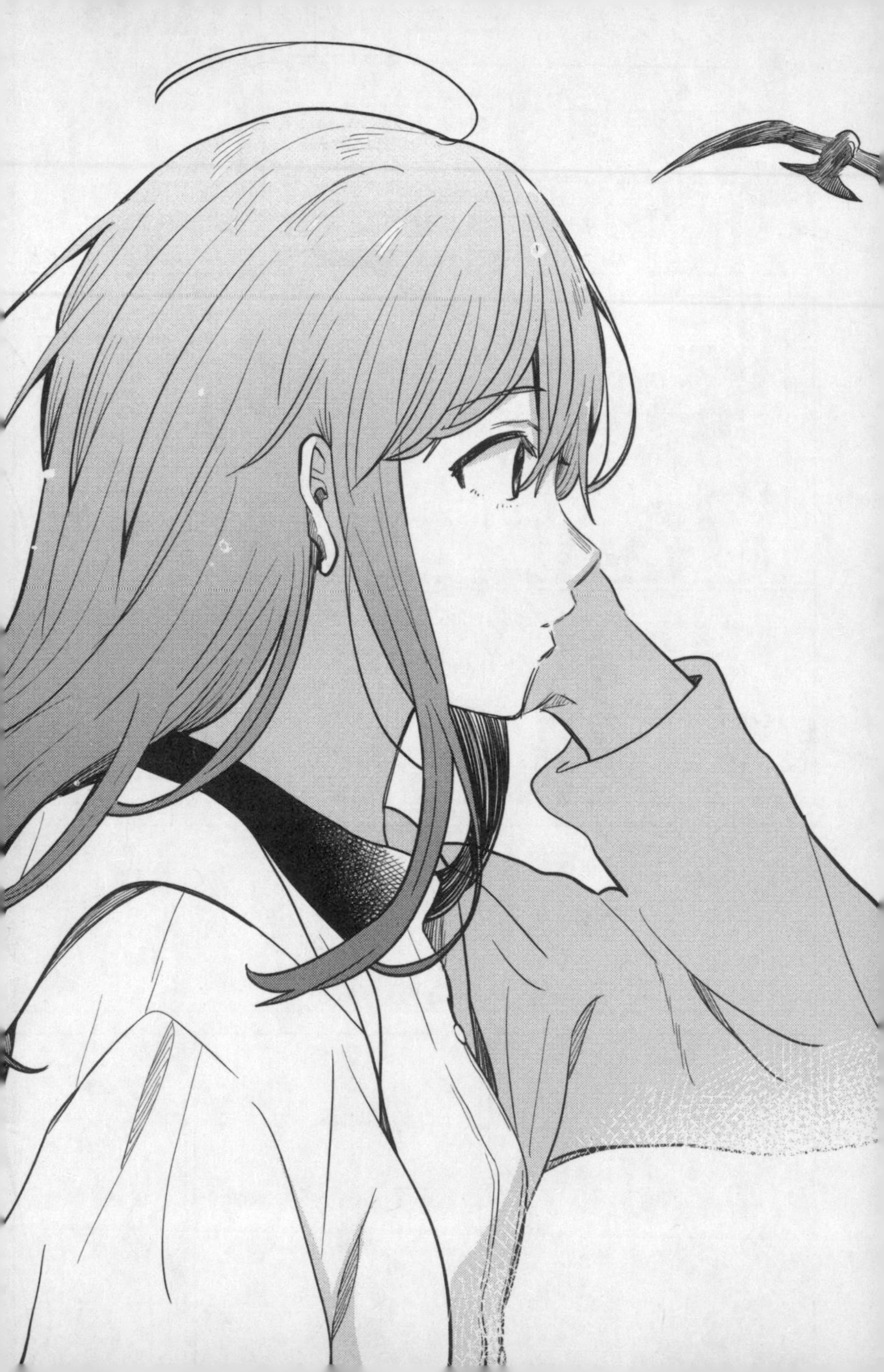

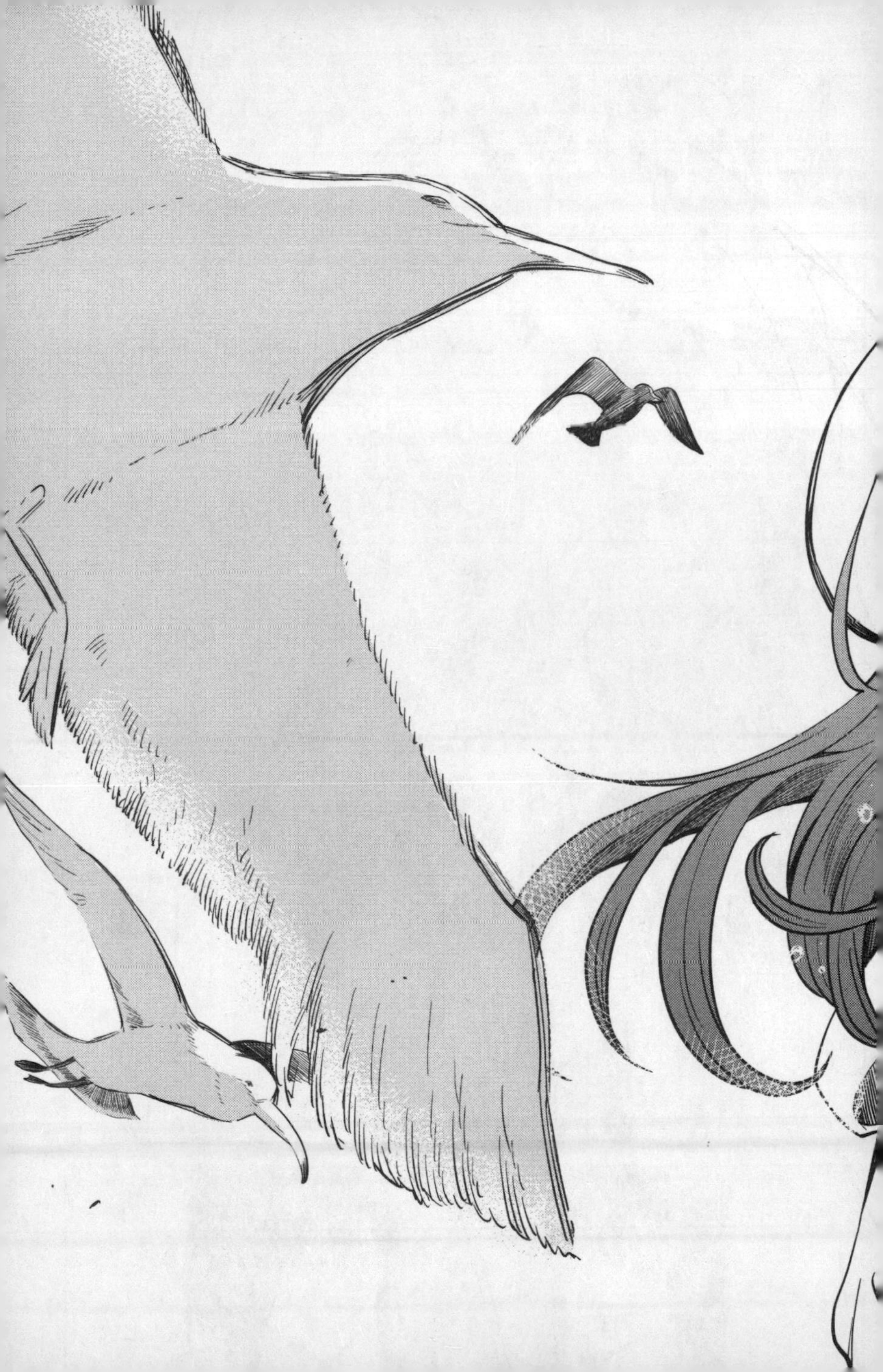

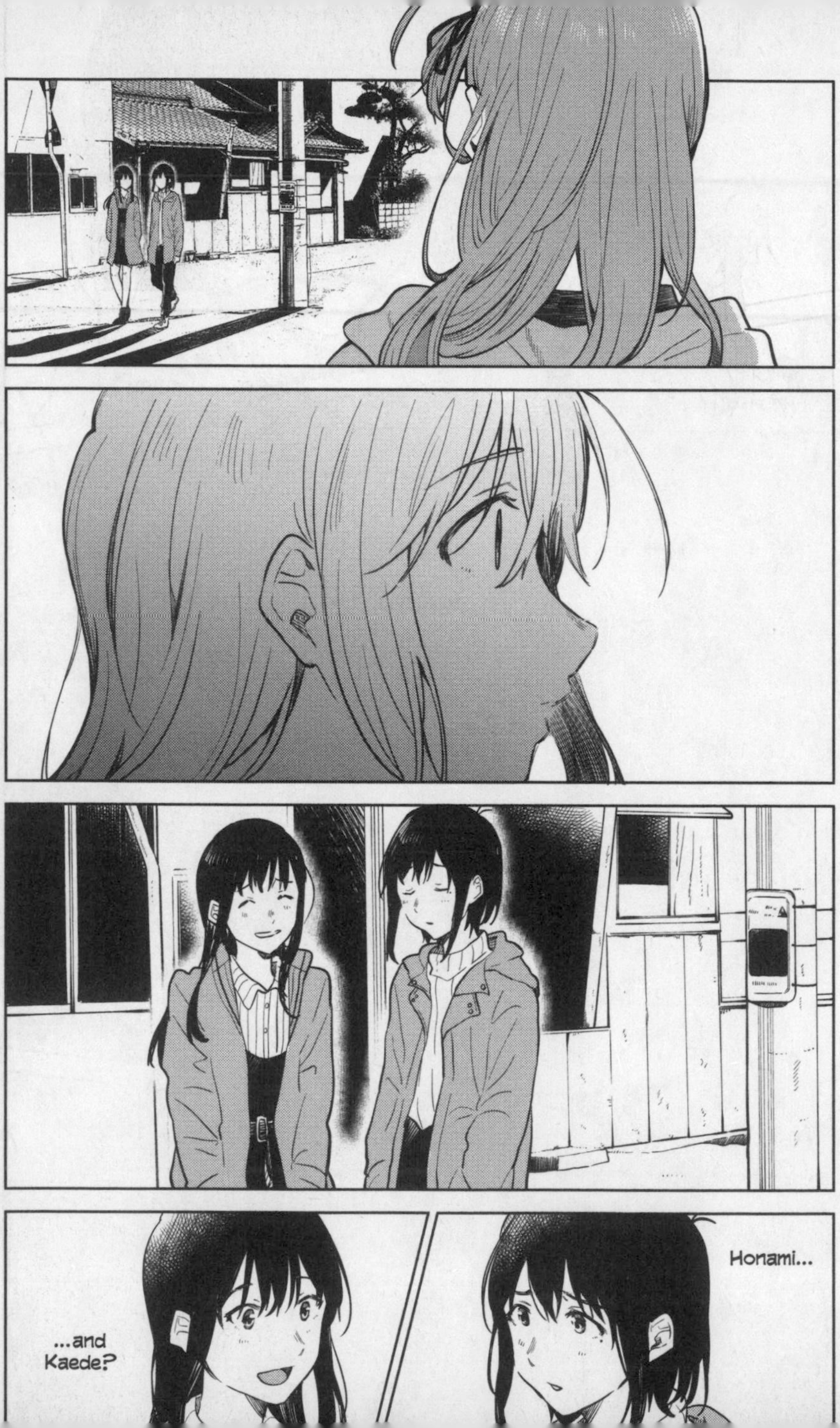
Honami...
...and Kaede?

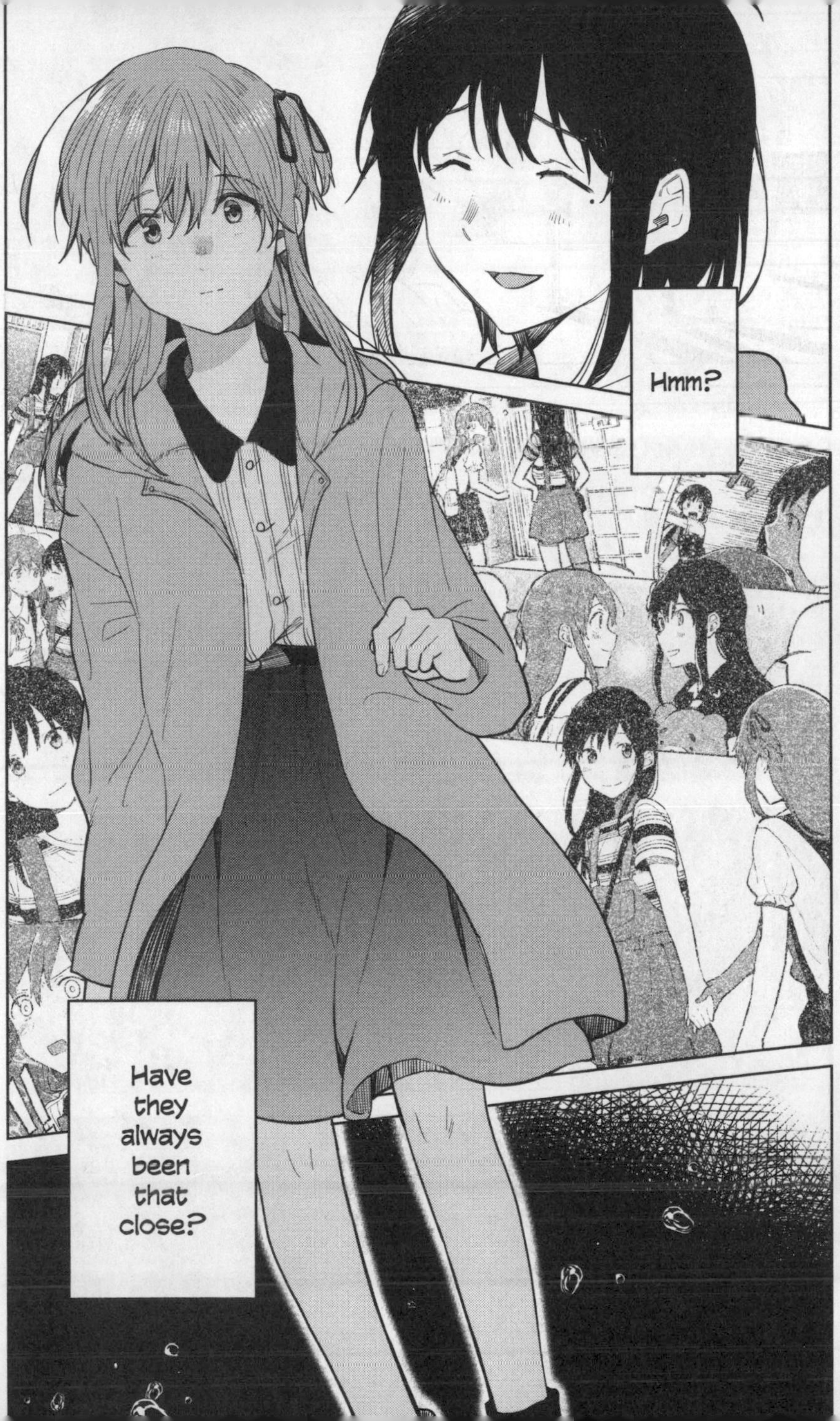
Hmm?
Have they always been that close?

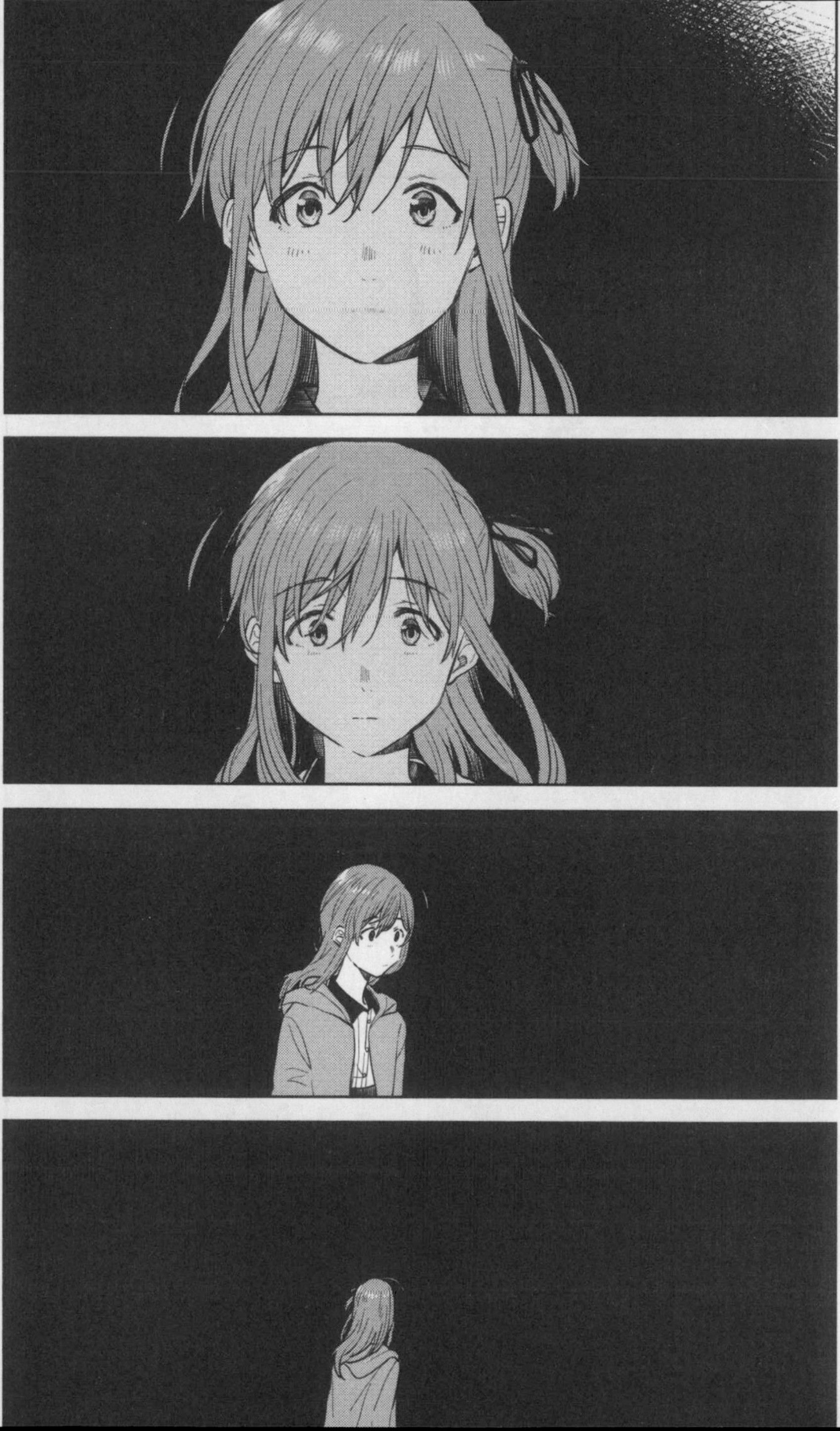

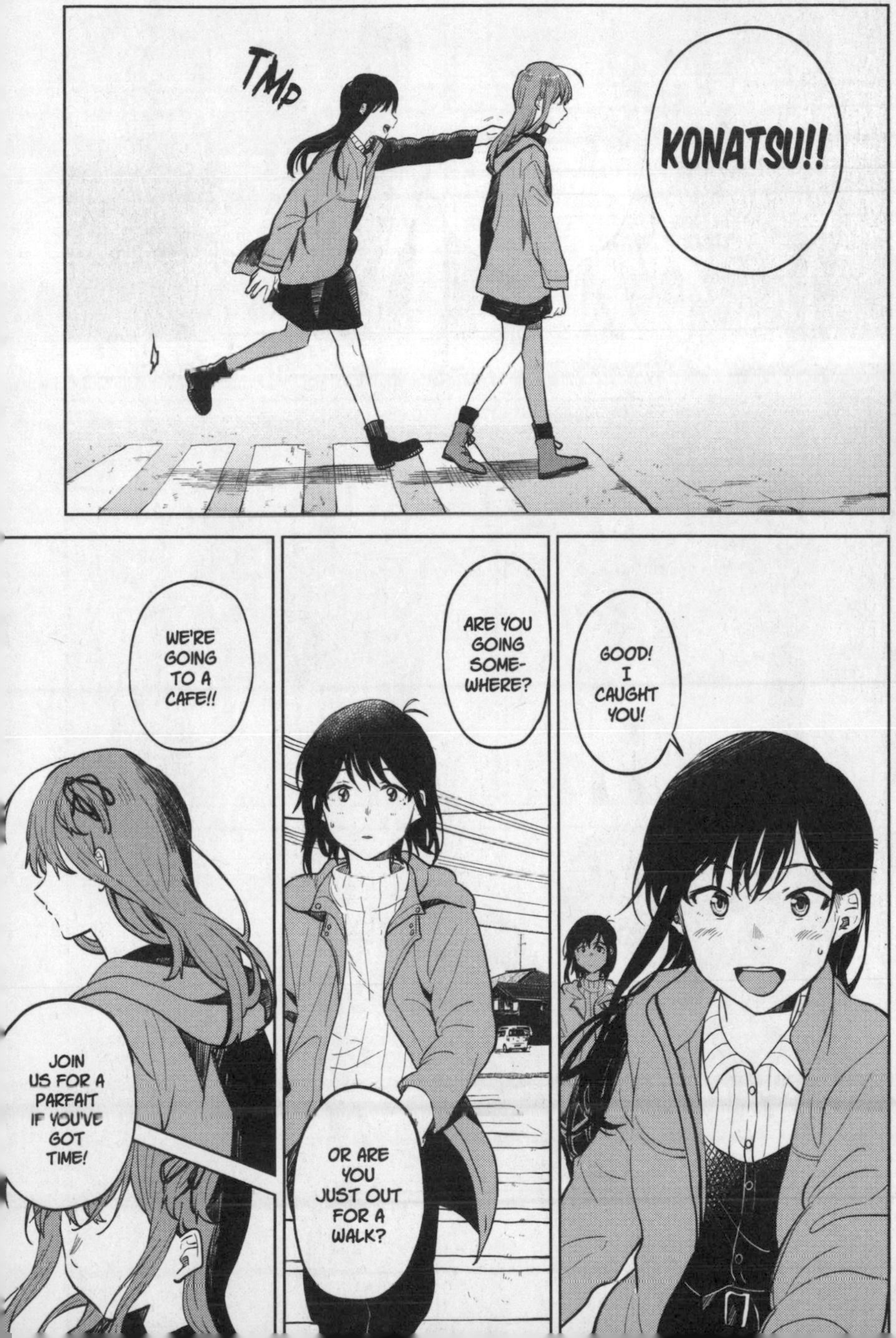
KONATSU!!
TMP
GOOD! I CAUGHT YOU!
ARE YOU GOING SOME-WHERE?
OR ARE YOU JUST OUT FOR A WALK?
WE'RE GOING TO A CAFE!!
JOIN US FOR A PARFAIT IF YOU'VE GOT TIME!

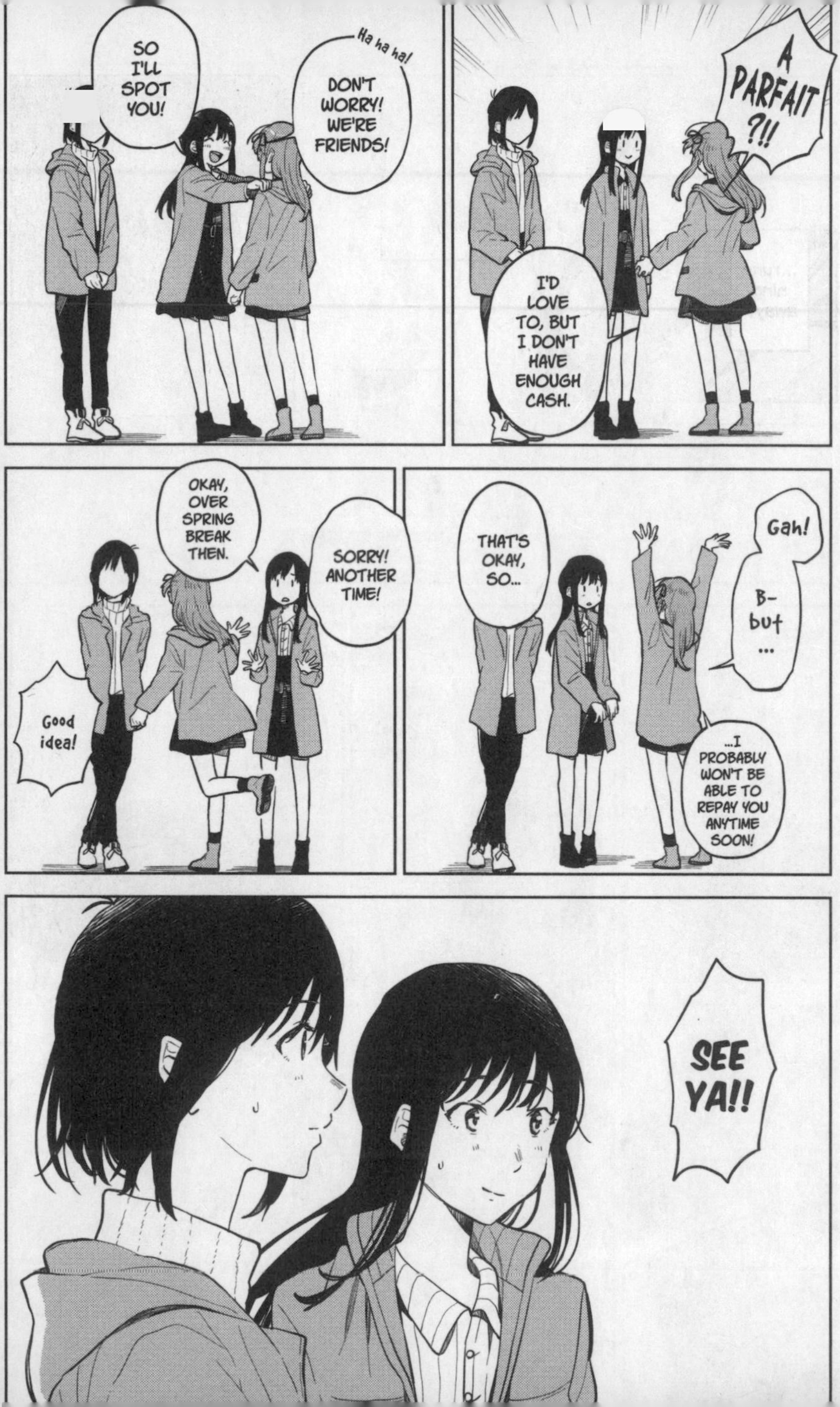
A PARFAIT?!!
I'D LOVE TO, BUT I DON'T HAVE ENOUGH CASH.
Ha ha ha!
DON'T WORRY! WE'RE FRIENDS!
SO I'LL SPOT YOU!
Gah!
B-but...
THAT'S OKAY, SO...
...I PROBABLY WON'T BE ABLE TO REPAY YOU ANYTIME SOON!
SORRY! ANOTHER TIME!
OKAY, OVER SPRING BREAK THEN.
Good idea!
SEE YA!!

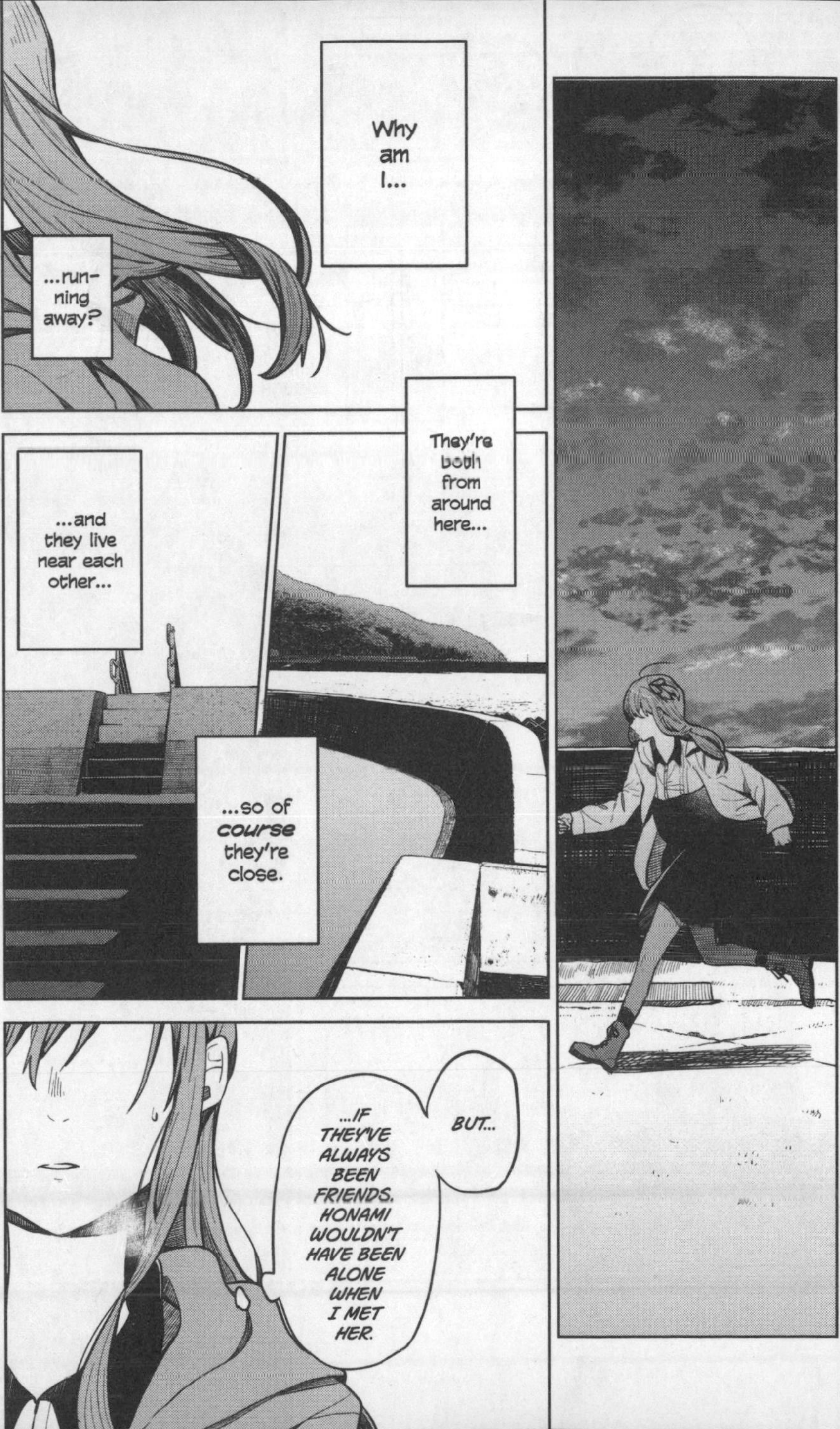

Why am I...
...running away?
They're both from around here...
...and they live near each other...
...so of *course* they're close.
BUT...
...IF THEY'VE ALWAYS BEEN FRIENDS, HONAMI WOULDN'T HAVE BEEN ALONE WHEN I MET HER.

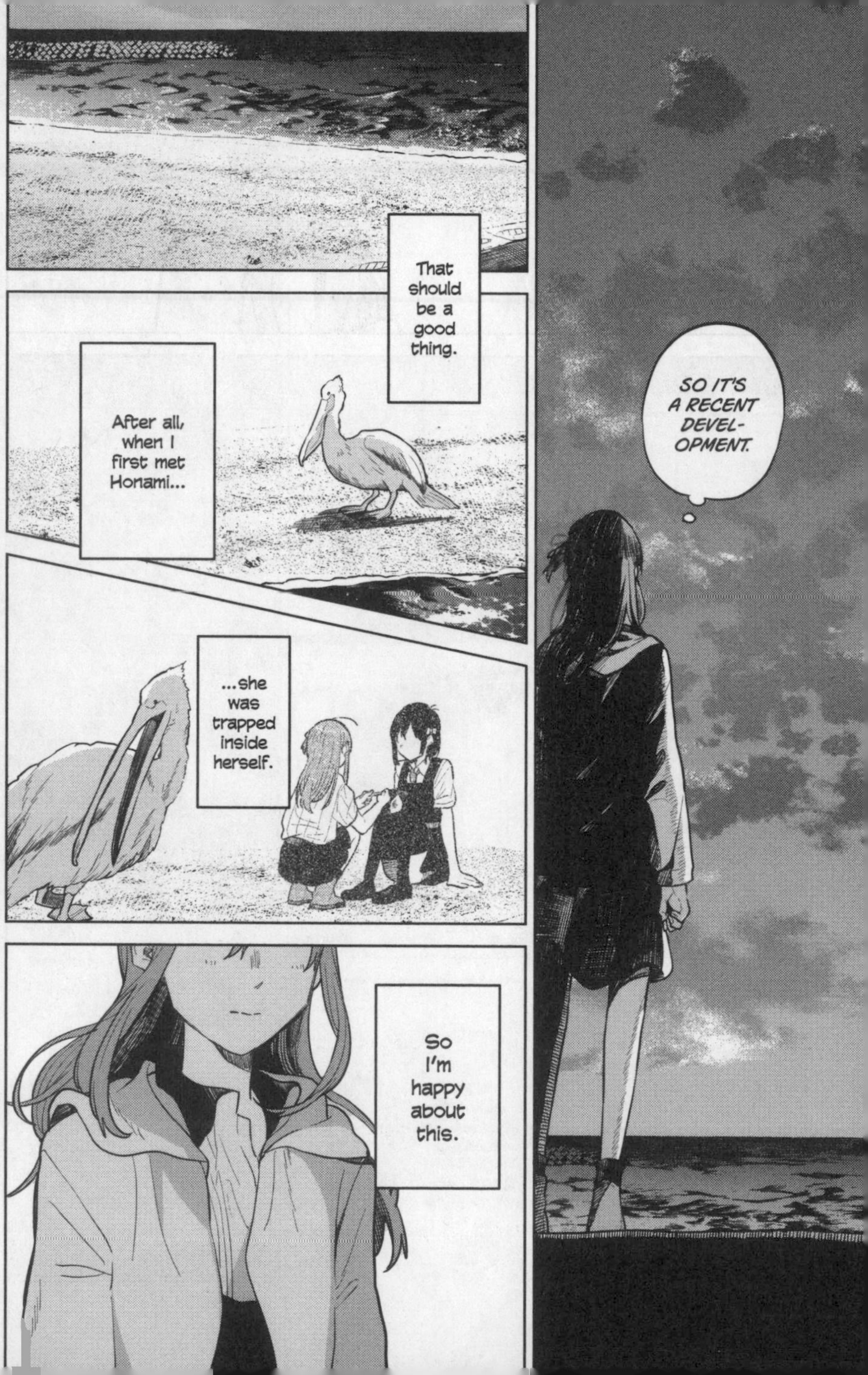
SO IT'S A RECENT DEVEL-OPMENT.
That should be a good thing.
After all, when I first met Honami...
...she was trapped inside herself.
So I'm happy about this.

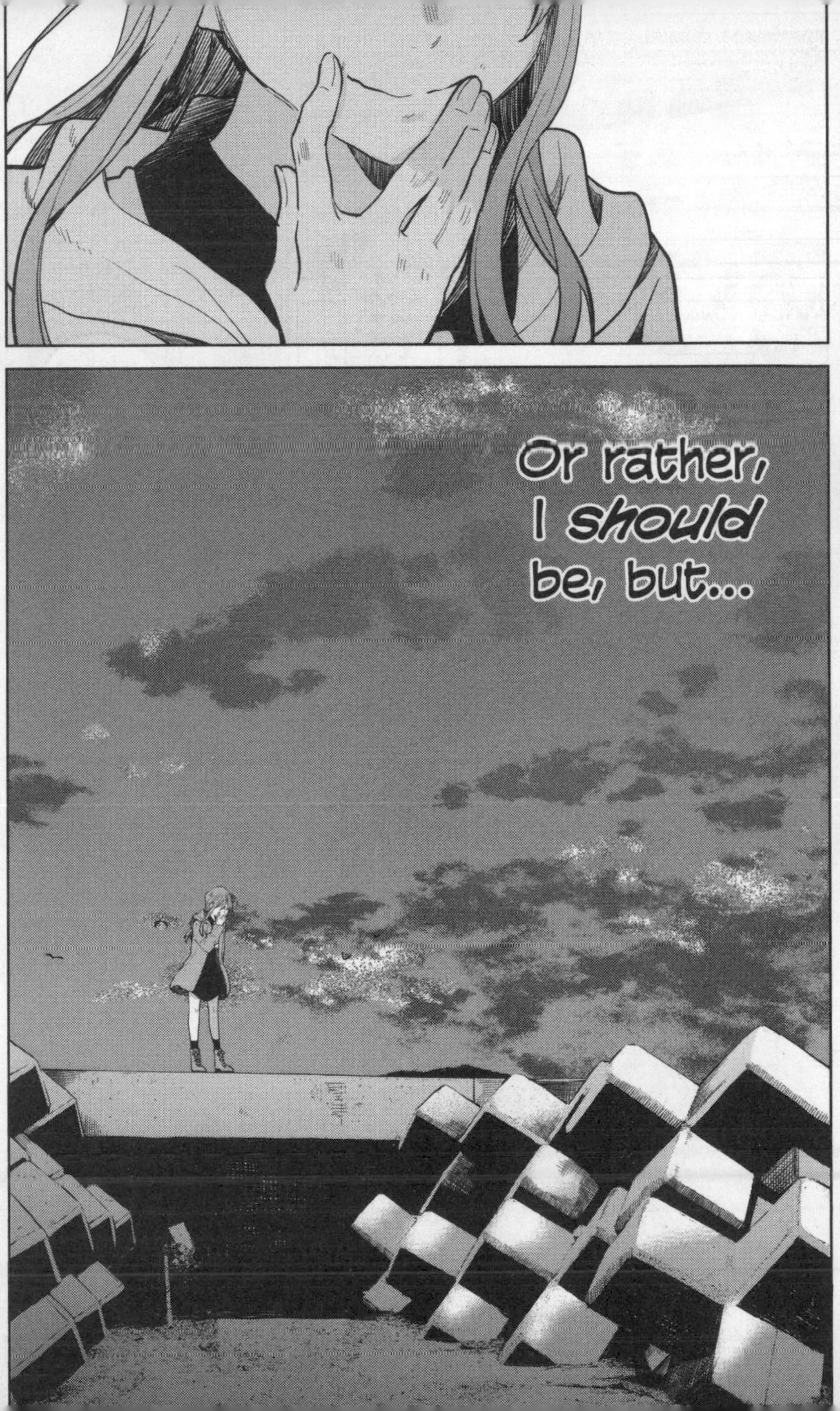
Or rather, I *should* be, but...

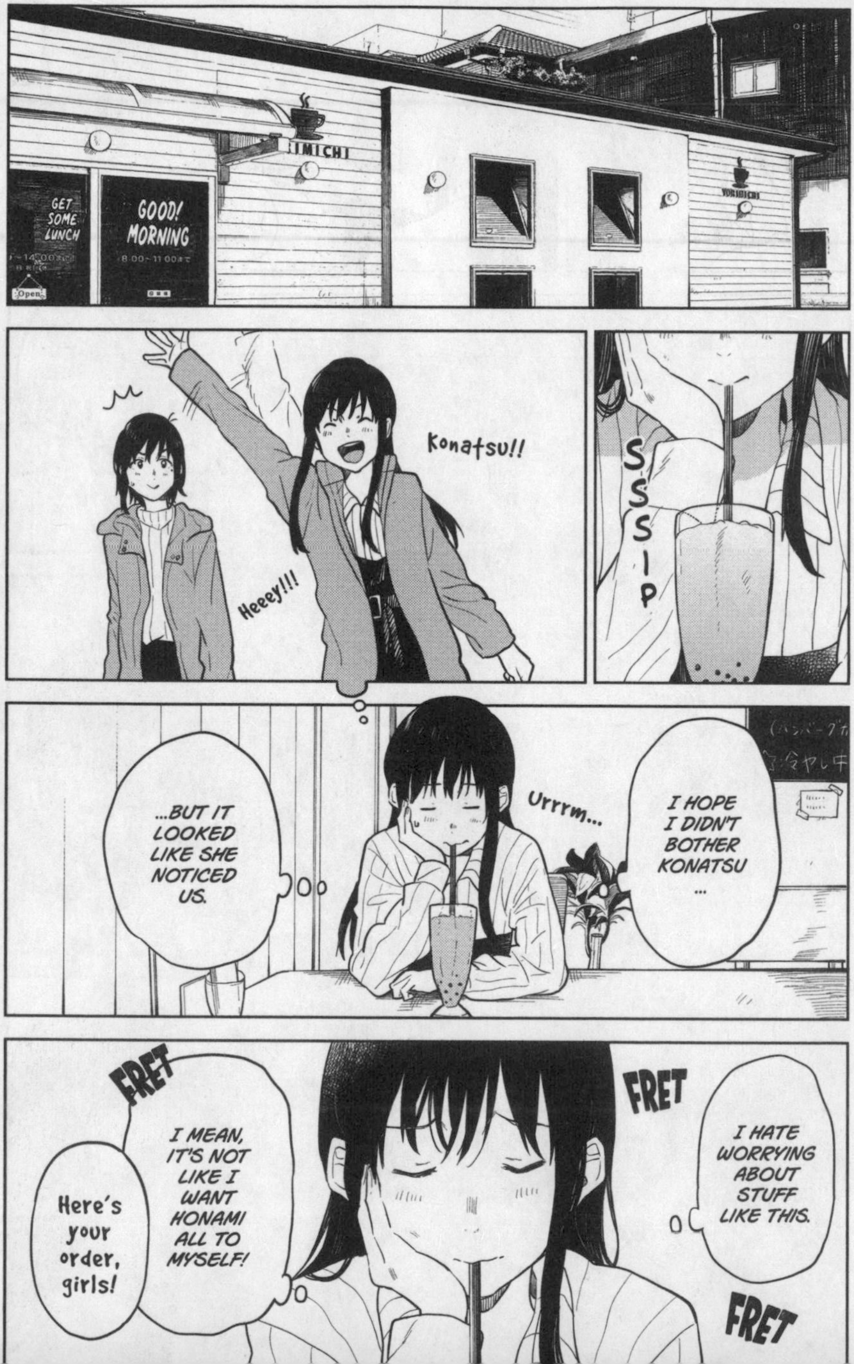
GET SOME LUNCH
GOOD! MORNING
8:00~11:00まで
Open
SSSIP
Konatsu!!
Heeey!!!
I HOPE I DIDN'T BOTHER KONATSU ...
Urrrm...
...BUT IT LOOKED LIKE SHE NOTICED US.
FRET
I HATE WORRYING ABOUT STUFF LIKE THIS.
FRET
I MEAN, IT'S NOT LIKE I WANT HONAMI ALL TO MYSELF!
FRET
Here's your order, girls!

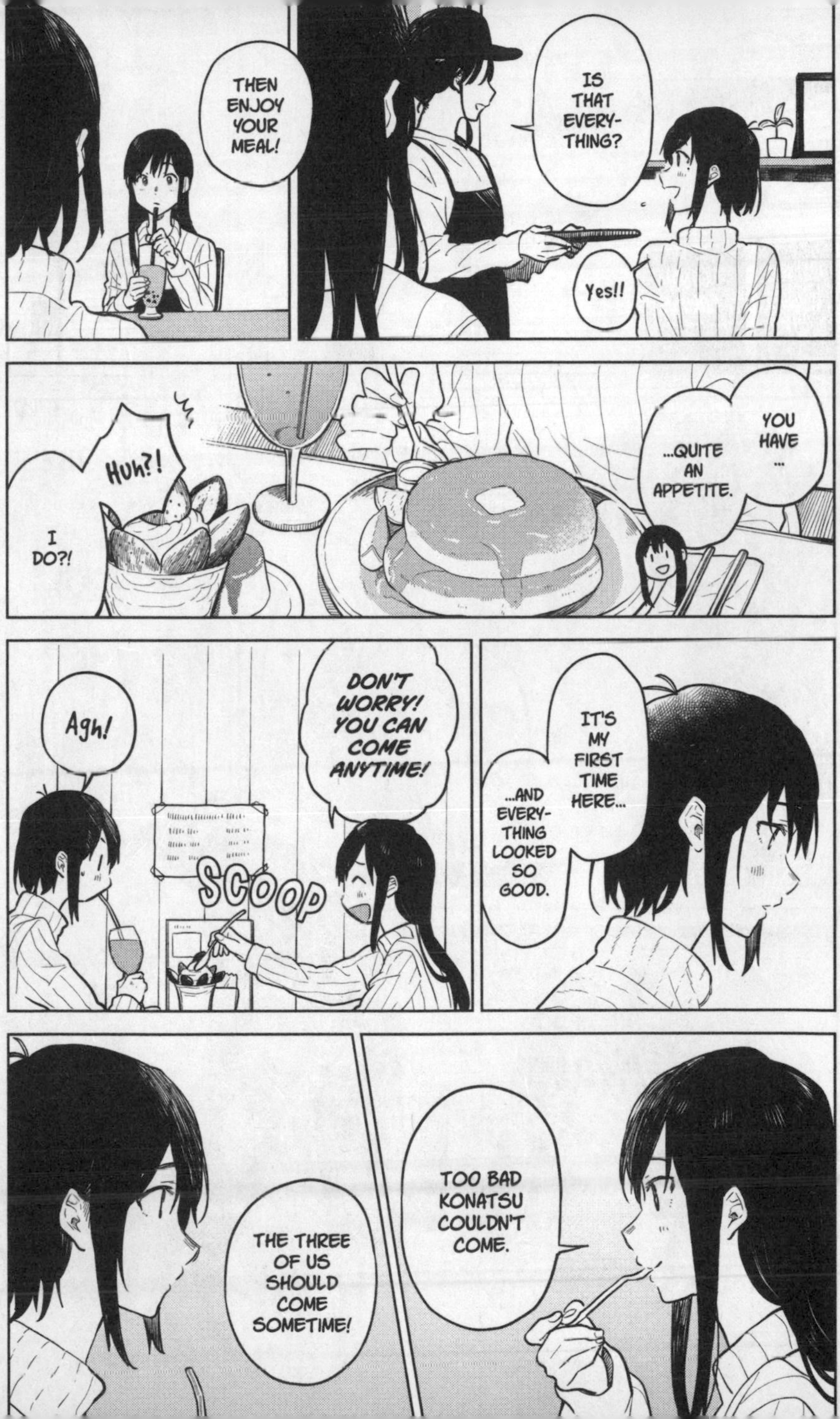
IS THAT EVERY-THING?
Yes!!
THEN ENJOY YOUR MEAL!
YOU HAVE ...
...QUITE AN APPETITE.
Huh?!
I DO?!
IT'S MY FIRST TIME HERE...
...AND EVERY-THING LOOKED SO GOOD.
DON'T WORRY! YOU CAN COME ANYTIME!
SCOOP
Agh!
TOO BAD KONATSU COULDN'T COME.
THE THREE OF US SHOULD COME SOMETIME!

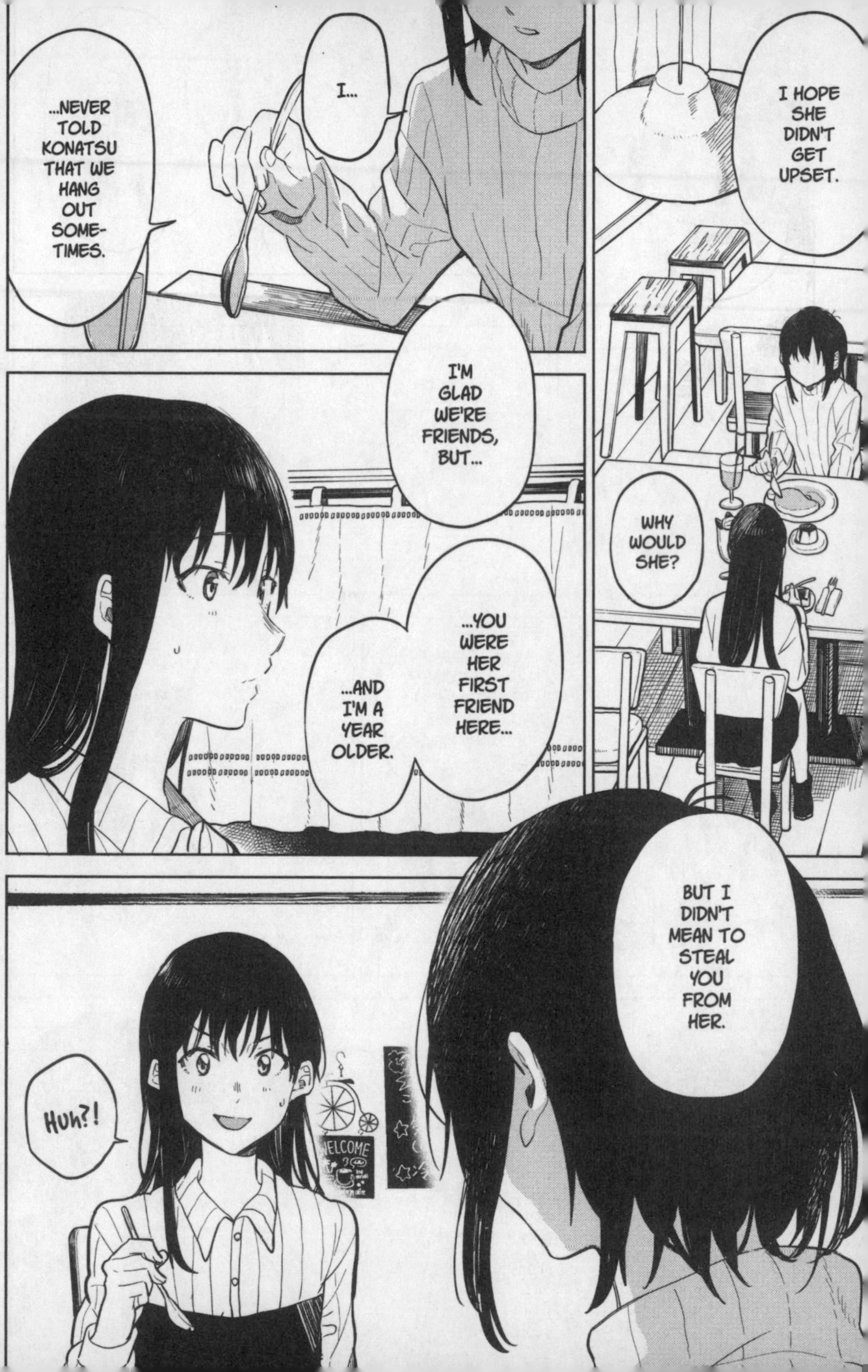
I HOPE SHE DIDN'T GET UPSET.
WHY WOULD SHE?
I...
...NEVER TOLD KONATSU THAT WE HANG OUT SOME-TIMES.
I'M GLAD WE'RE FRIENDS, BUT...
...YOU WERE HER FIRST FRIEND HERE...
...AND I'M A YEAR OLDER.
BUT I DIDN'T MEAN TO STEAL YOU FROM HER.
WELCOME
Huh?!

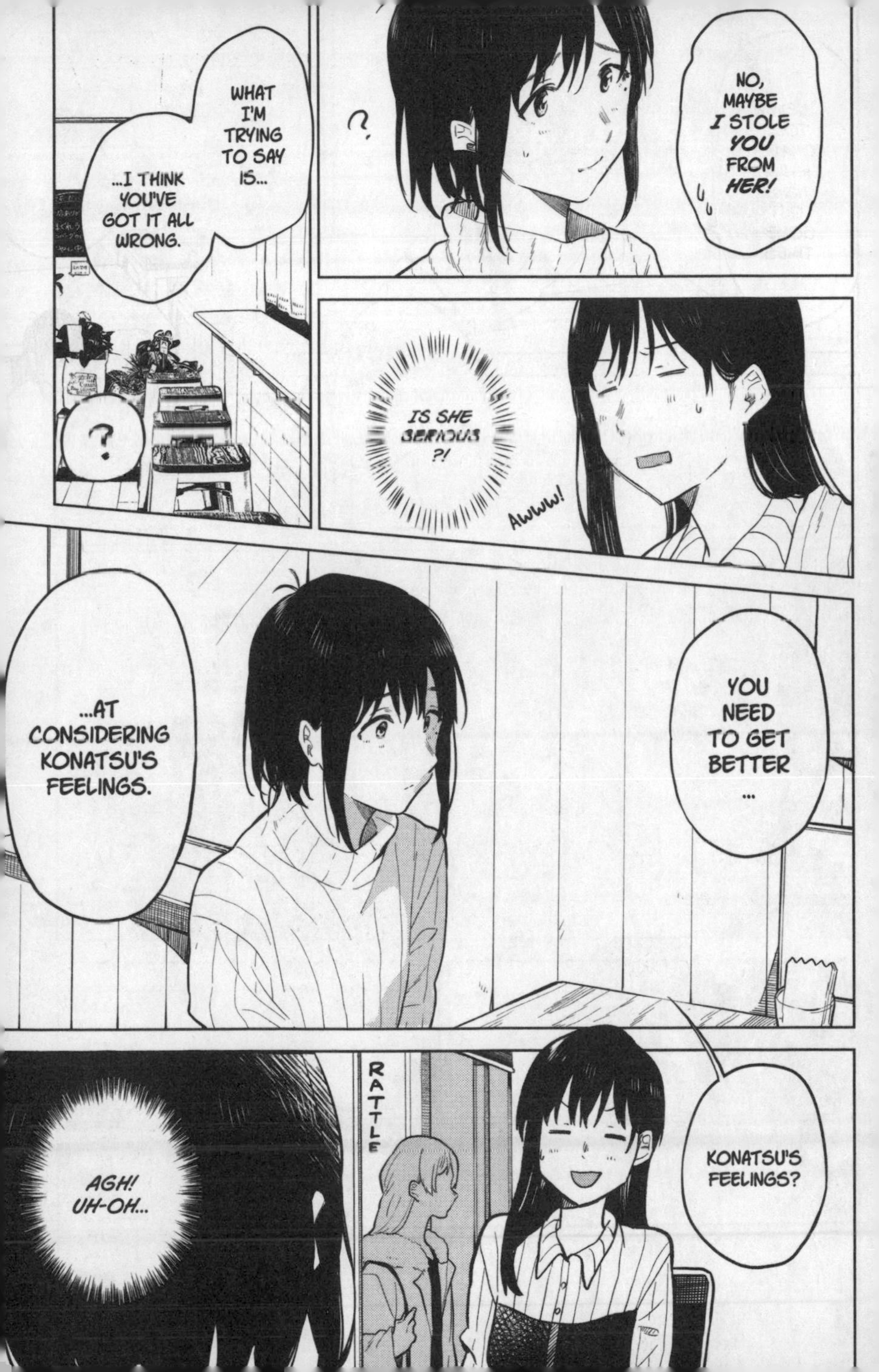
NO, MAYBE I STOLE YOU FROM HER!
?
IS SHE SERIOUS ?!
AWWW!
WHAT I'M TRYING TO SAY IS...
...I THINK YOU'VE GOT IT ALL WRONG.
?
YOU NEED TO GET BETTER ...
...AT CONSIDERING KONATSU'S FEELINGS.
KONATSU'S FEELINGS?
RATTLE
AGH! UH-OH...

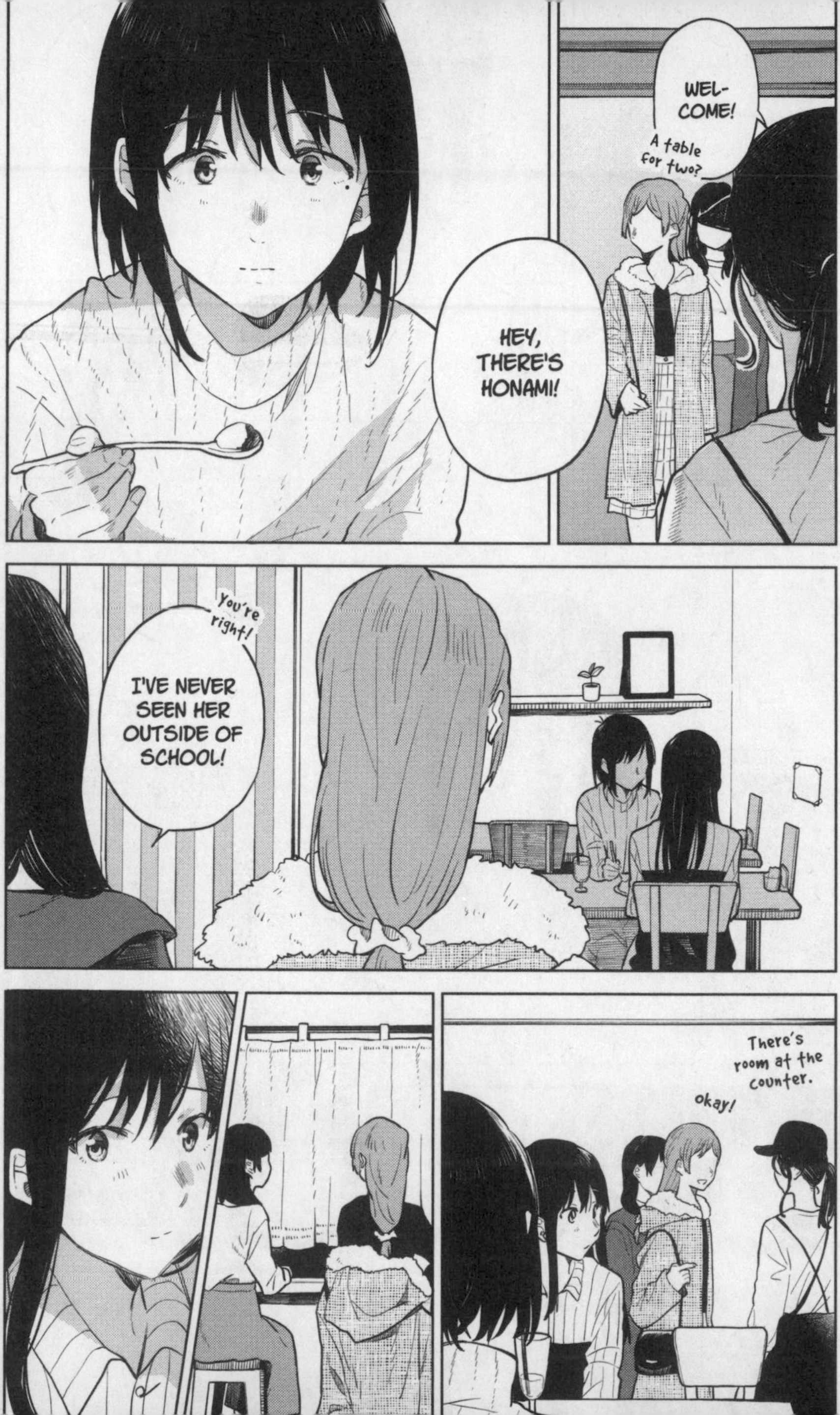
WEL-
COME!
A table for two?
HEY, THERE'S HONAMI!
You're right!
I'VE NEVER SEEN HER OUTSIDE OF SCHOOL!
There's room at the counter.
okay!

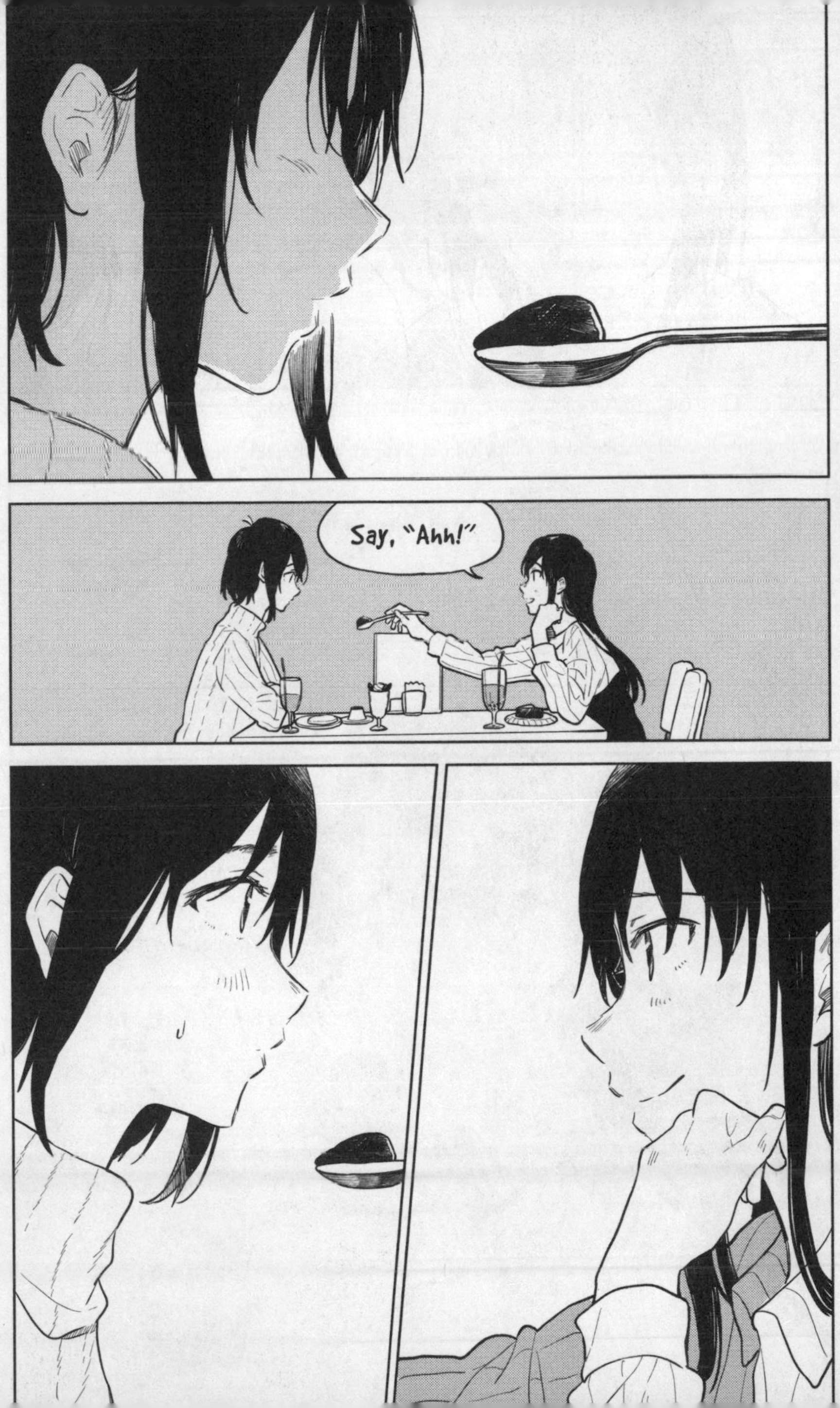
Say, "Ahh!"

UM...

C'MON, TAKE A BITE.

IT'S ALL RIGHT.

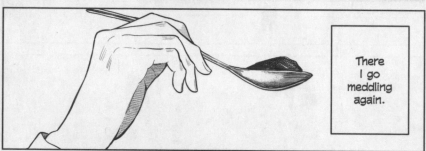

There I go meddling again.

BUT I JUST WANT TO BRING THEM TOGETHER.

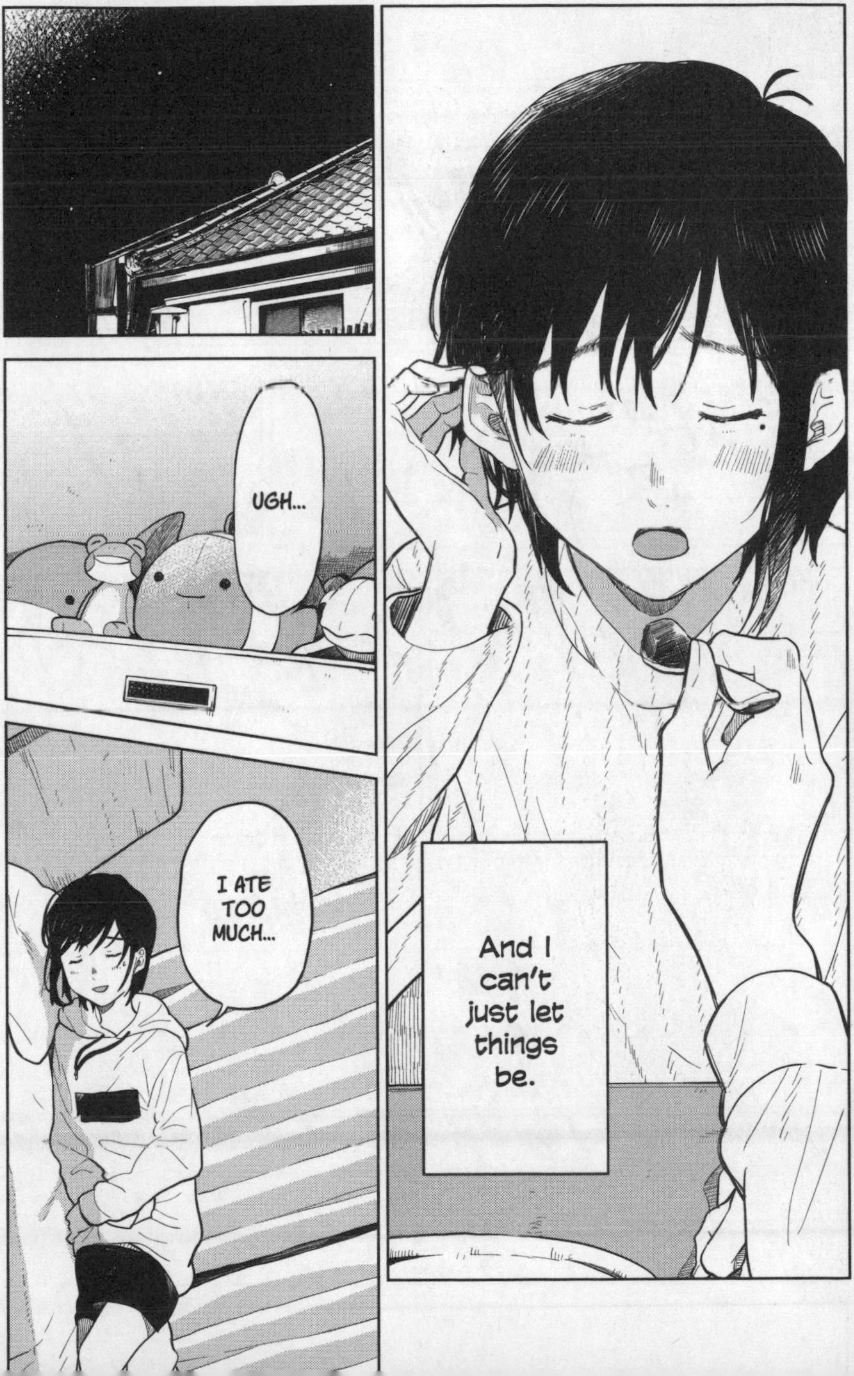
And I can't just let things be.
UGH...
I ATE TOO MUCH...

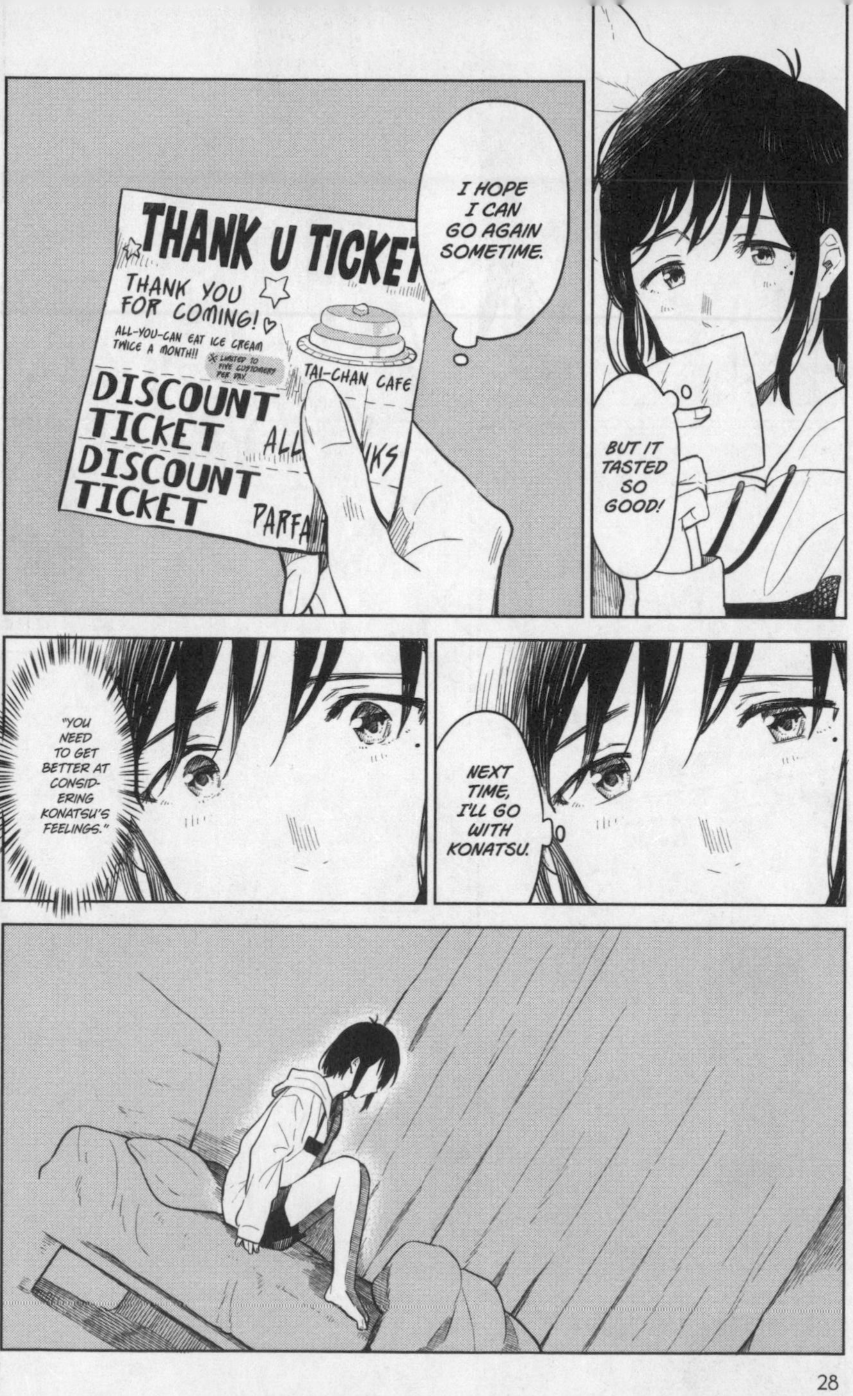
BUT IT TASTED SO GOOD!
I HOPE I CAN GO AGAIN SOMETIME.
THANK U TICKET
THANK YOU FOR COMING!
ALL-YOU-CAN EAT ICE CREAM TWICE A MONTH!!
※ LIMITED TO FIVE CUSTOMERS PER DAY.
TAI-CHAN CAFE
DISCOUNT TICKET
DISCOUNT TICKET
NEXT TIME, I'LL GO WITH KONATSU.
"YOU NEED TO GET BETTER AT CONSID-ERING KONATSU'S FEELINGS."

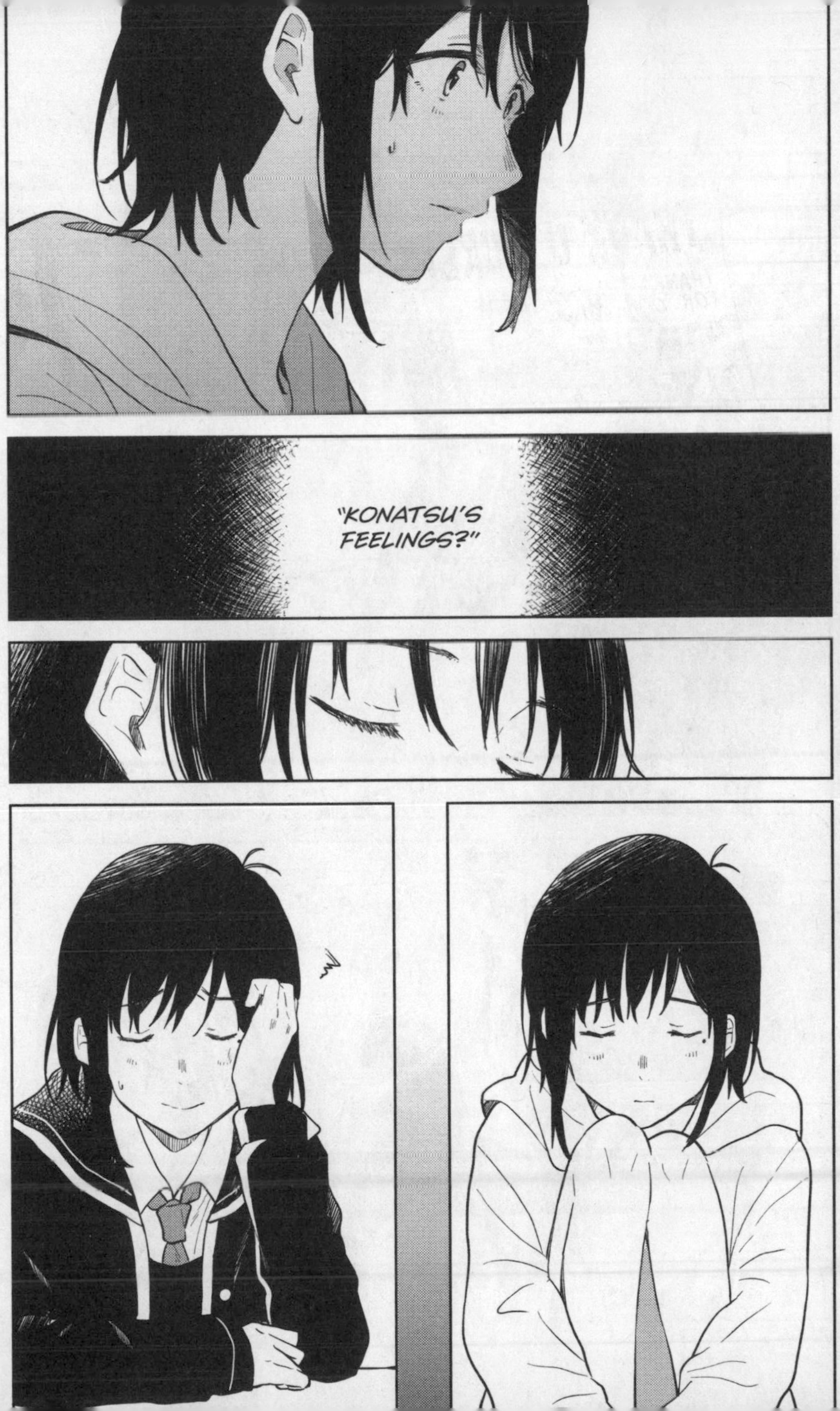
"KONATSU'S FEELINGS?"

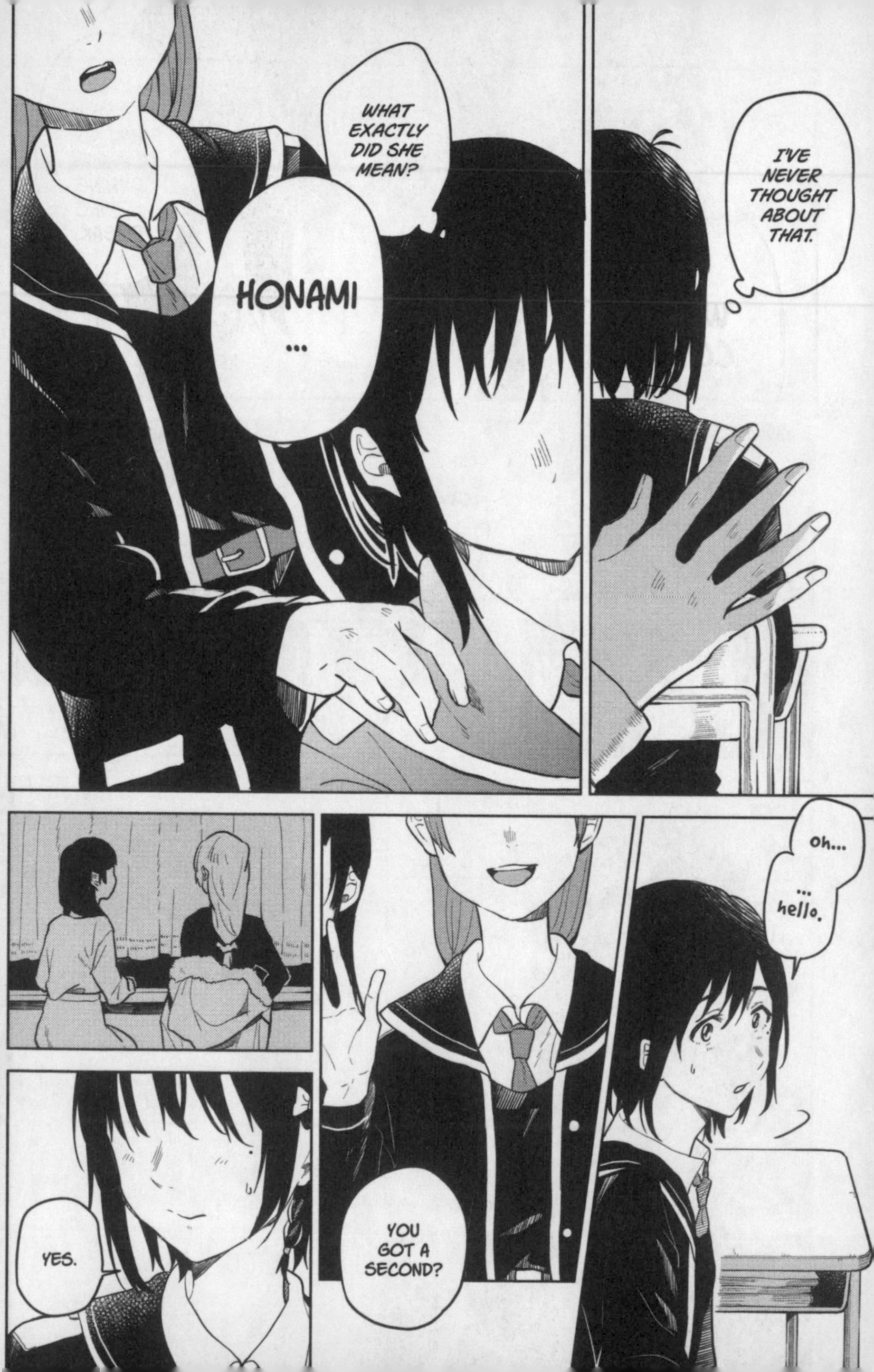
I'VE NEVER THOUGHT ABOUT THAT.
WHAT EXACTLY DID SHE MEAN?
HONAMI ...
oh...
... hello.
YOU GOT A SECOND?
YES.

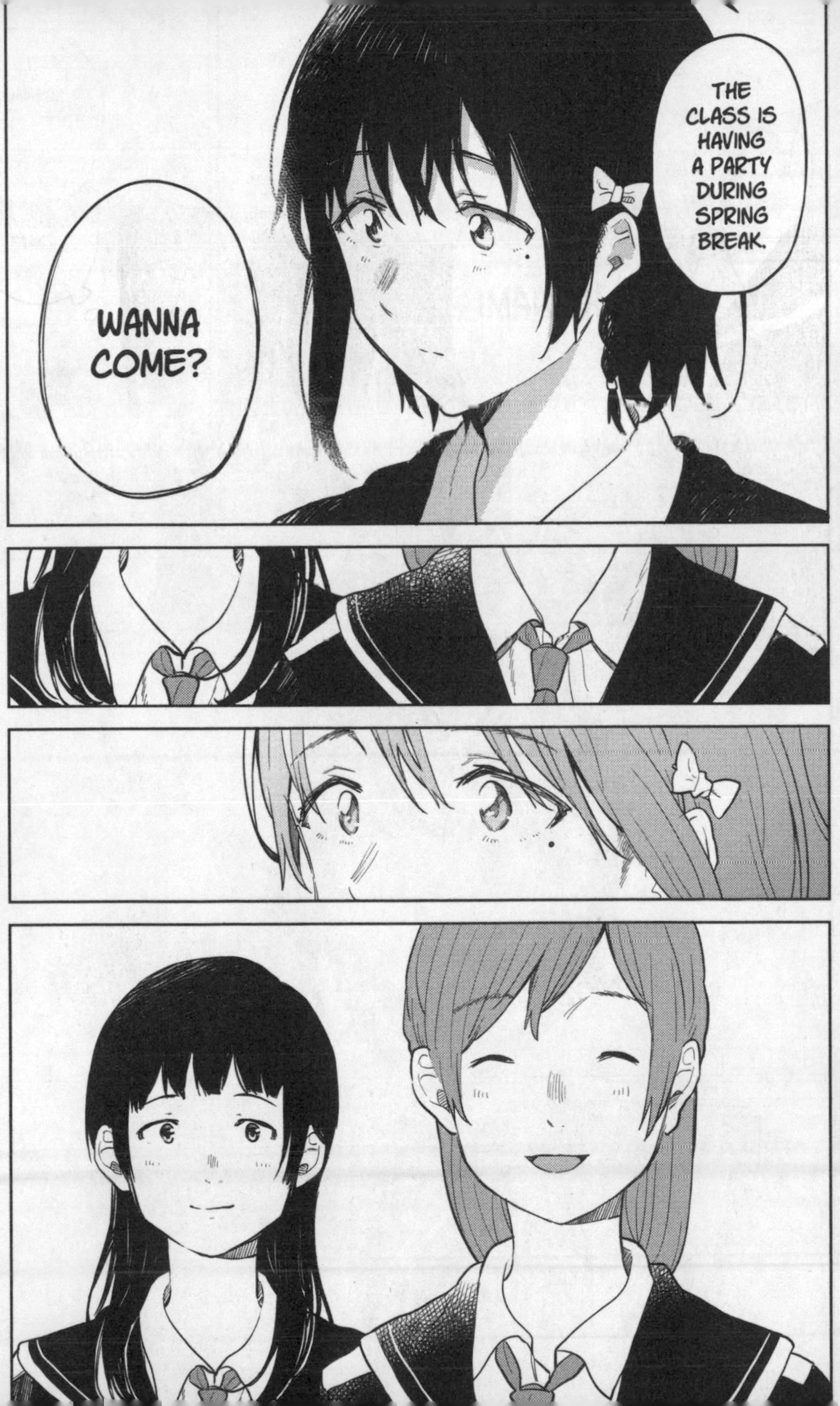
THE CLASS IS HAVING A PARTY DURING SPRING BREAK.
WANNA COME?

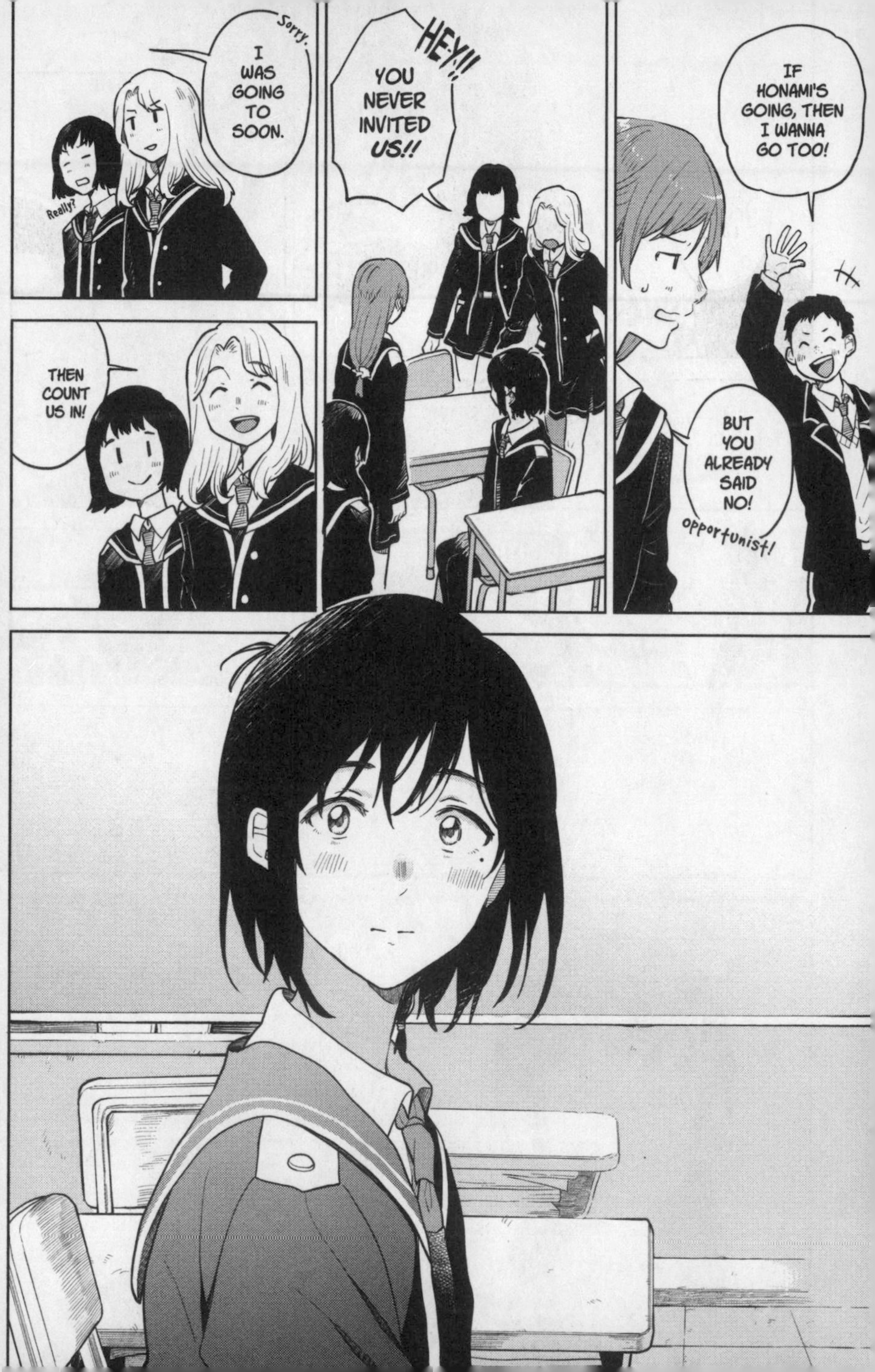
IF HONAMI'S GOING, THEN I WANNA GO TOO!
BUT YOU ALREADY SAID NO!
opportunist!
HEY!!!
YOU NEVER INVITED US!!
Sorry.
I WAS GOING TO SOON.
Really?
THEN COUNT US IN!

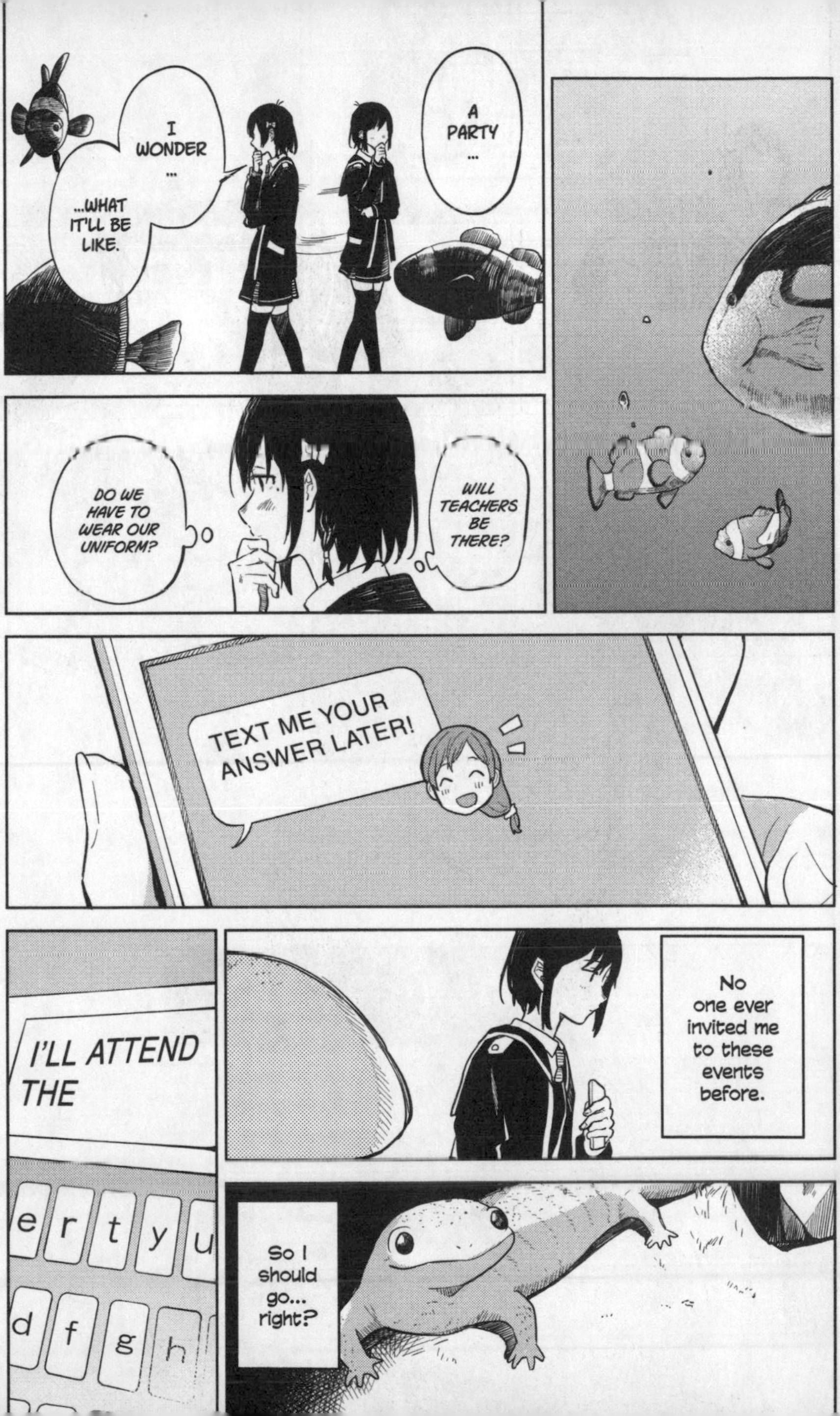
A PARTY ...
I WONDER ...
...WHAT IT'LL BE LIKE.
WILL TEACHERS BE THERE?
DO WE HAVE TO WEAR OUR UNIFORM?
TEXT ME YOUR ANSWER LATER!
No one ever invited me to these events before.
So I should go... right?
I'LL ATTEND THE
e r t y u
d f g h

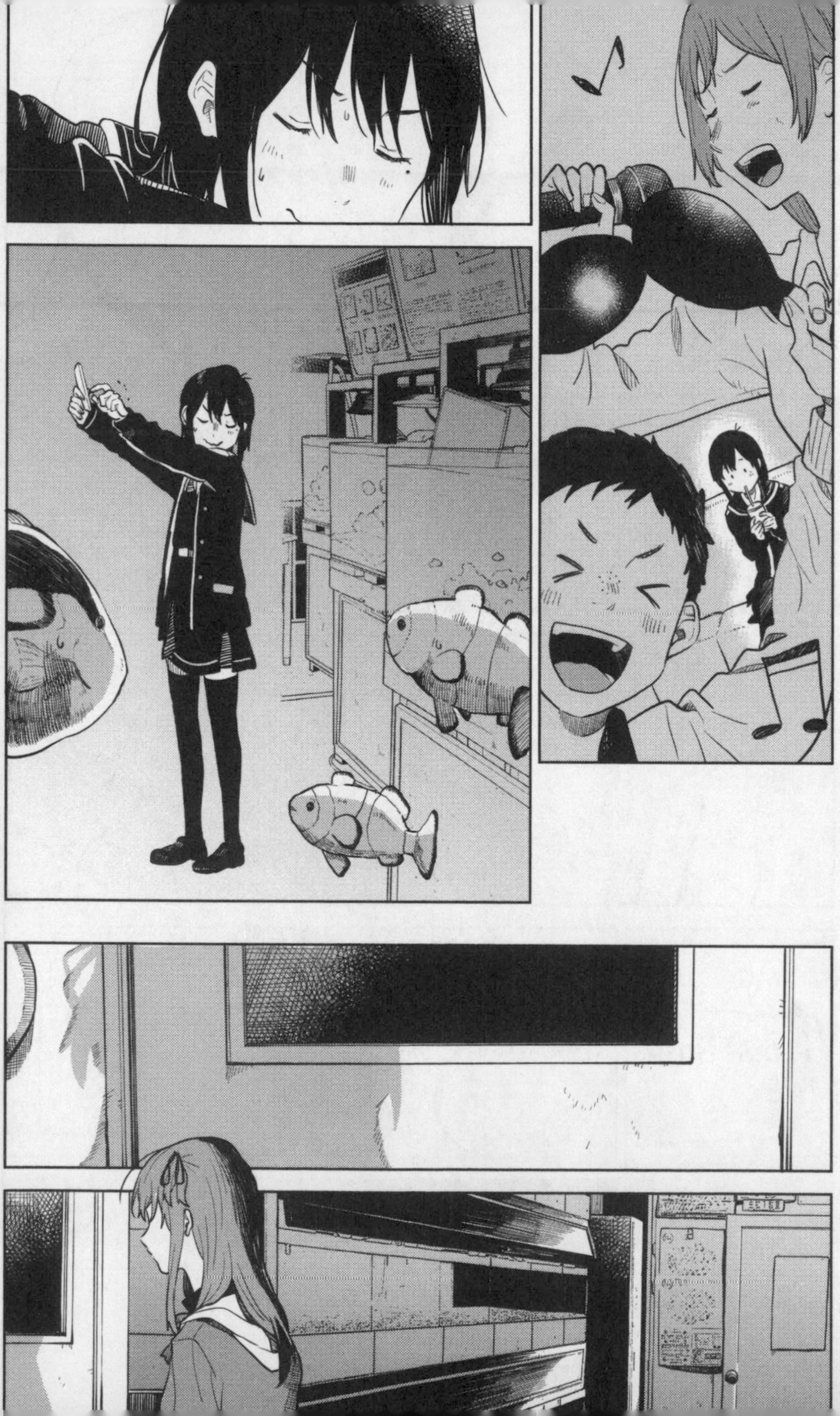

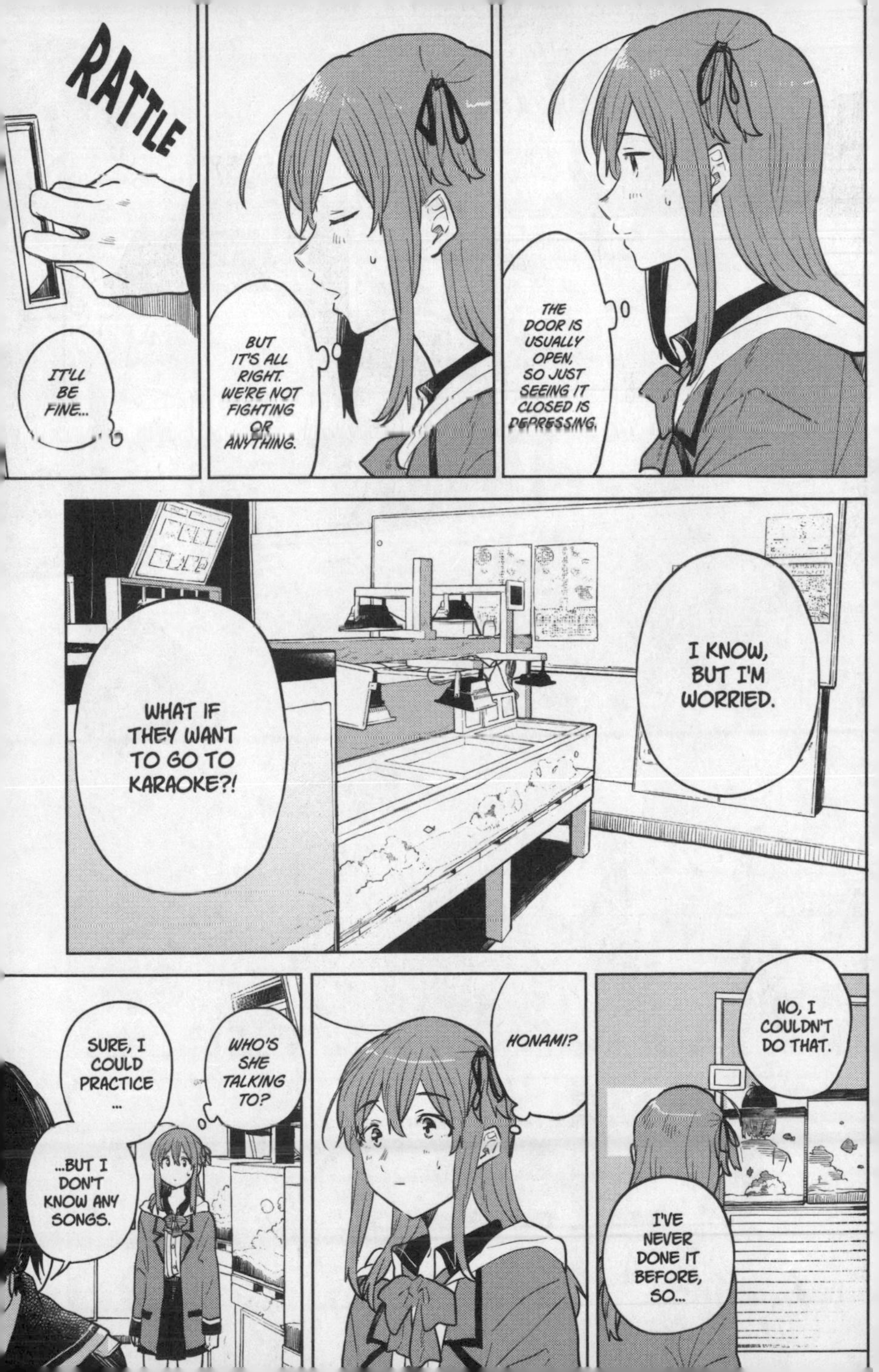
THE DOOR IS USUALLY OPEN, SO JUST SEEING IT CLOSED IS DEPRESSING.
BUT IT'S ALL RIGHT. WE'RE NOT FIGHTING OR ANYTHING.
RATTLE
IT'LL BE FINE...
I KNOW, BUT I'M WORRIED.
WHAT IF THEY WANT TO GO TO KARAOKE?!
NO, I COULDN'T DO THAT.
I'VE NEVER DONE IT BEFORE, SO...
HONAMI?
WHO'S SHE TALKING TO?
SURE, I COULD PRACTICE ...
...BUT I DON'T KNOW ANY SONGS.

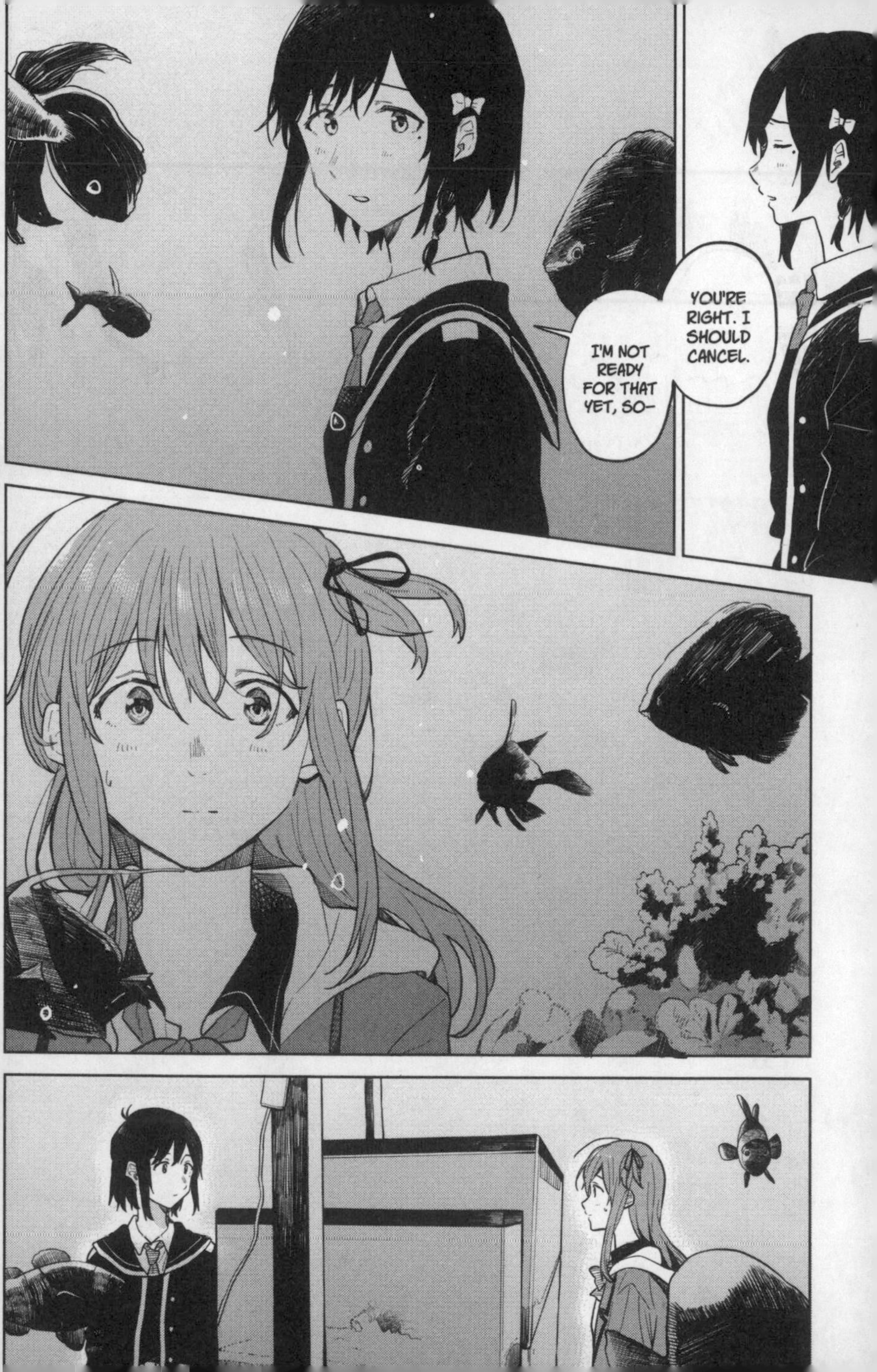
YOU'RE RIGHT. I SHOULD CANCEL.
I'M NOT READY FOR THAT YET, SO—

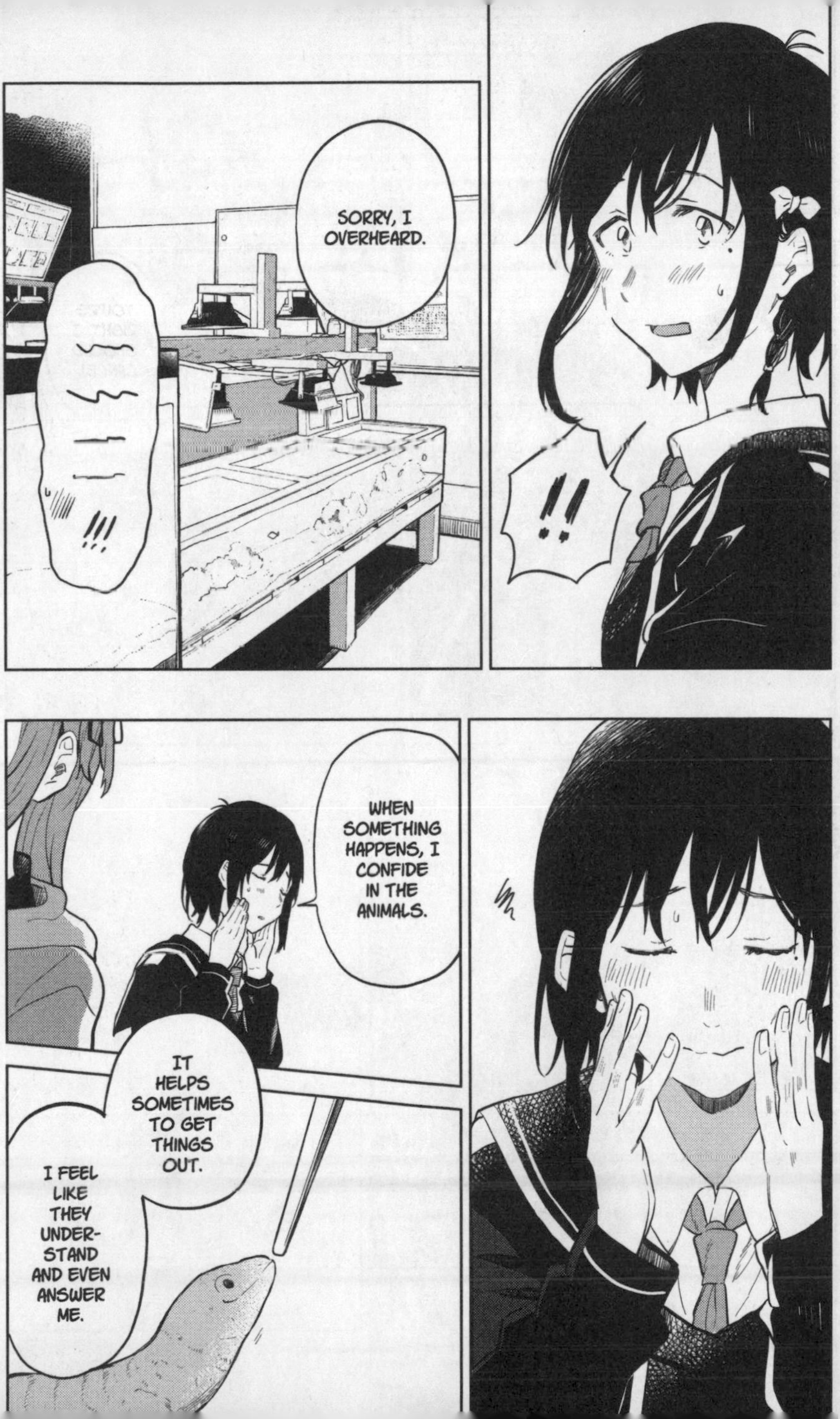
!!
SORRY, I OVERHEARD.
!!!
WHEN SOMETHING HAPPENS, I CONFIDE IN THE ANIMALS.
IT HELPS SOMETIMES TO GET THINGS OUT.
I FEEL LIKE THEY UNDER-STAND AND EVEN ANSWER ME.

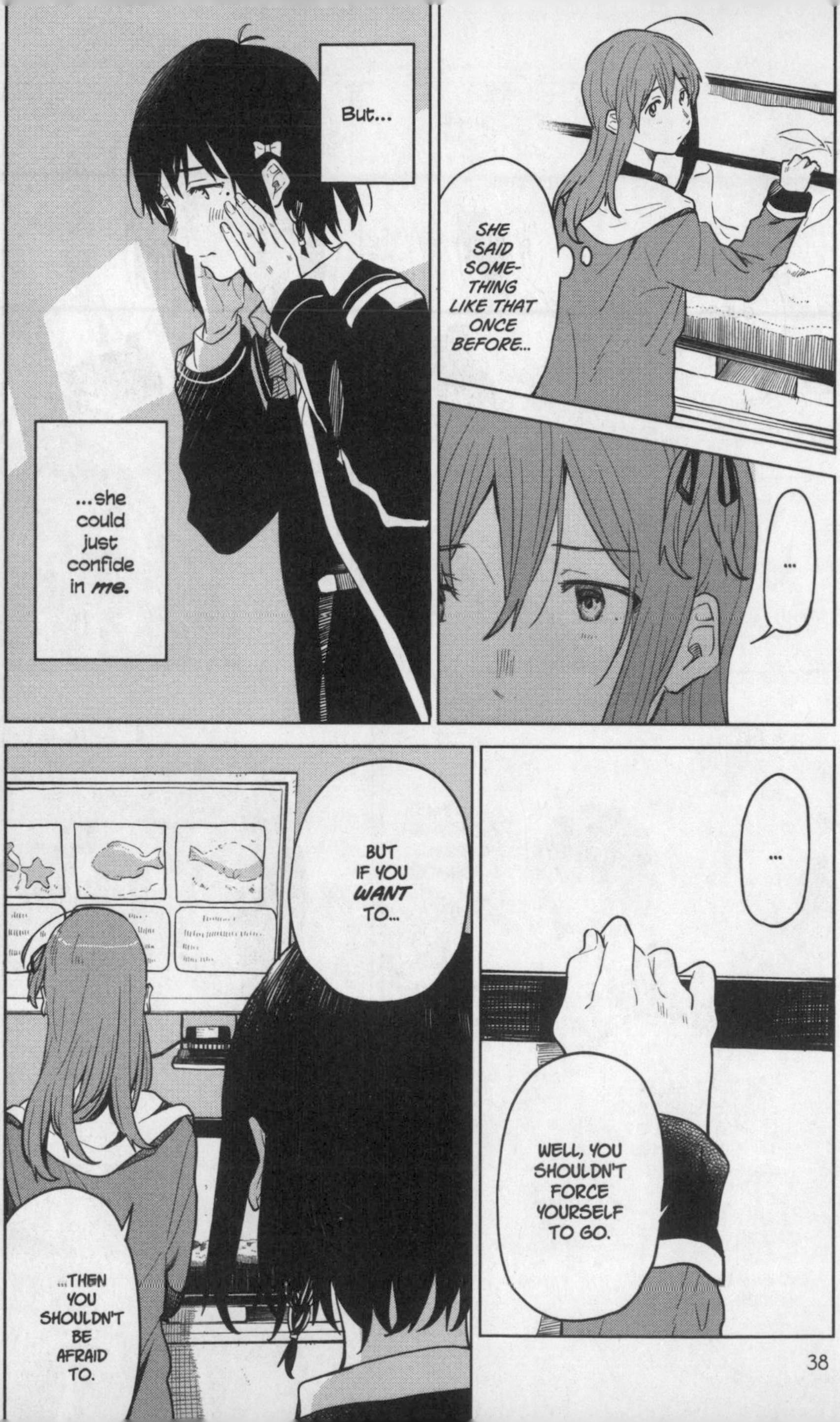
SHE SAID SOMETHING LIKE THAT ONCE BEFORE...
...
But...
...she could just confide in *me.*
...
WELL, YOU SHOULDN'T FORCE YOURSELF TO GO.
BUT IF YOU *WANT* TO...
...THEN YOU SHOULDN'T BE AFRAID TO.

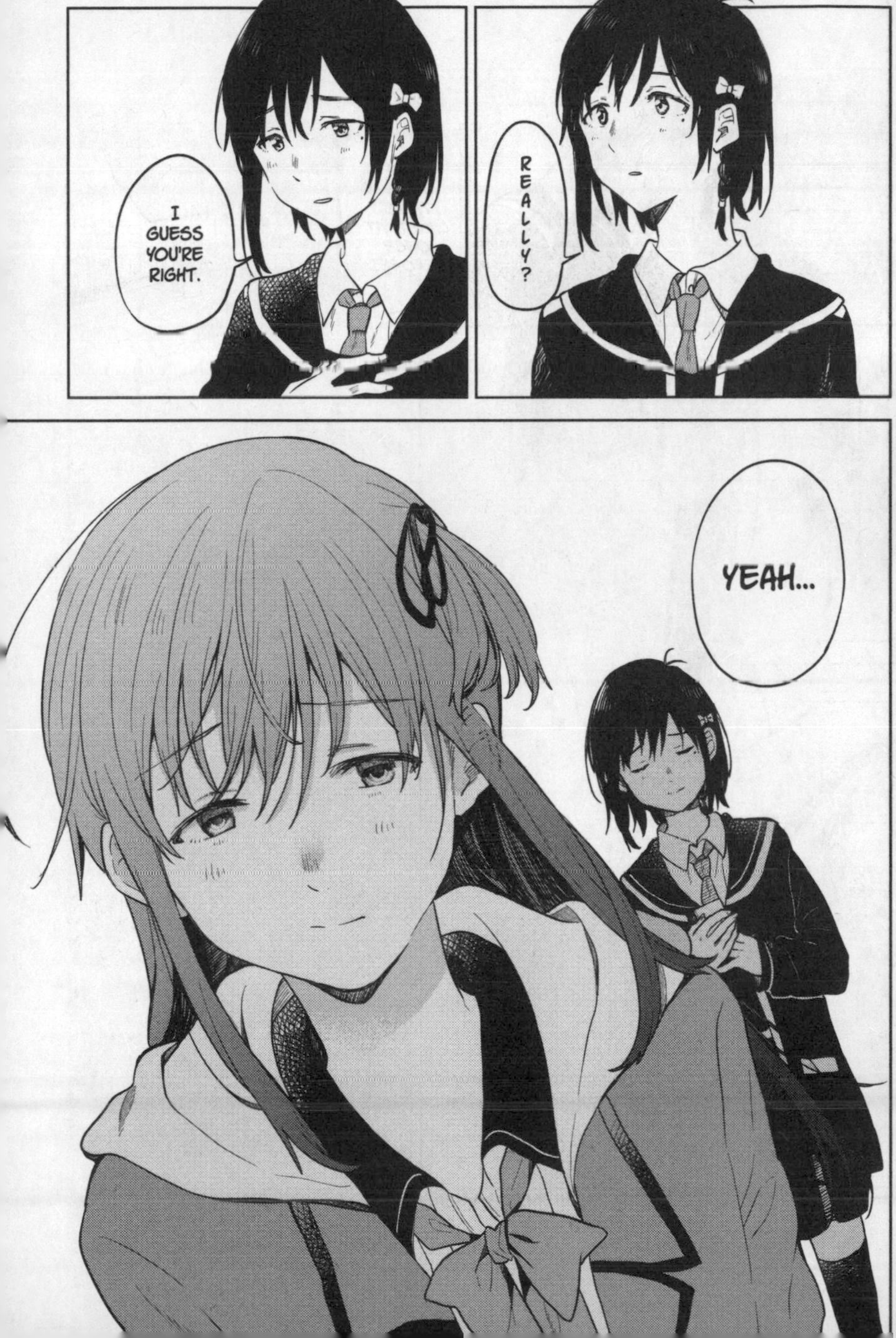
REALLY?
I GUESS YOU'RE RIGHT.
YEAH...

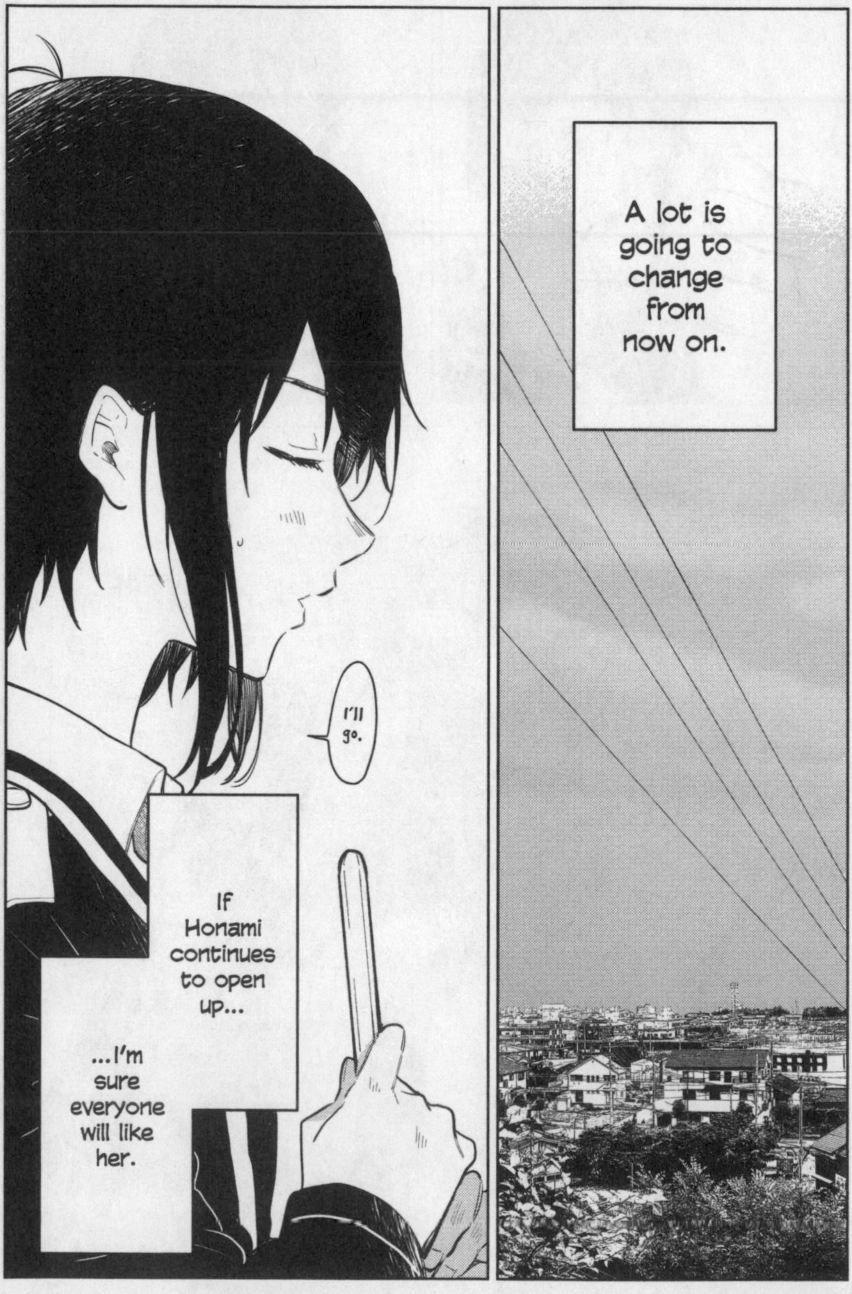
A lot is going to change from now on.
I'll go.
If Honami continues to open up...
...I'm sure everyone will like her.

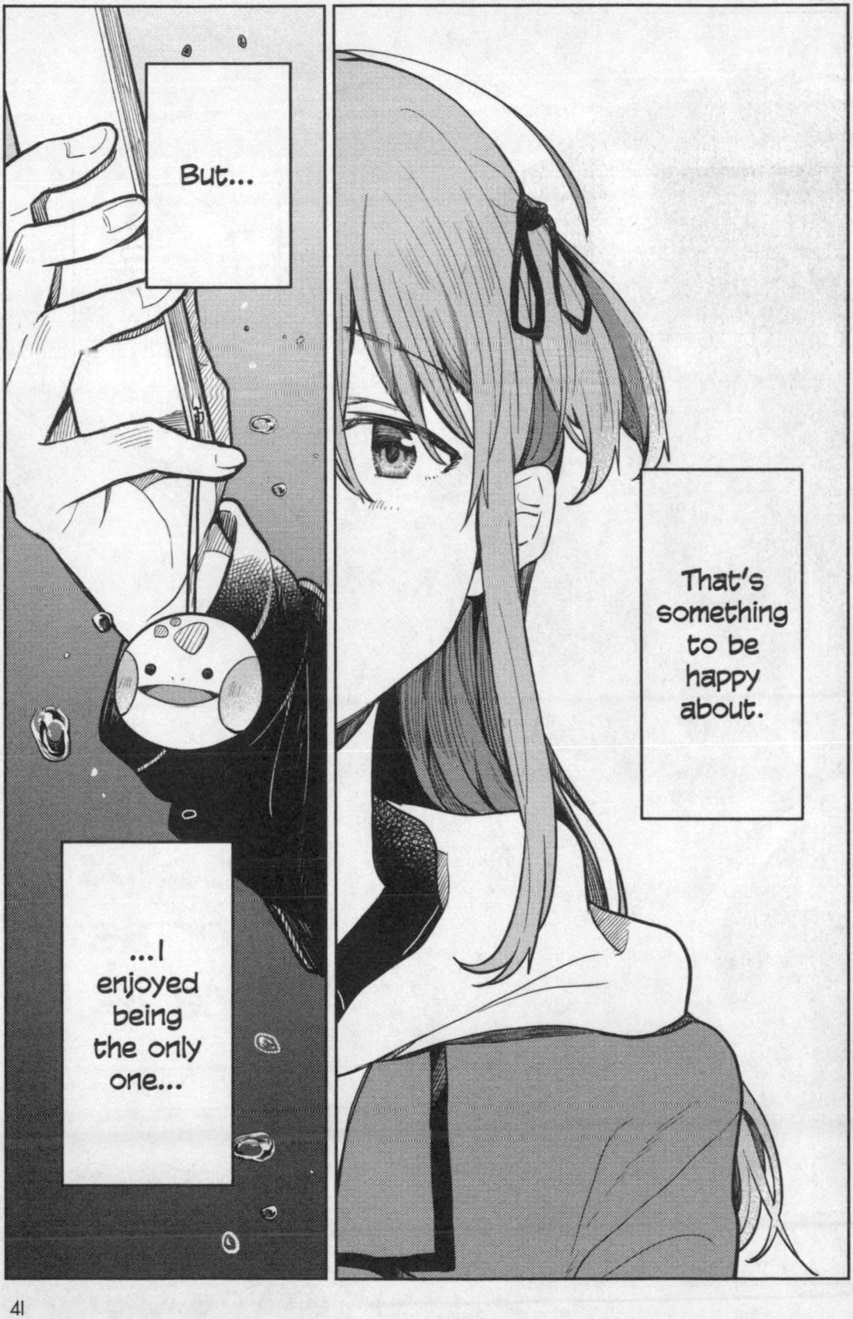
That's something to be happy about.
But...
...I enjoyed being the only one...

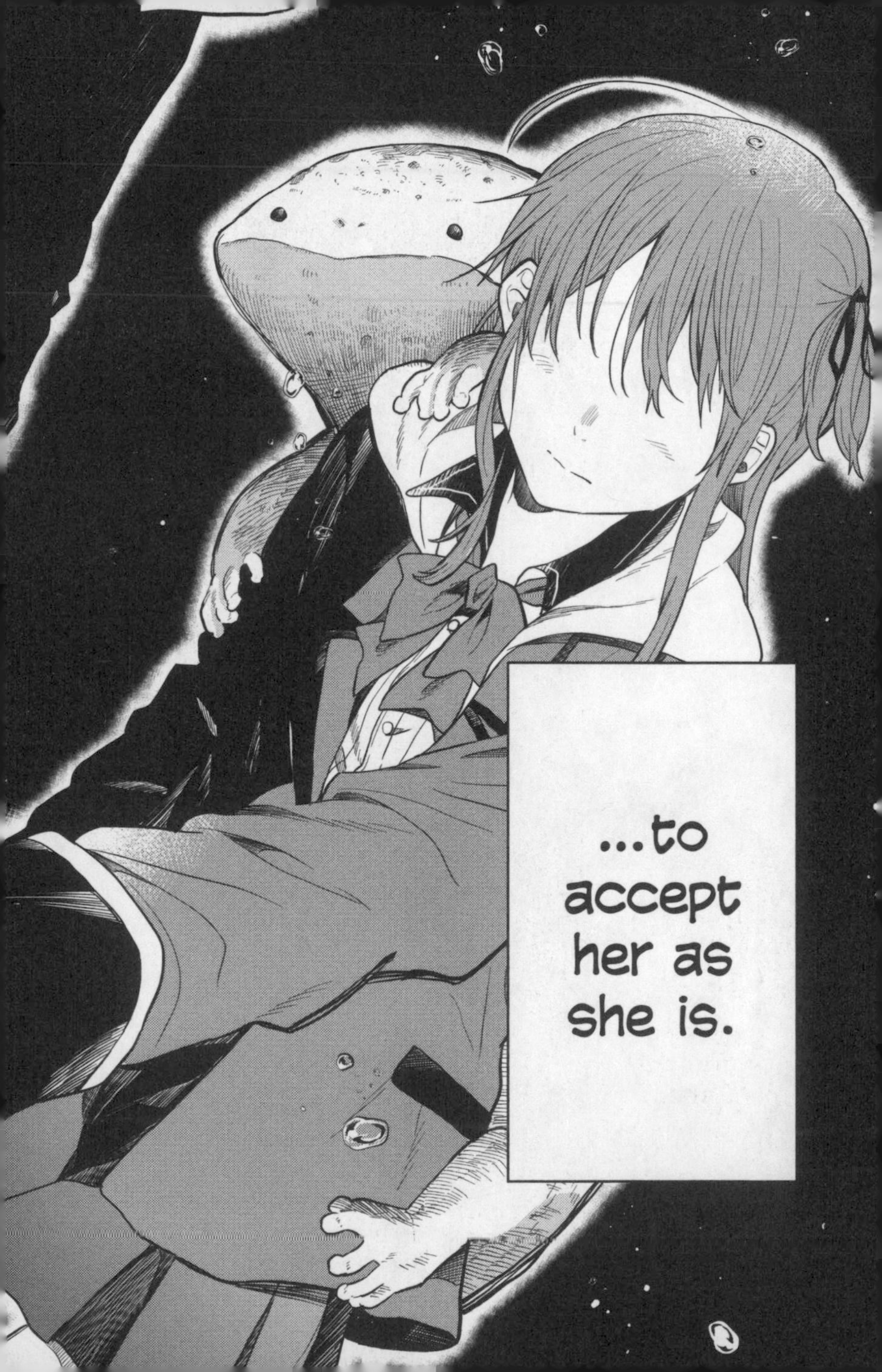
...to accept her as she is.

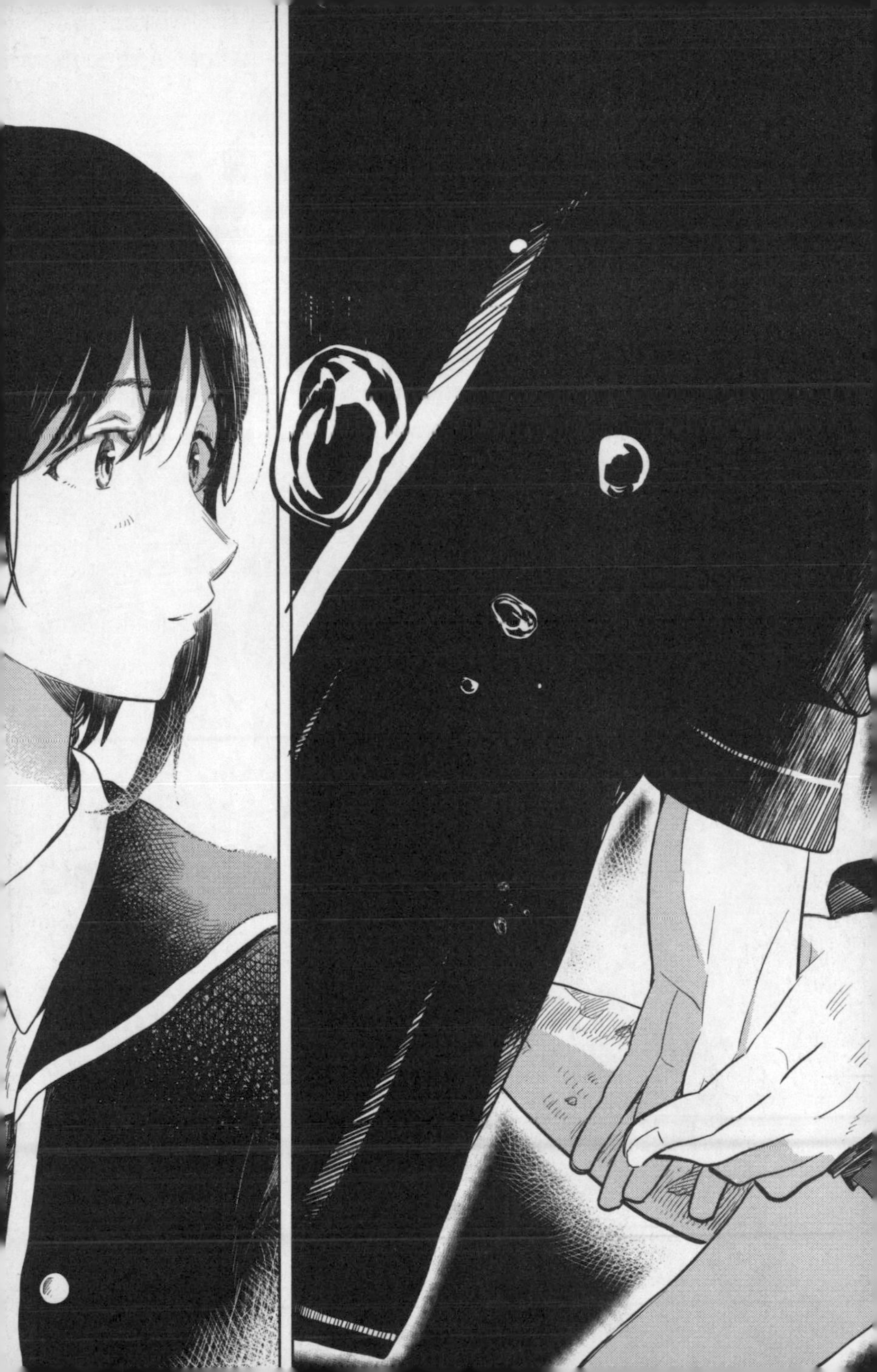

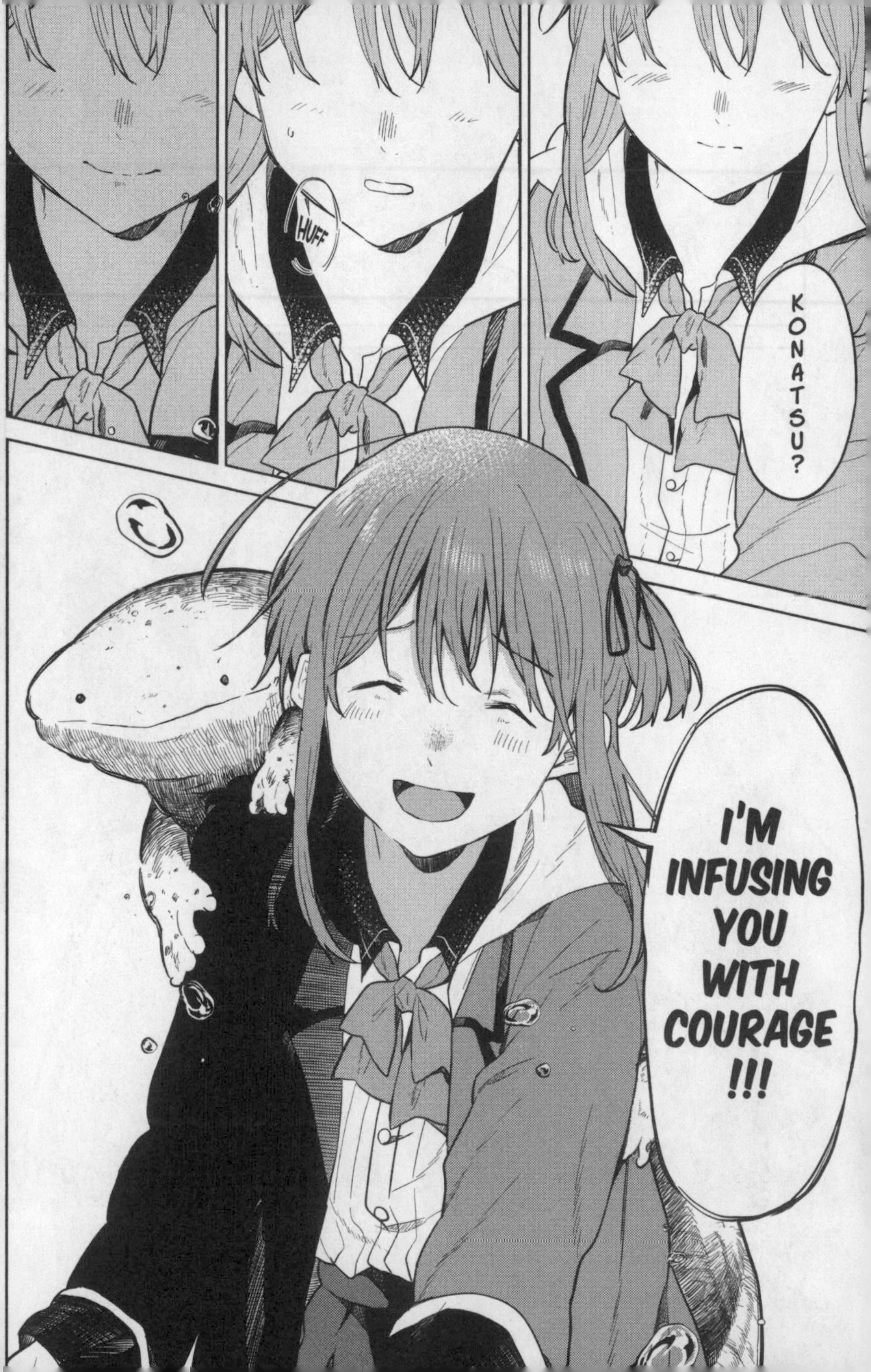
KONATSU?
HUFF
I'M INFUSING YOU WITH COURAGE!!!

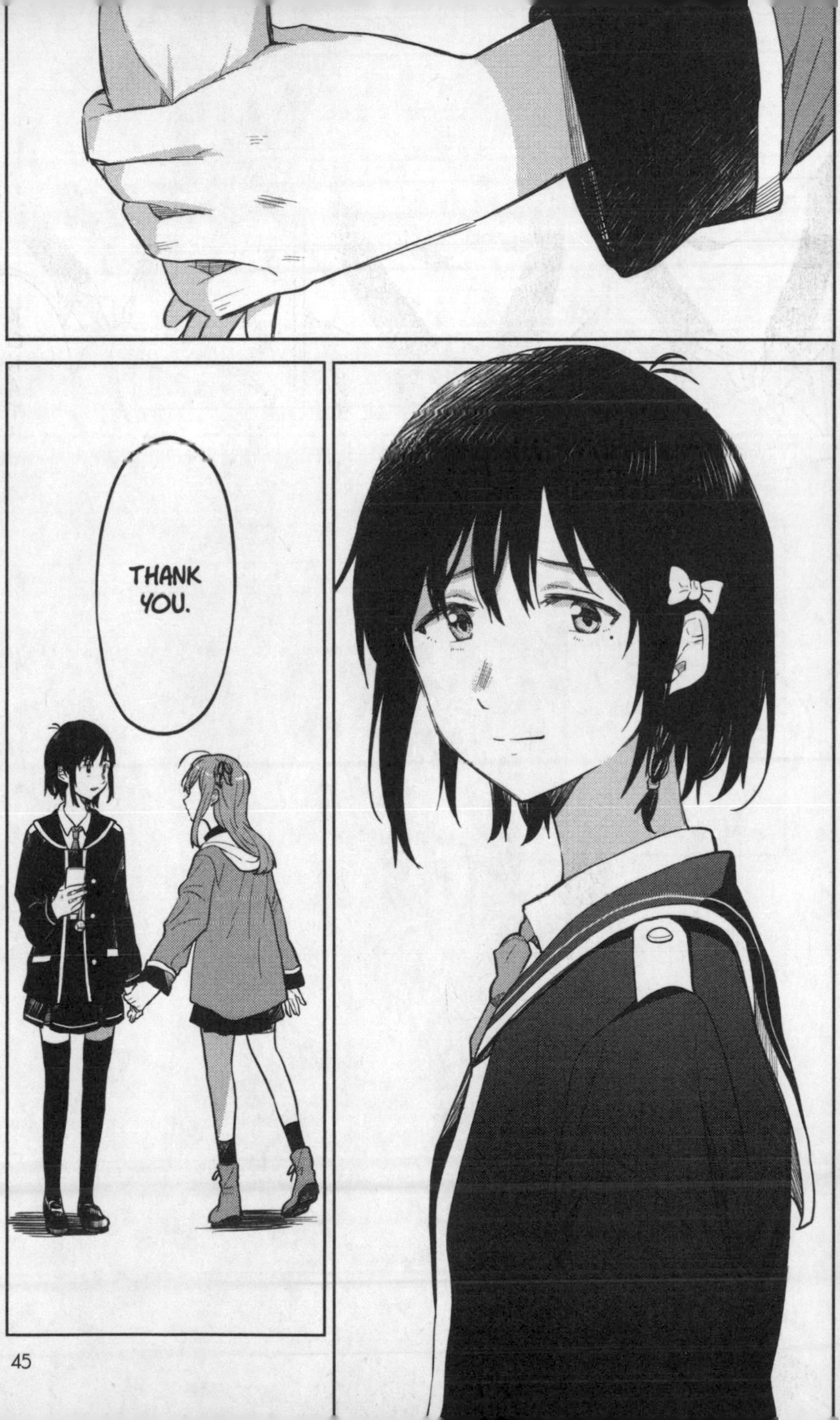
THANK YOU.

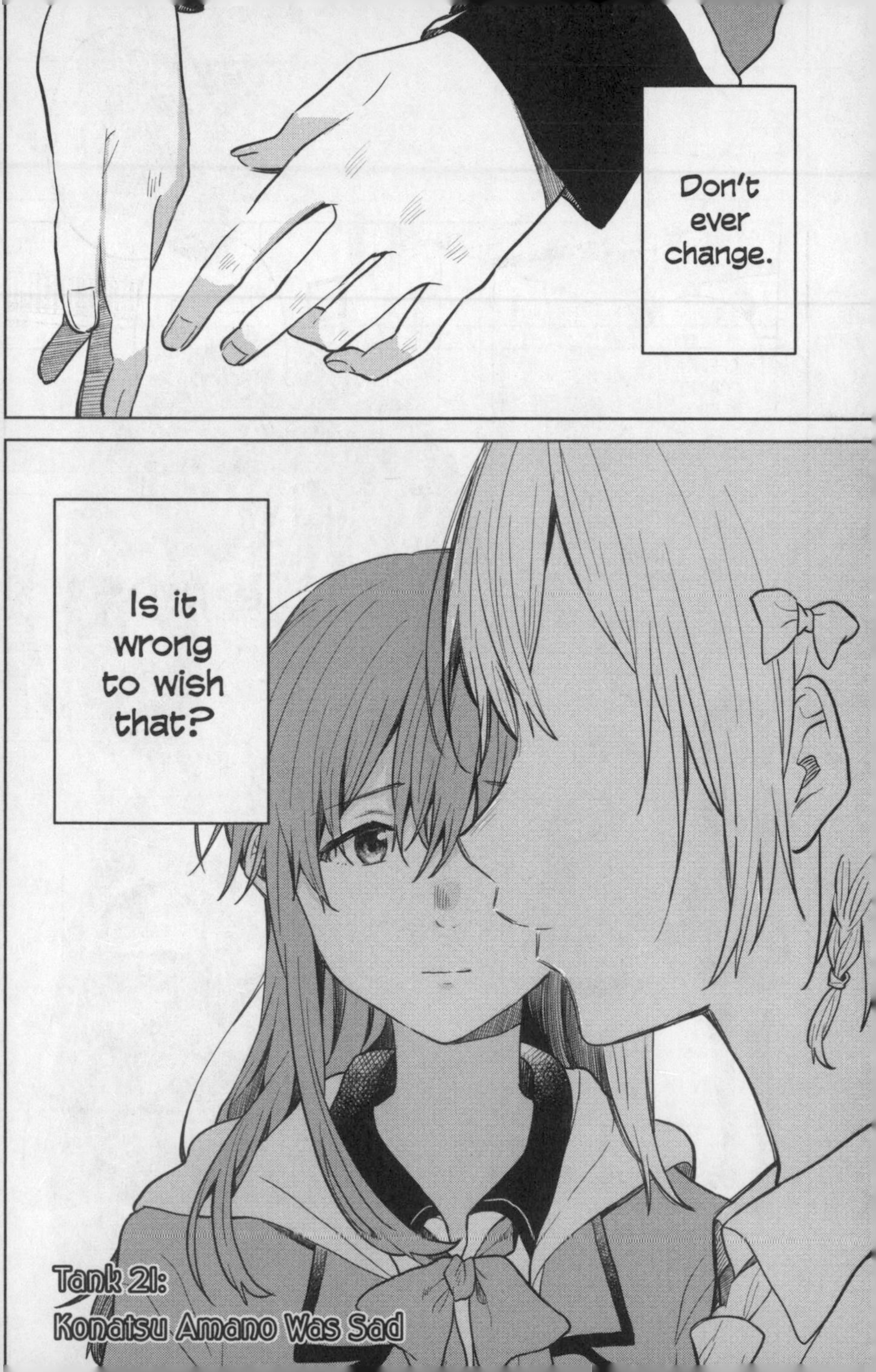
Don't ever change.
Is it wrong to wish that?
Tank 21:
Konatsu Amano Was Sad

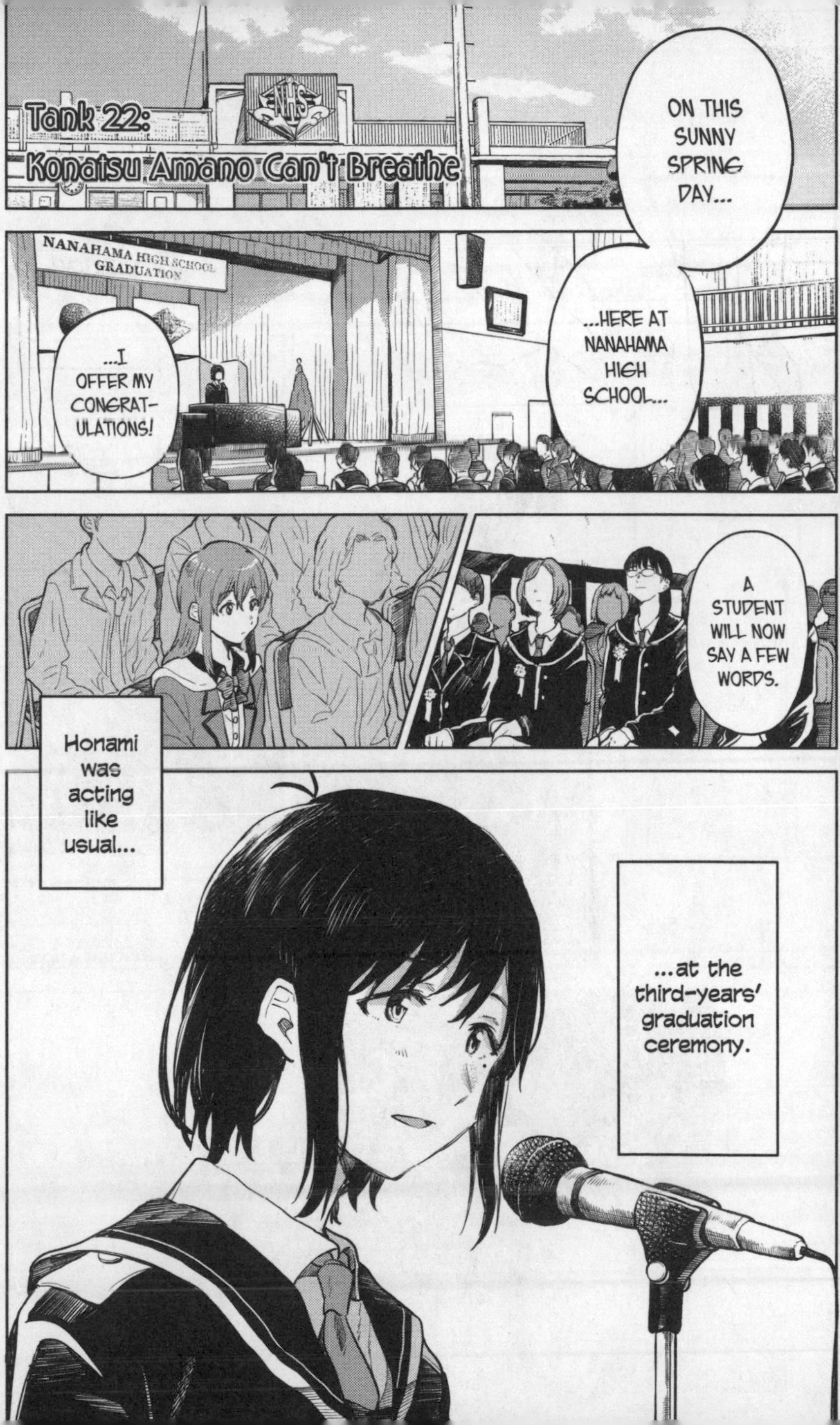
ON THIS SUNNY SPRING DAY...
Tank 22: Konatsu Amano Can't Breathe
...HERE AT NANAHAMA HIGH SCHOOL...
NANAHAMA HIGH SCHOOL GRADUATION
...I OFFER MY CONGRAT-ULATIONS!
A STUDENT WILL NOW SAY A FEW WORDS.
Honami was acting like usual...
...at the third-years' graduation ceremony.

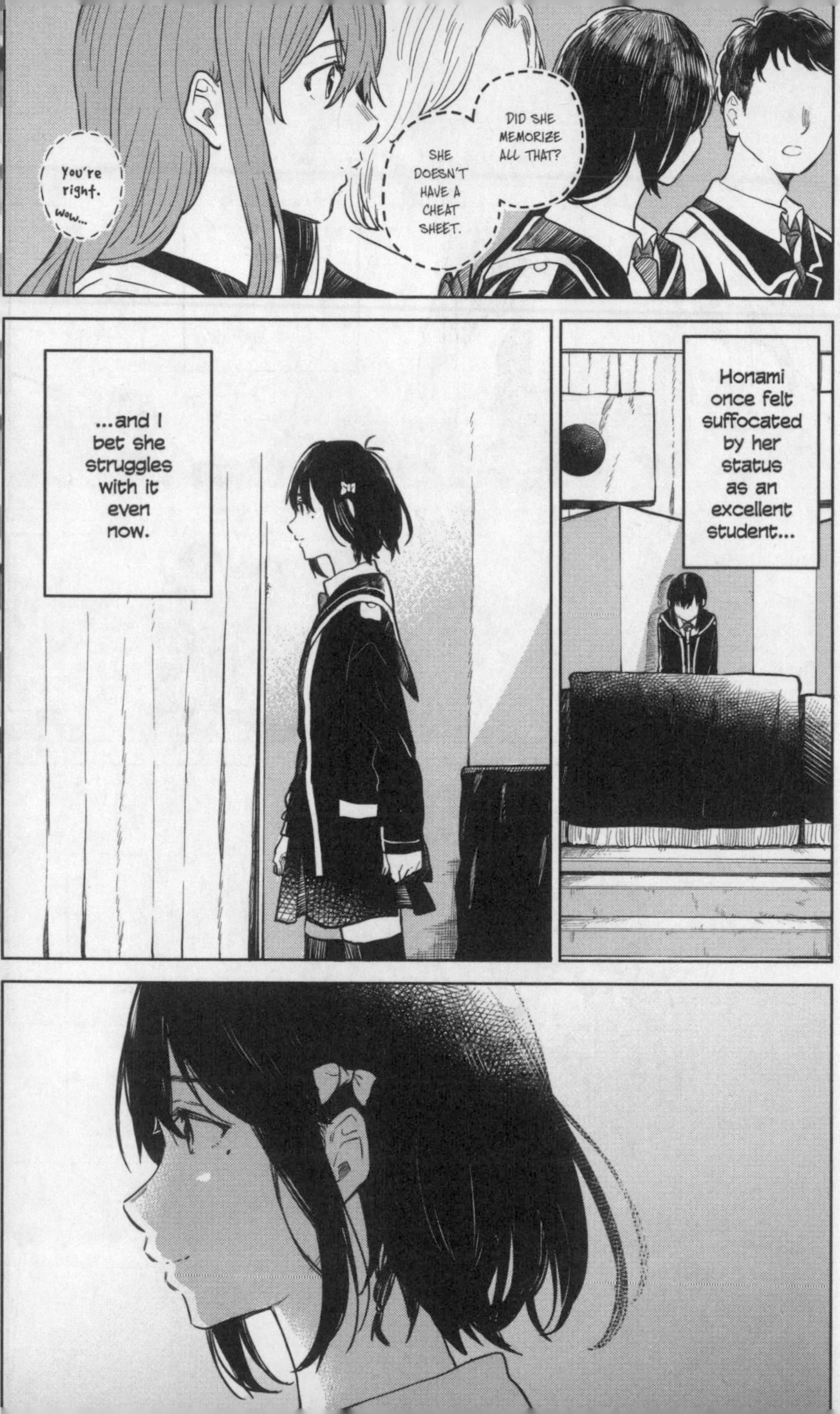
DID SHE MEMORIZE ALL THAT?
SHE DOESN'T HAVE A CHEAT SHEET.
You're right.
wow...
Honami once felt suffocated by her status as an excellent student...
...and I bet she struggles with it even now.

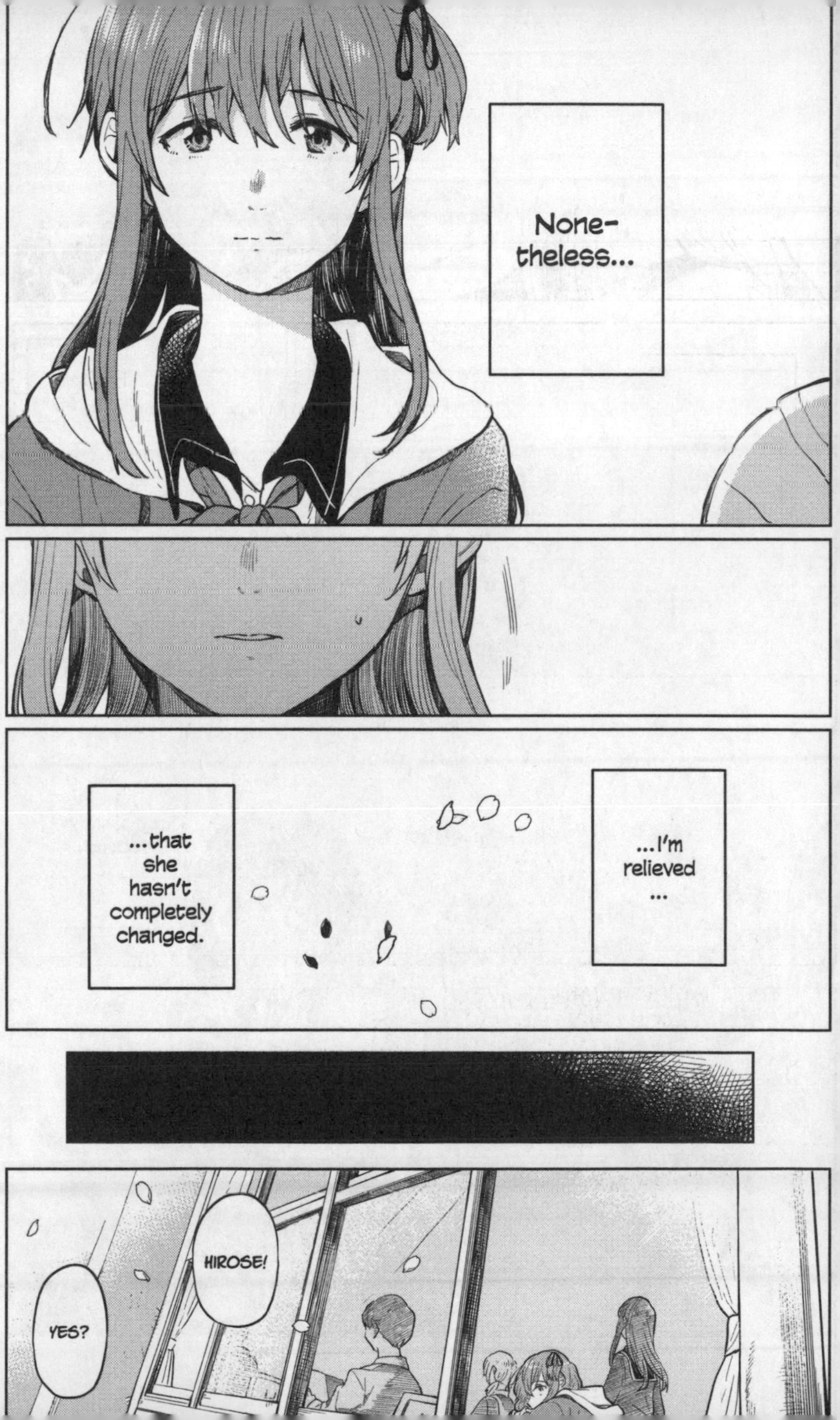
None-theless...
...I'm relieved ...
...that she hasn't completely changed.
HIROSE!
YES?

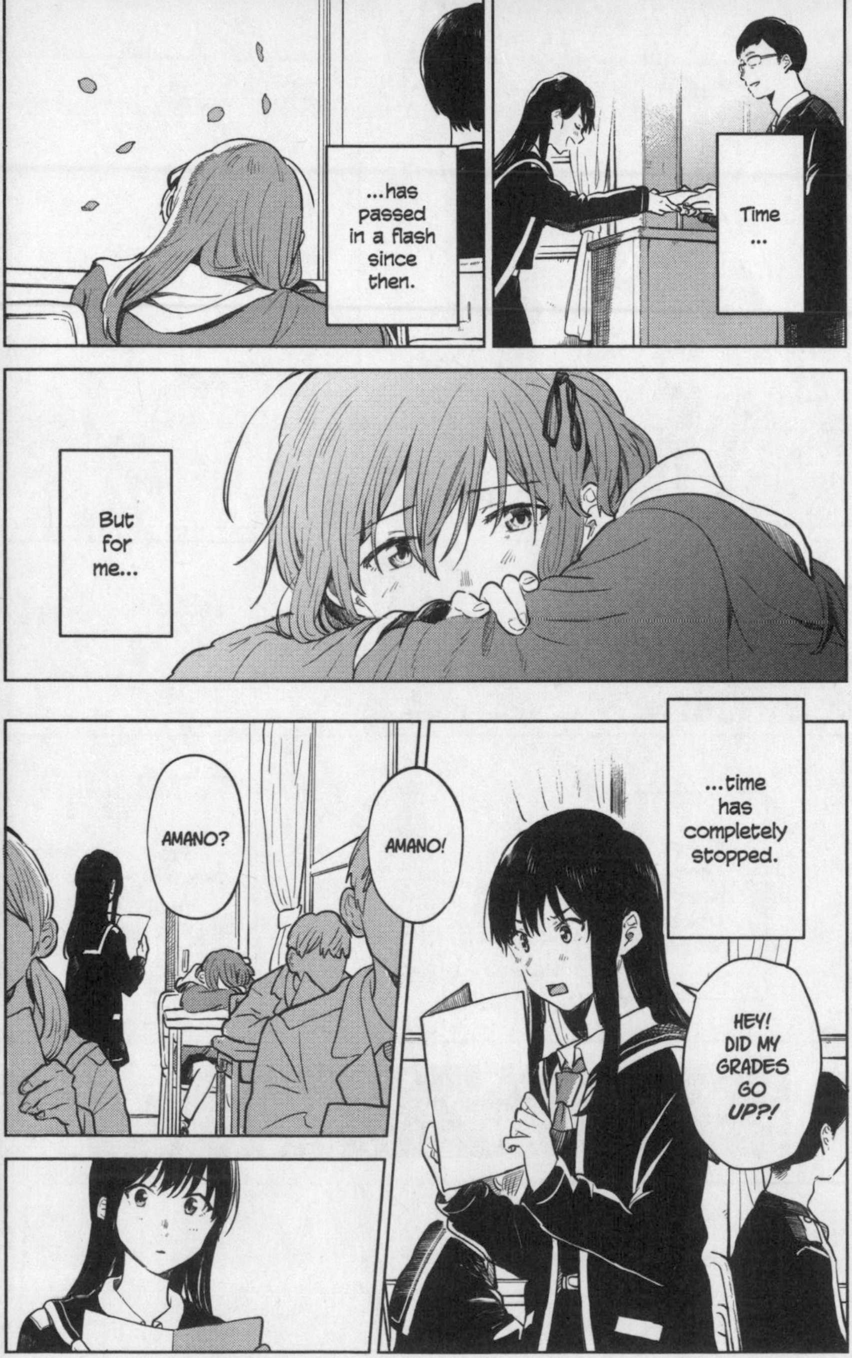
Time ...
...has passed in a flash since then.
But for me...
...time has completely stopped.
HEY! DID MY GRADES GO UP?!
AMANO!
AMANO?

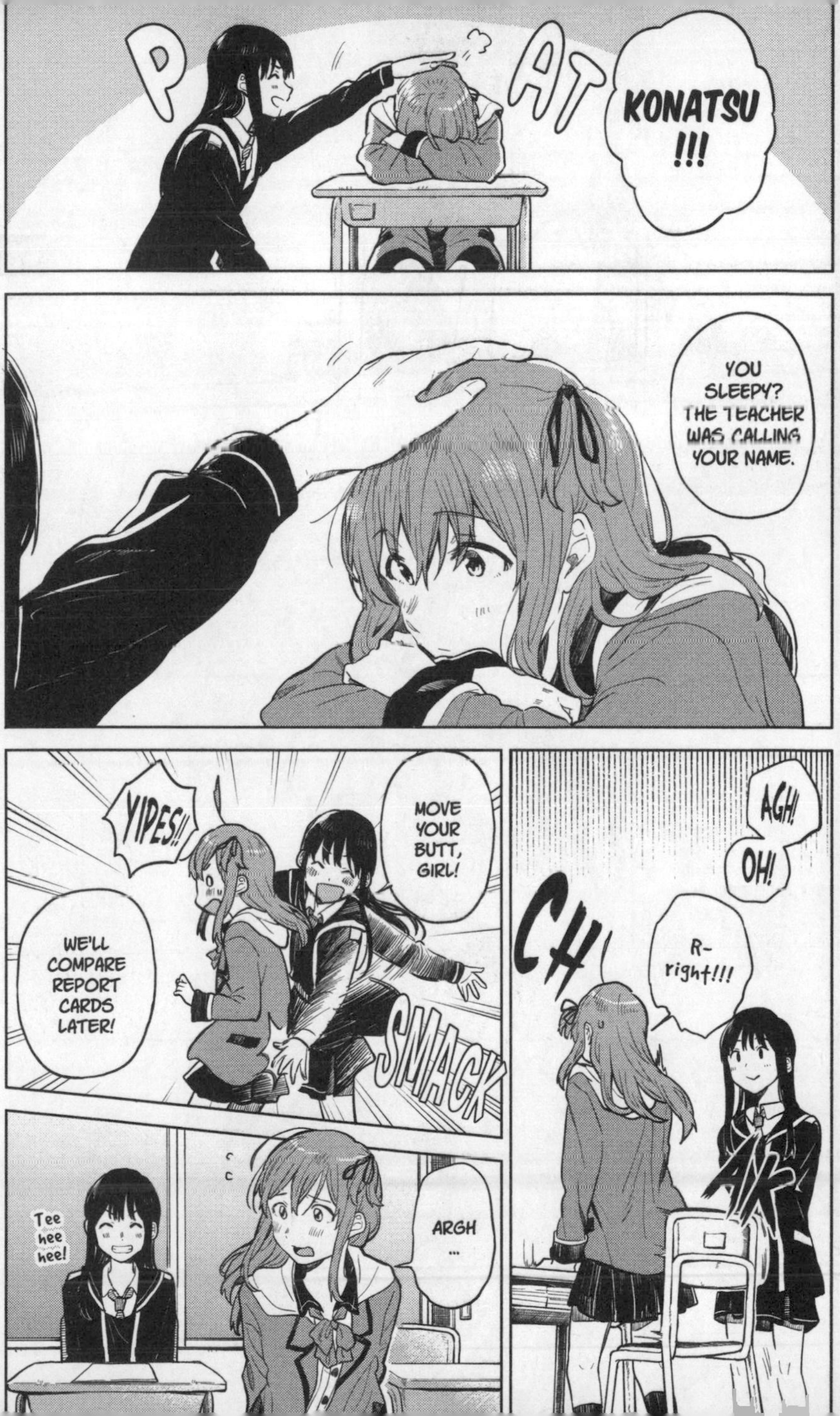
KONATSU !!!
P
AT
YOU SLEEPY? THE TEACHER WAS CALLING YOUR NAME.
AGH!
OH!
R-right!!!
CH
MOVE YOUR BUTT, GIRL!
YIPES!!
WE'LL COMPARE REPORT CARDS LATER!
SMACK
ARGH ...
Tee hee hee!

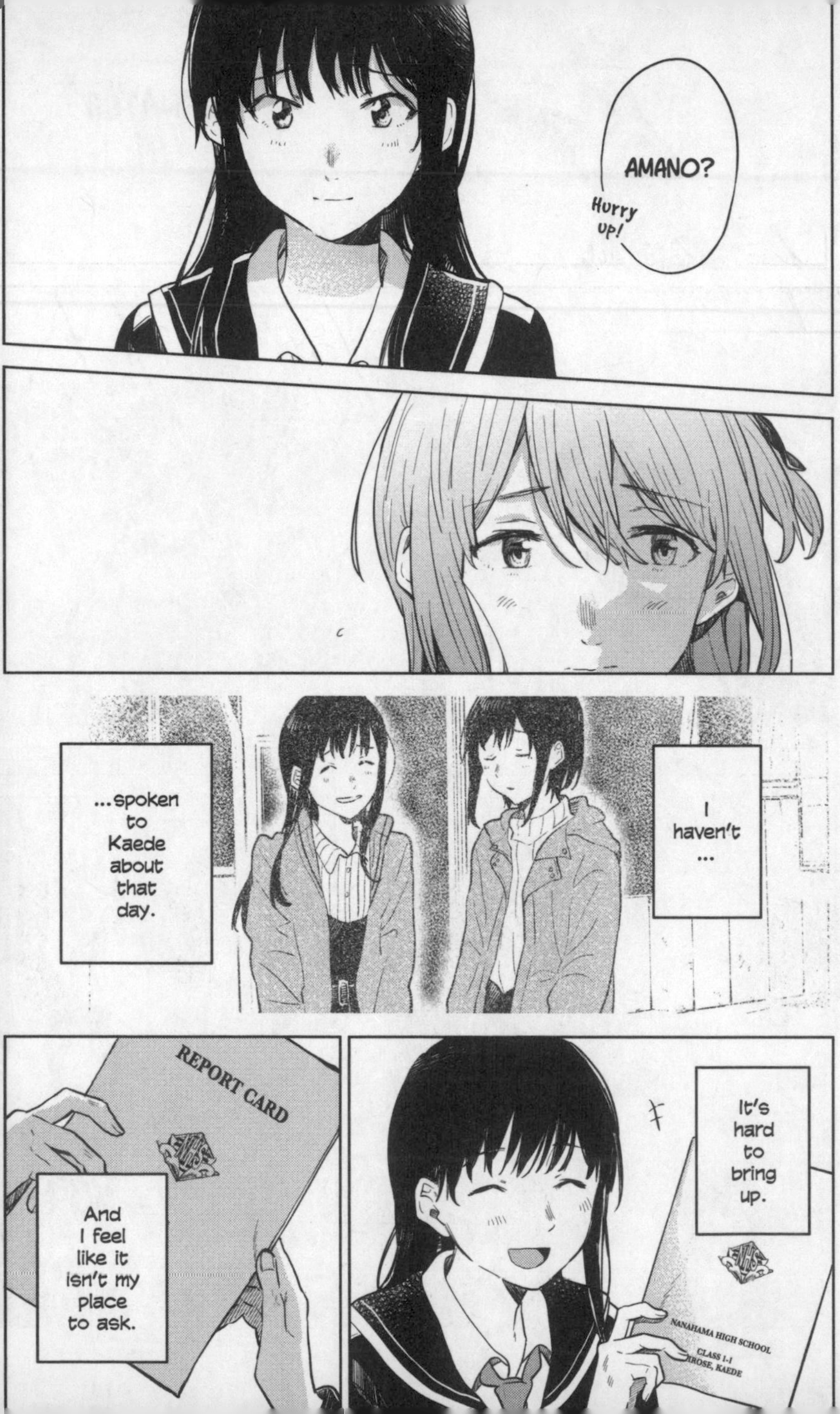
AMANO?
Hurry up!
I haven't ...
...spoken to Kaede about that day.
It's hard to bring up.
NANAHAMA HIGH SCHOOL
CLASS 1-1
REPORT CARD
And I feel like it isn't my place to ask.

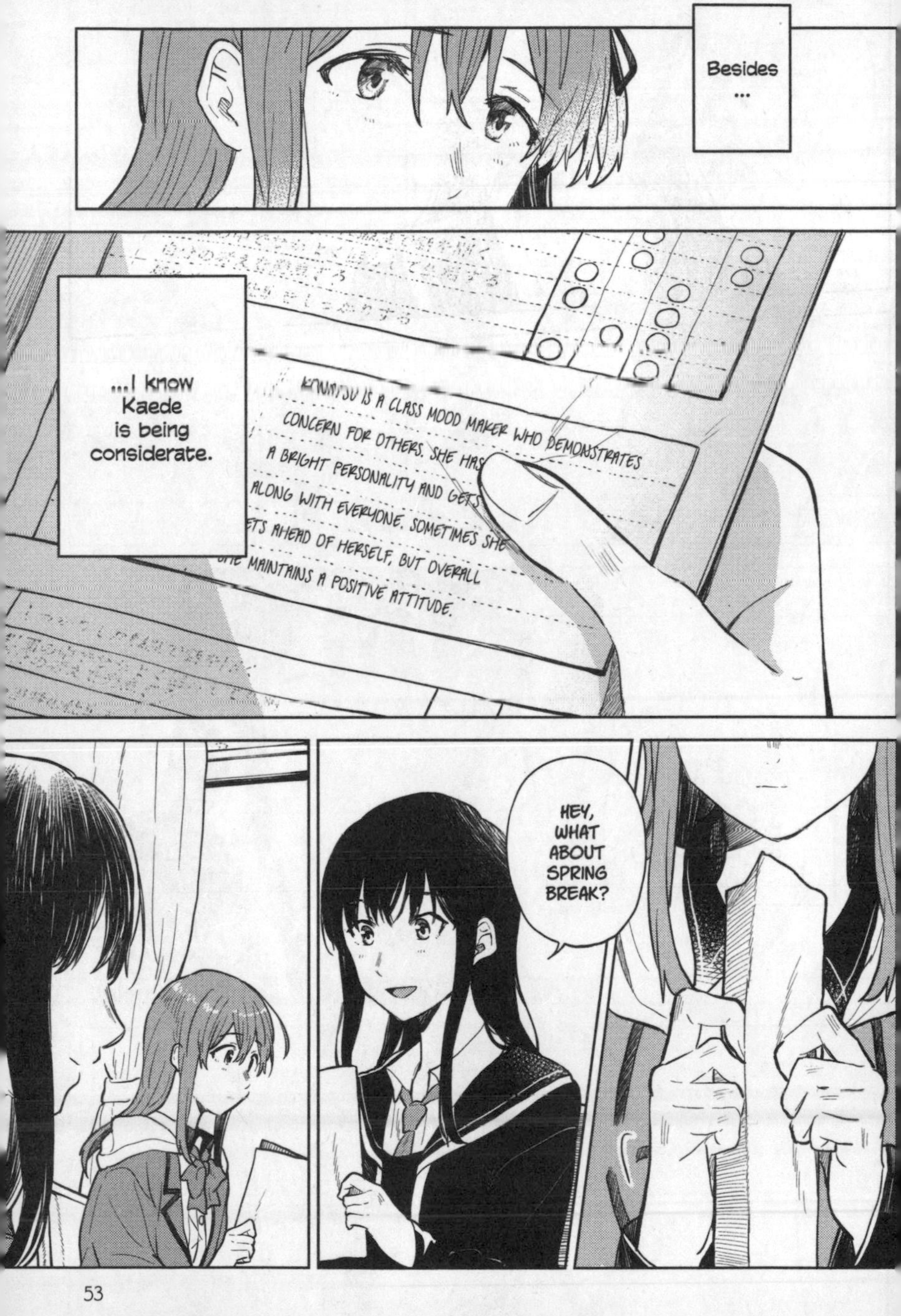
Besides ...
IS A CLASS MOOD MAKER WHO DEMONSTRATES CONCERN FOR OTHERS. SHE HAS A BRIGHT PERSONALITY AND GETS ALONG WITH EVERYONE. SOMETIMES SHE GETS AHEAD OF HERSELF, BUT OVERALL SHE MAINTAINS A POSITIVE ATTITUDE.
...I know Kaede is being considerate.
HEY, WHAT ABOUT SPRING BREAK?

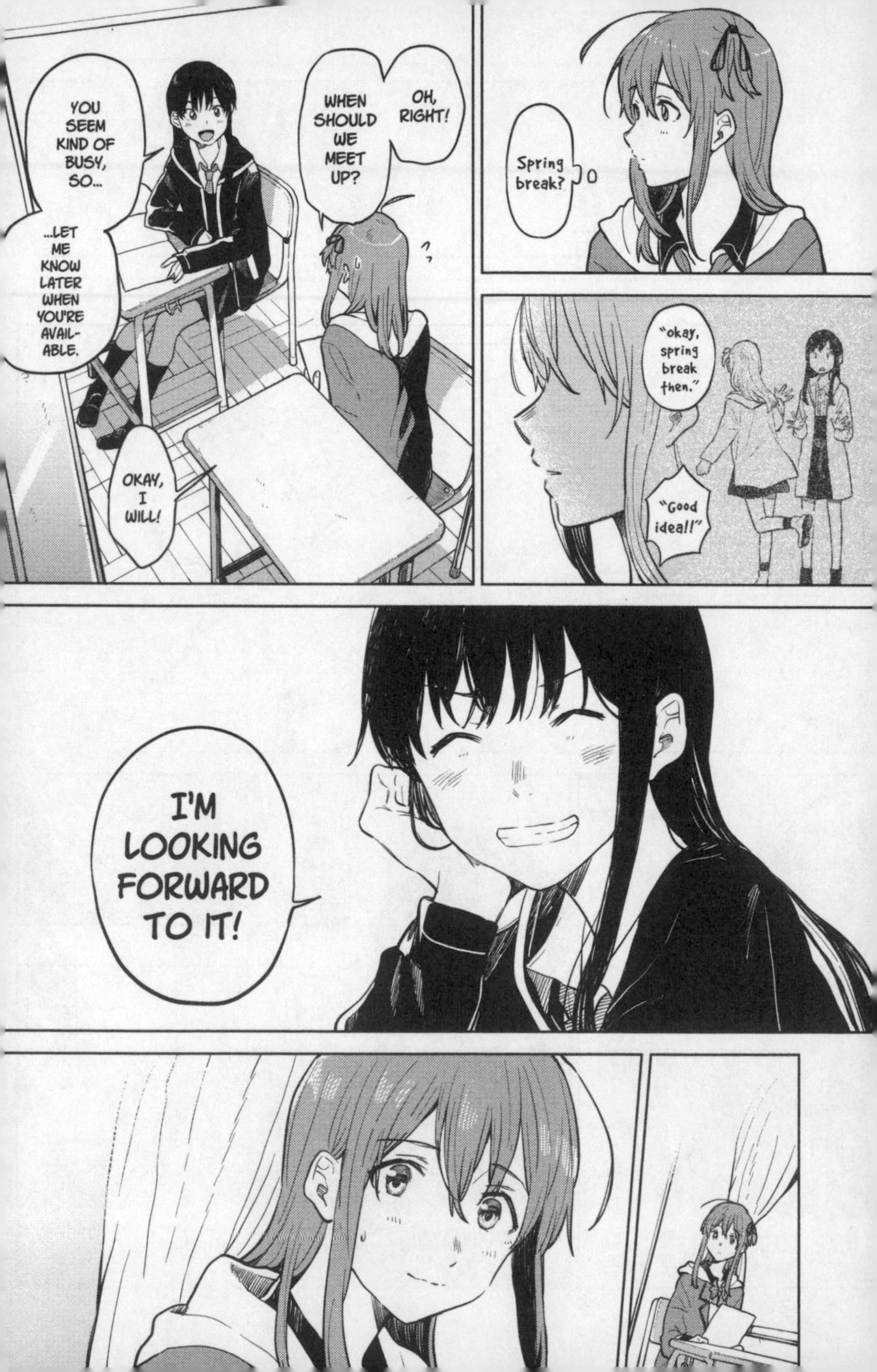
Spring break?
"okay, spring break then."
"Good idea!!"
OH, RIGHT!
WHEN SHOULD WE MEET UP?
YOU SEEM KIND OF BUSY, SO...
...LET ME KNOW LATER WHEN YOU'RE AVAIL-ABLE.
OKAY, I WILL!
I'M LOOKING FORWARD TO IT!

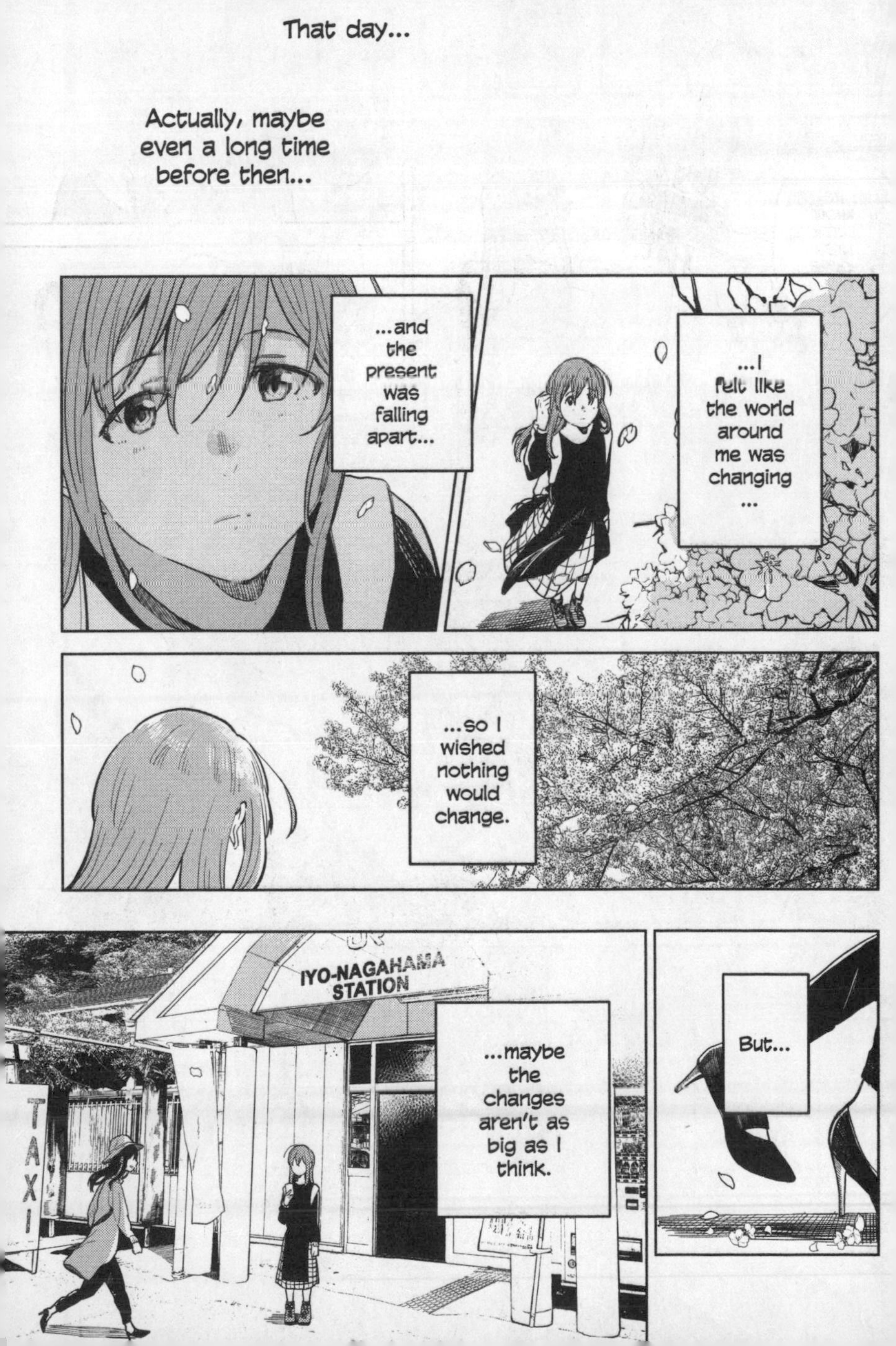
That day...
Actually, maybe even a long time before then...
...I felt like the world around me was changing...
...and the present was falling apart...
...so I wished nothing would change.
But...
IYO-NAGAHAMA STATION
TAXI
...maybe the changes aren't as big as I think.

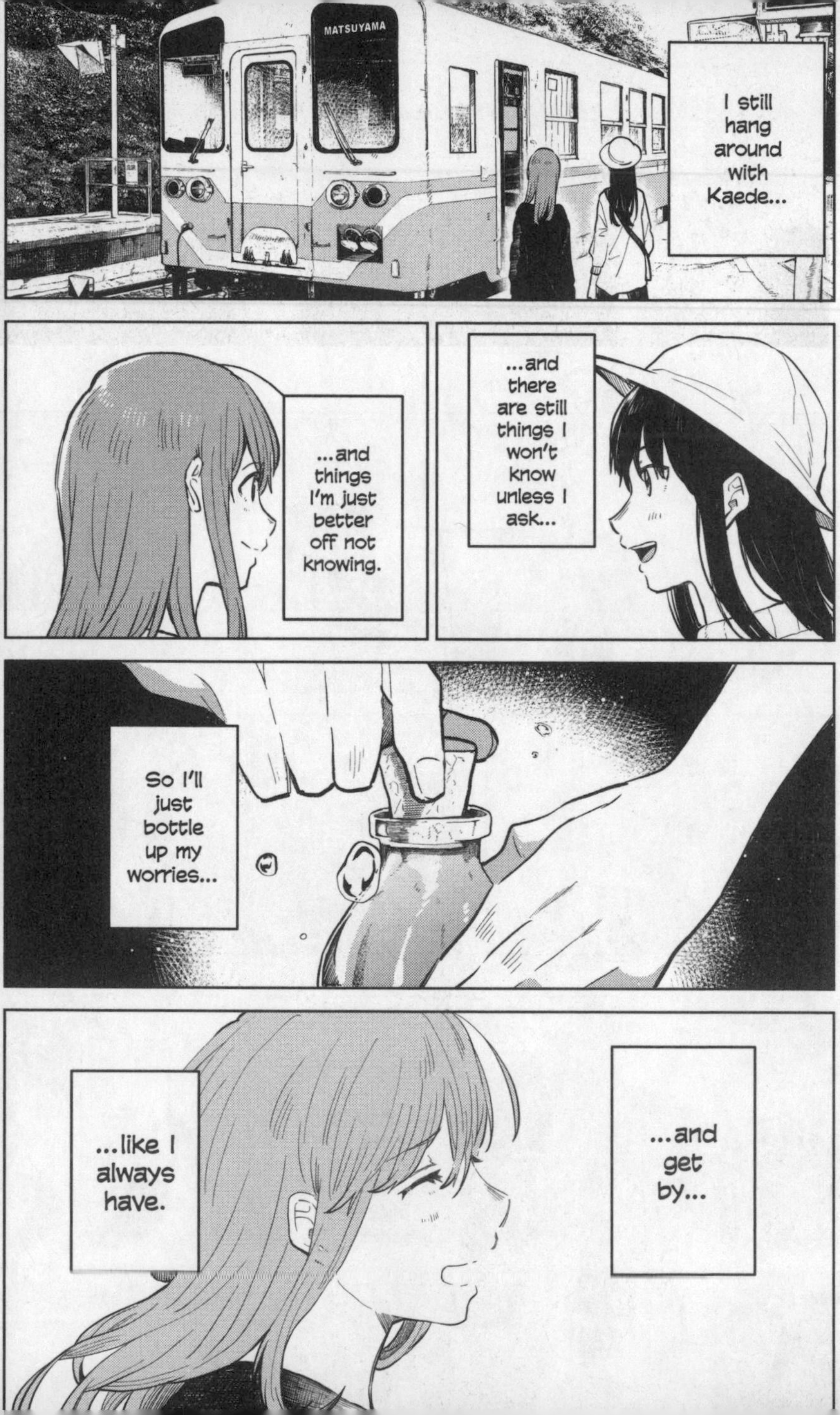
MATSUYAMA
I still hang around with Kaede...
...and there are still things I won't know unless I ask...
...and things I'm just better off not knowing.
So I'll just bottle up my worries...
...and get by...
...like I always have.

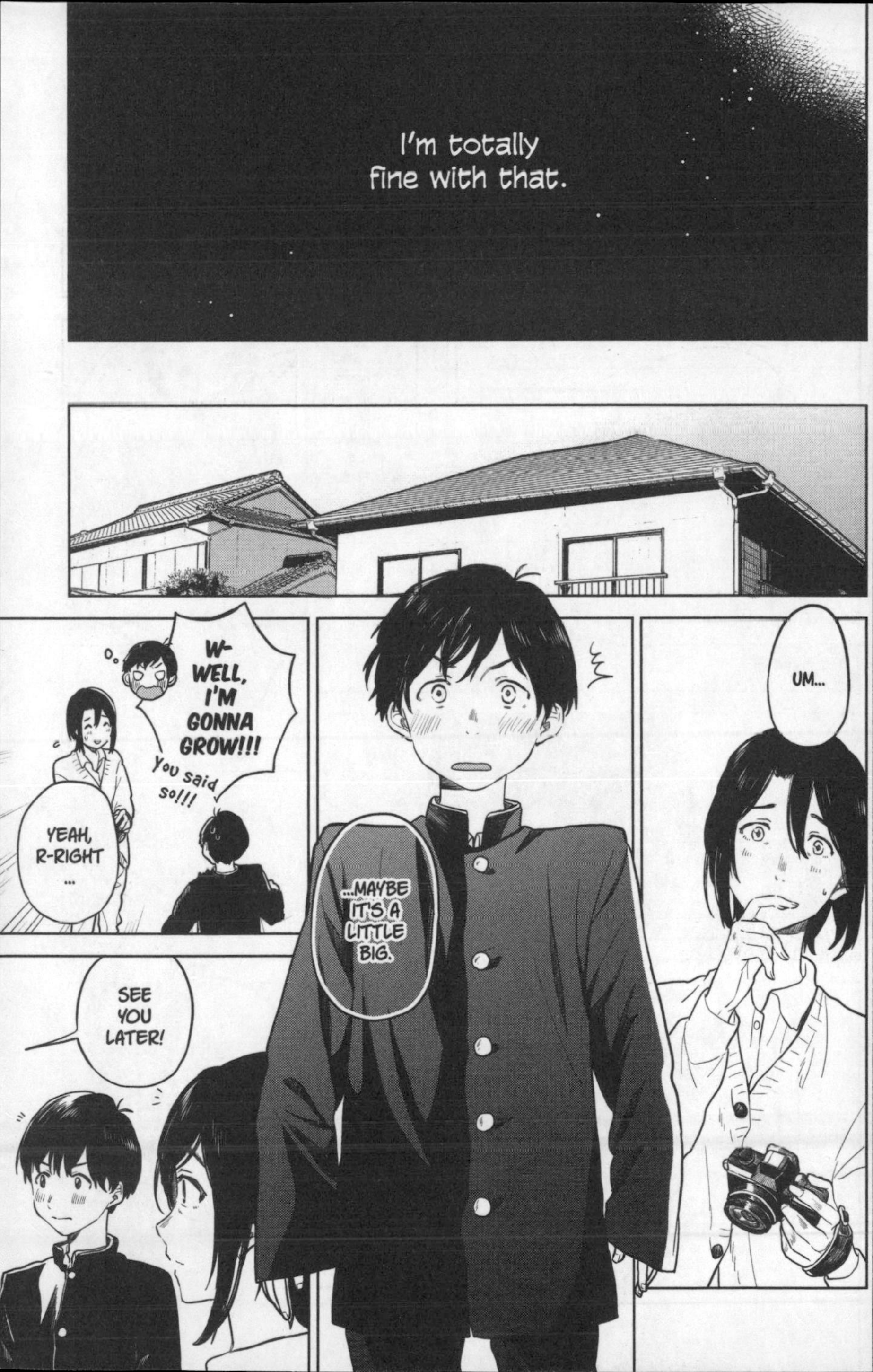
I'm totally fine with that.
UM...
...MAYBE IT'S A LITTLE BIG.
W-WELL, I'M GONNA GROW!!!
You said so!!!
YEAH, R-RIGHT...
SEE YOU LATER!

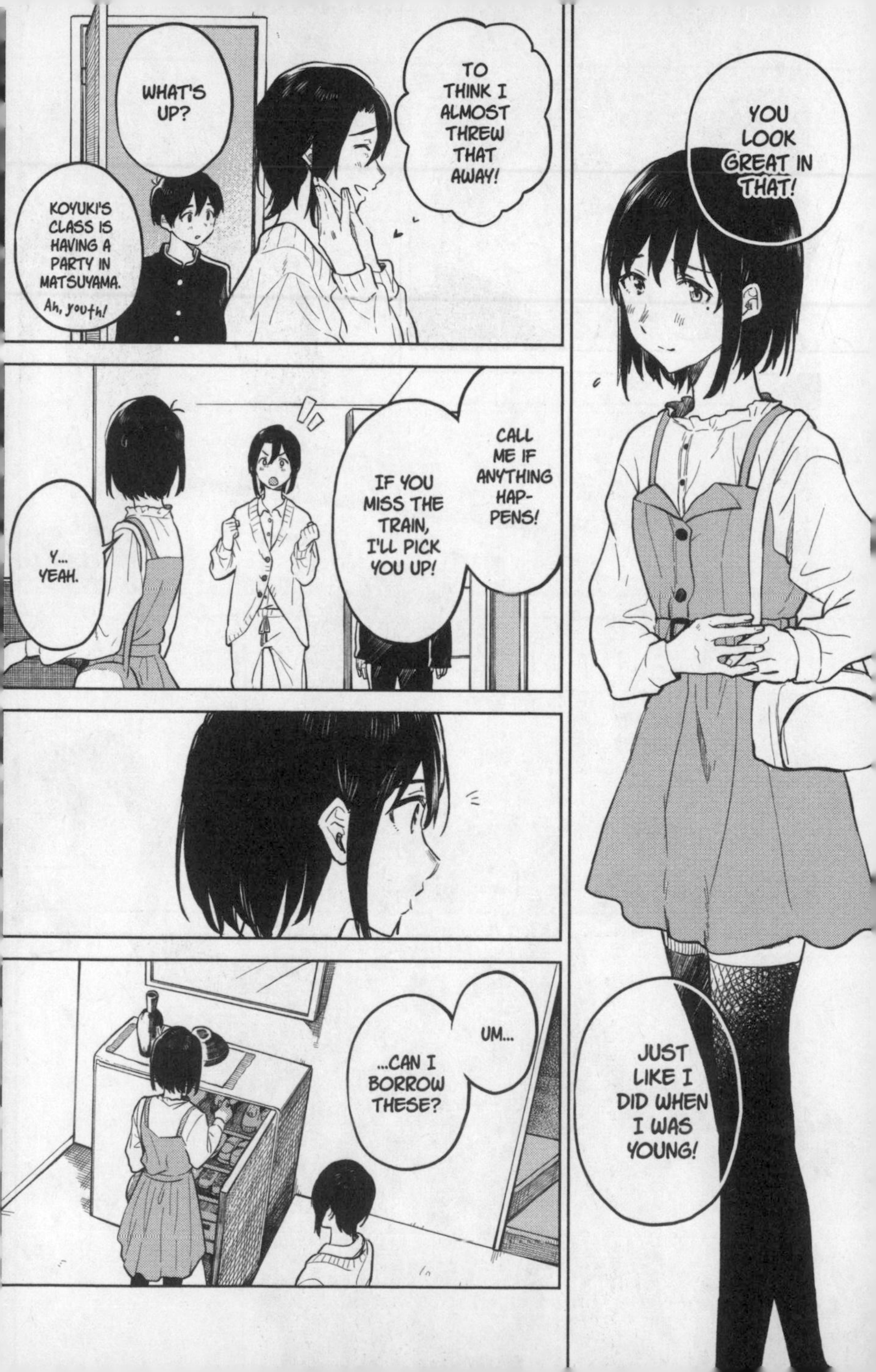
YOU LOOK GREAT IN THAT!
JUST LIKE I DID WHEN I WAS YOUNG!
TO THINK I ALMOST THREW THAT AWAY!
WHAT'S UP?
KOYUKI'S CLASS IS HAVING A PARTY IN MATSUYAMA.
Ah, youth!
CALL ME IF ANYTHING HAP-PENS!
IF YOU MISS THE TRAIN, I'LL PICK YOU UP!
Y... YEAH.
UM...
...CAN I BORROW THESE?

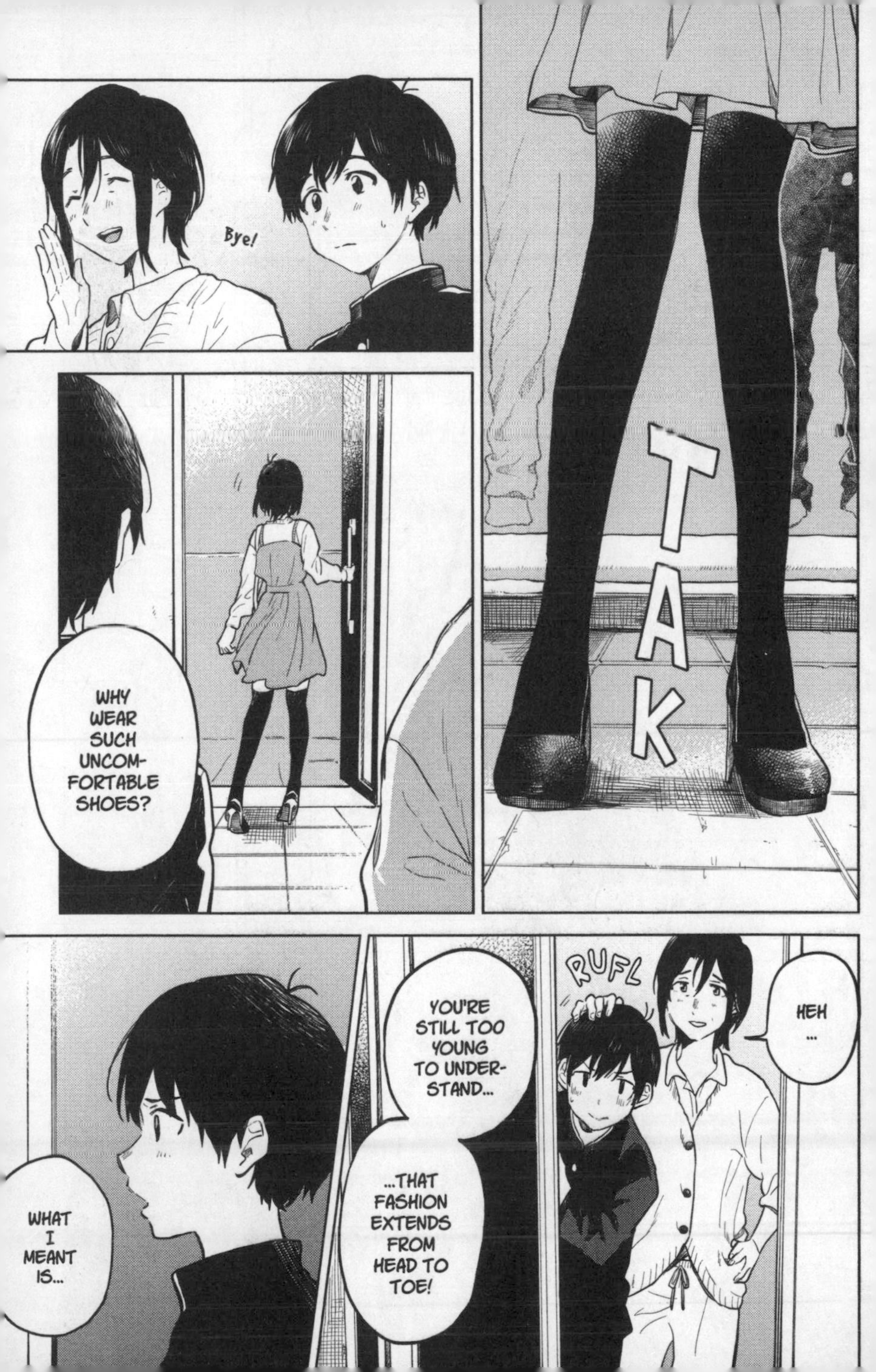
TAK
Bye!
WHY WEAR SUCH UNCOM-FORTABLE SHOES?
HEH ...
RUFL
YOU'RE STILL TOO YOUNG TO UNDER-STAND...
...THAT FASHION EXTENDS FROM HEAD TO TOE!
WHAT I MEANT IS...

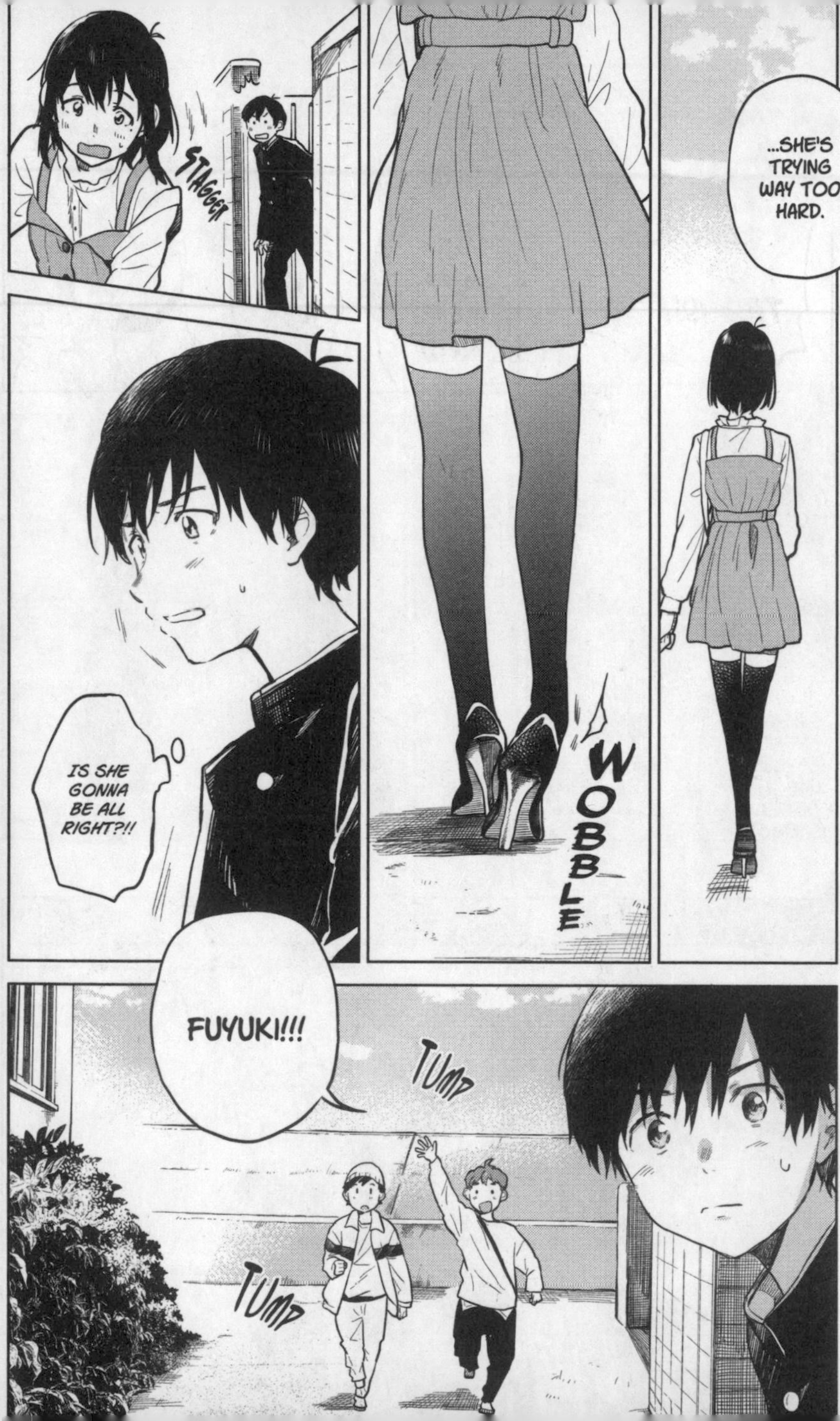
...SHE'S TRYING WAY TOO HARD.
WOBBLE
STAGGER
IS SHE GONNA BE ALL RIGHT?!!
FUYUKI!!!
TUMP
TUMP

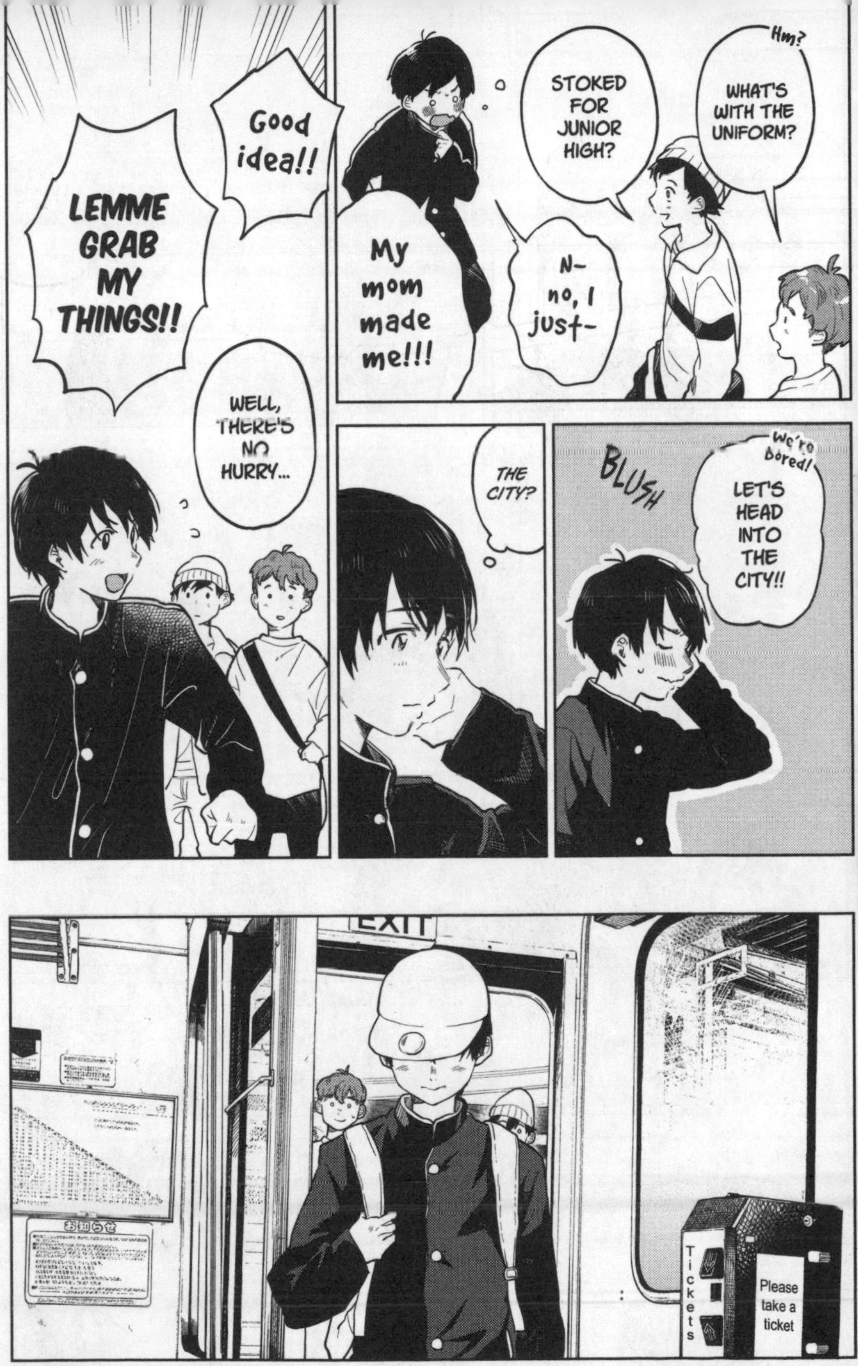
Hm?
WHAT'S WITH THE UNIFORM?
STOKED FOR JUNIOR HIGH?
N-no, I just-
My mom made me!!!
We're bored!
LET'S HEAD INTO THE CITY!!
BLUSH
THE CITY?
Good idea!!
LEMME GRAB MY THINGS!!
WELL, THERE'S NO HURRY...
EXIT
お知らせ
Tickets
Please take a ticket

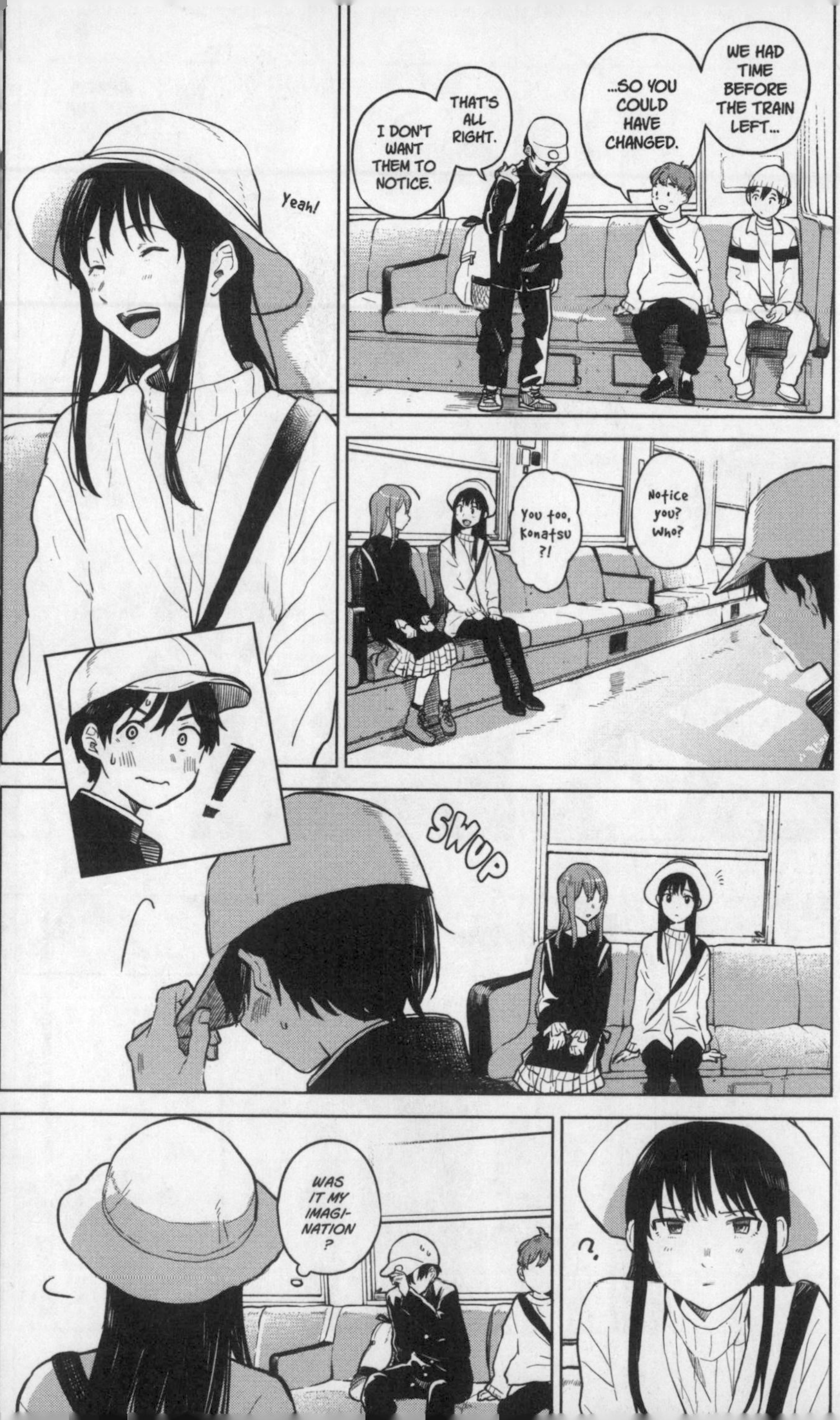
WE HAD TIME BEFORE THE TRAIN LEFT...
...SO YOU COULD HAVE CHANGED.
THAT'S ALL RIGHT.
I DON'T WANT THEM TO NOTICE.
Notice you? Who?
You too, Konatsu?!
Yeah!
!
SWUP
?
WAS IT MY IMAGINATION?

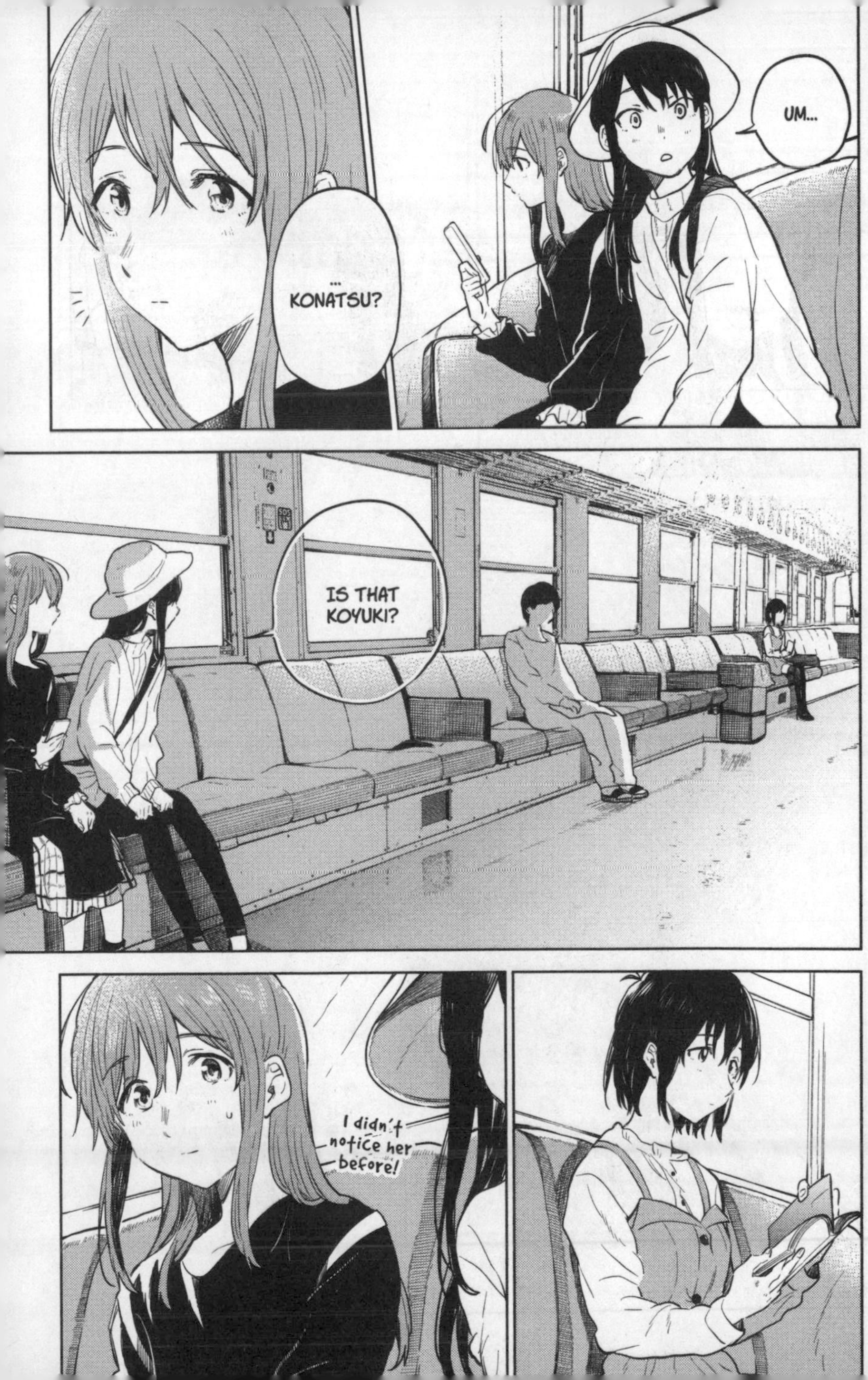
UM...
... KONATSU?
IS THAT KOYUKI?
I didn't notice her before!

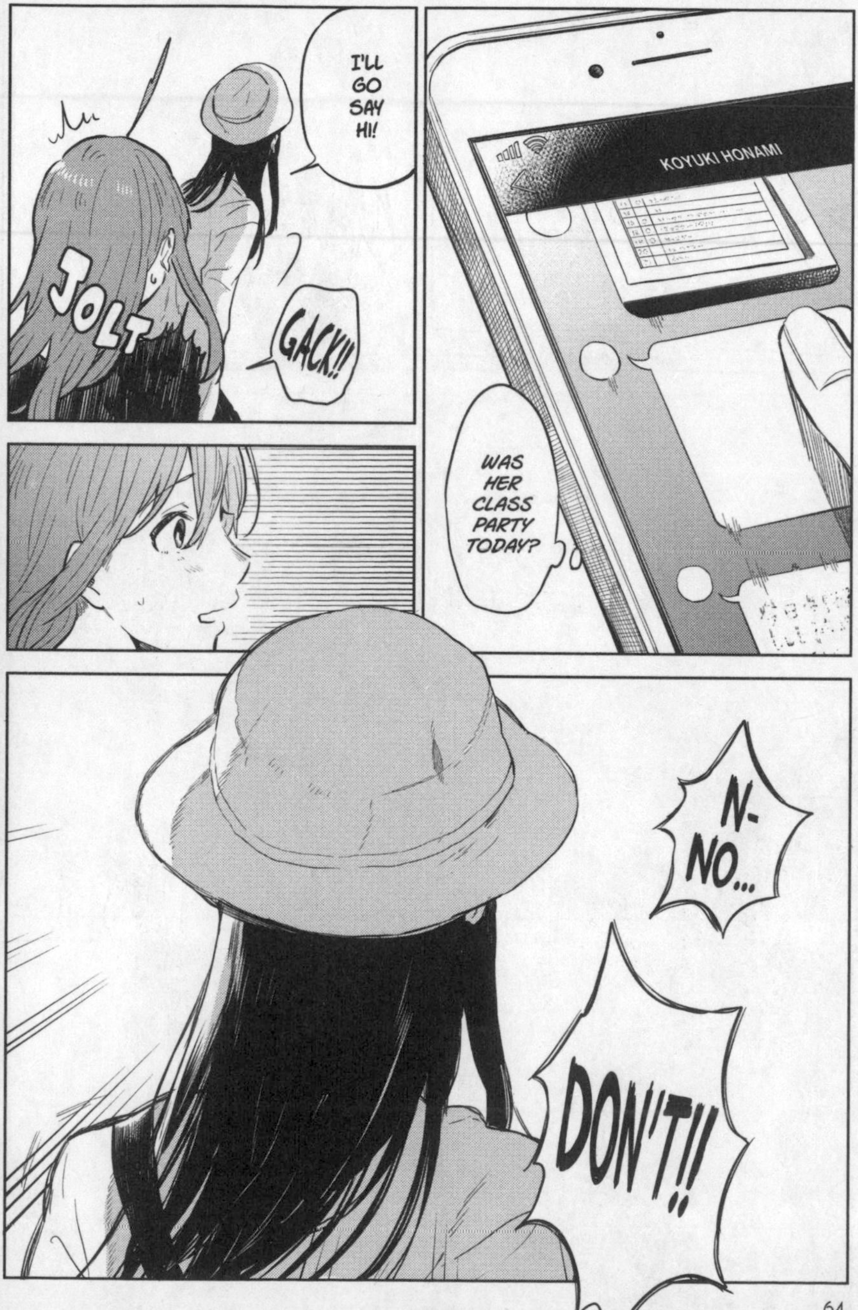
KOYUKI HONAMI
WAS HER CLASS PARTY TODAY?
I'LL GO SAY HI!
JOLT
GACK!!
N-NO...
DON'T!!

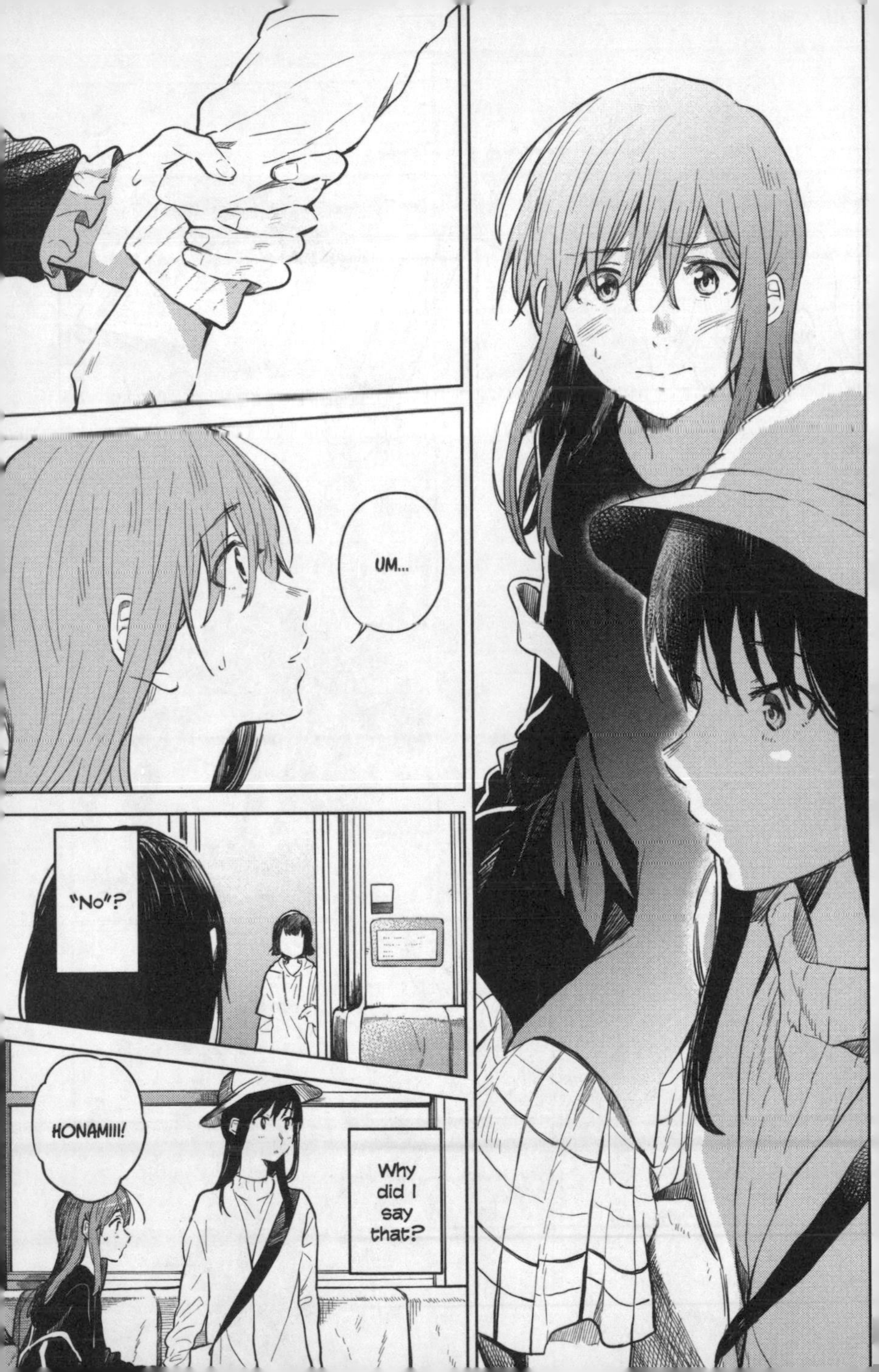
UM...
"No"?
Why did I say that?
HONAMIII!

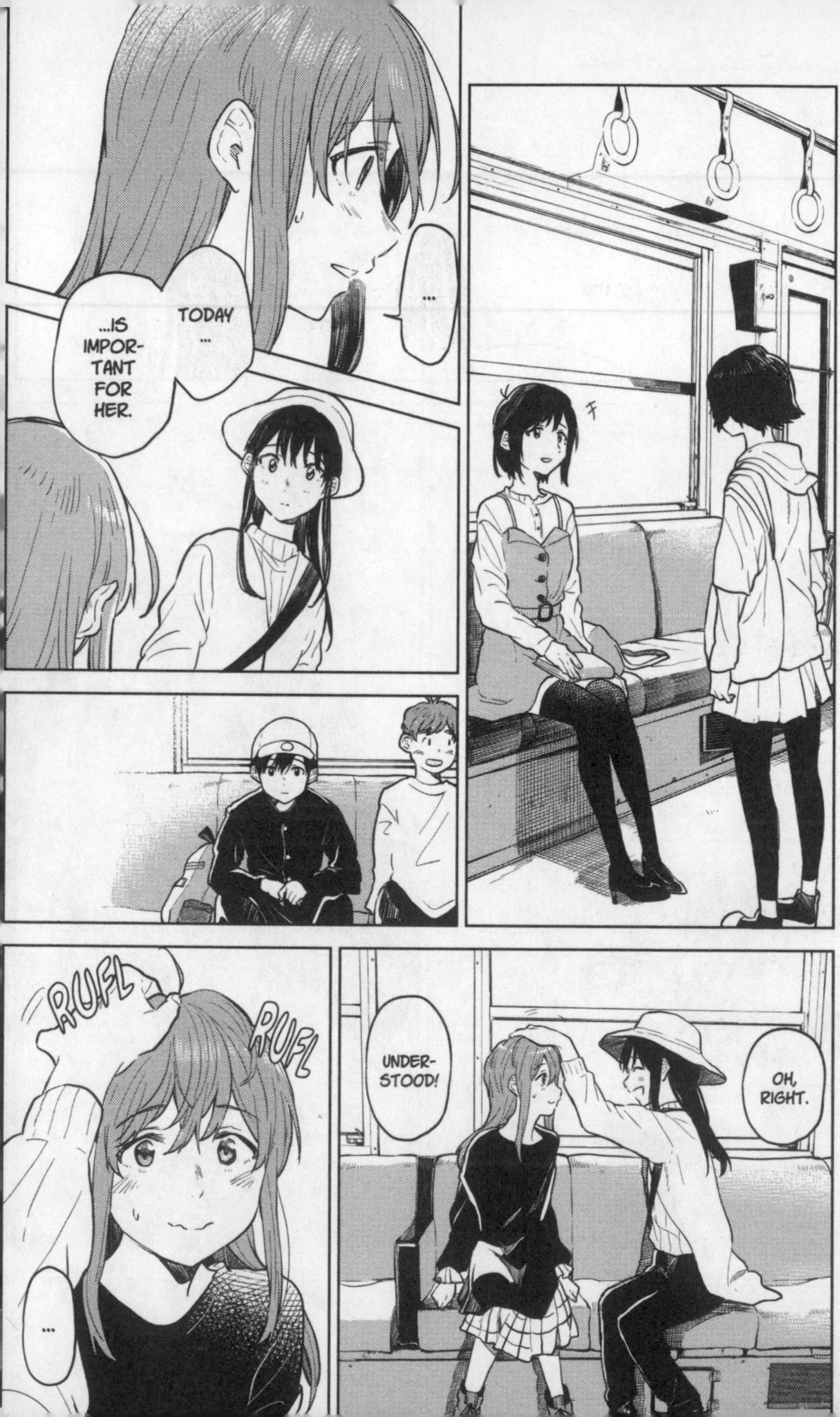
...
TODAY ...
...IS IMPORTANT FOR HER.
OH, RIGHT.
UNDER-STOOD!
RUFL
RUFL
...

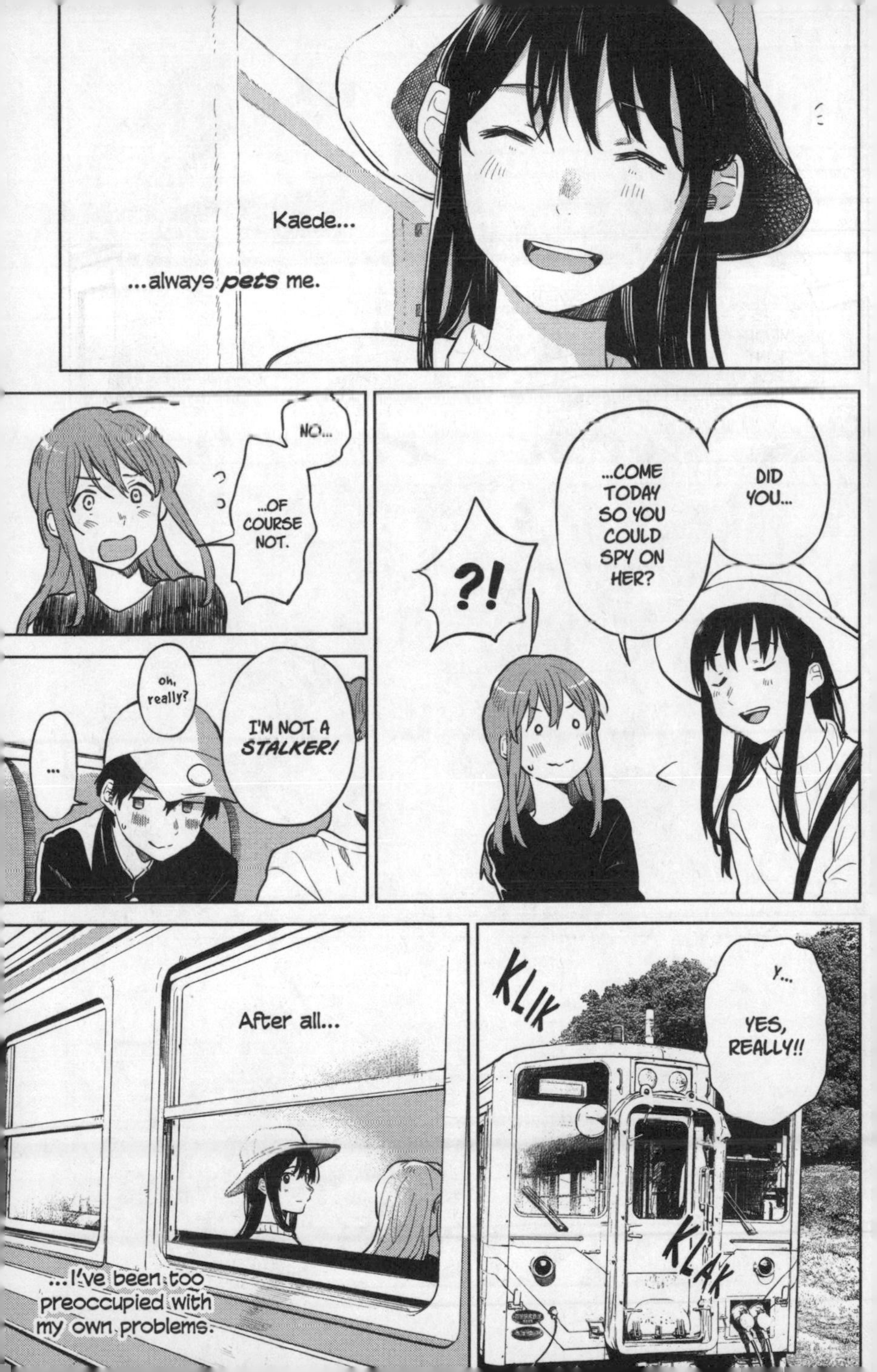
Kaede...
...always *pets* me.
DID YOU...
...COME TODAY SO YOU COULD SPY ON HER?
?!
NO...
...OF COURSE NOT.
I'M NOT A *STALKER!*
oh, really?
...
KLIK
Y...
YES, REALLY!!
KLAK
After all...
...I've been too preoccupied with my own problems.

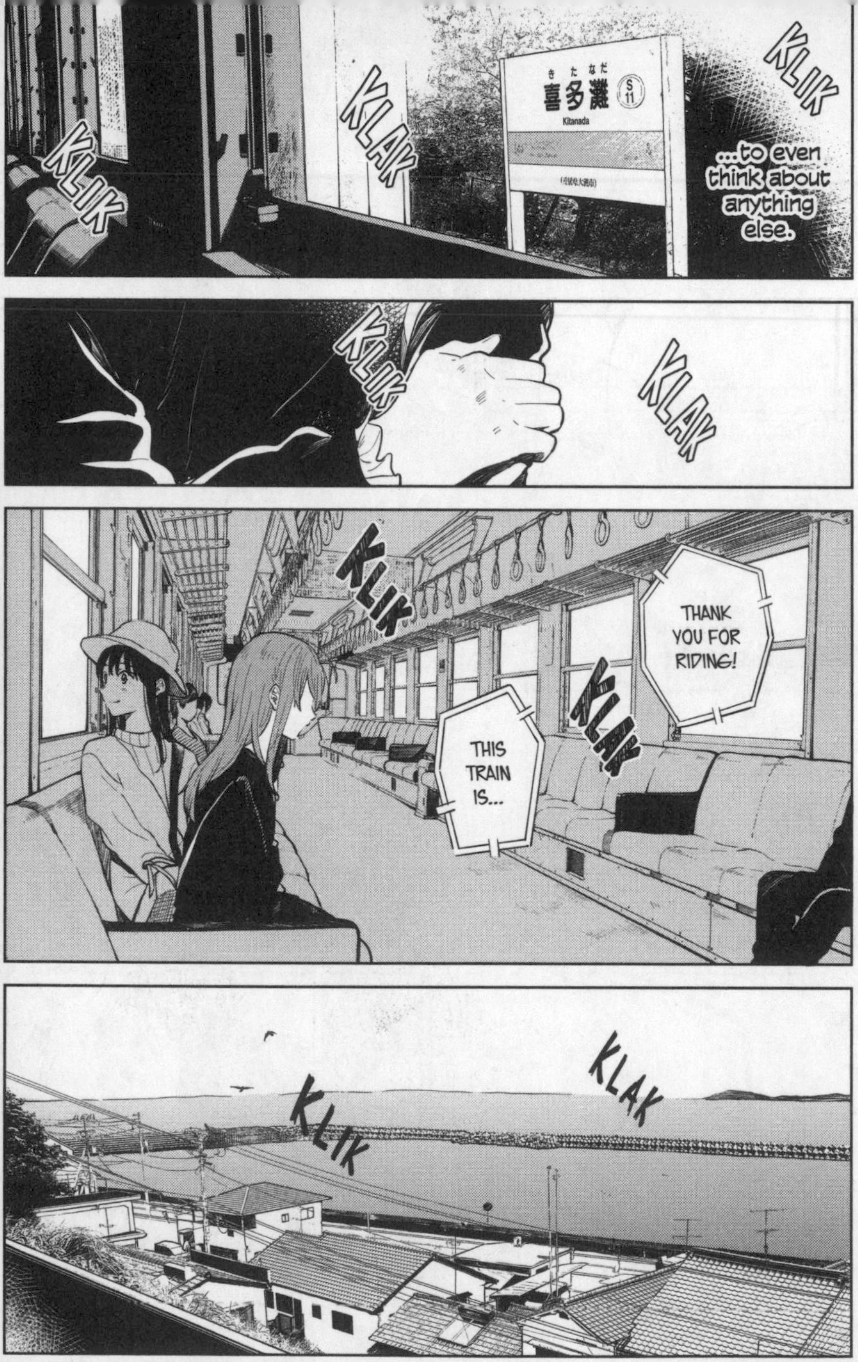
KLIK
...to even think about anything else.
きたなだ
喜多灘
S11
Kitanada
KLAK
KLIK
KLAK
KLIK
THANK YOU FOR RIDING!
KLAK
KLIK
THIS TRAIN IS...
KLAK
KLIK

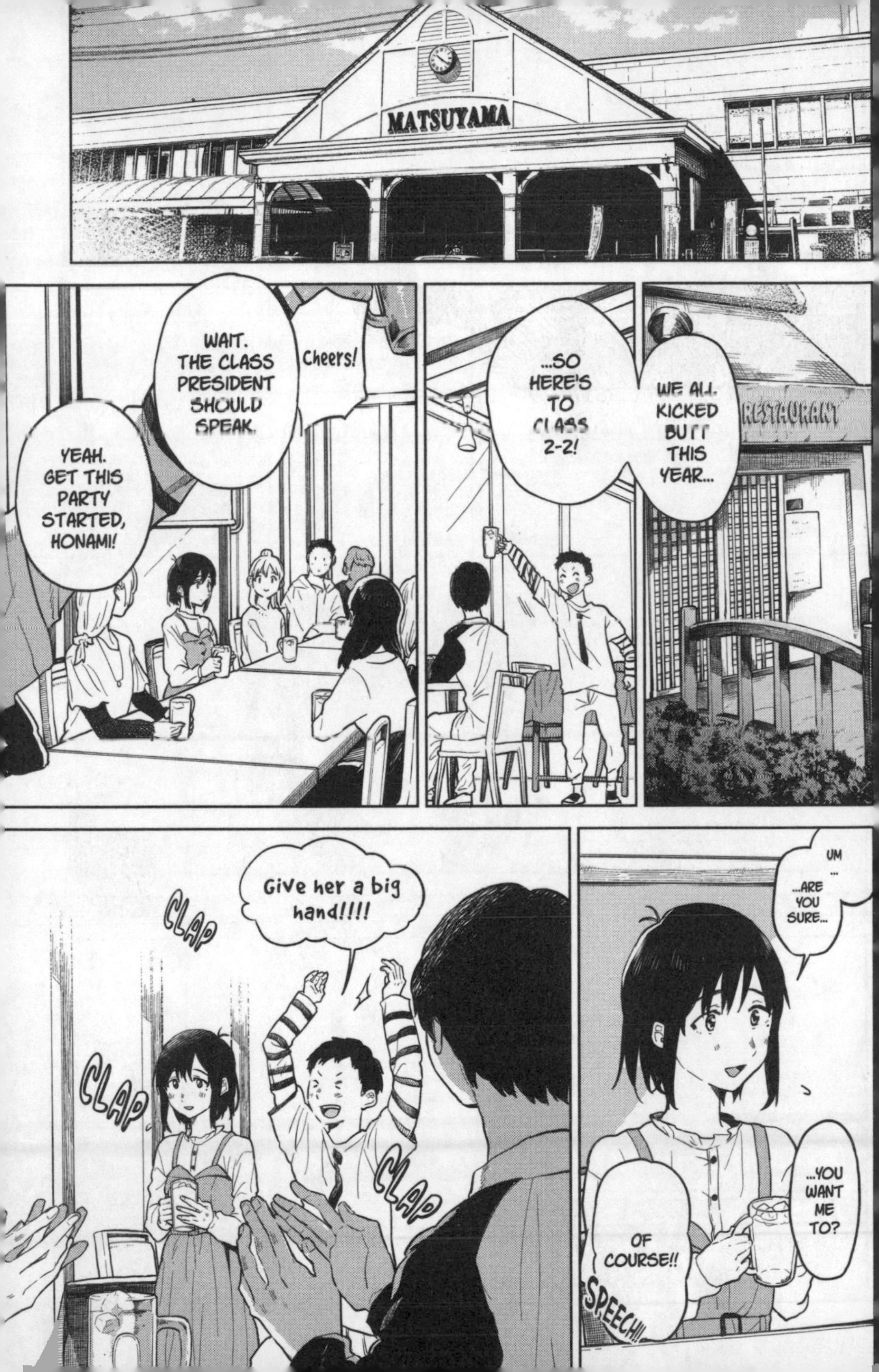
MATSUYAMA
RESTAURANT
WE ALL KICKED BUTT THIS YEAR...
...SO HERE'S TO CLASS 2-2!
Cheers!
WAIT. THE CLASS PRESIDENT SHOULD SPEAK.
YEAH. GET THIS PARTY STARTED, HONAMI!
UM... ...ARE YOU SURE...
...YOU WANT ME TO?
OF COURSE!!
SPEECH!!
Give her a big hand!!!!
CLAP
CLAP
CLAP

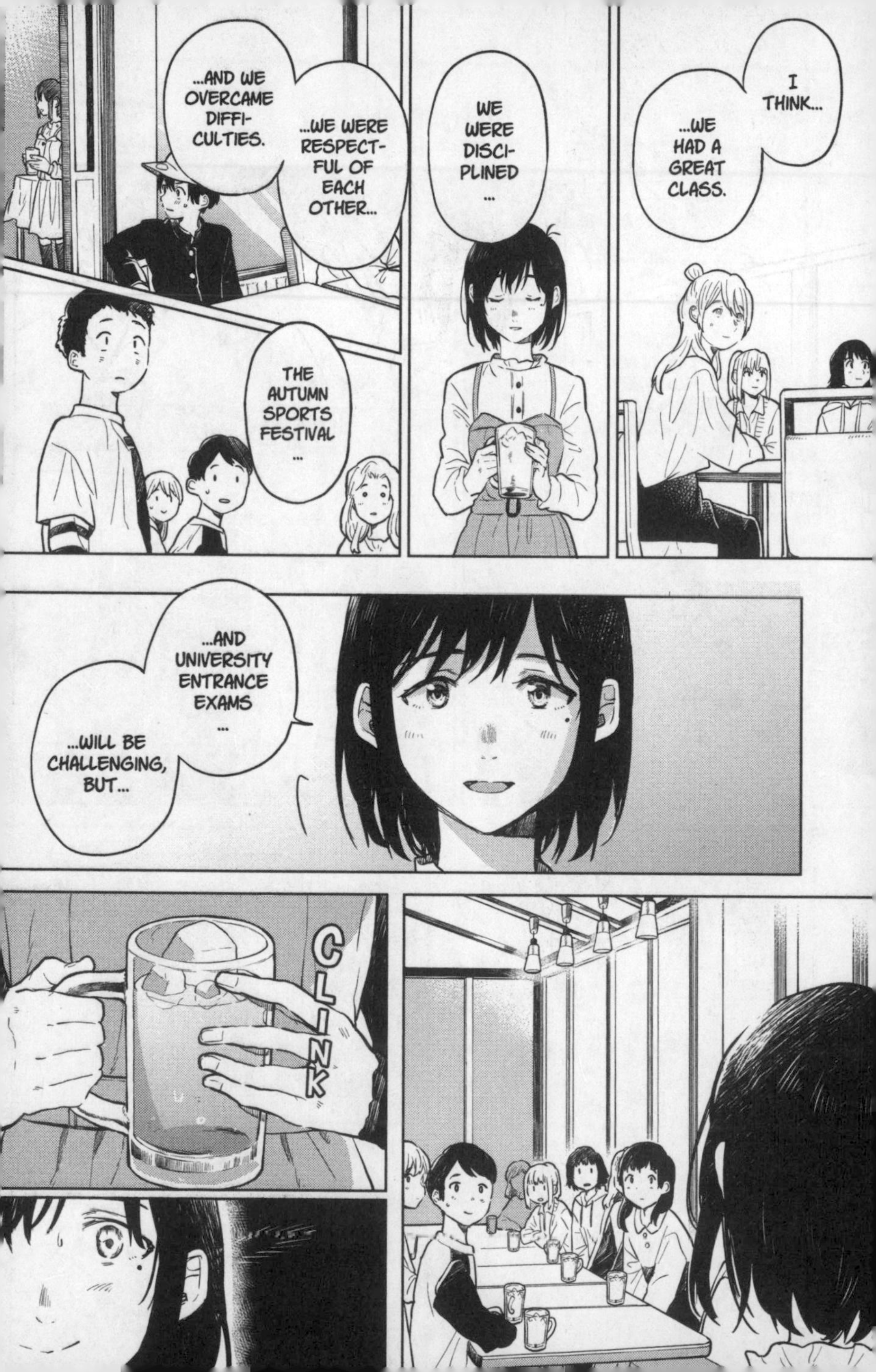
I THINK...
...WE HAD A GREAT CLASS.
WE WERE DISCI-PLINED ...
...WE WERE RESPECT-FUL OF EACH OTHER...
...AND WE OVERCAME DIFFI-CULTIES.
THE AUTUMN SPORTS FESTIVAL ...
...AND UNIVERSITY ENTRANCE EXAMS ...
...WILL BE CHALLENGING, BUT...
CLINK

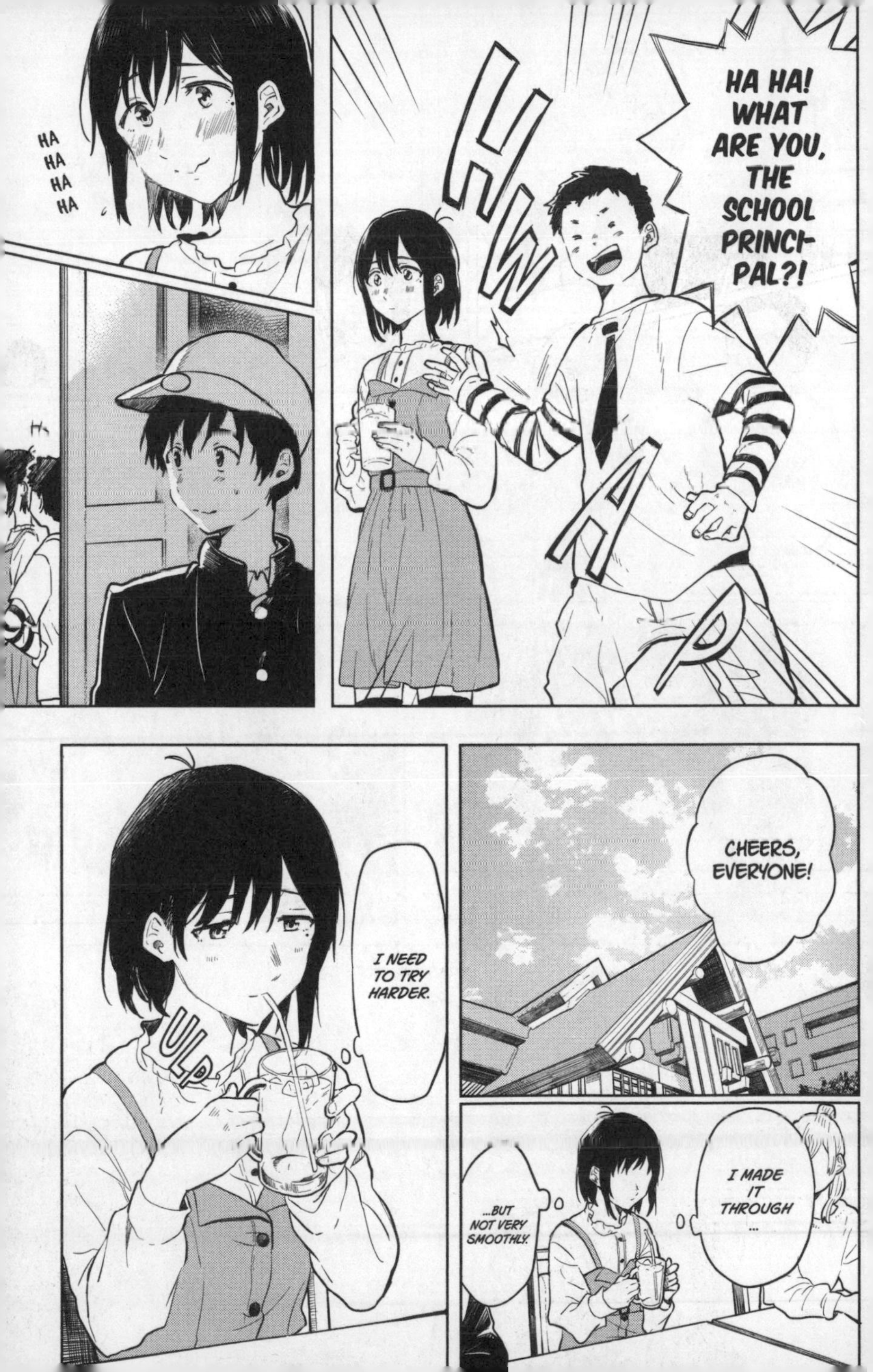
HA HA! WHAT ARE YOU, THE SCHOOL PRINCI-PAL?!
HWAAP
HA HA HA HA
CHEERS, EVERYONE!
I MADE IT THROUGH ...
...BUT NOT VERY SMOOTHLY.
I NEED TO TRY HARDER.
ULP

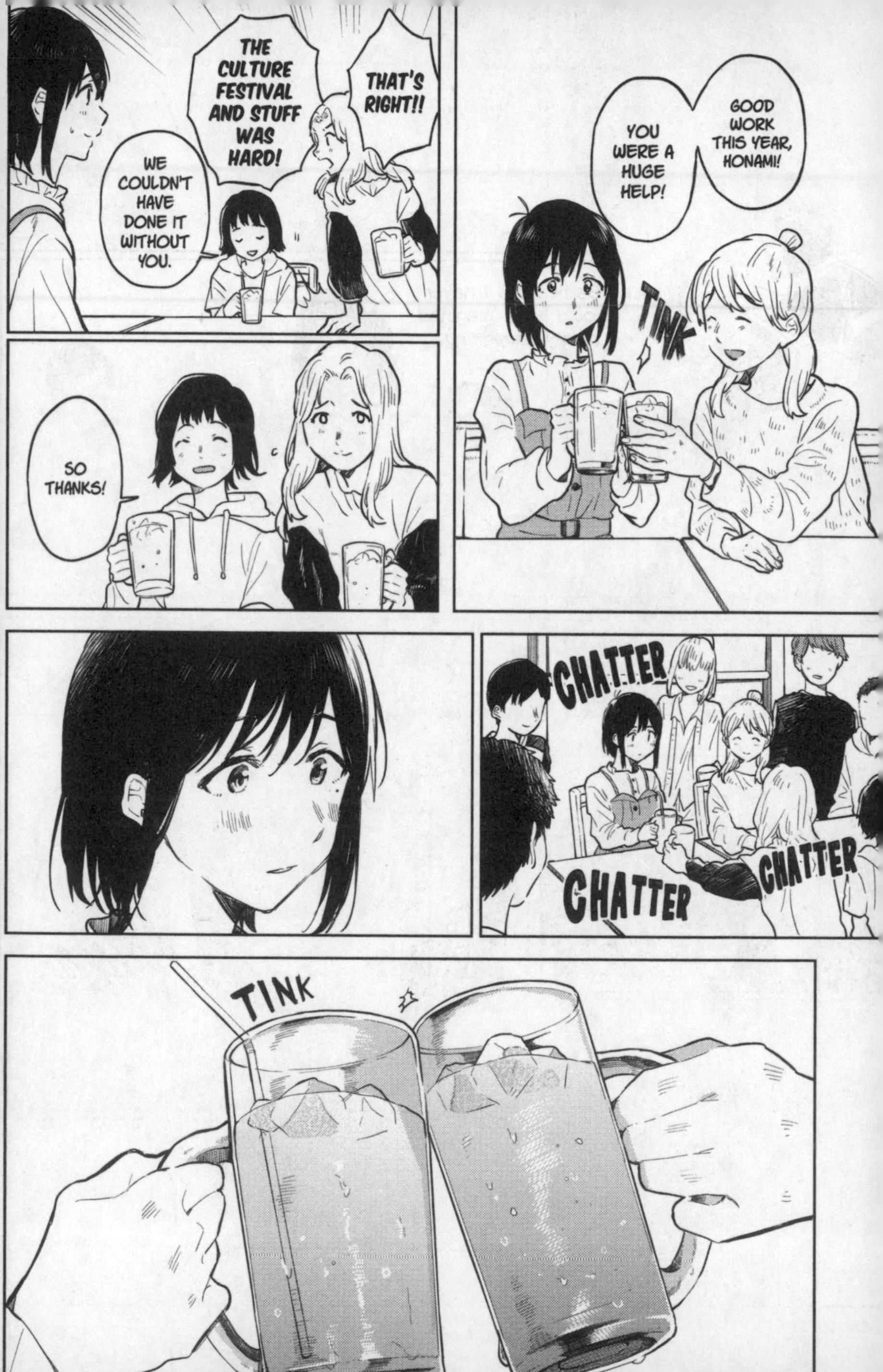
GOOD WORK THIS YEAR, HONAMI!
YOU WERE A HUGE HELP!
TINK
THAT'S RIGHT!!
THE CULTURE FESTIVAL AND STUFF WAS HARD!
WE COULDN'T HAVE DONE IT WITHOUT YOU.
SO THANKS!
CHATTER
CHATTER
CHATTER
TINK

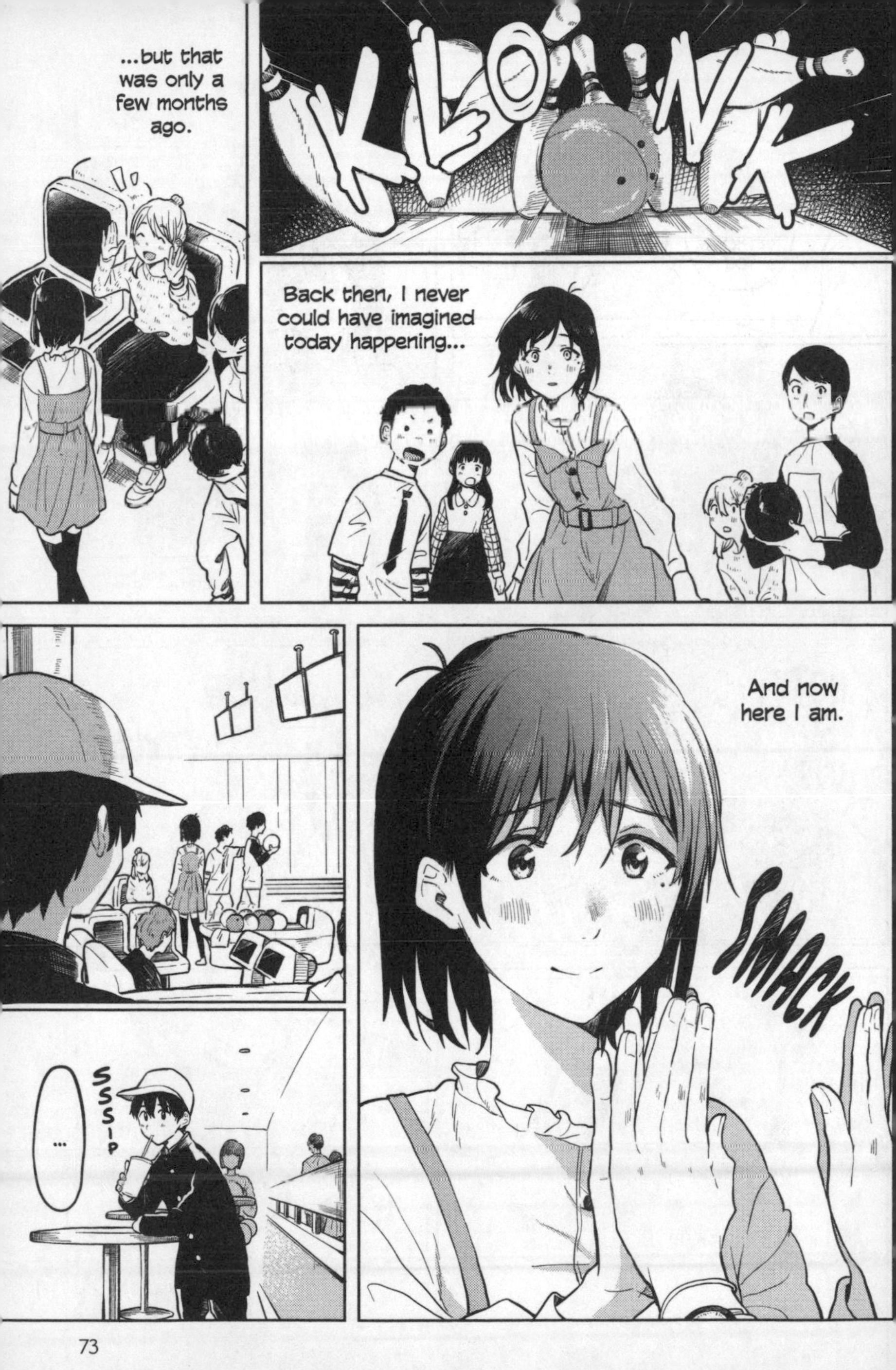
KLONK
Back then, I never could have imagined today happening...
...but that was only a few months ago.
And now here I am.
SMACK
SSSIP
...

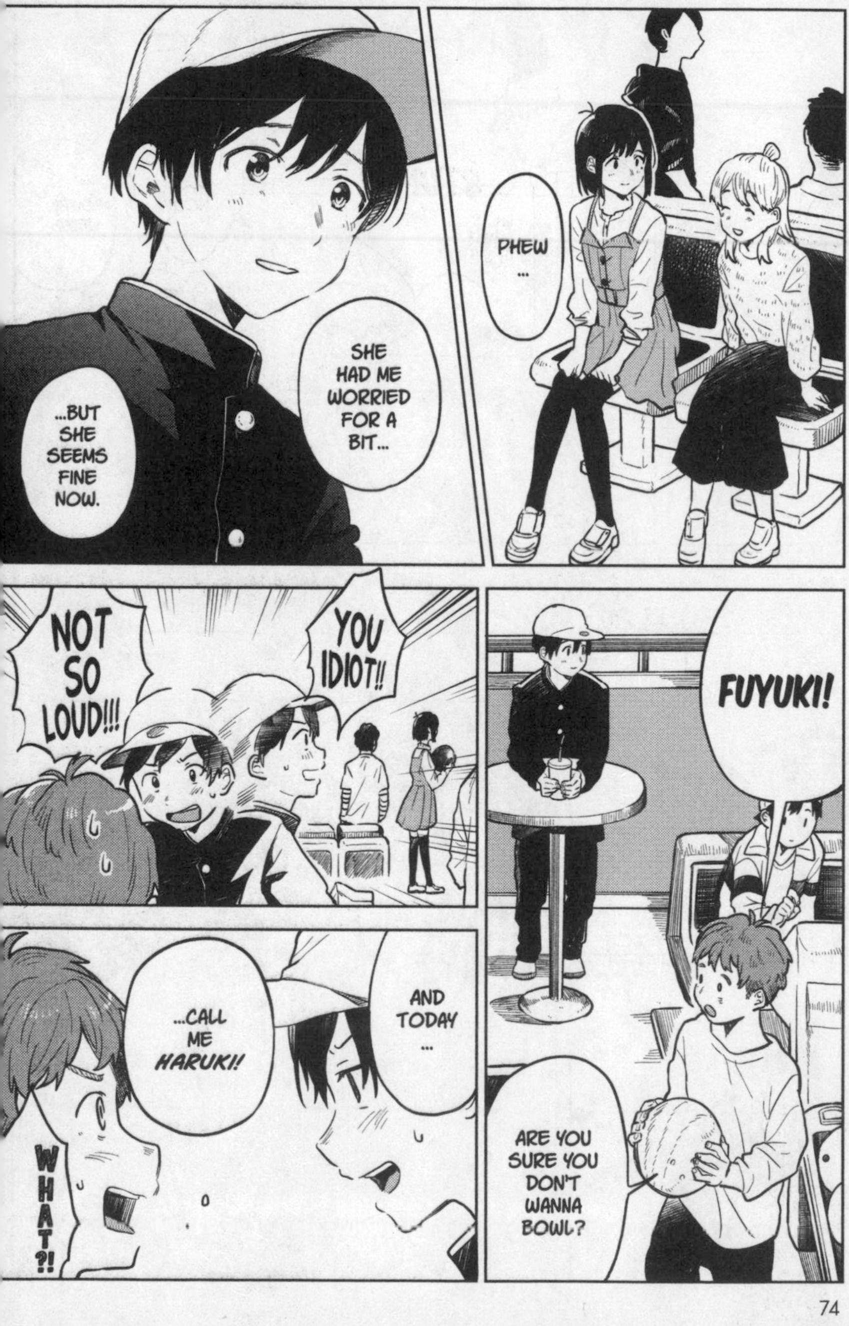
PHEW ...
SHE HAD ME WORRIED FOR A BIT...
...BUT SHE SEEMS FINE NOW.
FUYUKI!
ARE YOU SURE YOU DON'T WANNA BOWL?
YOU IDIOT!!
NOT SO LOUD!!!
AND TODAY ...
...CALL ME HARUKI!
WHAT?!

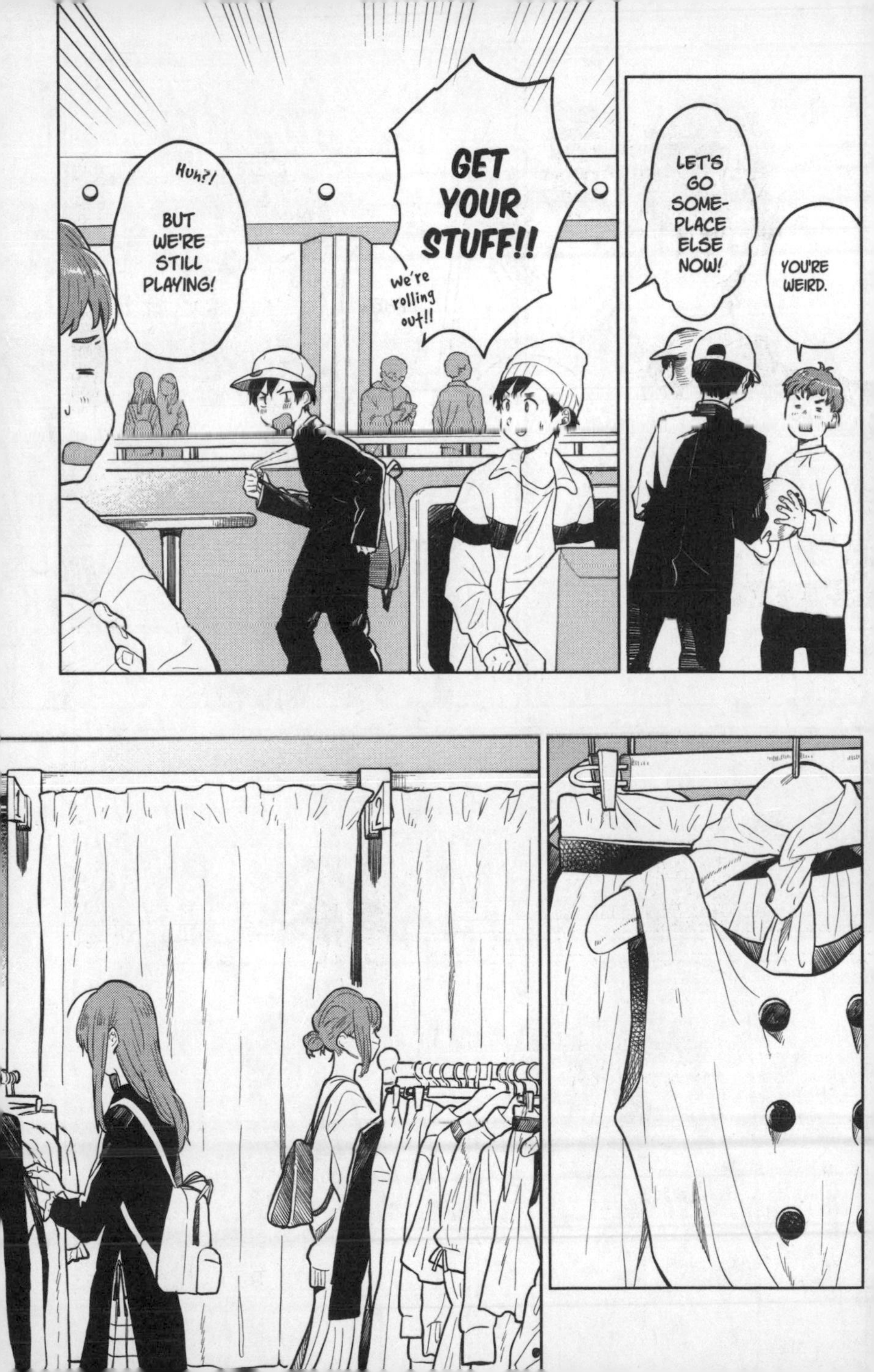
LET'S GO SOME-PLACE ELSE NOW!
YOU'RE WEIRD.
GET YOUR STUFF!!
We're rolling out!!
Huh?!
BUT WE'RE STILL PLAYING!

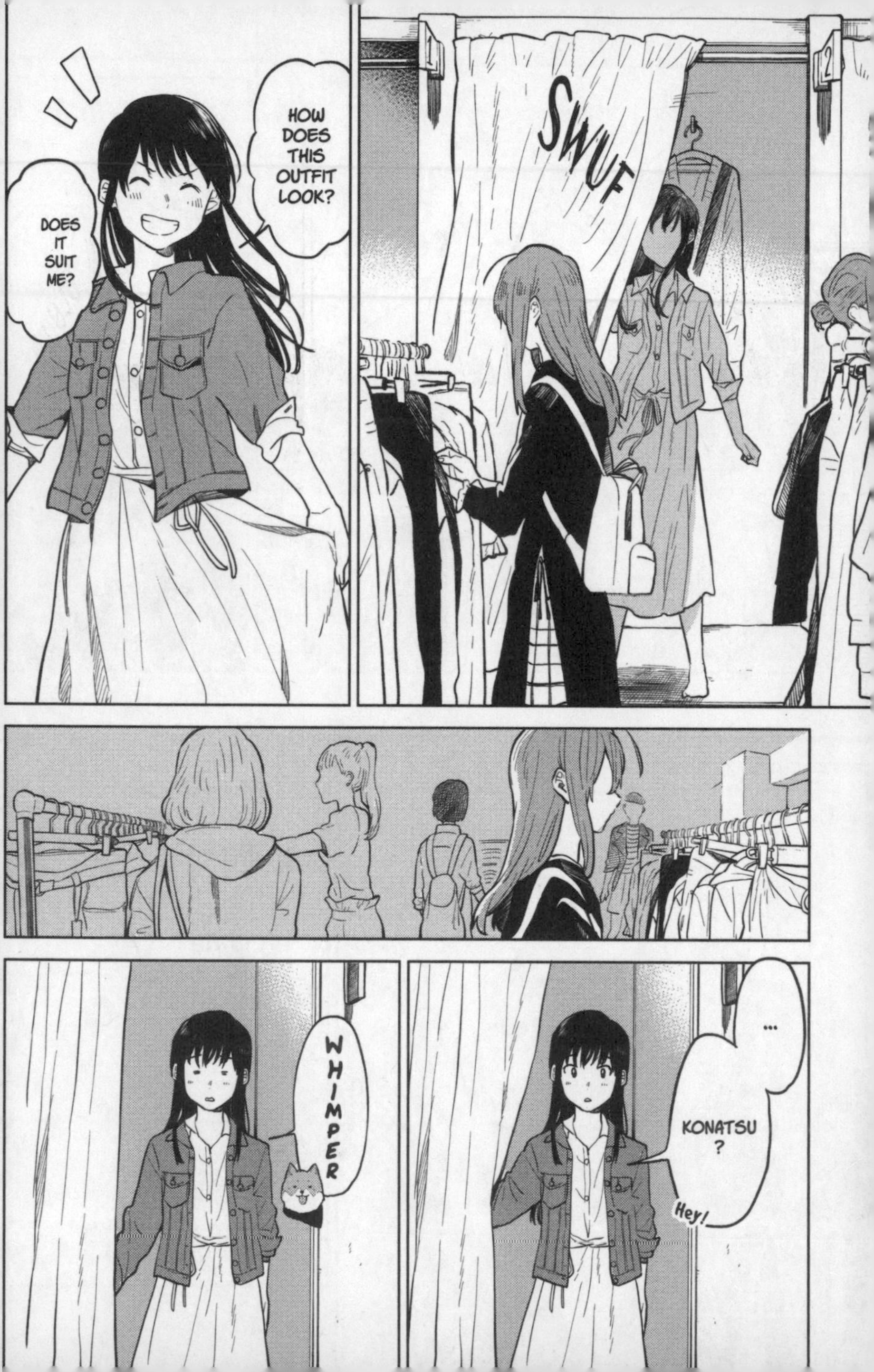
SWUF
HOW DOES THIS OUTFIT LOOK?
DOES IT SUIT ME?
...
KONATSU?
Hey!
WHIMPER

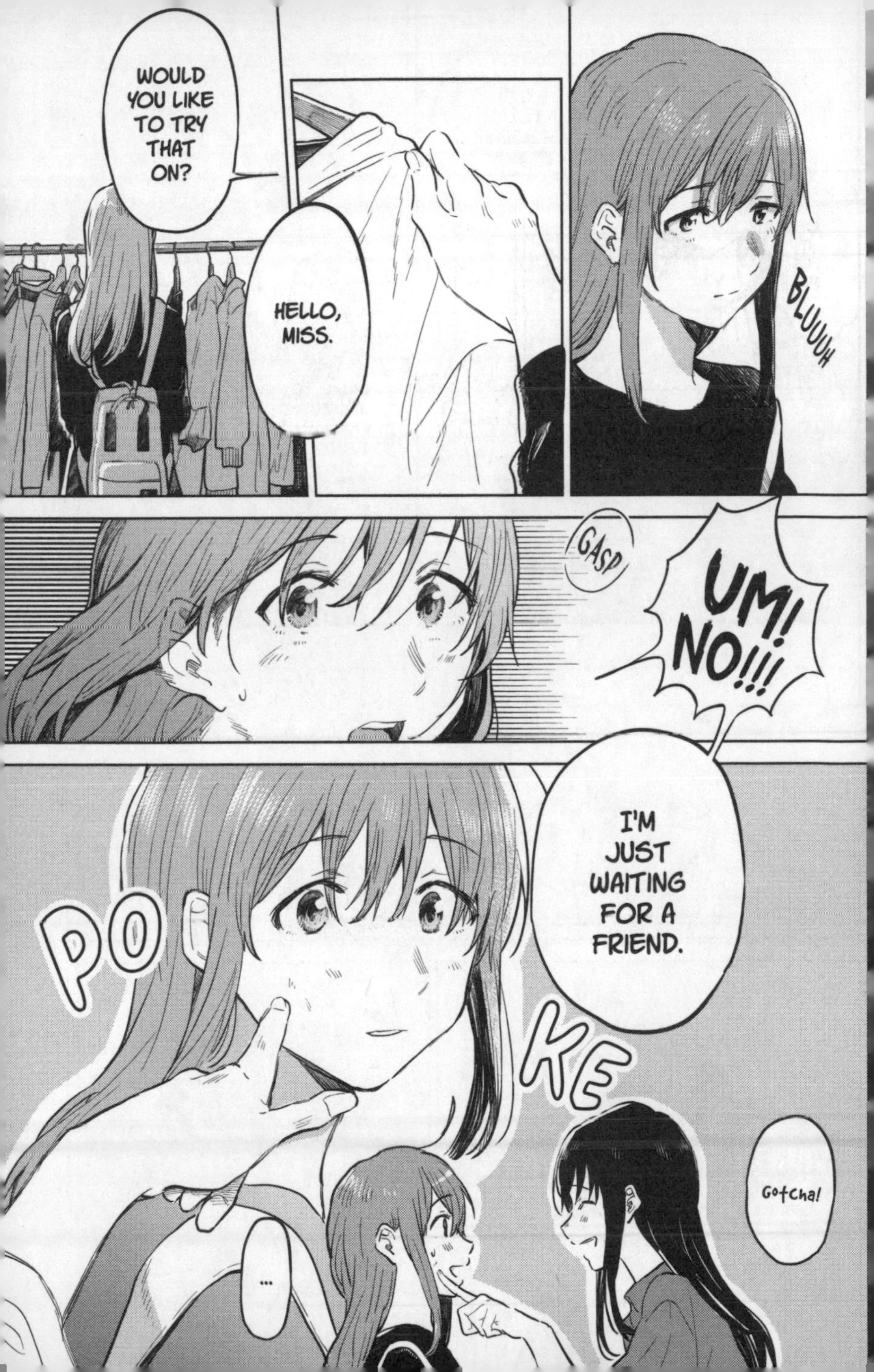
BLUUUH
HELLO, MISS.
WOULD YOU LIKE TO TRY THAT ON?
GASP
UM! NO!!!
I'M JUST WAITING FOR A FRIEND.
POKE
Gotcha!
...

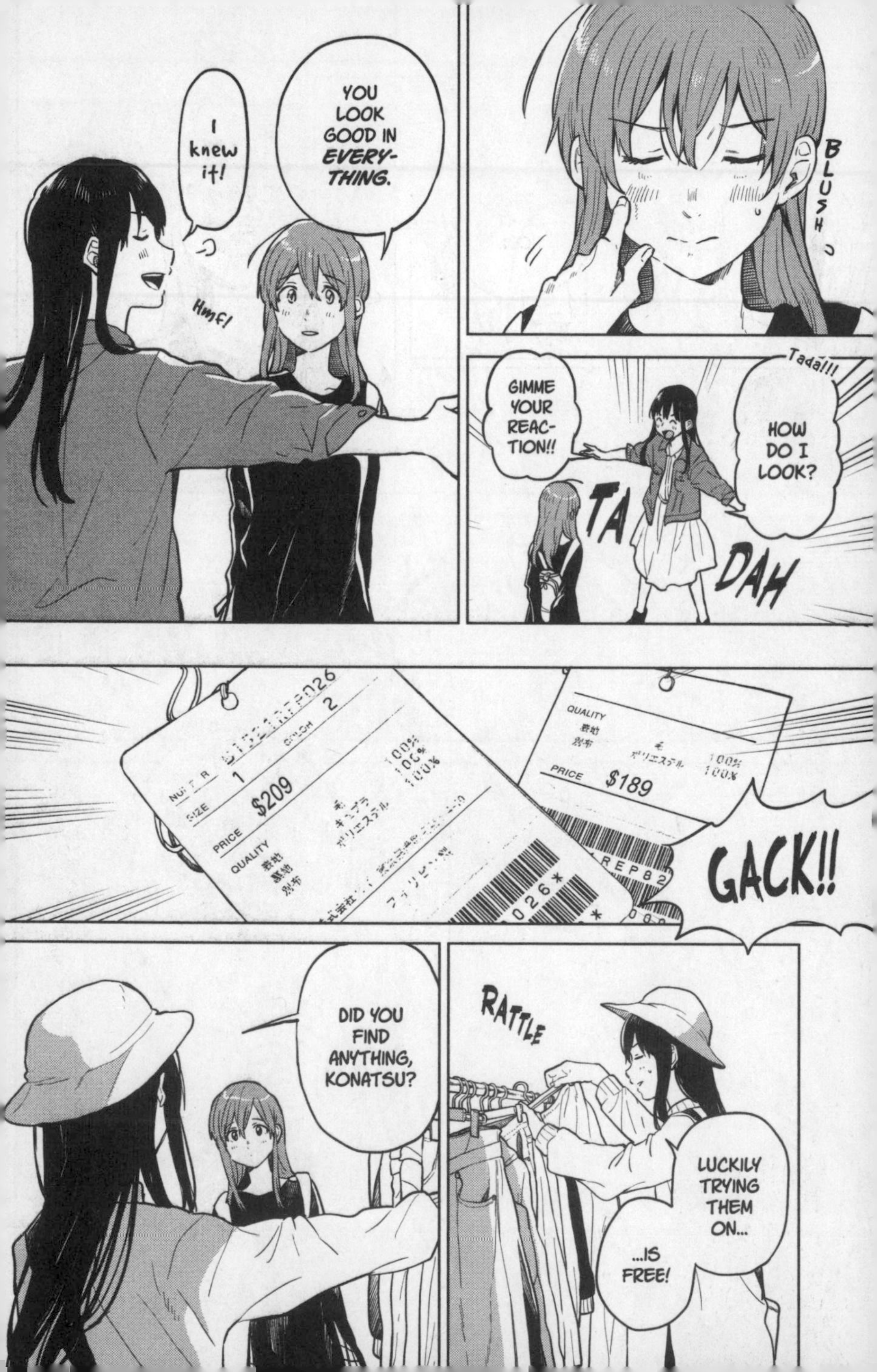
BLUSH
Tada!!!
HOW DO I LOOK?
GIMME YOUR REACTION!!
TA DAH
YOU LOOK GOOD IN EVERYTHING.
I knew it!
Hmf!
QUALITY
PRICE $189
SIZE 1
COLOR 2
PRICE $209
QUALITY
GACK!!
RATTLE
LUCKILY TRYING THEM ON...
...IS FREE!
DID YOU FIND ANYTHING, KONATSU?

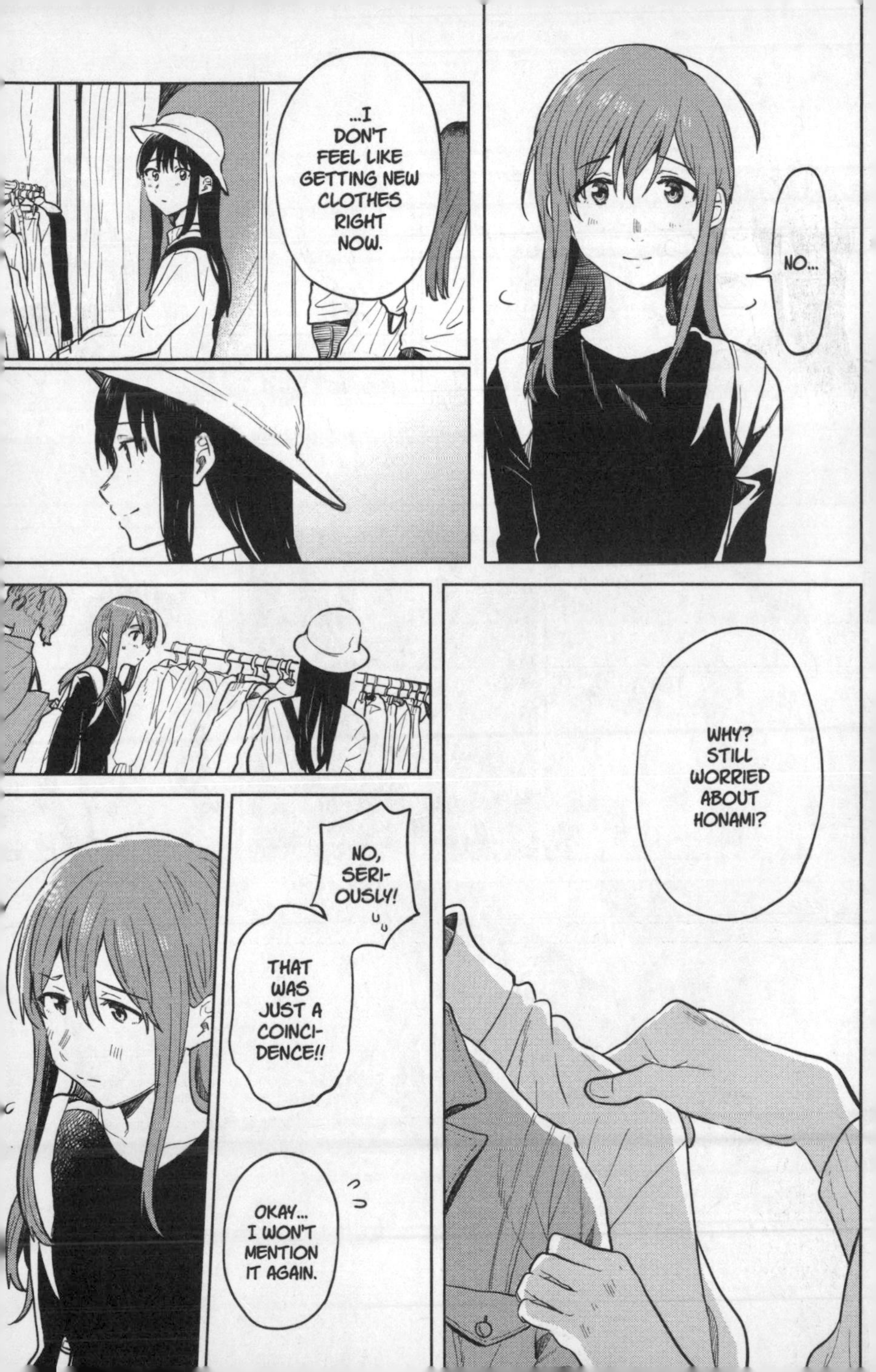
NO...
...I DON'T FEEL LIKE GETTING NEW CLOTHES RIGHT NOW.
WHY? STILL WORRIED ABOUT HONAMI?
NO, SERI-OUSLY!
THAT WAS JUST A COINCI-DENCE!!
OKAY... I WON'T MENTION IT AGAIN.

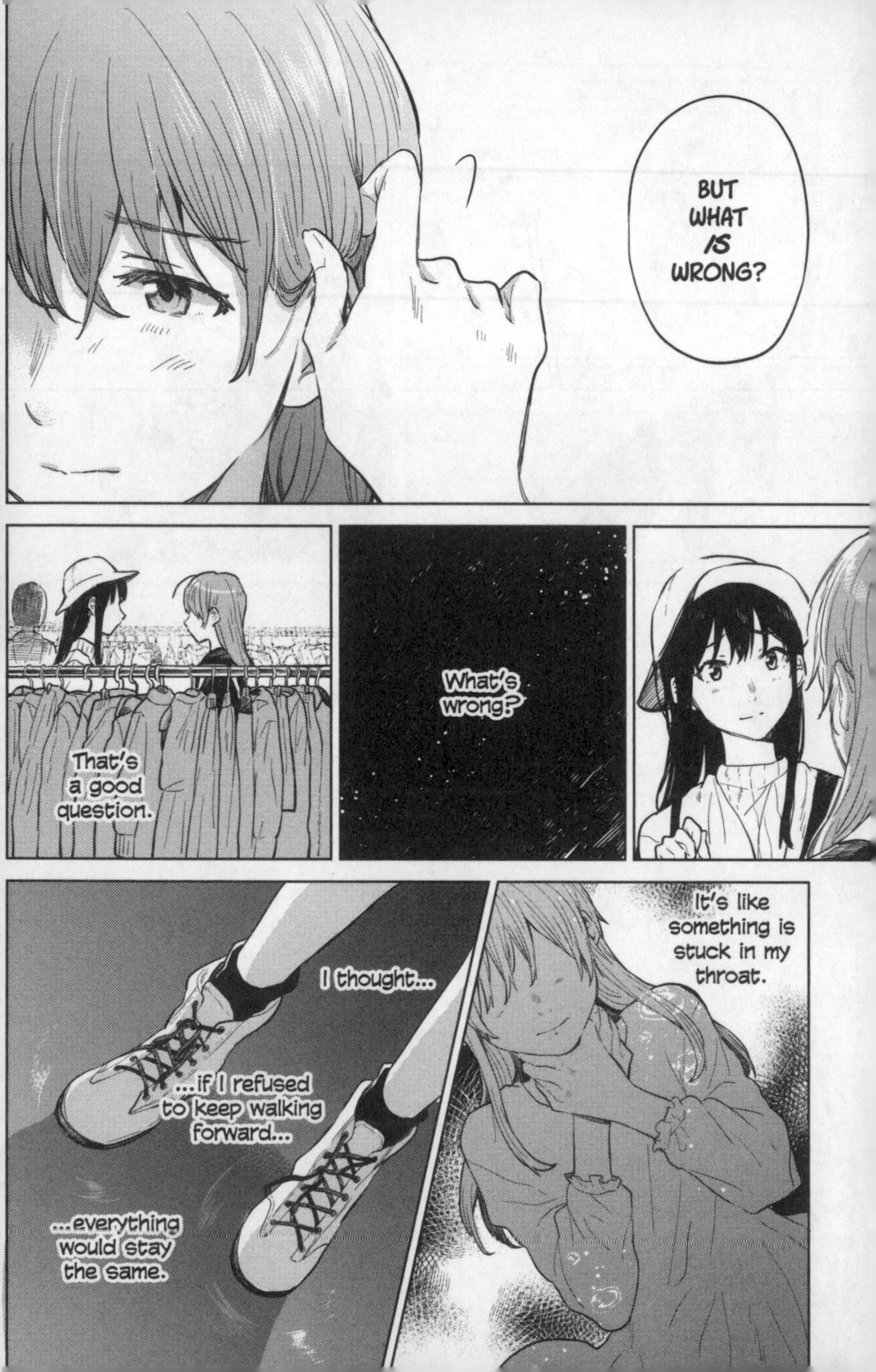
BUT WHAT IS WRONG?
What's wrong?
That's a good question.
It's like something is stuck in my throat.
I thought...
...if I refused to keep walking forward...
...everything would stay the same.

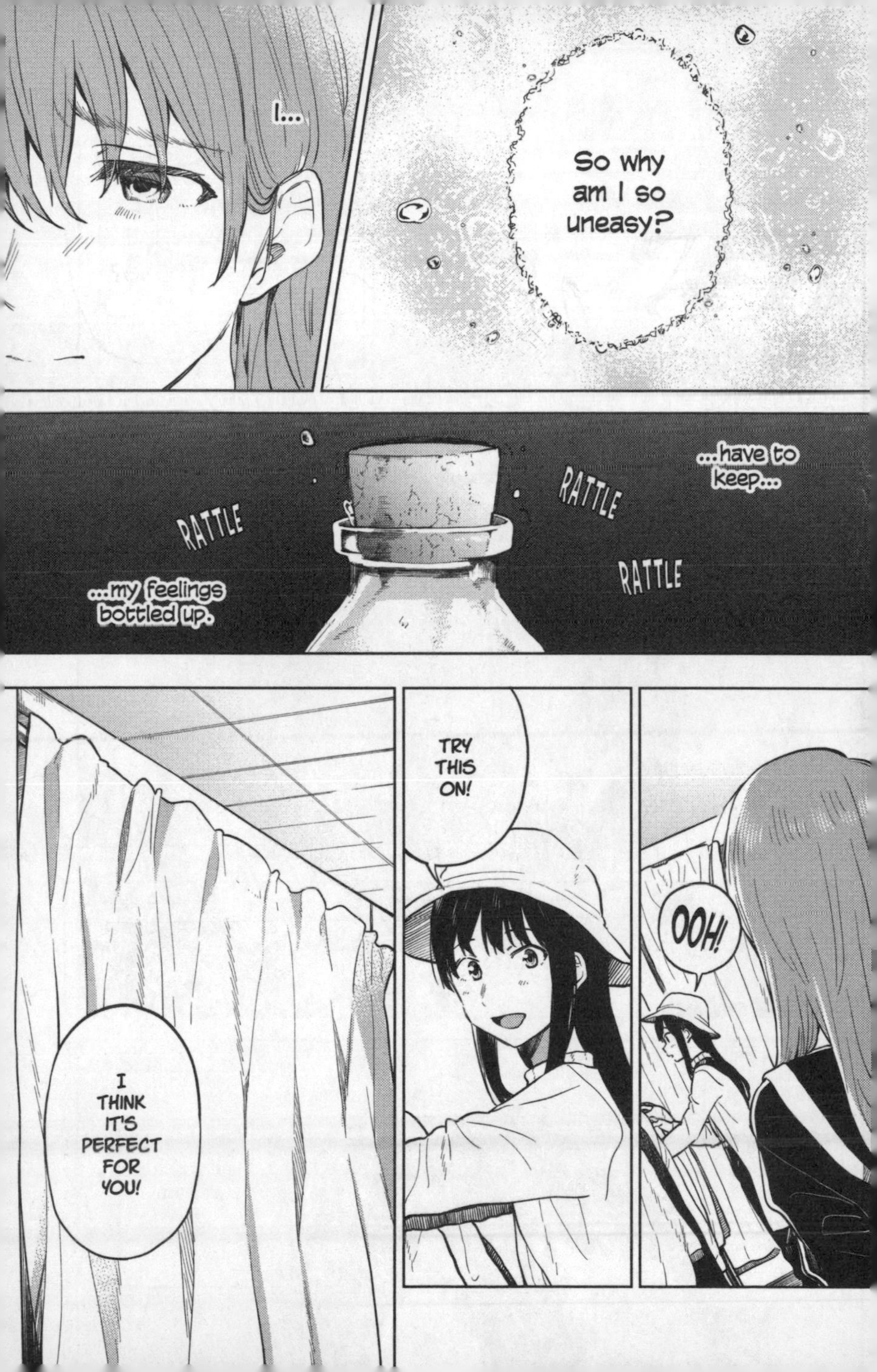
So why am I so uneasy?
I...
...have to keep...
RATTLE
RATTLE
RATTLE
...my feelings bottled up.
OOH!
TRY THIS ON!
I THINK IT'S PERFECT FOR YOU!

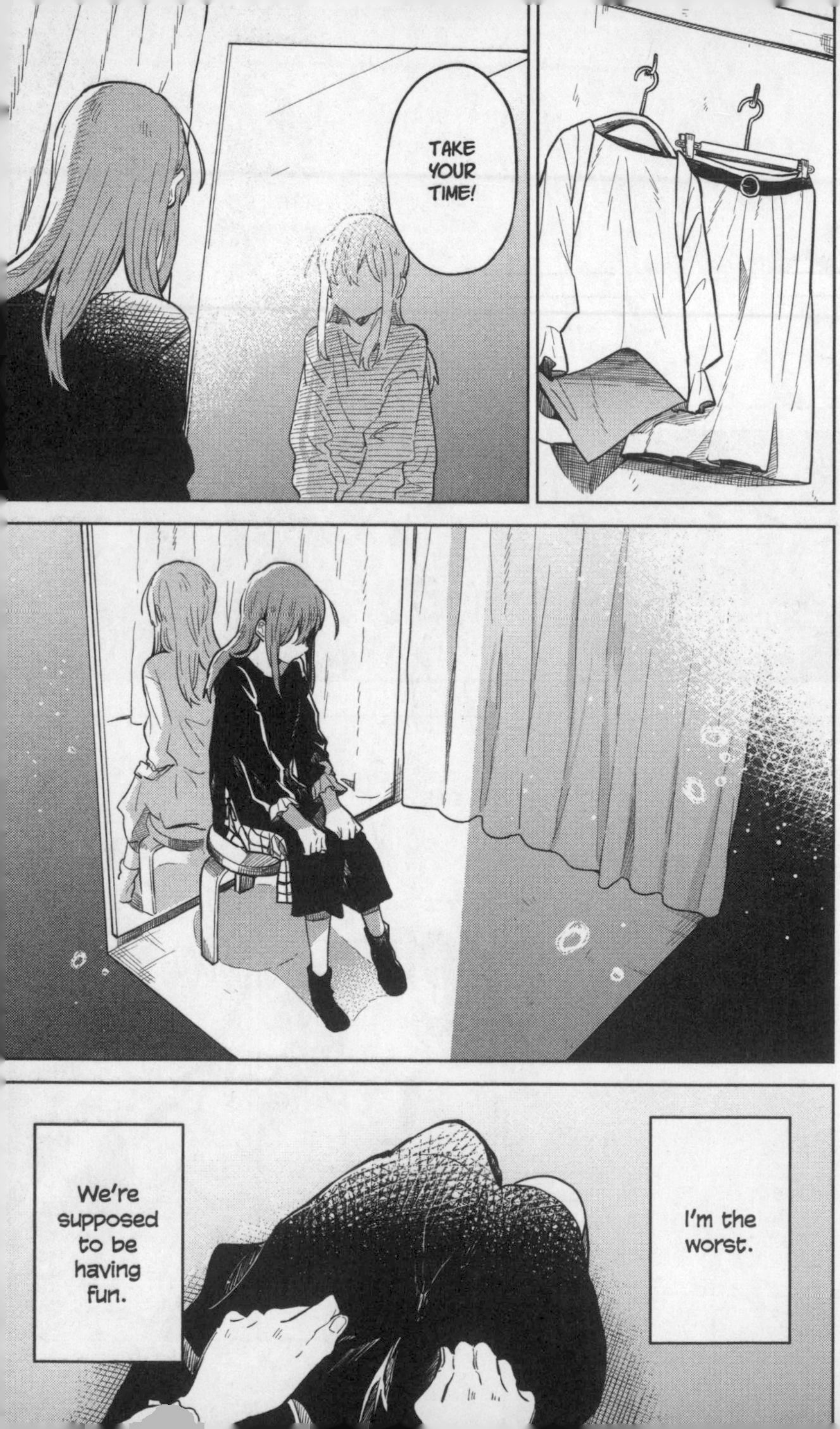
TAKE YOUR TIME!
I'm the worst.
We're supposed to be having fun.

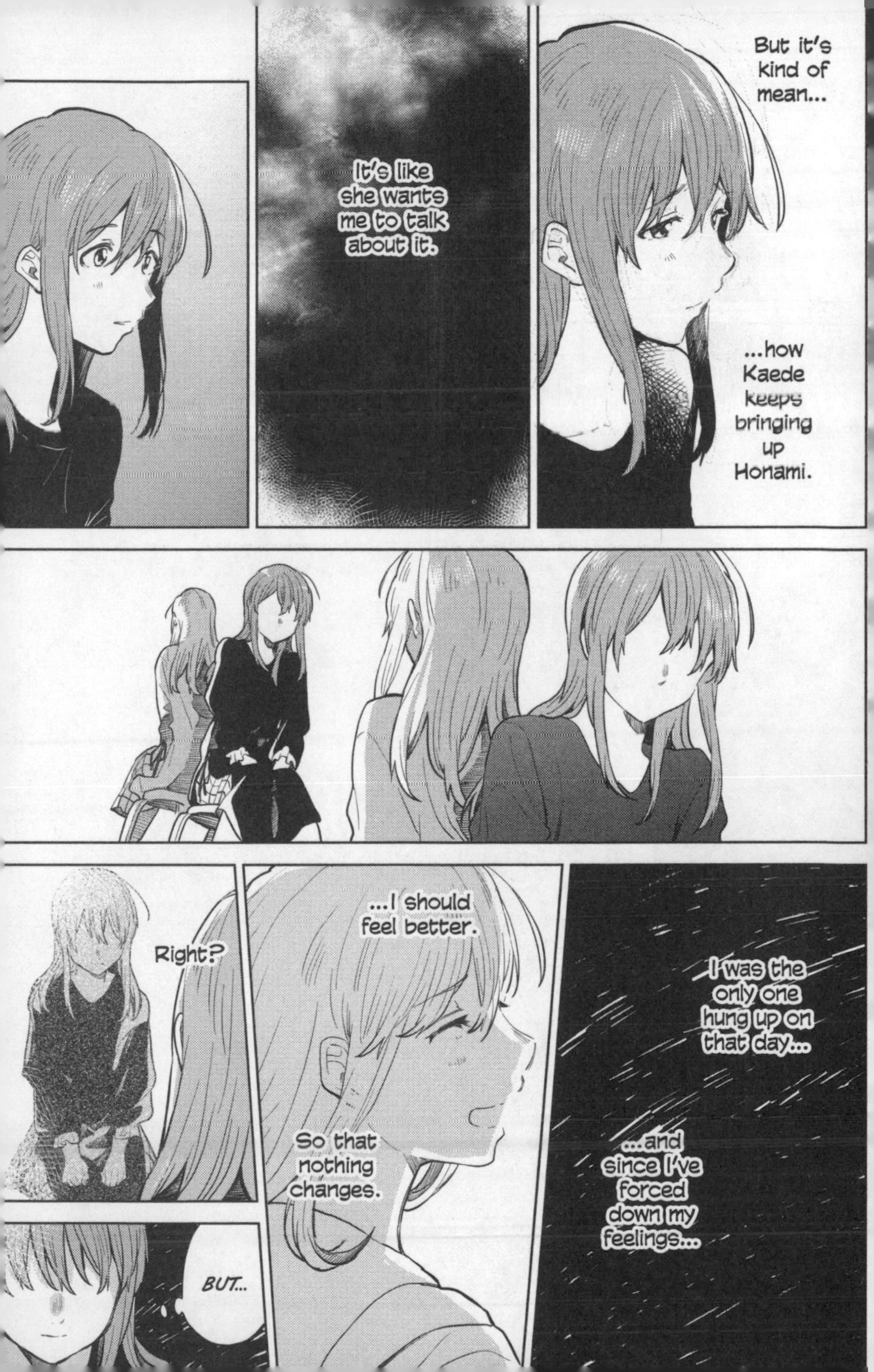
But it's kind of mean...
...how Kaede keeps bringing up Honami.
It's like she wants me to talk about it.
I was the only one hung up on that day...
...and since I've forced down my feelings...
...I should feel better.
So that nothing changes.
Right?
BUT...

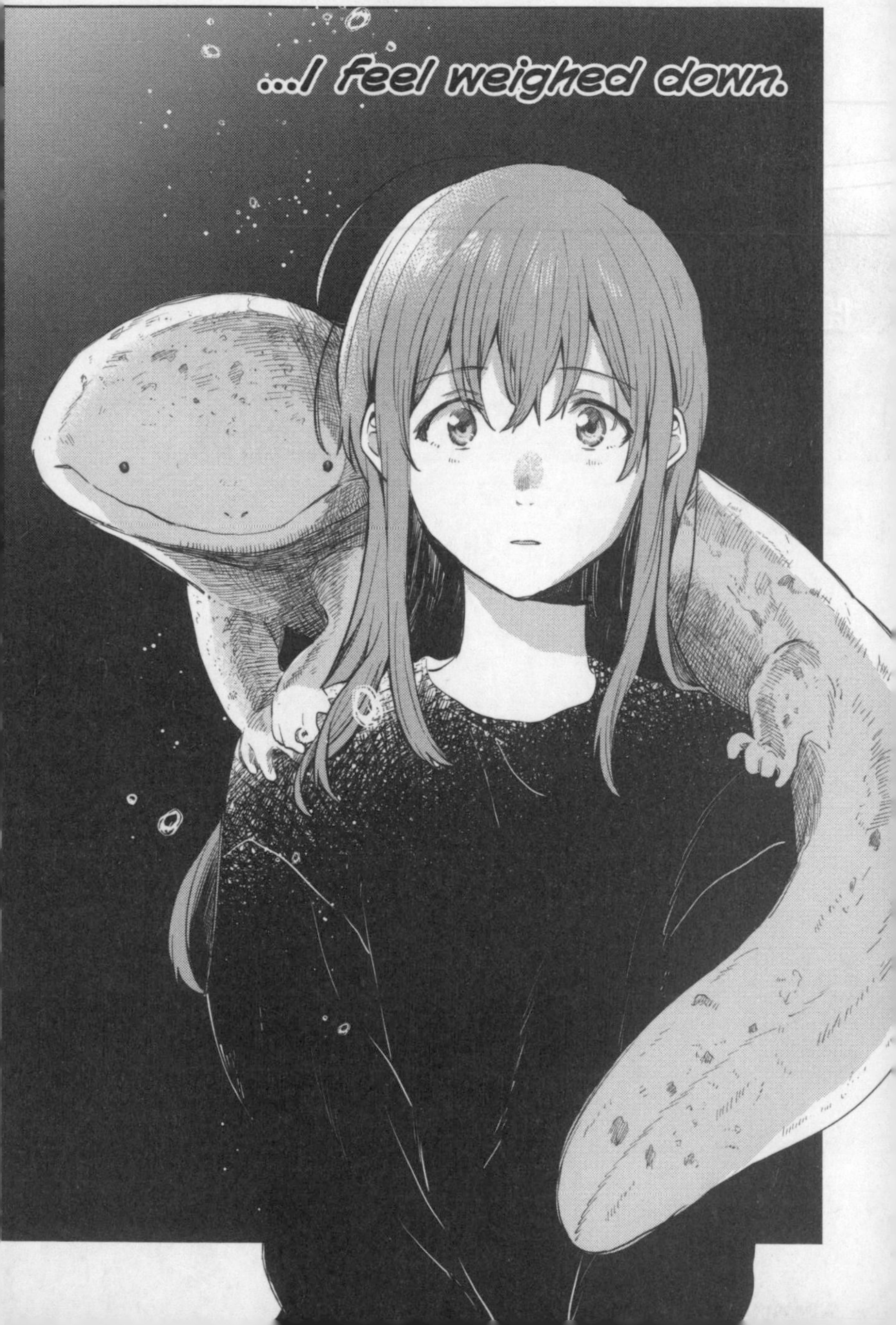
...I feel weighed down.

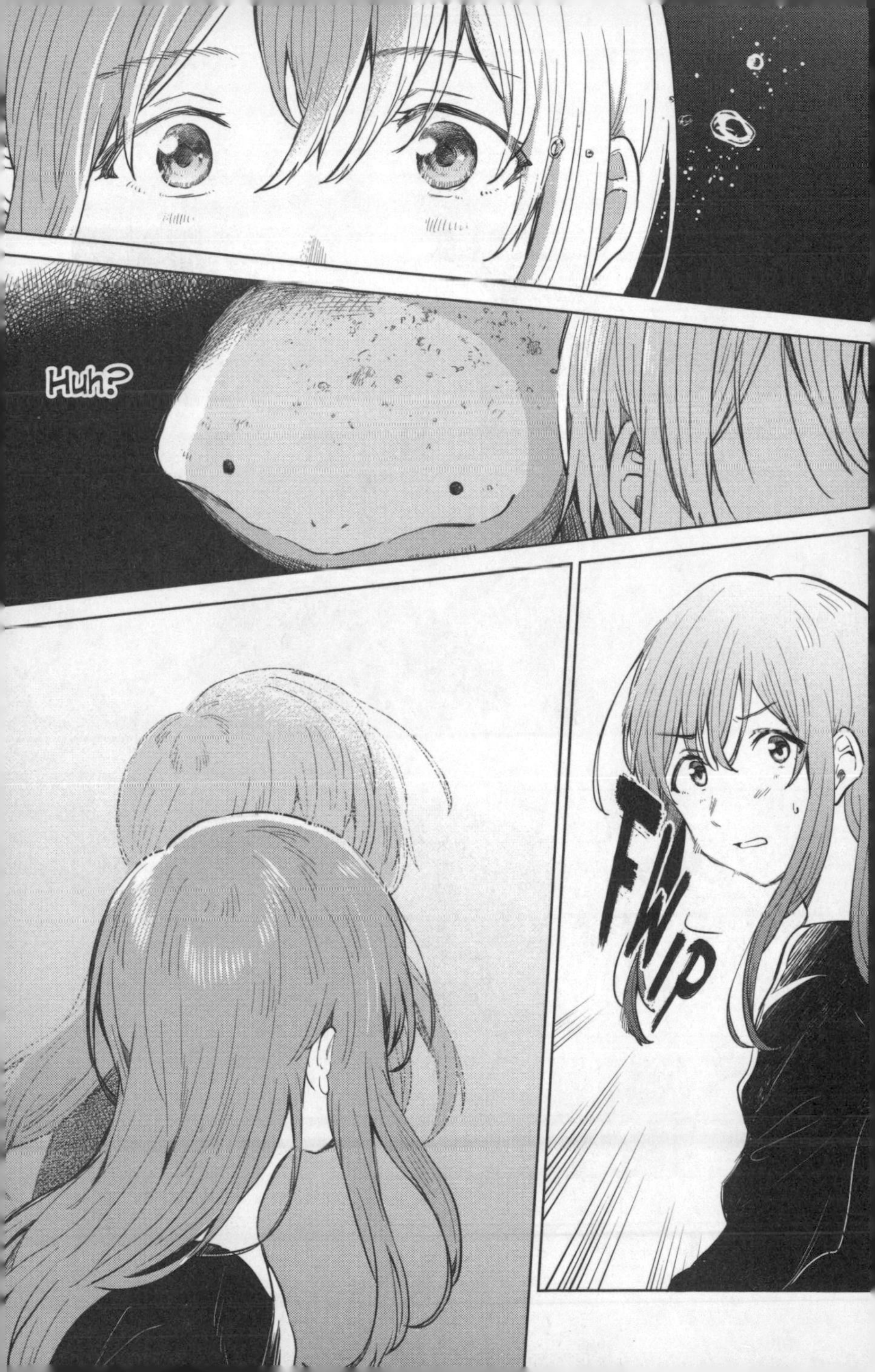
Huh?
FWIP

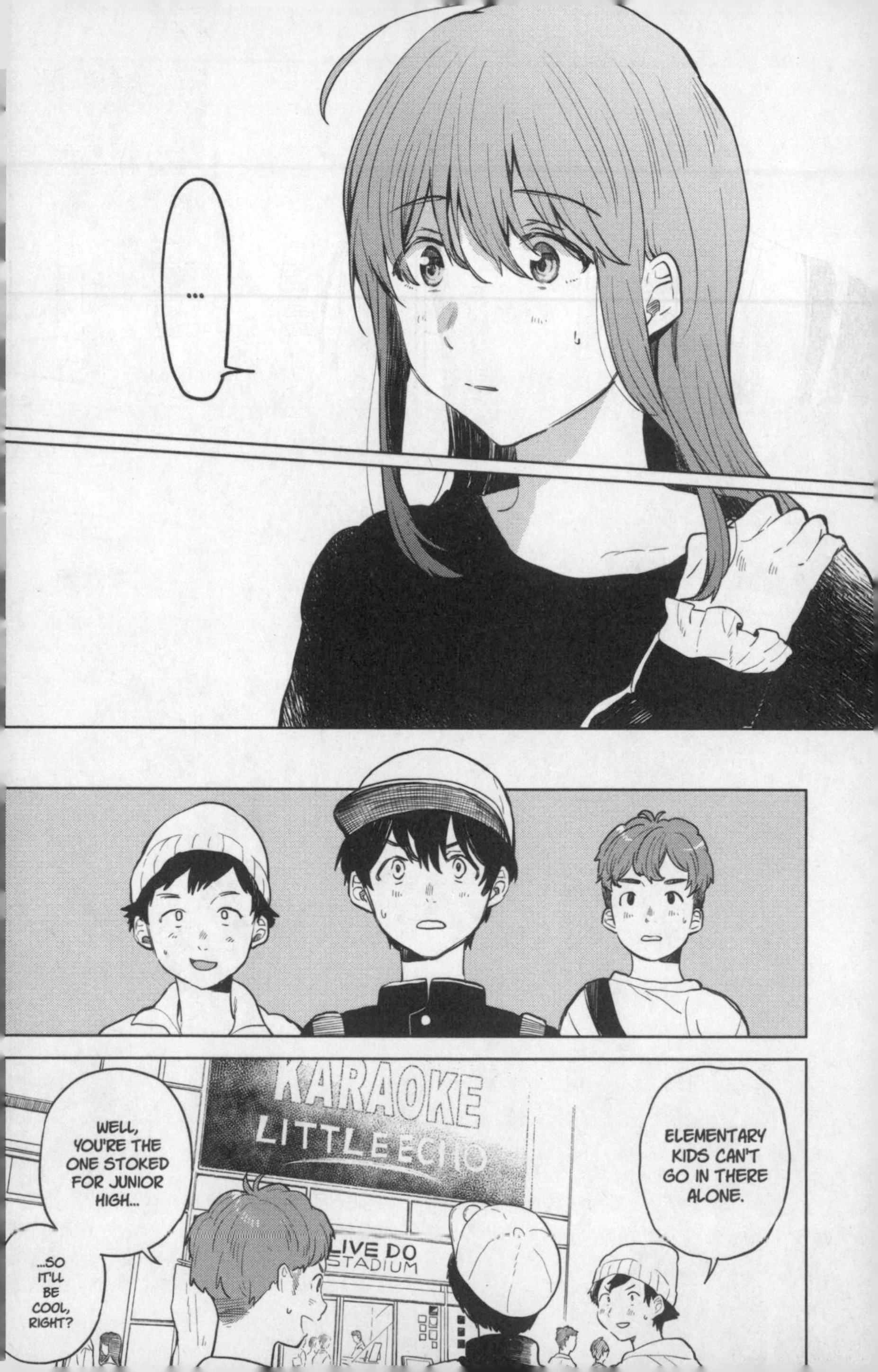
...
ELEMENTARY KIDS CAN'T GO IN THERE ALONE.
KARAOKE
WELL, YOU'RE THE ONE STOKED FOR JUNIOR HIGH...
...SO IT'LL BE COOL, RIGHT?
LIVE DO STADIUM

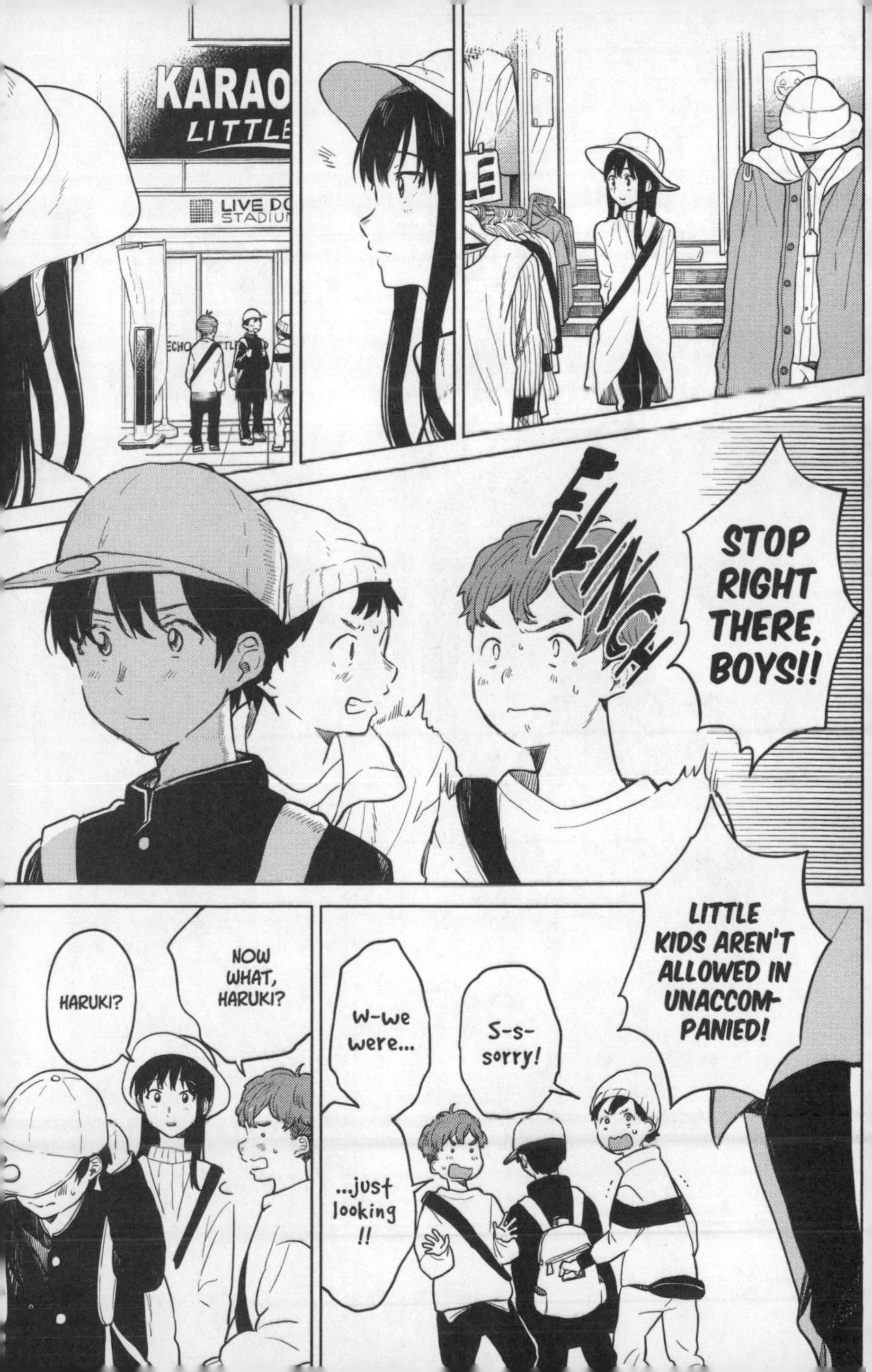
FLINCH
STOP RIGHT THERE, BOYS!!
LITTLE KIDS AREN'T ALLOWED IN UNACCOM-PANIED!
S-s-sorry!
W-we were...
...just looking!!
NOW WHAT, HARUKI?
HARUKI?

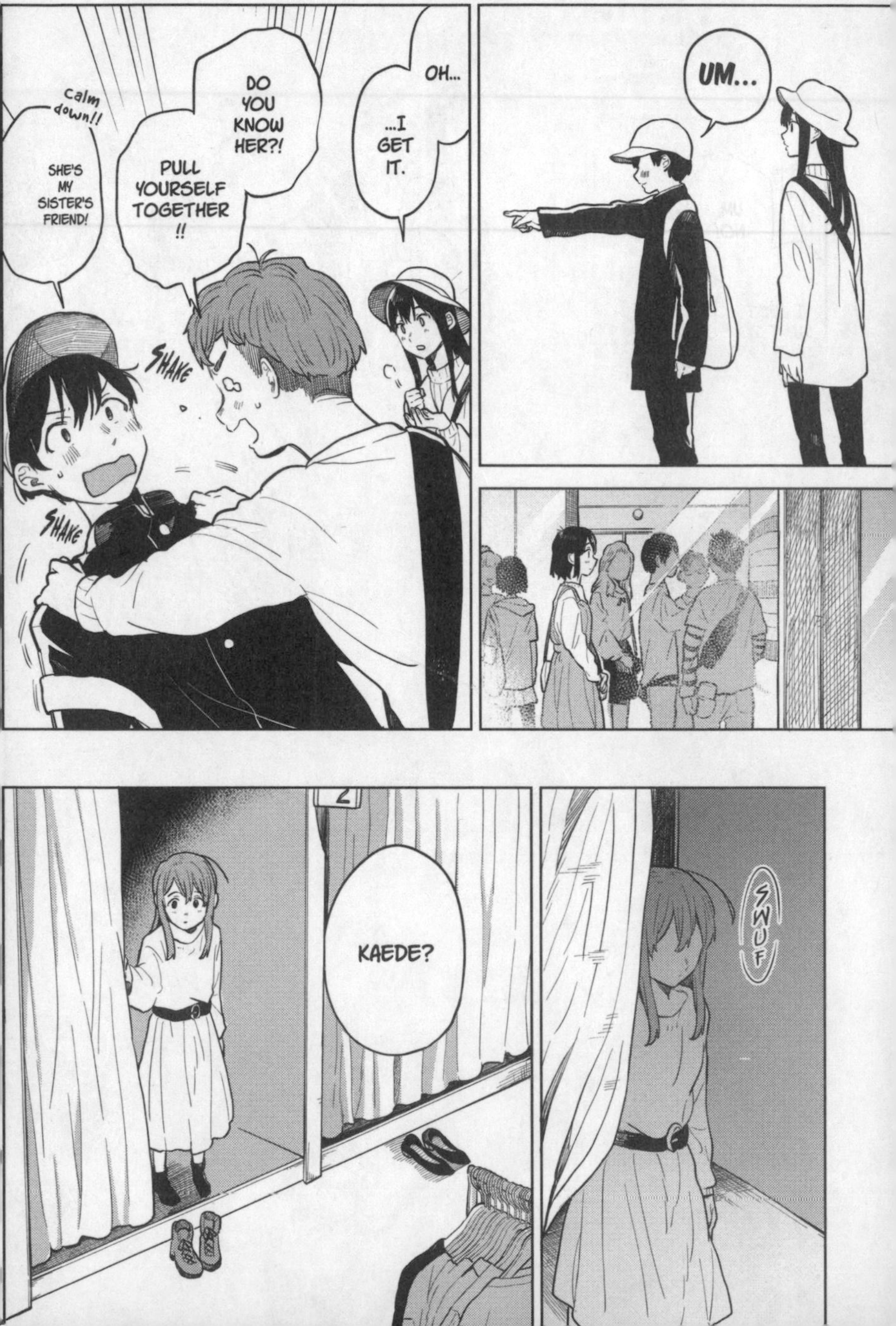
UM...
OH...
...I GET IT.
DO YOU KNOW HER?!
PULL YOURSELF TOGETHER!!
Calm down!!
SHE'S MY SISTER'S FRIEND!
SHAKE
SHAKE
SWUF
KAEDE?

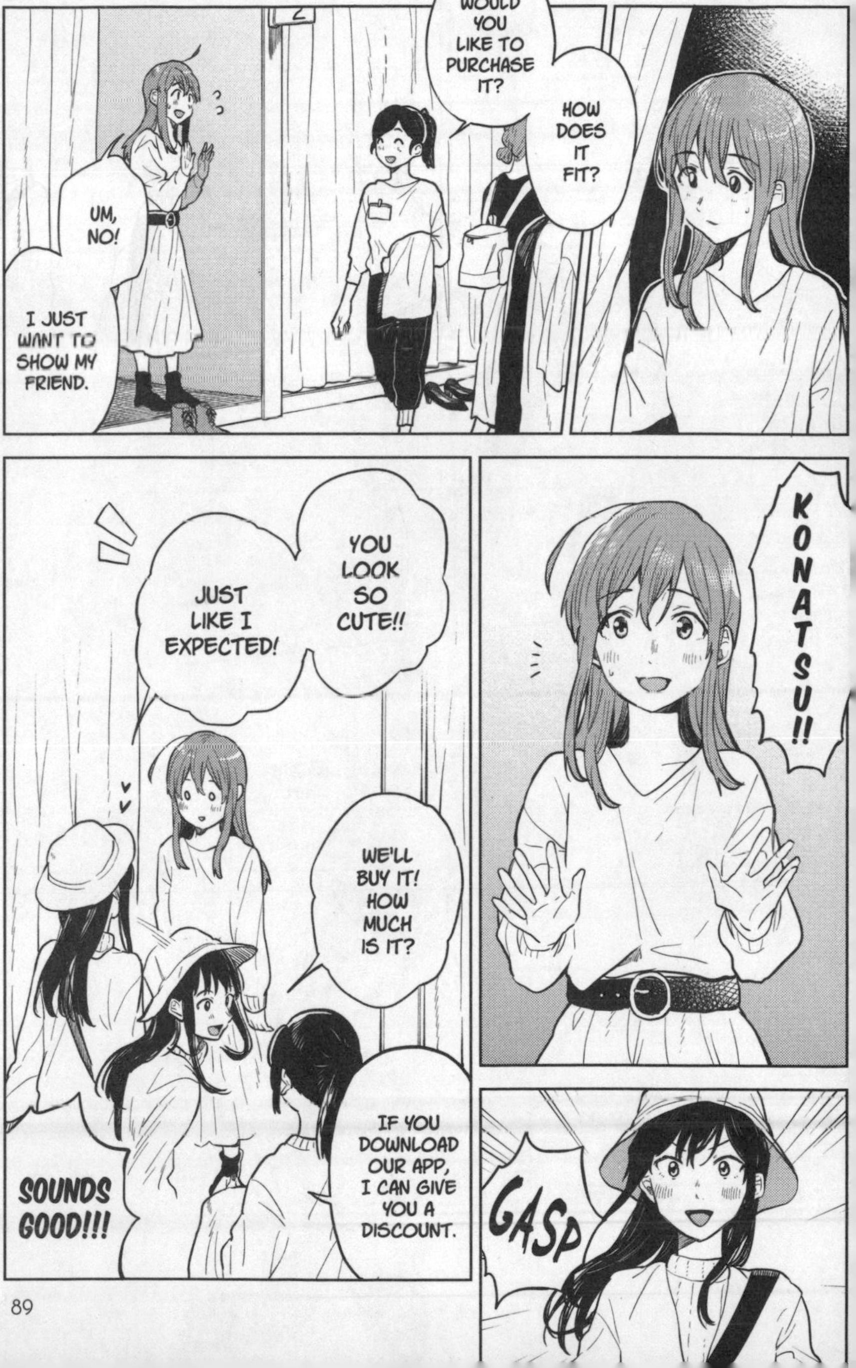
HOW DOES IT FIT?
WOULD YOU LIKE TO PURCHASE IT?
UM, NO!
I JUST WANT TO SHOW MY FRIEND.
KONATSU!!
GASP
YOU LOOK SO CUTE!!
JUST LIKE I EXPECTED!
WE'LL BUY IT! HOW MUCH IS IT?
IF YOU DOWNLOAD OUR APP, I CAN GIVE YOU A DISCOUNT.
SOUNDS GOOD!!!

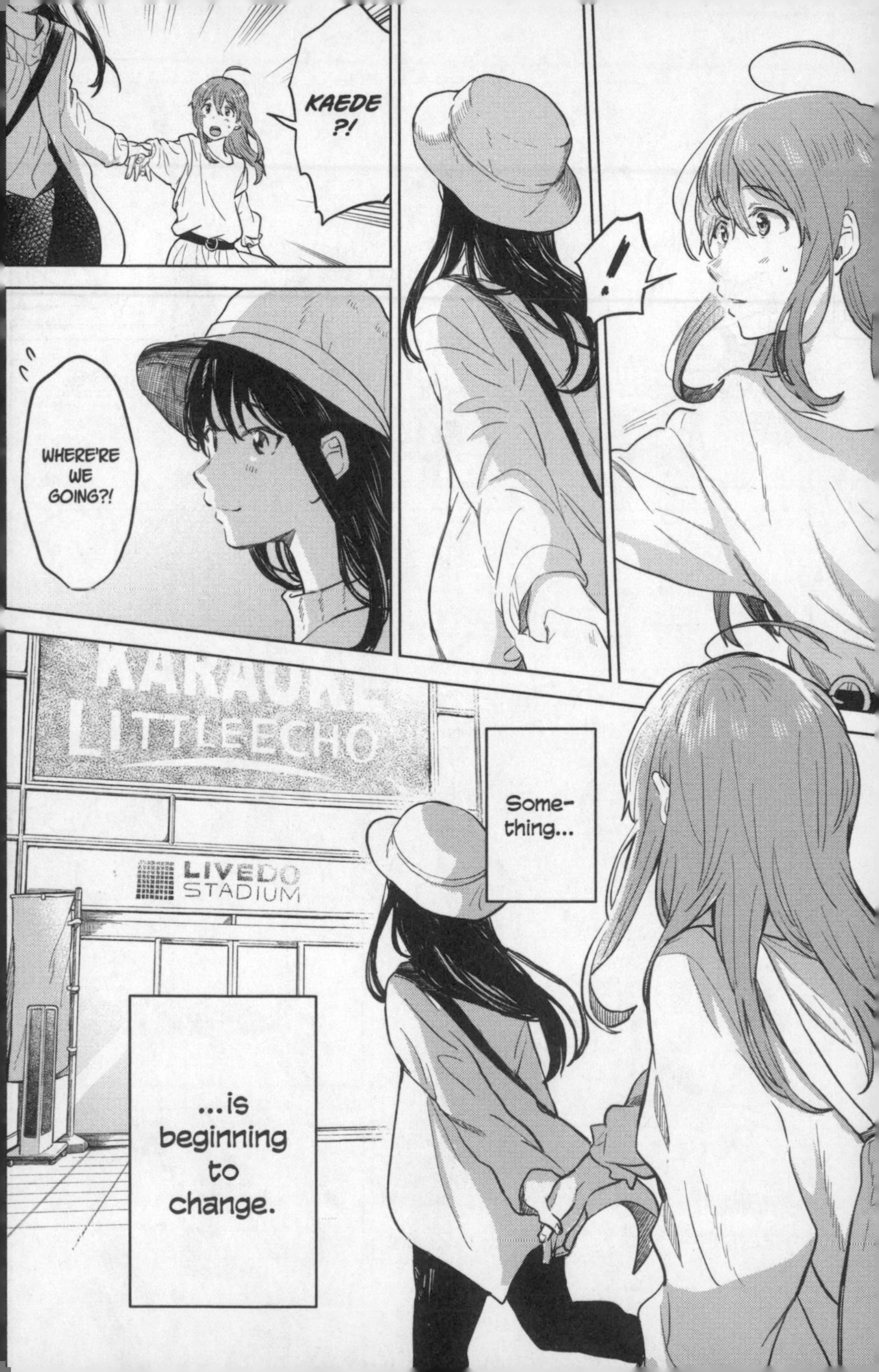
!
KAEDE ?!
WHERE'RE WE GOING?!
KARAOKE LITTLEECHO
LIVEDO STADIUM
Some-thing...
...is beginning to change.

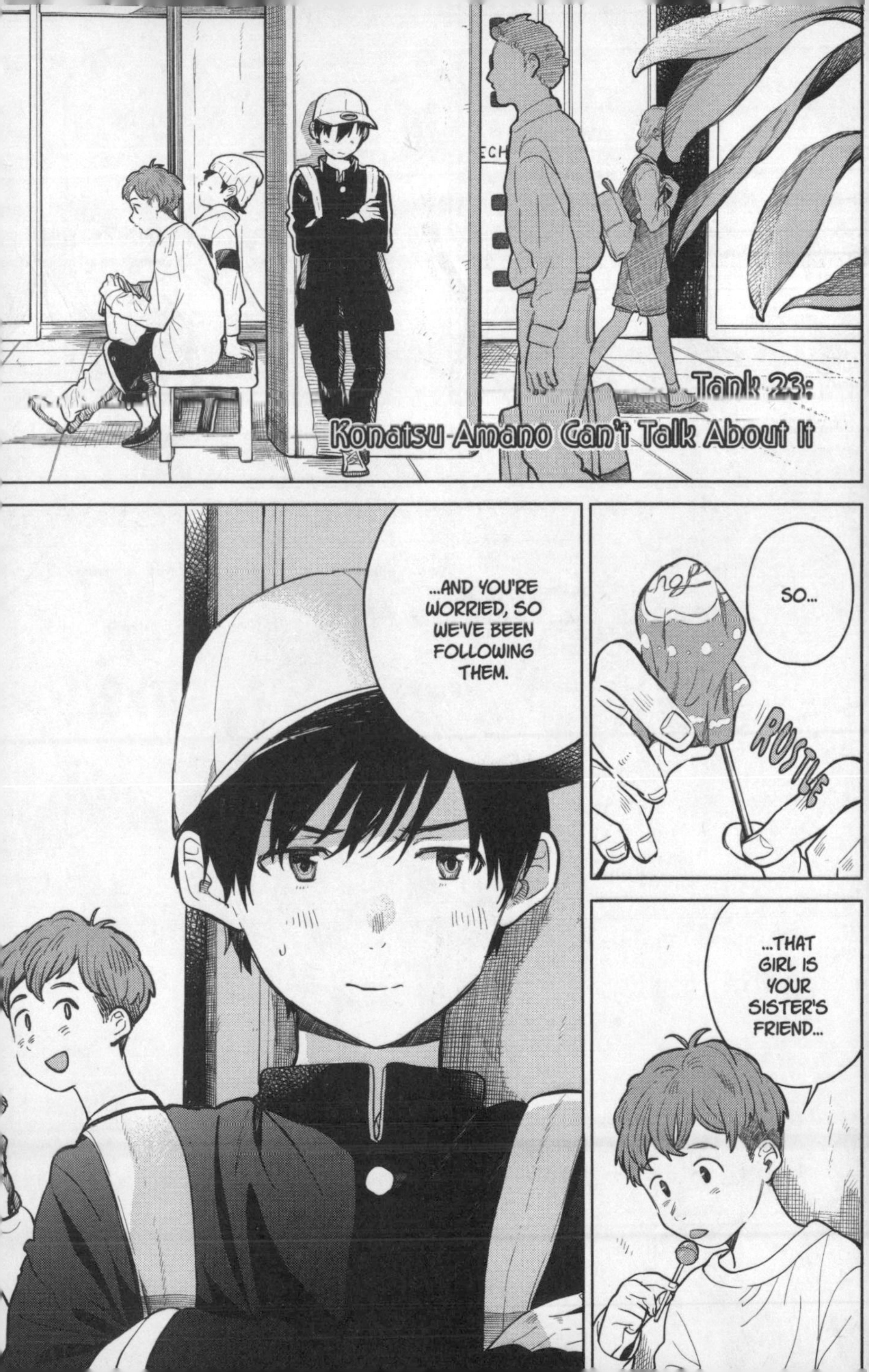
ECH
Tank 23:
Konatsu Amano Can't Talk About It
SO...
RUSTLE
...THAT GIRL IS YOUR SISTER'S FRIEND...
...AND YOU'RE WORRIED, SO WE'VE BEEN FOLLOWING THEM.

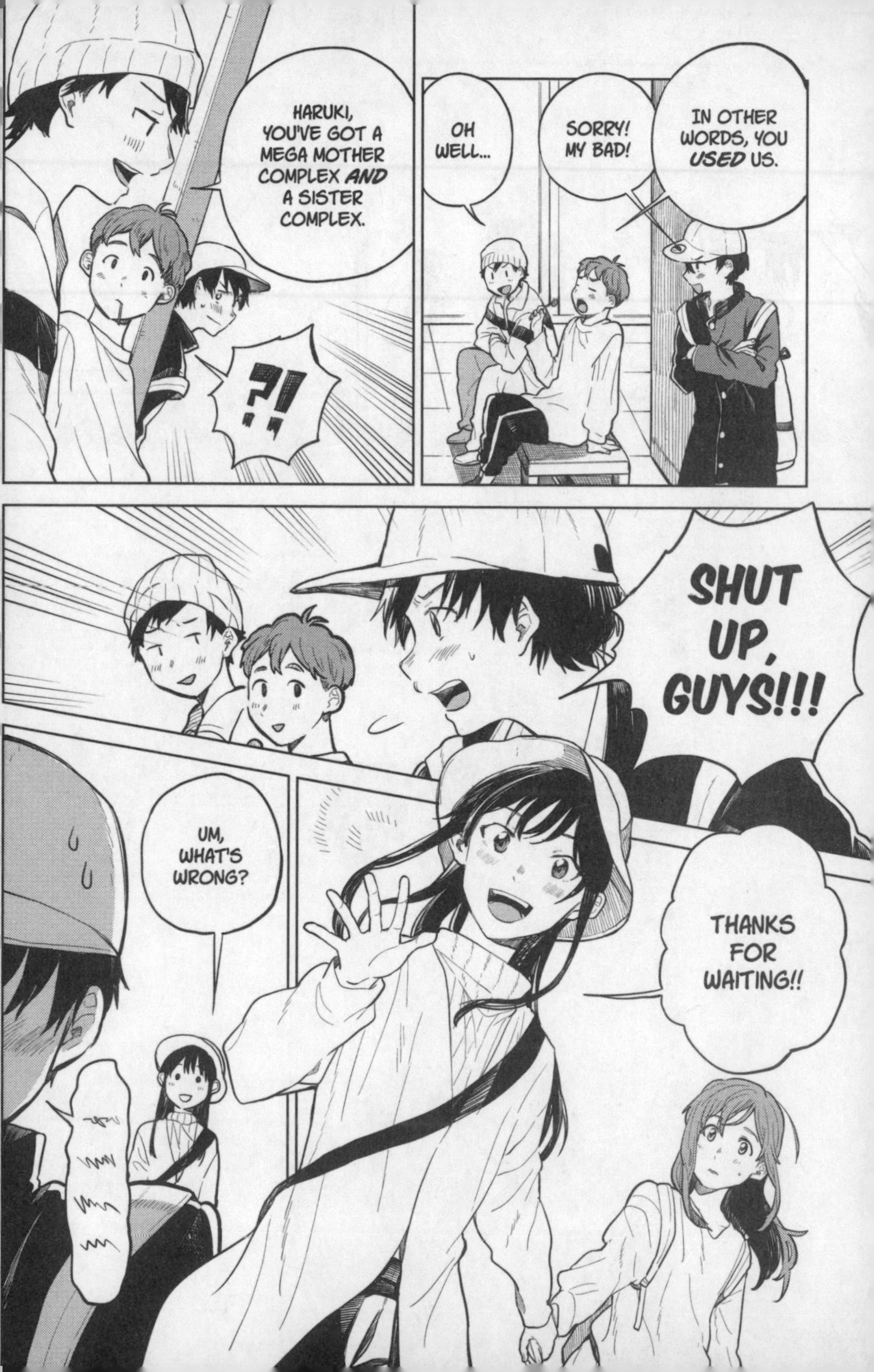
IN OTHER WORDS, YOU USED US.
SORRY! MY BAD!
OH WELL...
HARUKI, YOU'VE GOT A MEGA MOTHER COMPLEX AND A SISTER COMPLEX.
?!
SHUT UP, GUYS!!!
THANKS FOR WAITING!!
UM, WHAT'S WRONG?

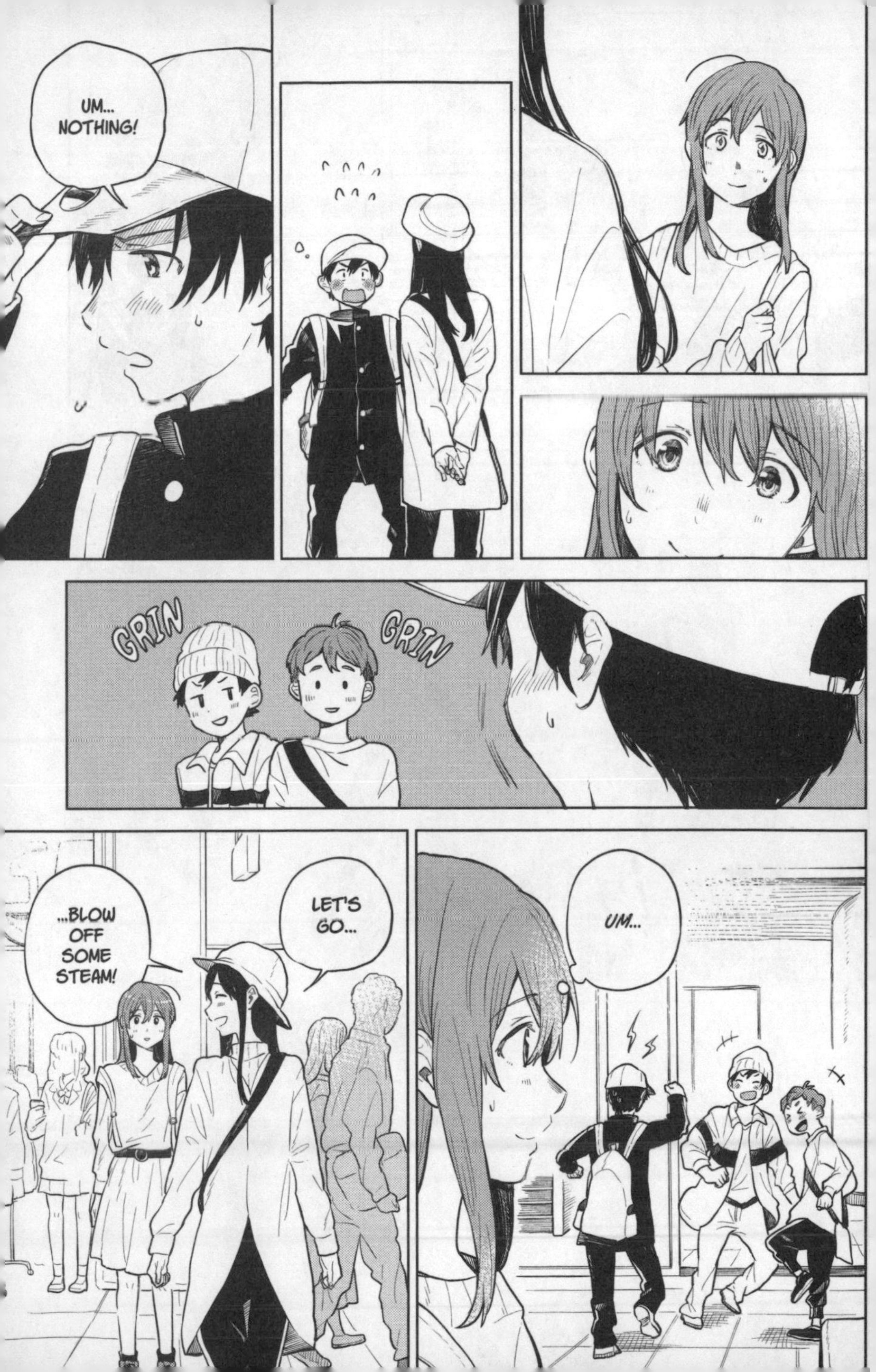
UM... NOTHING!
GRIN
GRIN
UM...
LET'S GO...
...BLOW OFF SOME STEAM!

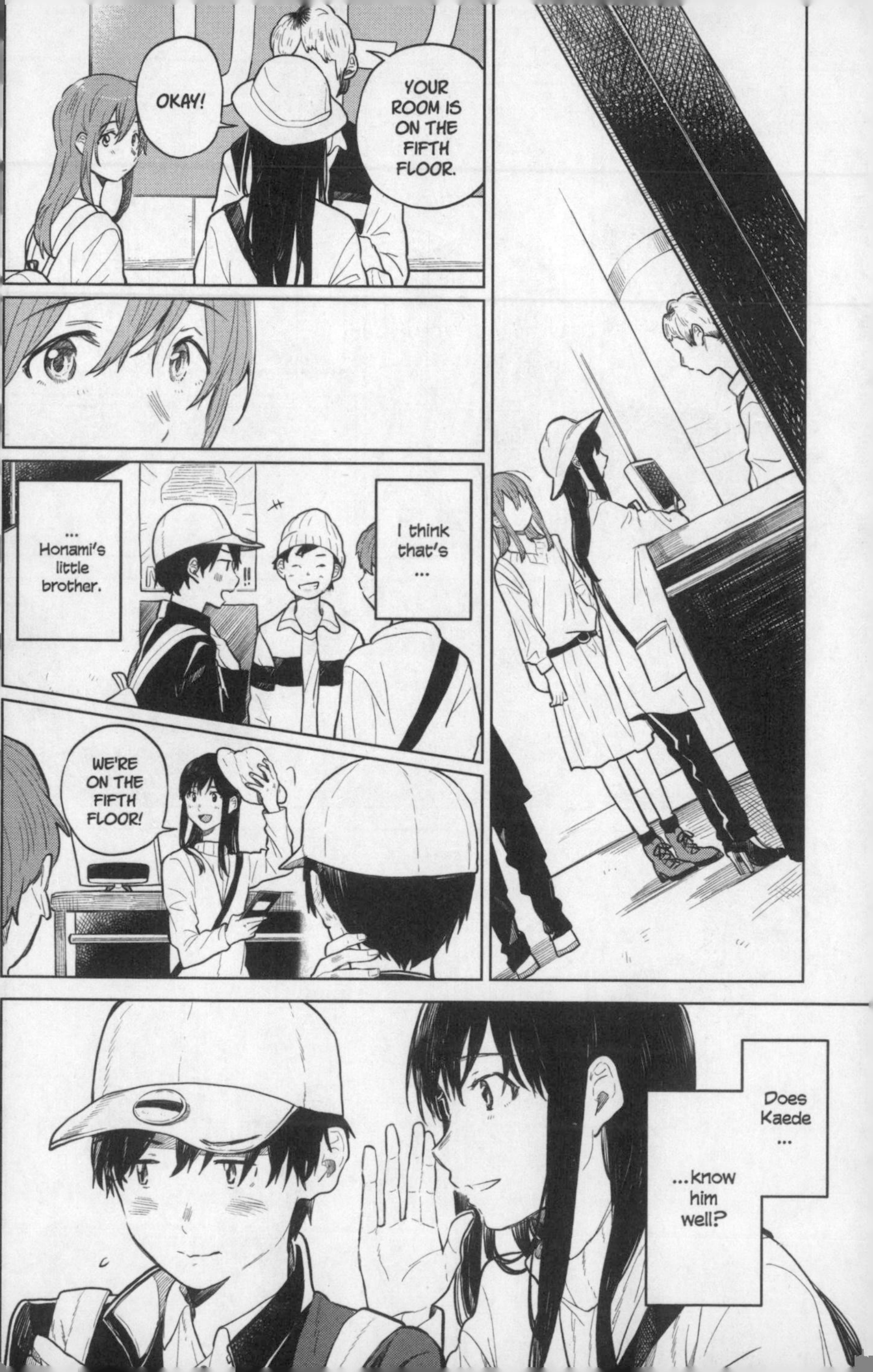
YOUR ROOM IS ON THE FIFTH FLOOR.
OKAY!
I think that's ...
... Honami's little brother.
WE'RE ON THE FIFTH FLOOR!
Does Kaede ...
...know him well?

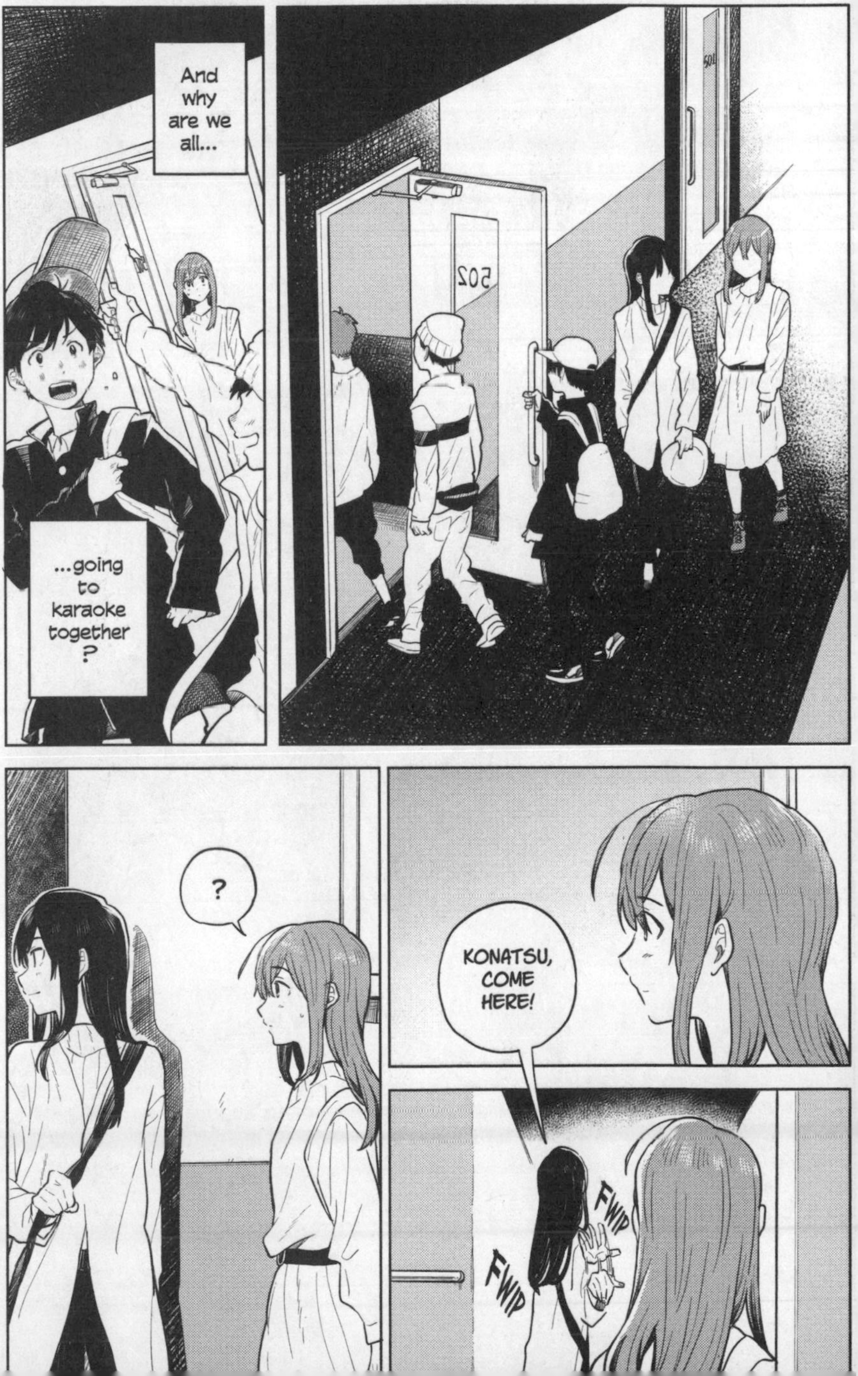
And why are we all...
...going to karaoke together?
KONATSU, COME HERE!
FWIP
FWIP
?

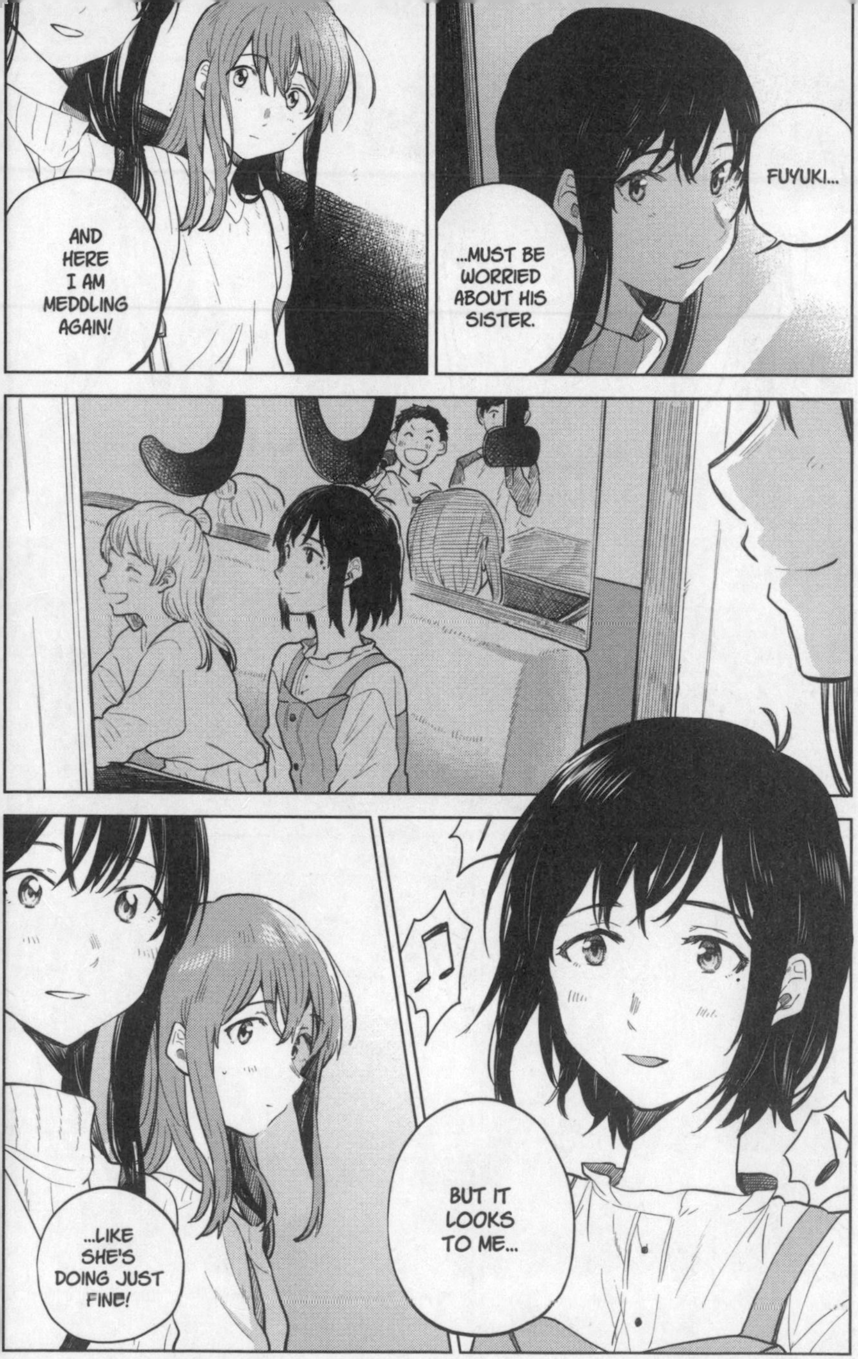
FUYUKI...
...MUST BE WORRIED ABOUT HIS SISTER.
AND HERE I AM MEDDLING AGAIN!
BUT IT LOOKS TO ME...
...LIKE SHE'S DOING JUST FINE!

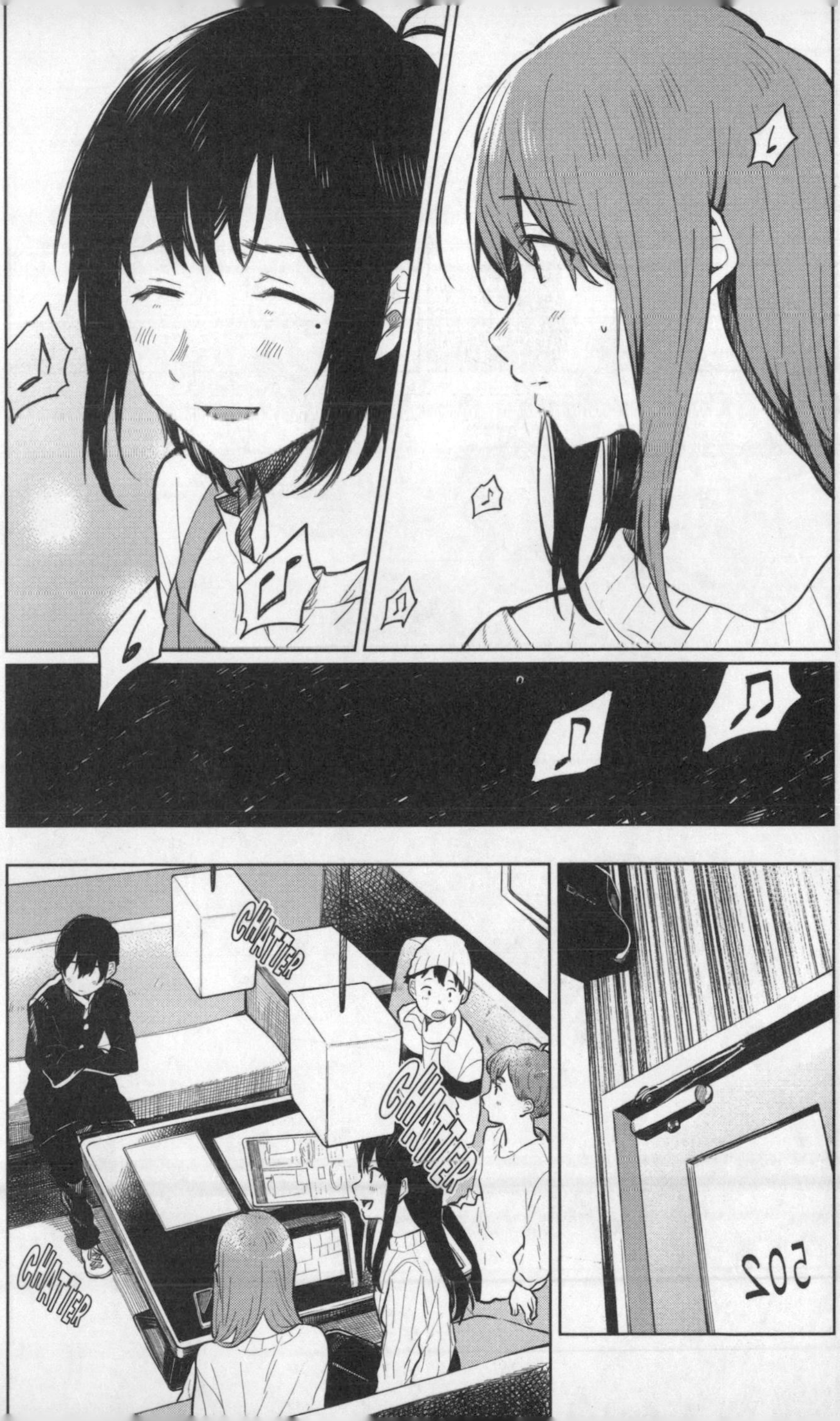
CHATTER
CHATTER
CHATTER

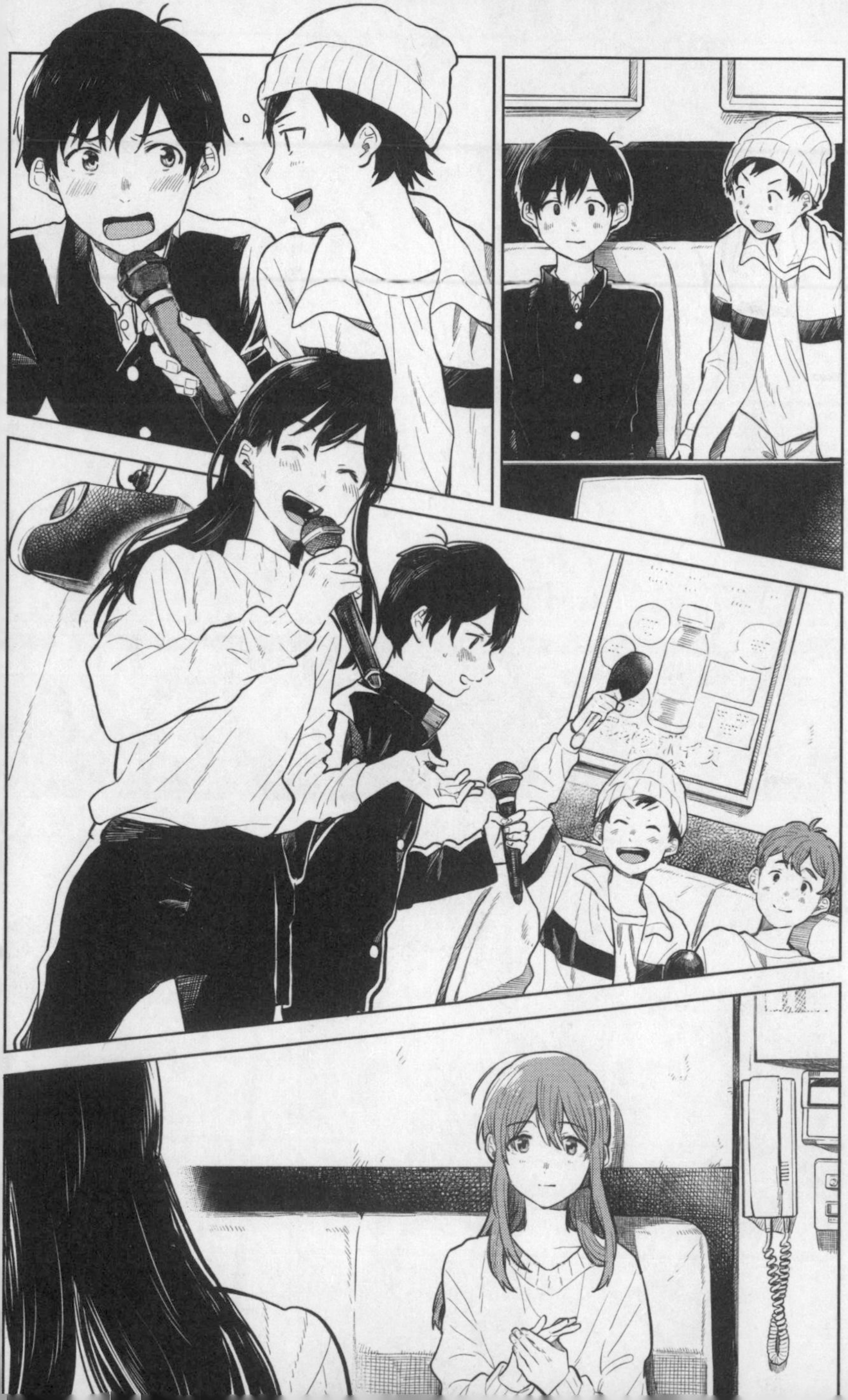

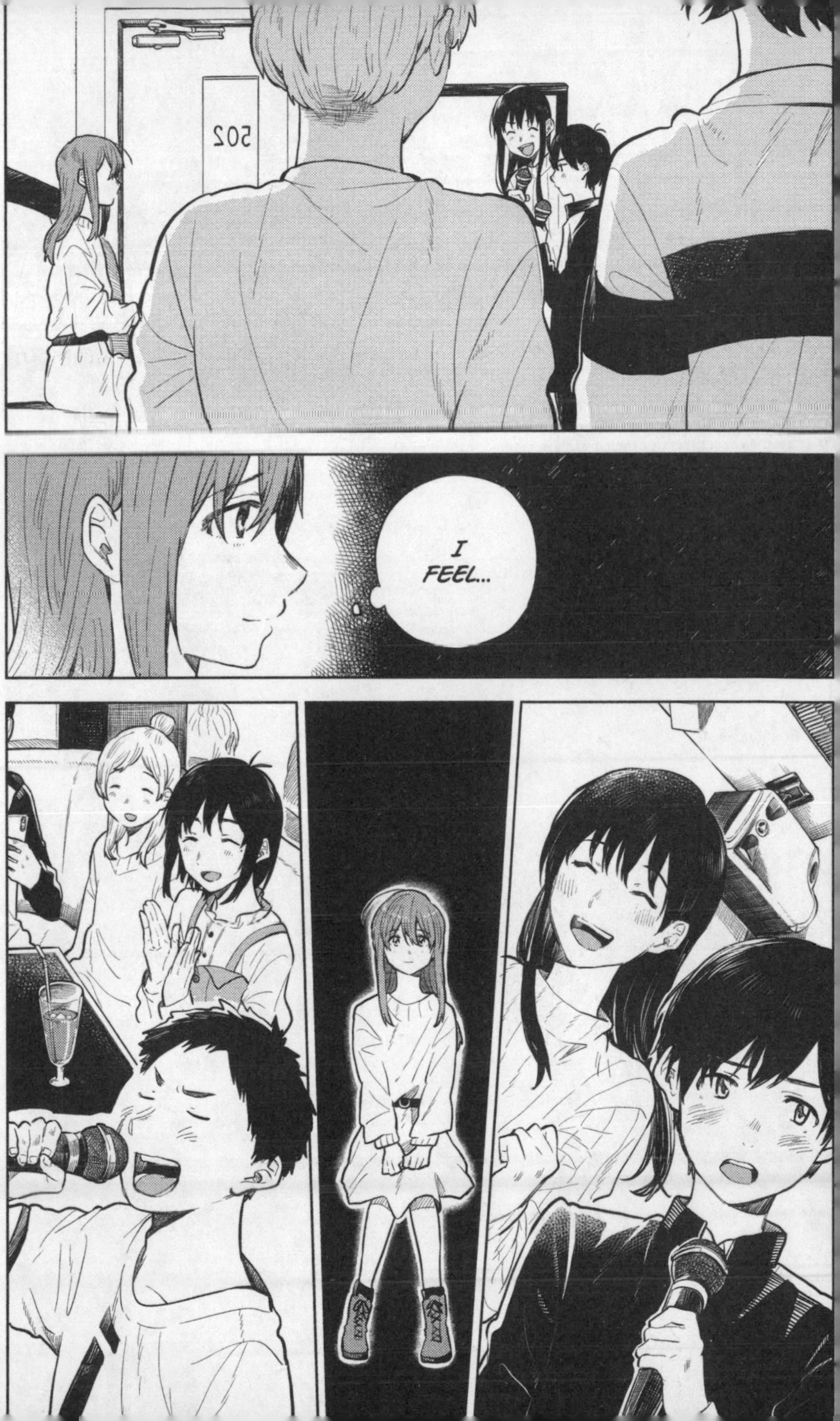
502
I FEEL...

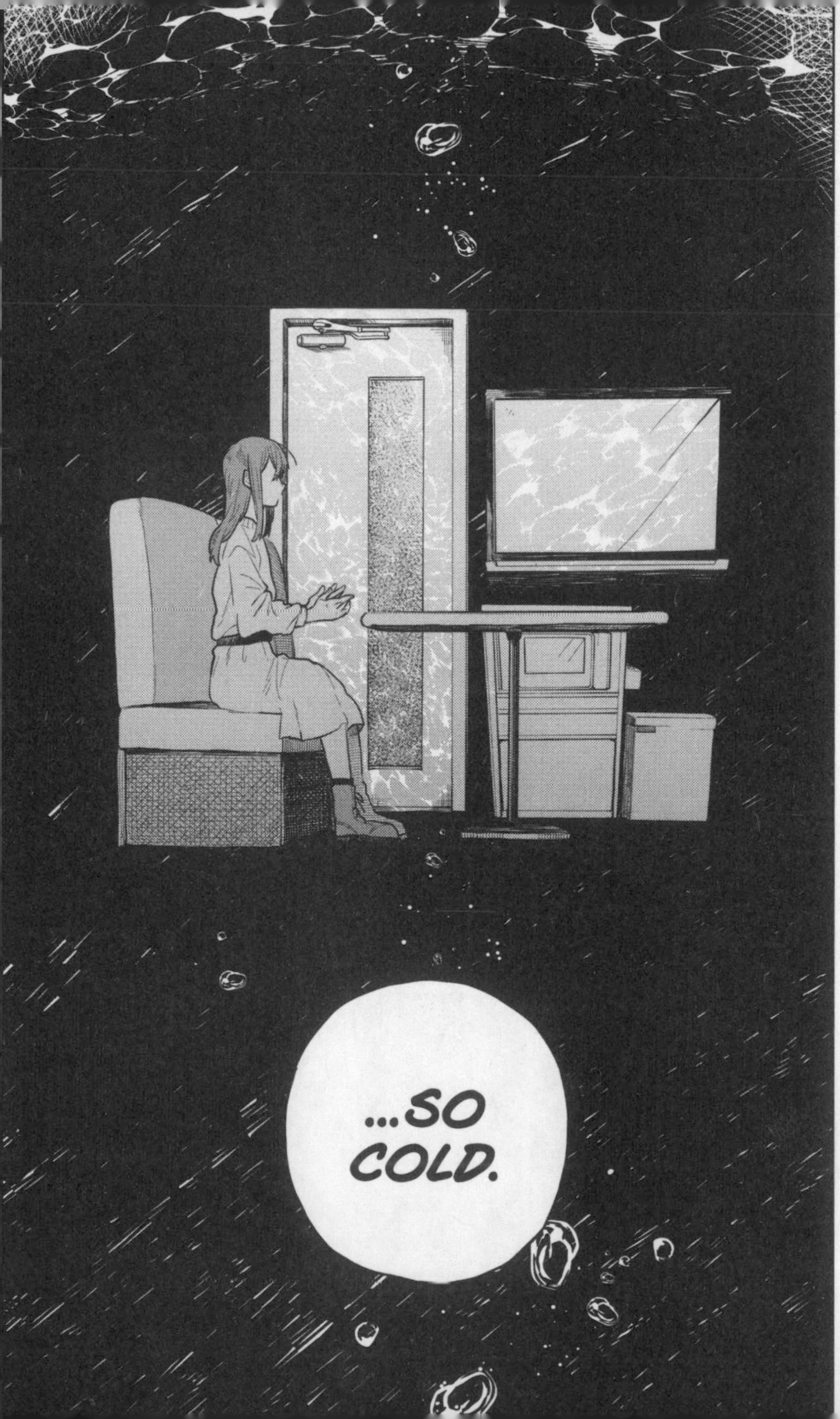
...SO COLD.

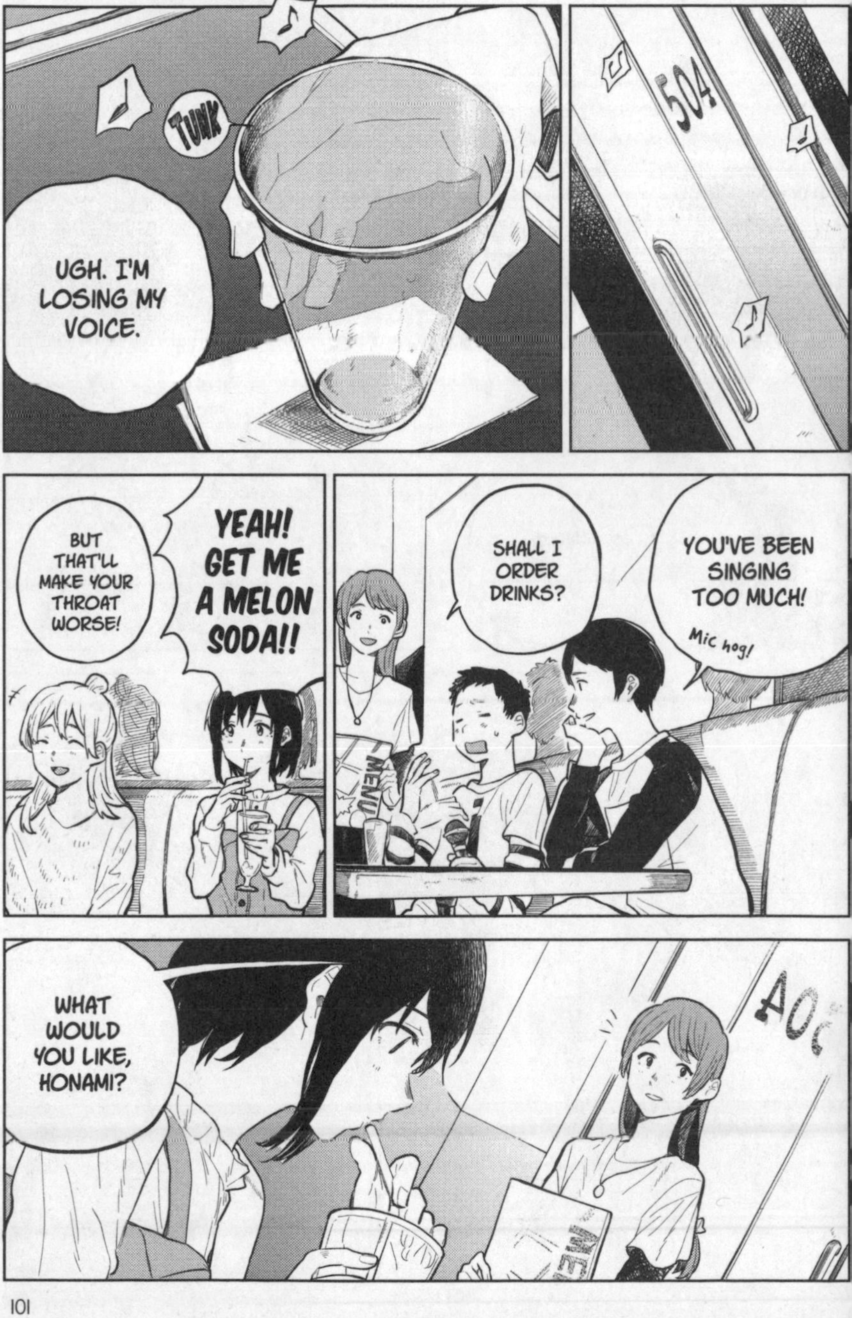
504
TUNK
UGH. I'M LOSING MY VOICE.
YOU'VE BEEN SINGING TOO MUCH!
Mic hog!
SHALL I ORDER DRINKS?
MENU
YEAH! GET ME A MELON SODA!!
BUT THAT'LL MAKE YOUR THROAT WORSE!
WHAT WOULD YOU LIKE, HONAMI?

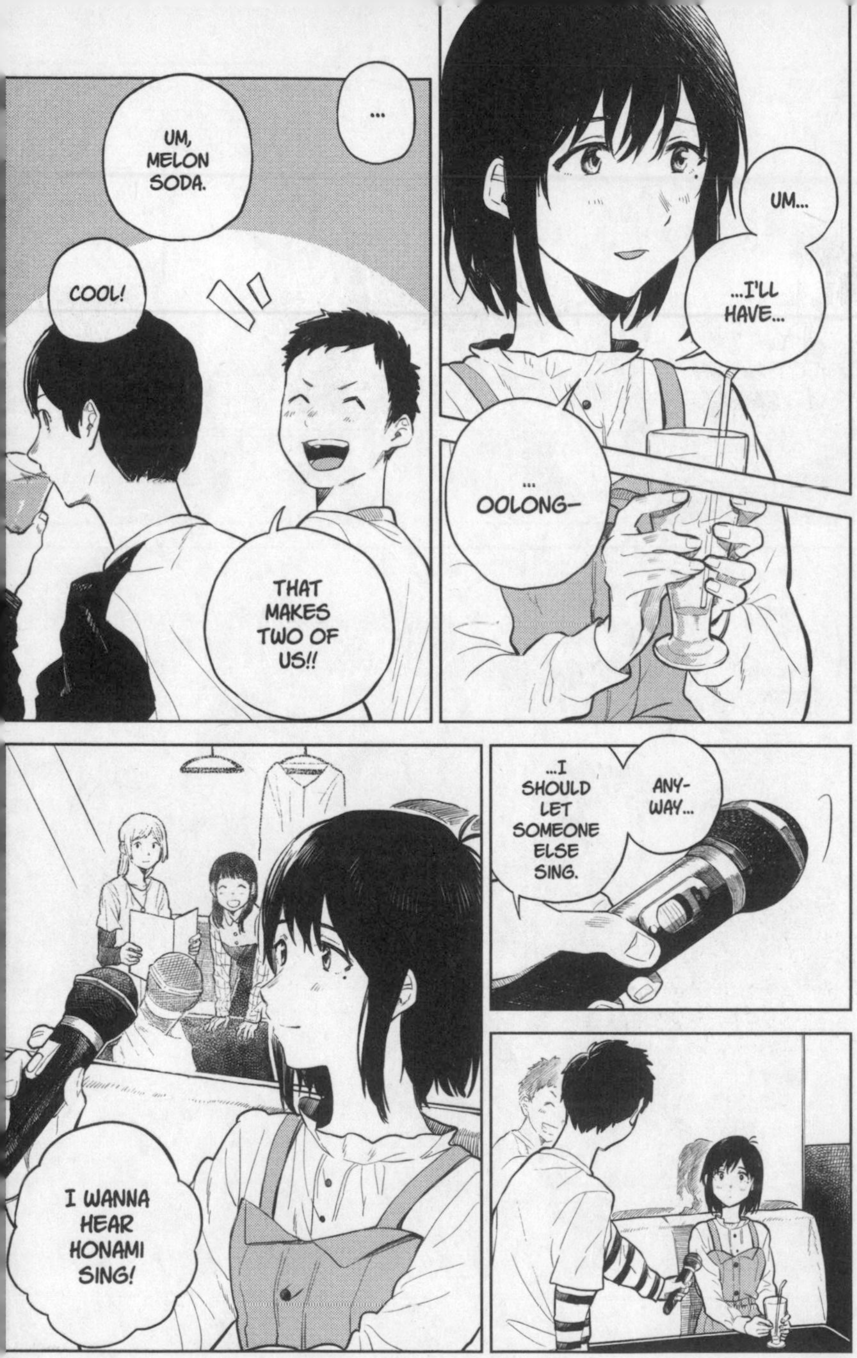
UM...
...I'LL HAVE...
... OOLONG-
...
UM, MELON SODA.
COOL!
THAT MAKES TWO OF US!!
ANY-WAY...
...I SHOULD LET SOMEONE ELSE SING.
I WANNA HEAR HONAMI SING!

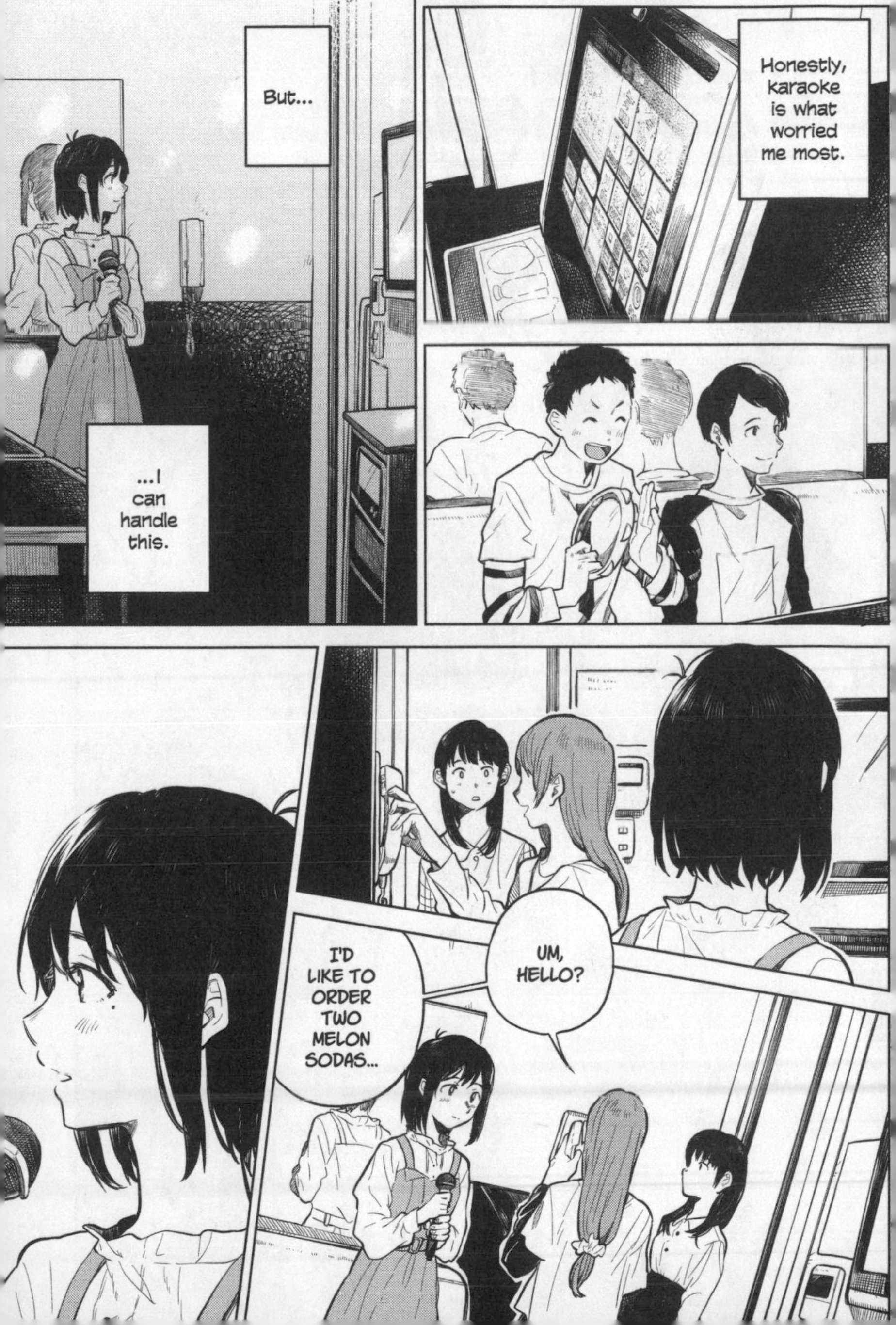
Honestly, karaoke is what worried me most.
But...
...I can handle this.
UM, HELLO?
I'D LIKE TO ORDER TWO MELON SODAS...

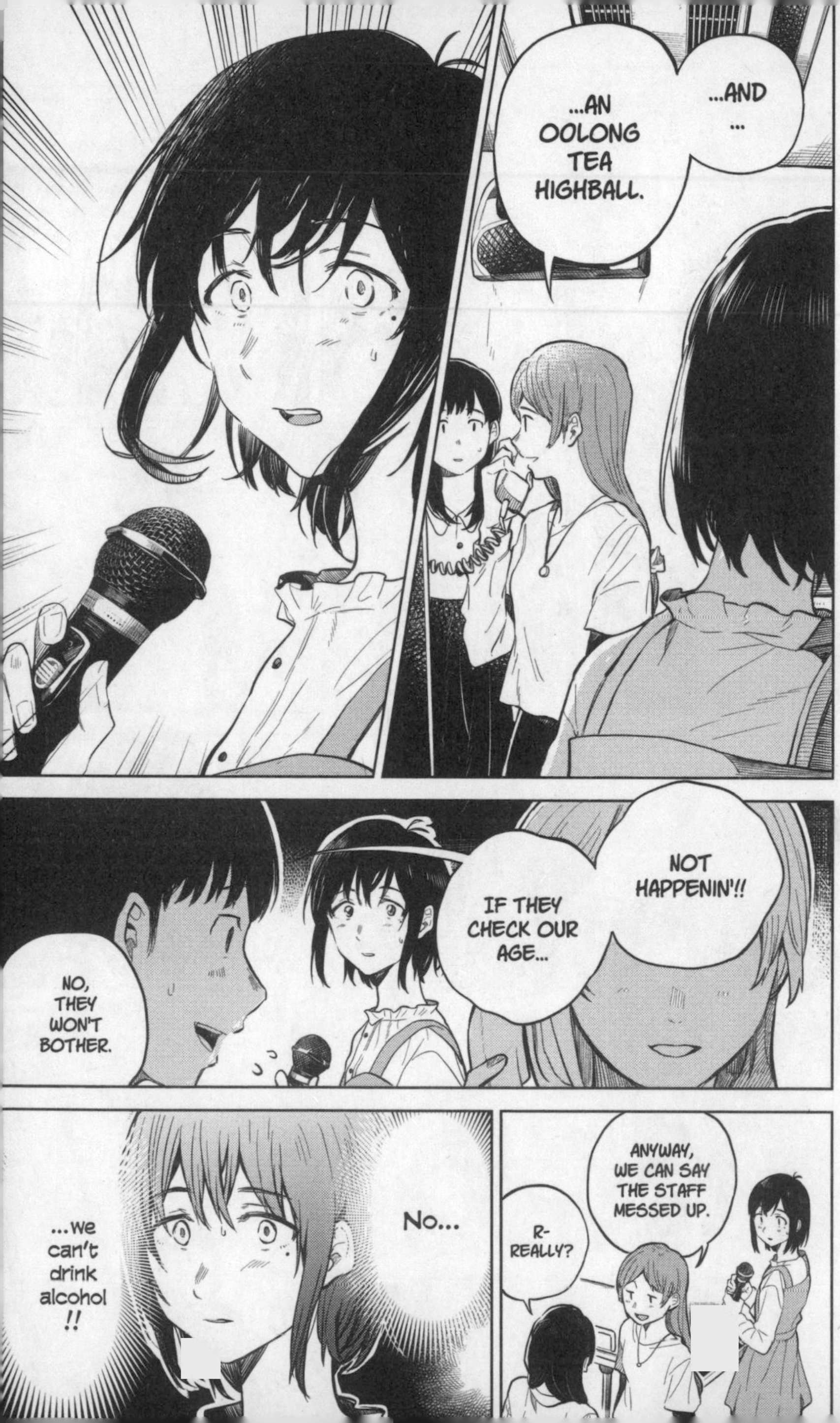
...AND ...
...AN OOLONG TEA HIGHBALL.
NOT HAPPENIN'!!
IF THEY CHECK OUR AGE...
NO, THEY WON'T BOTHER.
ANYWAY, WE CAN SAY THE STAFF MESSED UP.
R-REALLY?
No...
...we can't drink alcohol!!

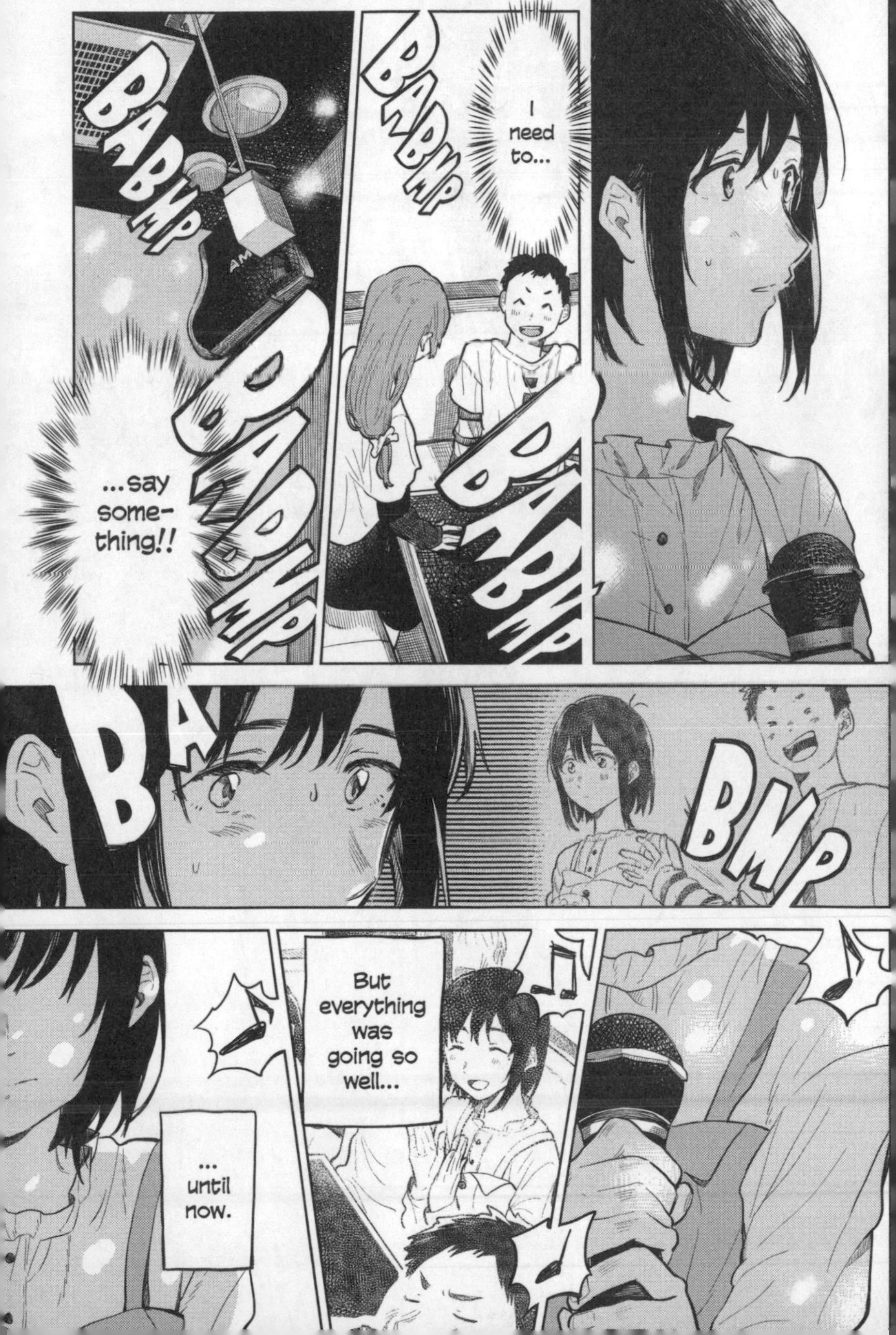
I need to...
BABMP
BABMP
BABMP
...say some-thing!!
BABMP
BA
BMP
But everything was going so well...
... until now.

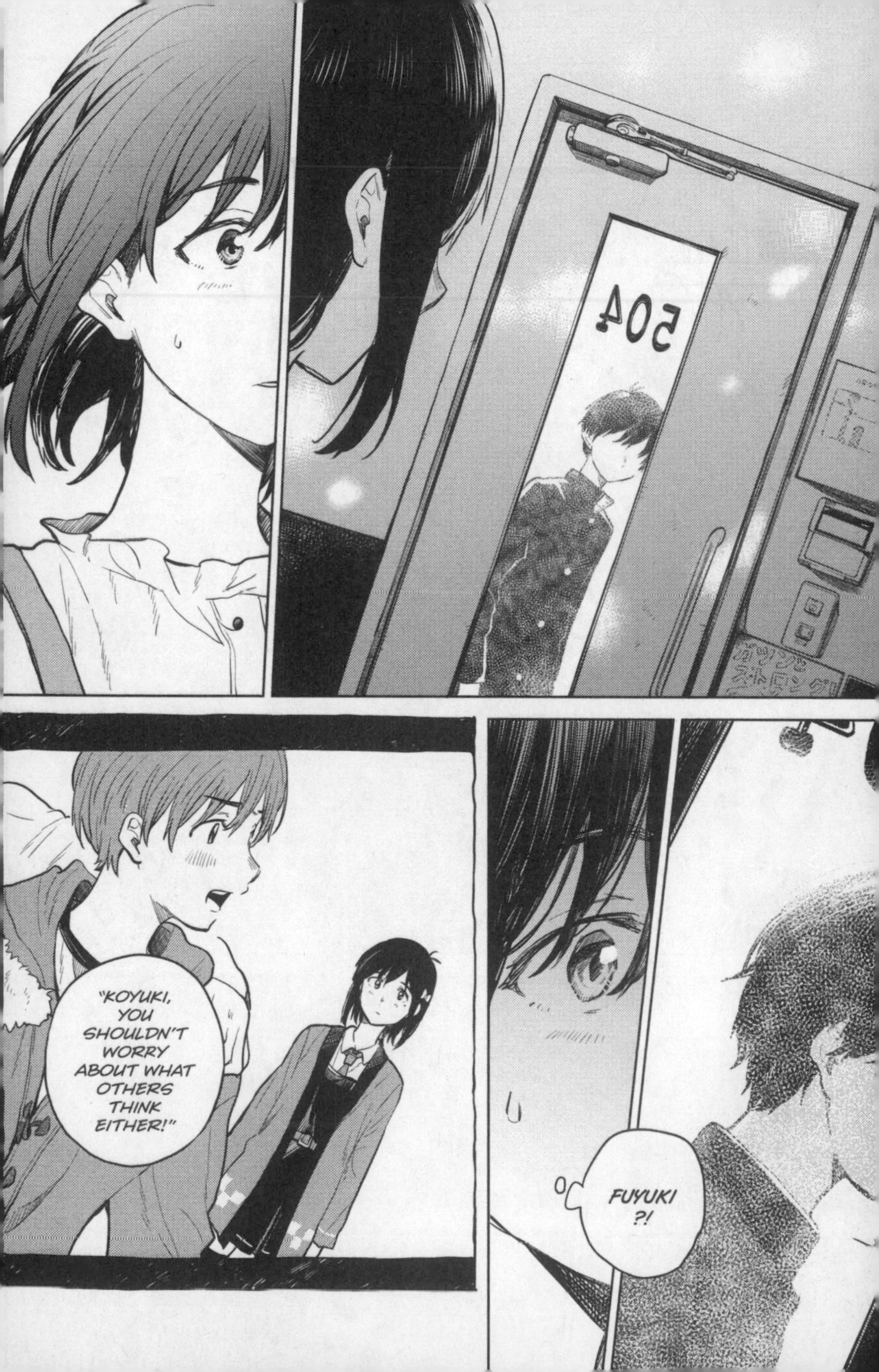
504
FUYUKI ?!
"KOYUKI, YOU SHOULDN'T WORRY ABOUT WHAT OTHERS THINK EITHER!"

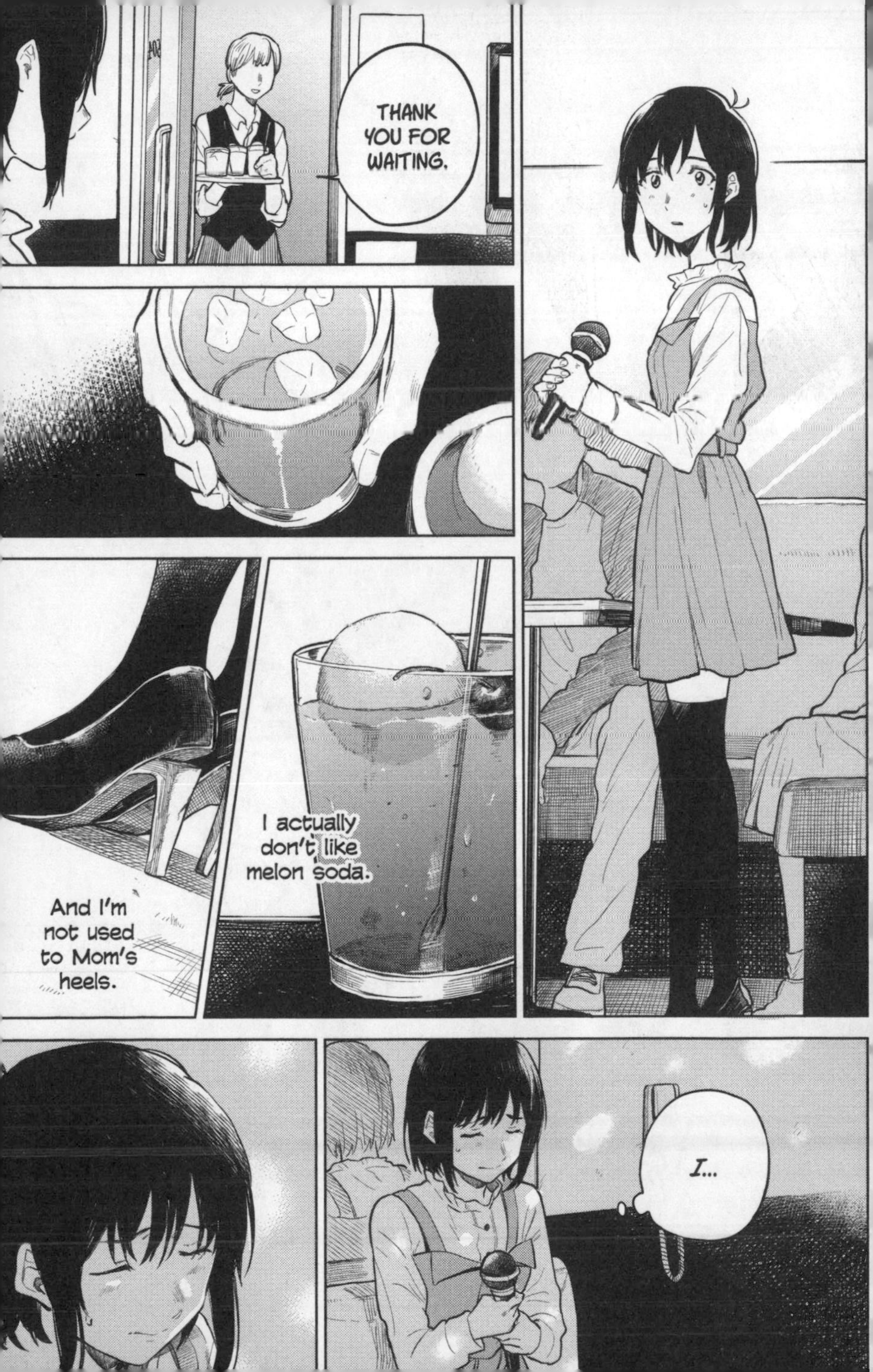
THANK YOU FOR WAITING.
I actually don't like melon soda.
And I'm not used to Mom's heels.
I...

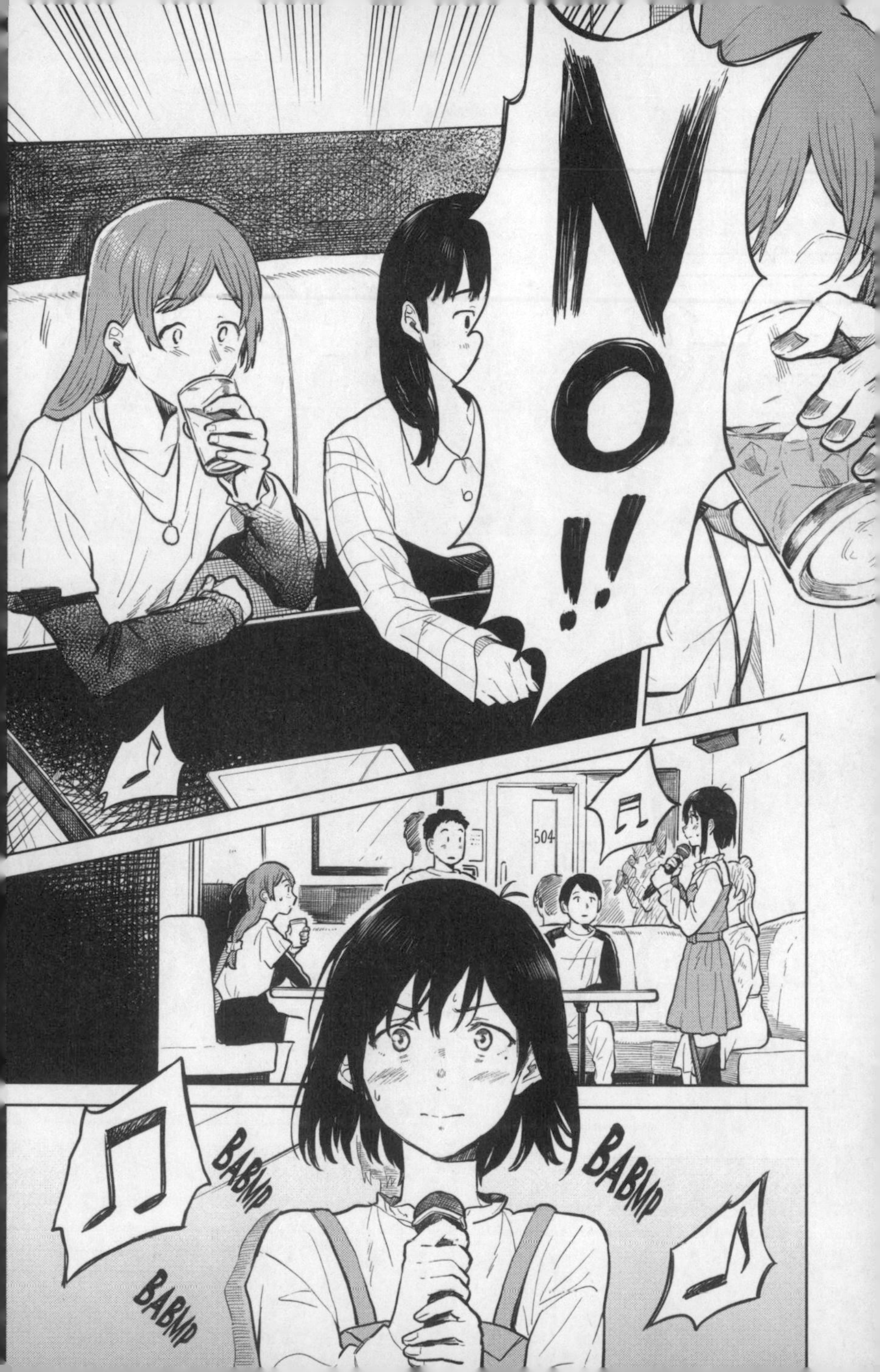
NO!!
BABMP
BABMP
BABMP

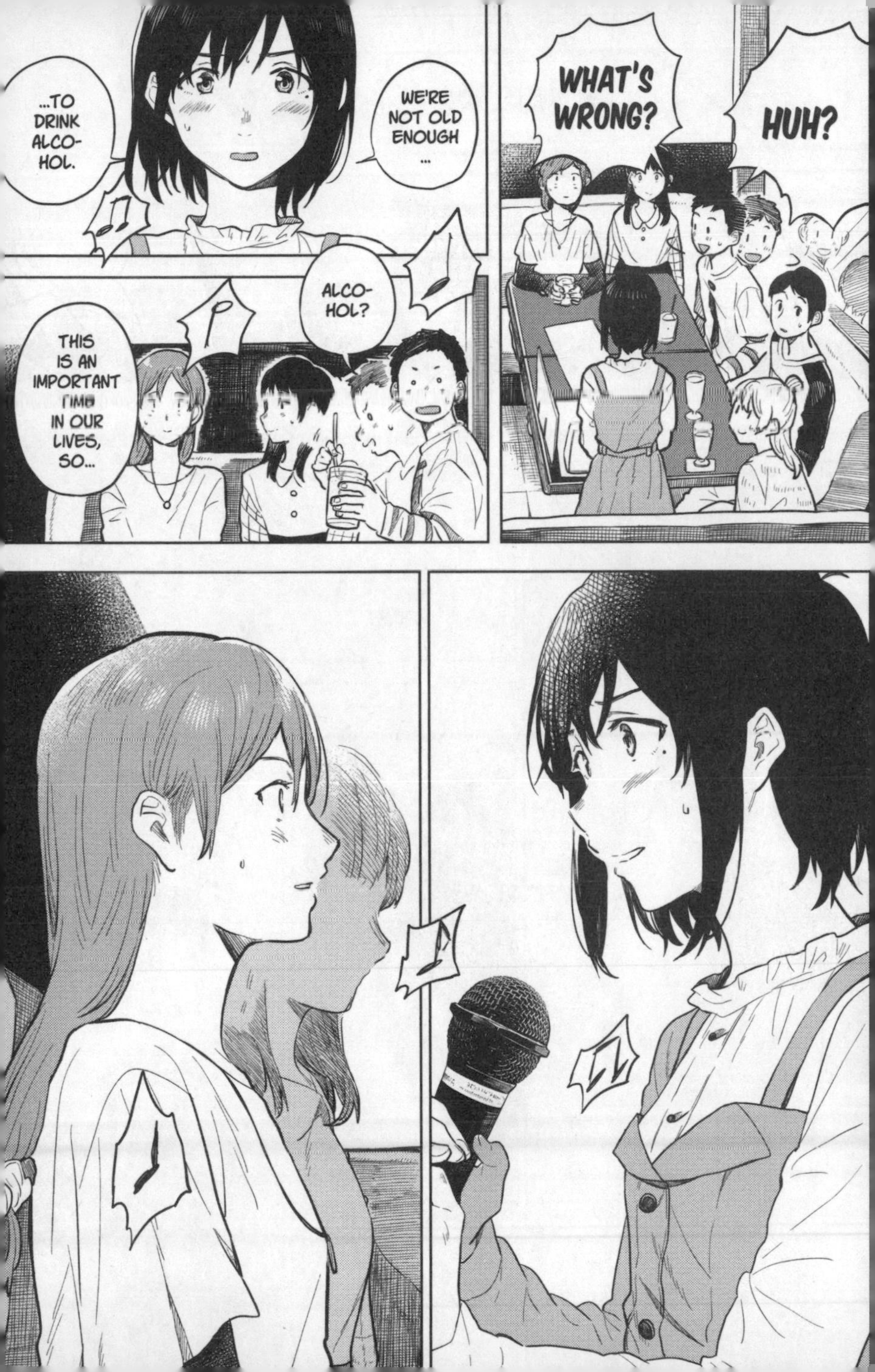

HUH?
WHAT'S WRONG?
WE'RE NOT OLD ENOUGH ...
...TO DRINK ALCO-HOL.
ALCO-HOL?
THIS IS AN IMPORTANT TIME IN OUR LIVES, SO...

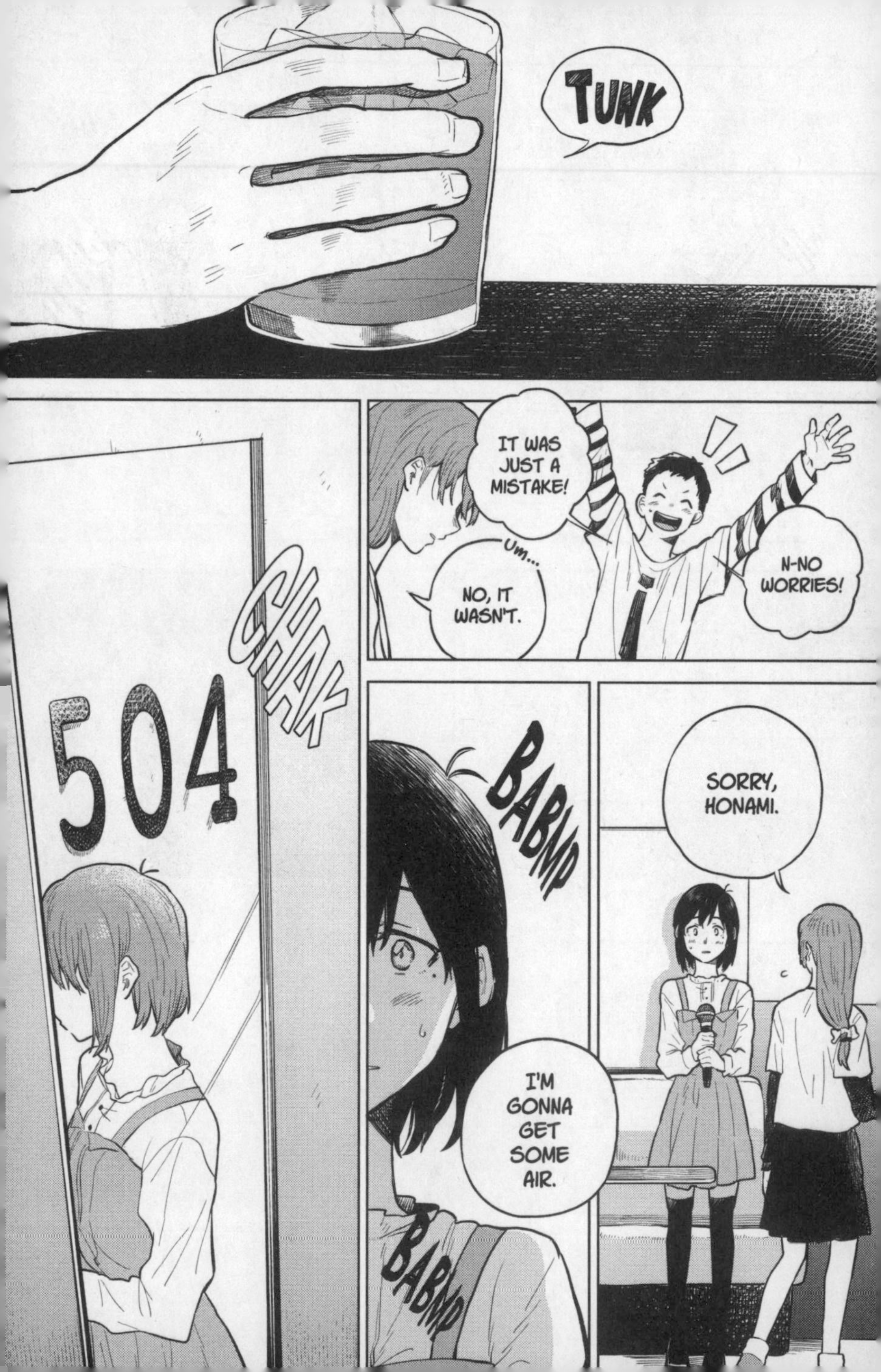
TUNK
IT WAS JUST A MISTAKE!
N-NO WORRIES!
Um...
NO, IT WASN'T.
SORRY, HONAMI.
BABMP
I'M GONNA GET SOME AIR.
BABMP
504
CHAK

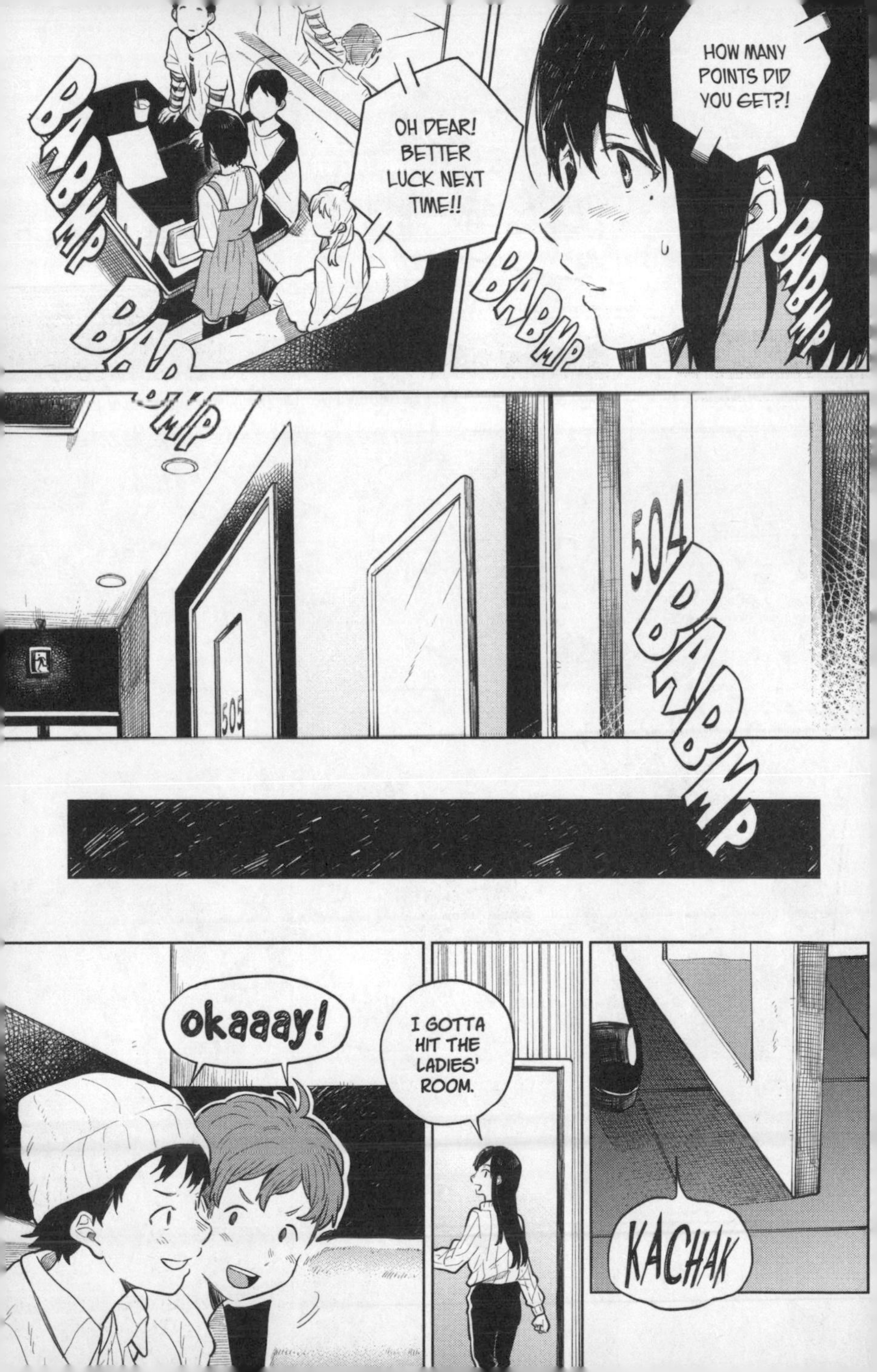
HOW MANY POINTS DID YOU GET?!
BABUMP
BABUMP
OH DEAR! BETTER LUCK NEXT TIME!!
BABUMP
BABUMP
BABUMP
504
505
BABUMP
KACHAK
I GOTTA HIT THE LADIES' ROOM.
okaaay!

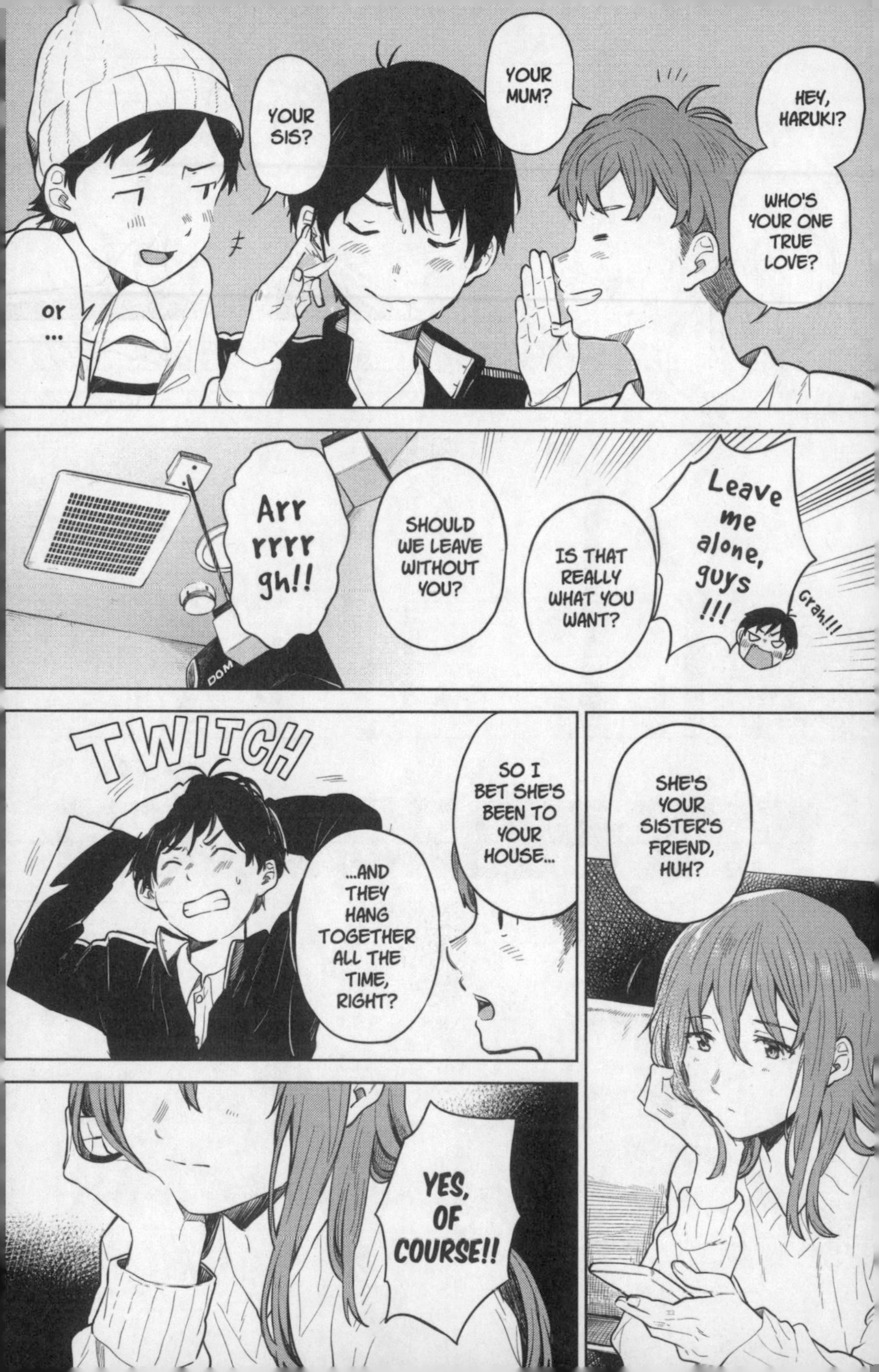
HEY, HARUKI?
WHO'S YOUR ONE TRUE LOVE?
YOUR MUM?
YOUR SIS?
or ...
Leave me alone, guys!!!
Graw!!!
IS THAT REALLY WHAT YOU WANT?
SHOULD WE LEAVE WITHOUT YOU?
Arrrrrrgh!!
SHE'S YOUR SISTER'S FRIEND, HUH?
SO I BET SHE'S BEEN TO YOUR HOUSE...
...AND THEY HANG TOGETHER ALL THE TIME, RIGHT?
TWITCH
YES, OF COURSE!!

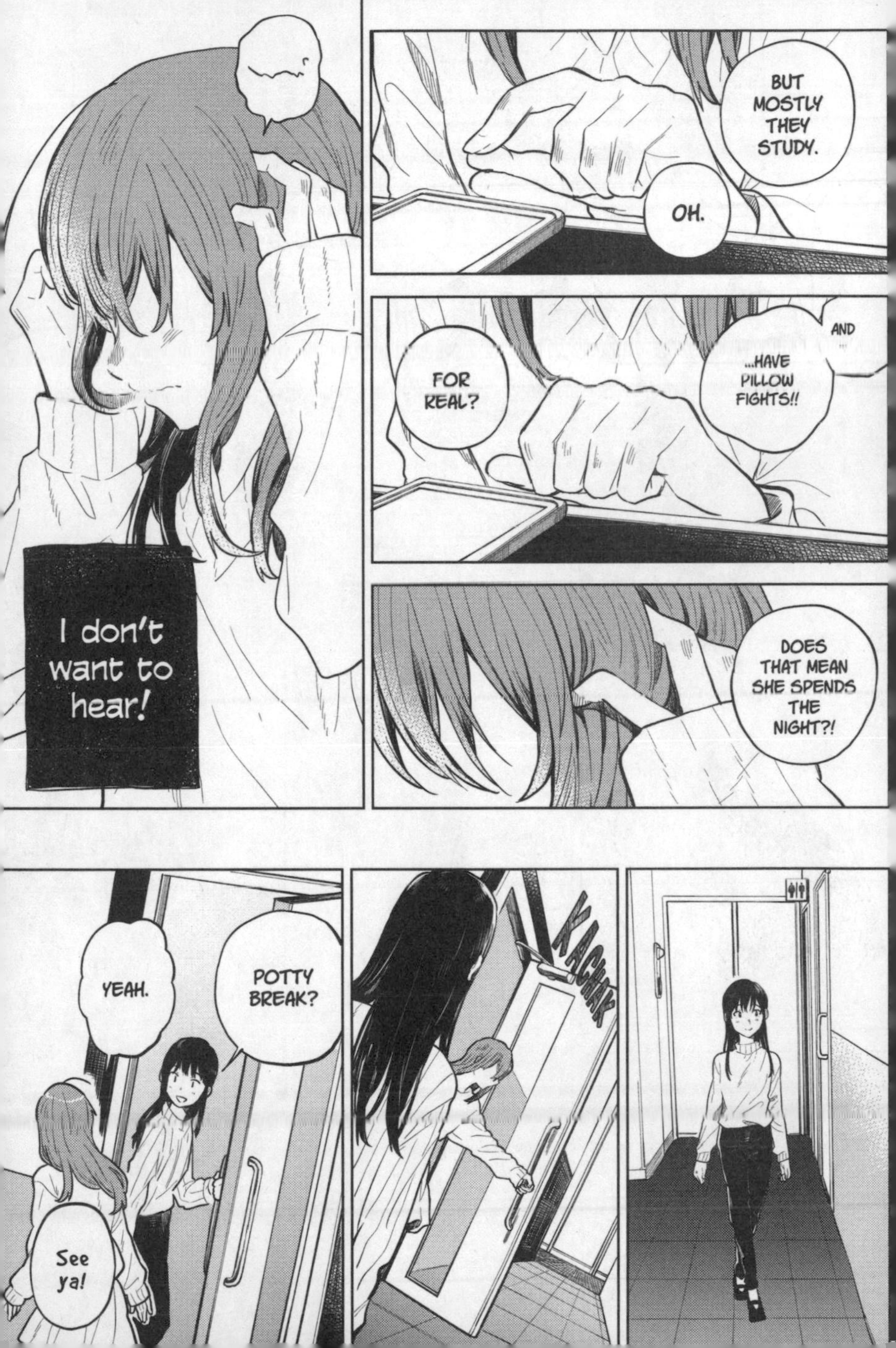
BUT MOSTLY THEY STUDY.
OH.
AND
...HAVE PILLOW FIGHTS!!
FOR REAL?
DOES THAT MEAN SHE SPENDS THE NIGHT?!
I don't want to hear!
KACHAK
POTTY BREAK?
YEAH.
See ya!

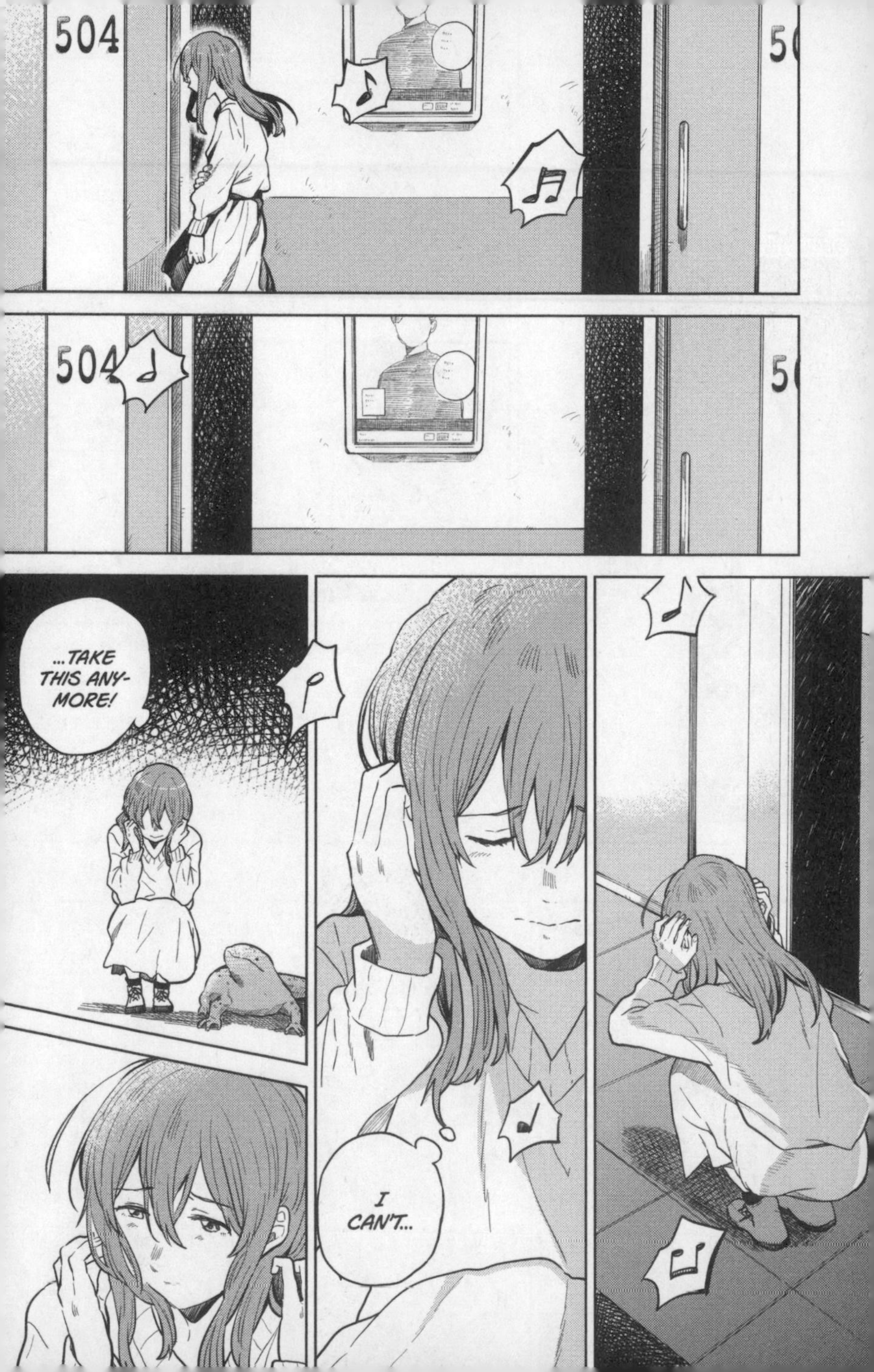
504
504
I CAN'T...
...TAKE THIS ANY-MORE!

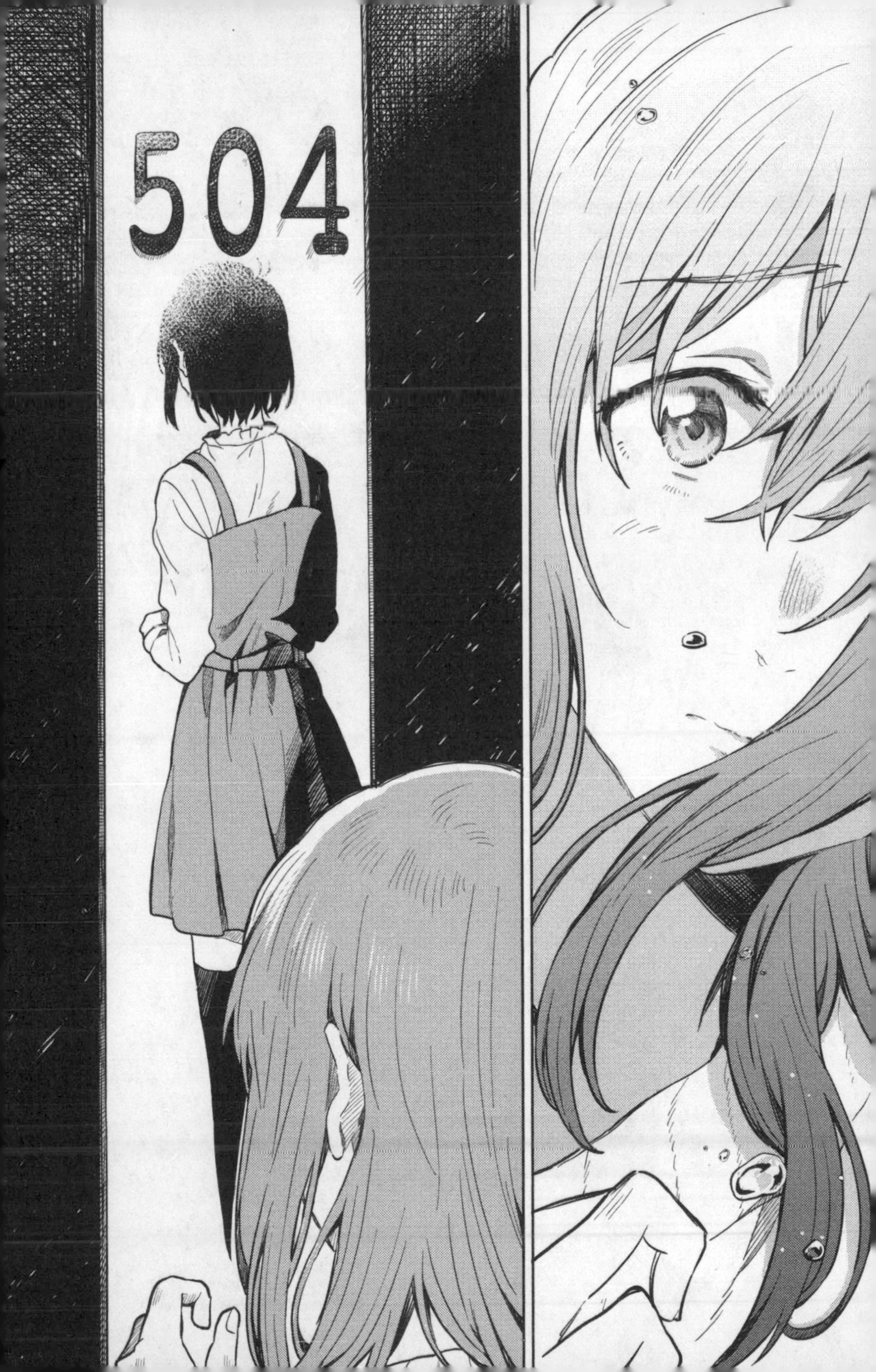
504

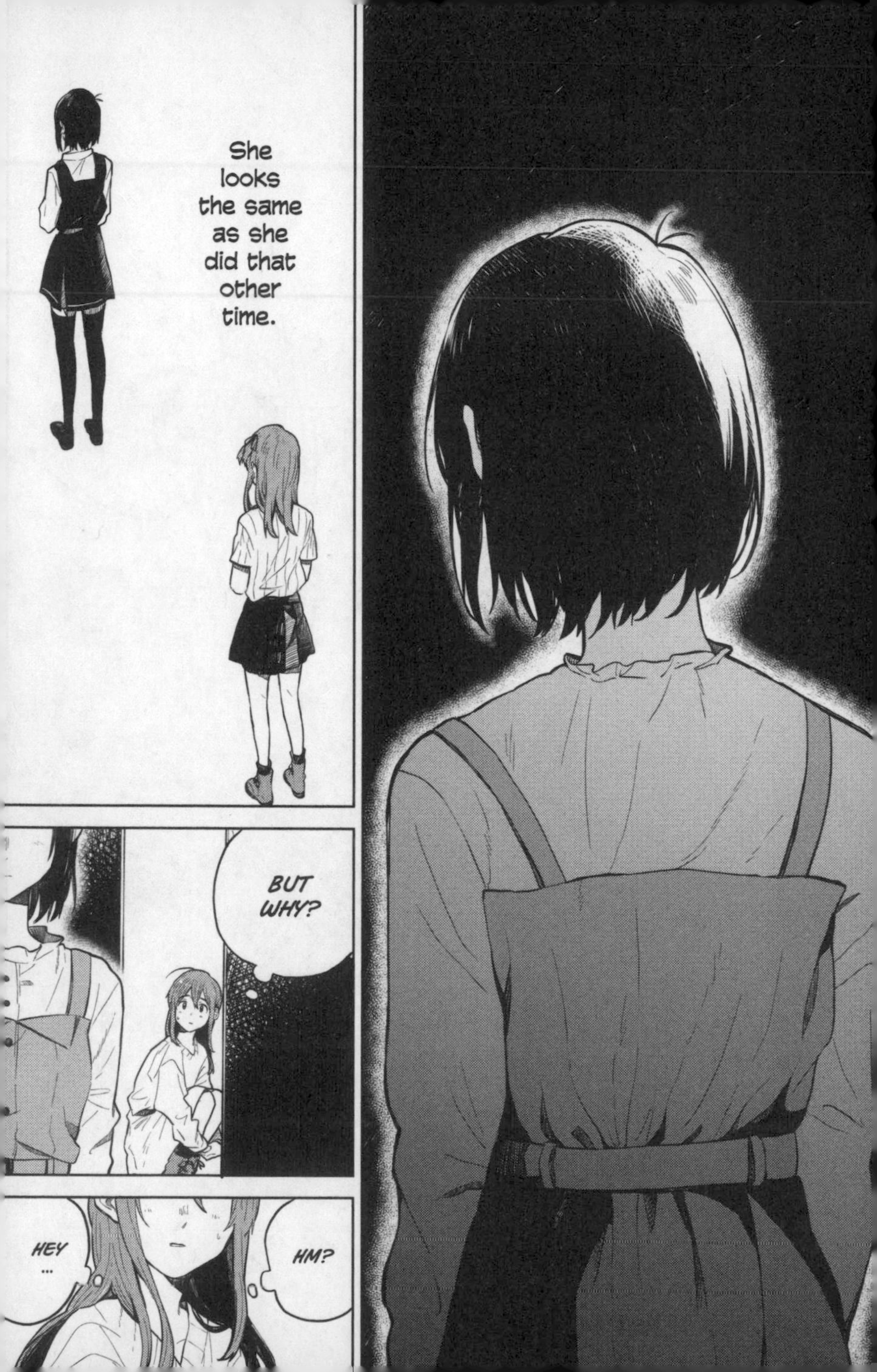
She looks the same as she did that other time.
BUT WHY?
HM?
HEY ...

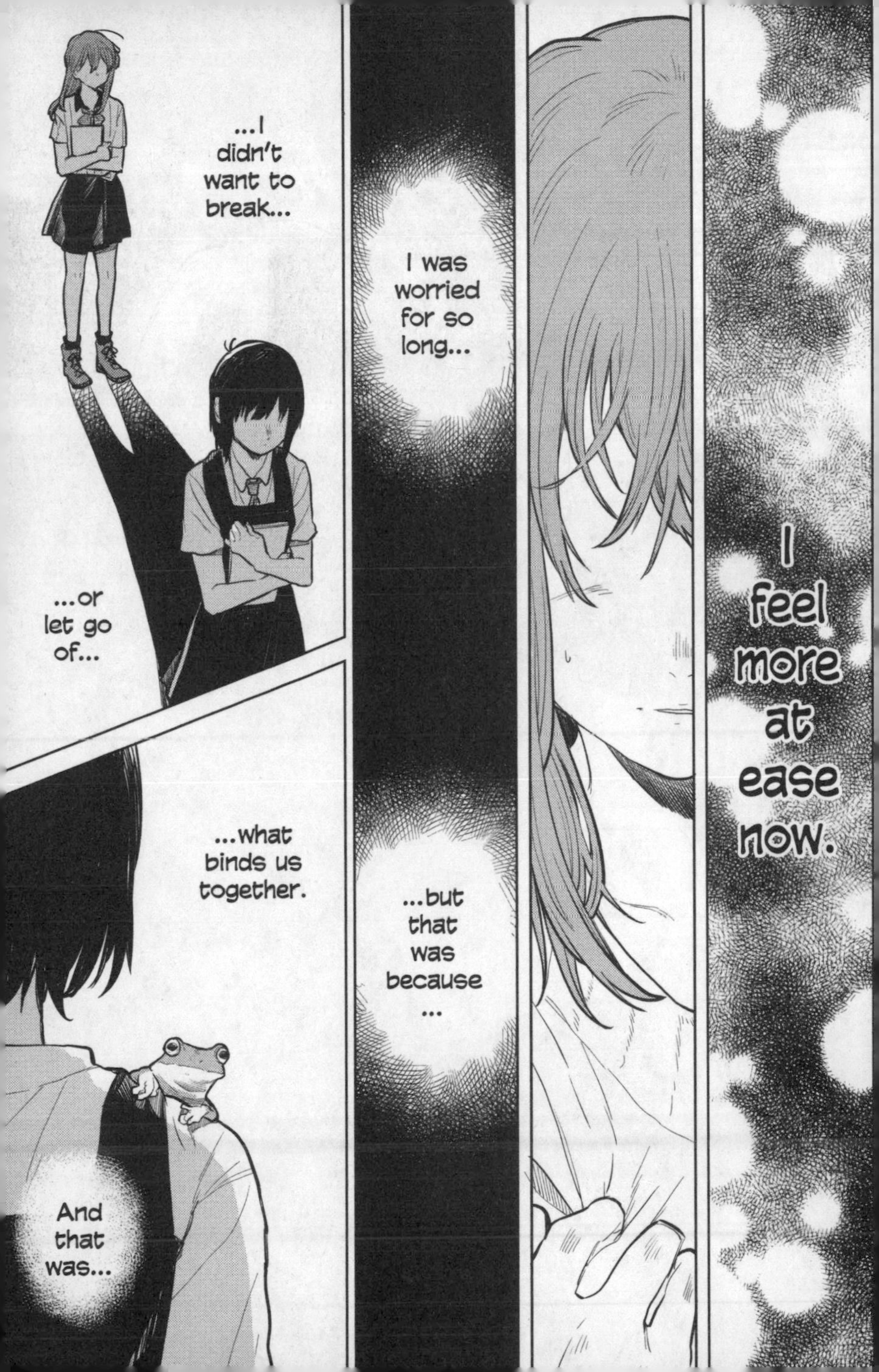
I feel more at ease now.
I was worried for so long...
...but that was because ...
...I didn't want to break...
...or let go of...
...what binds us together.
And that was...

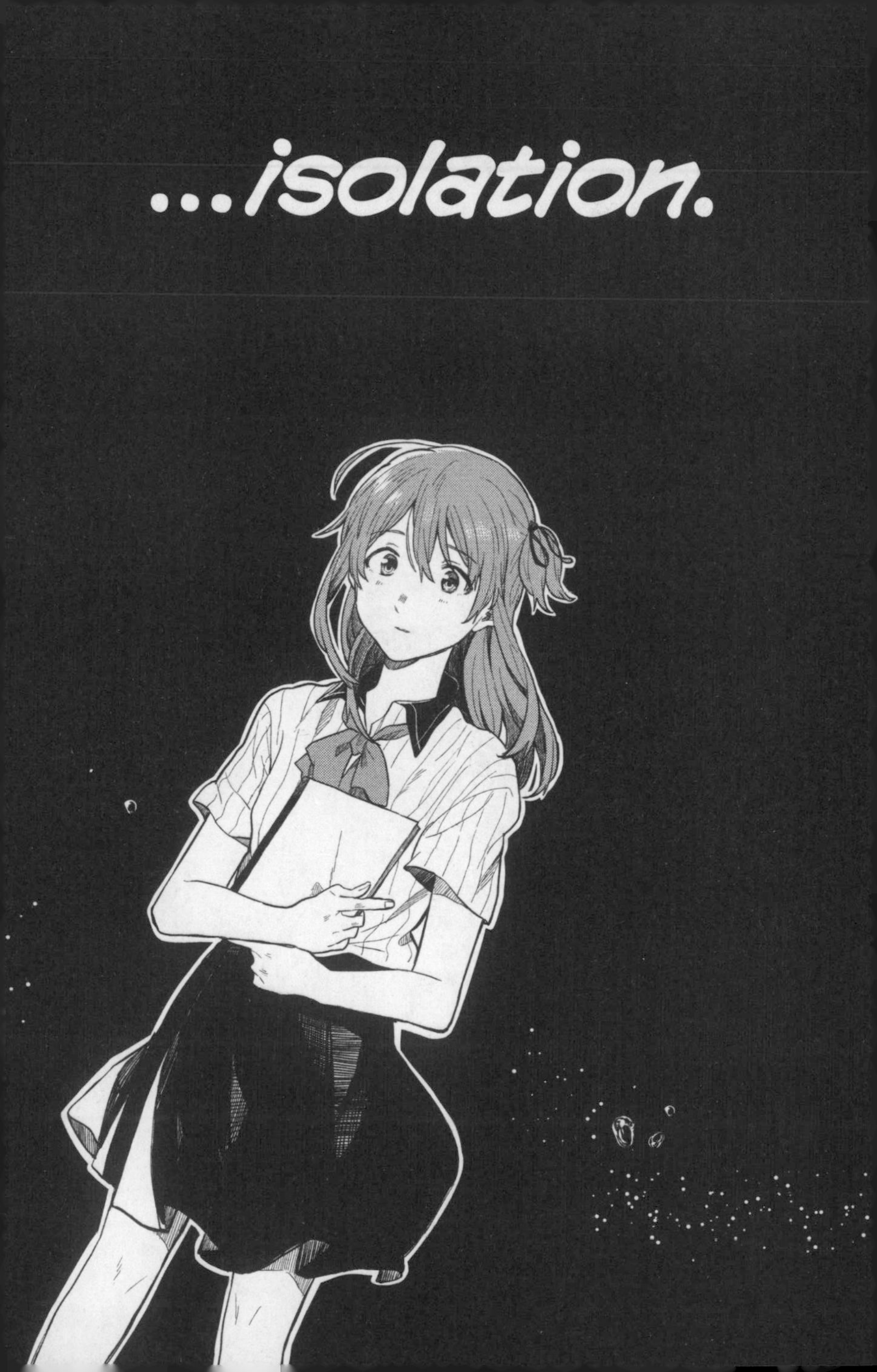
...isolation.

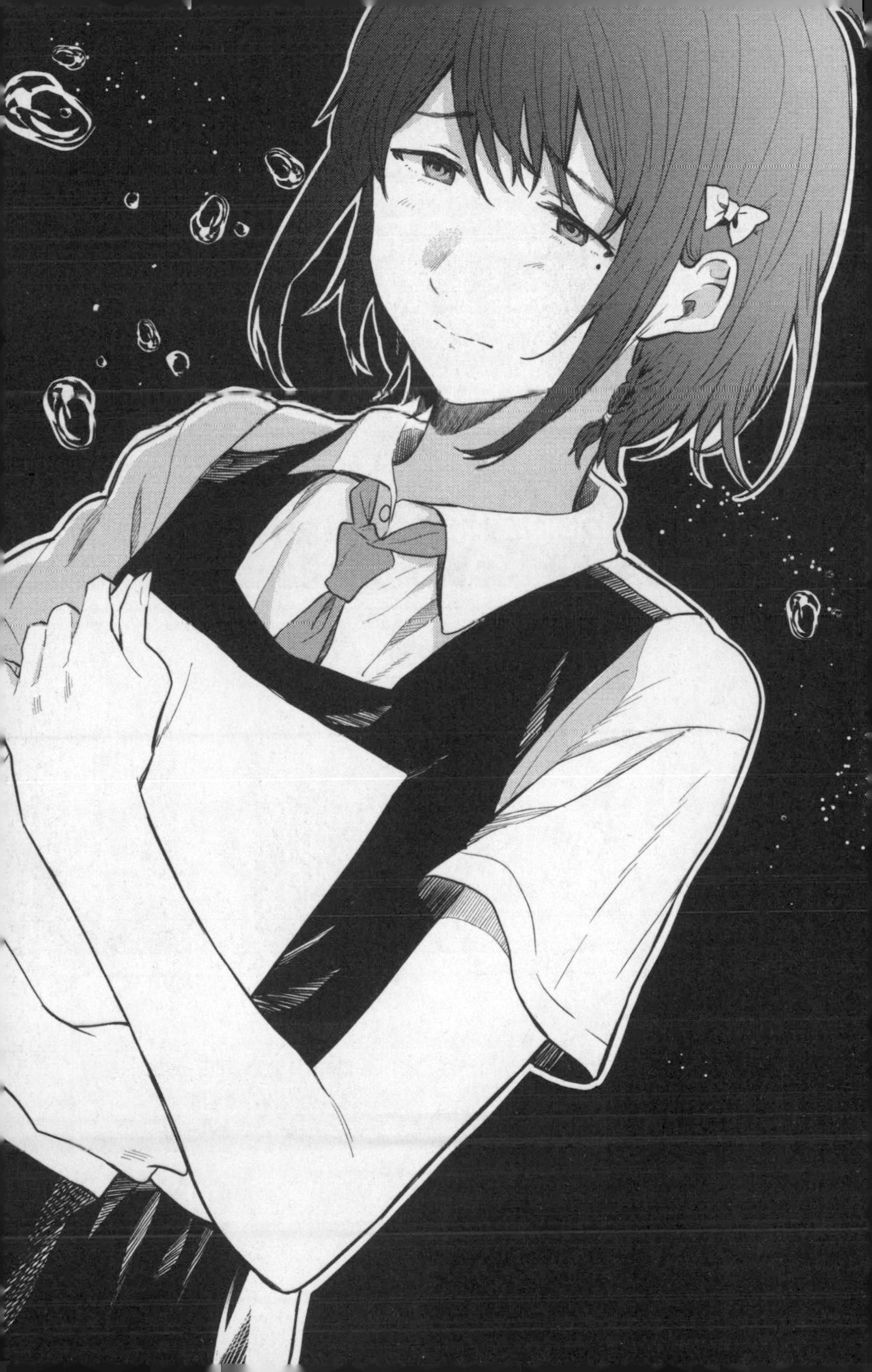

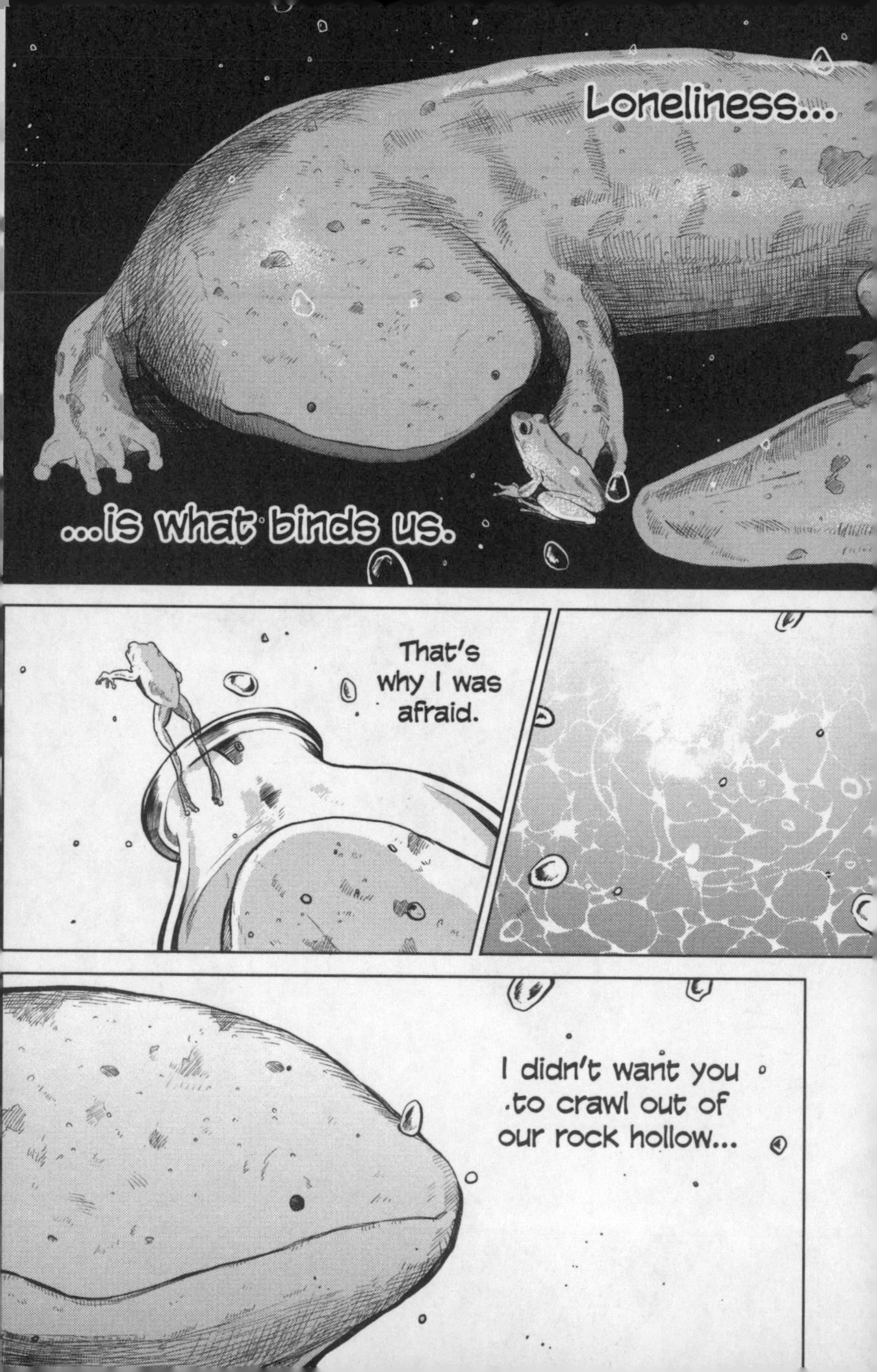
Loneliness...
...is what binds us.
That's why I was afraid.
I didn't want you to crawl out of our rock hollow...

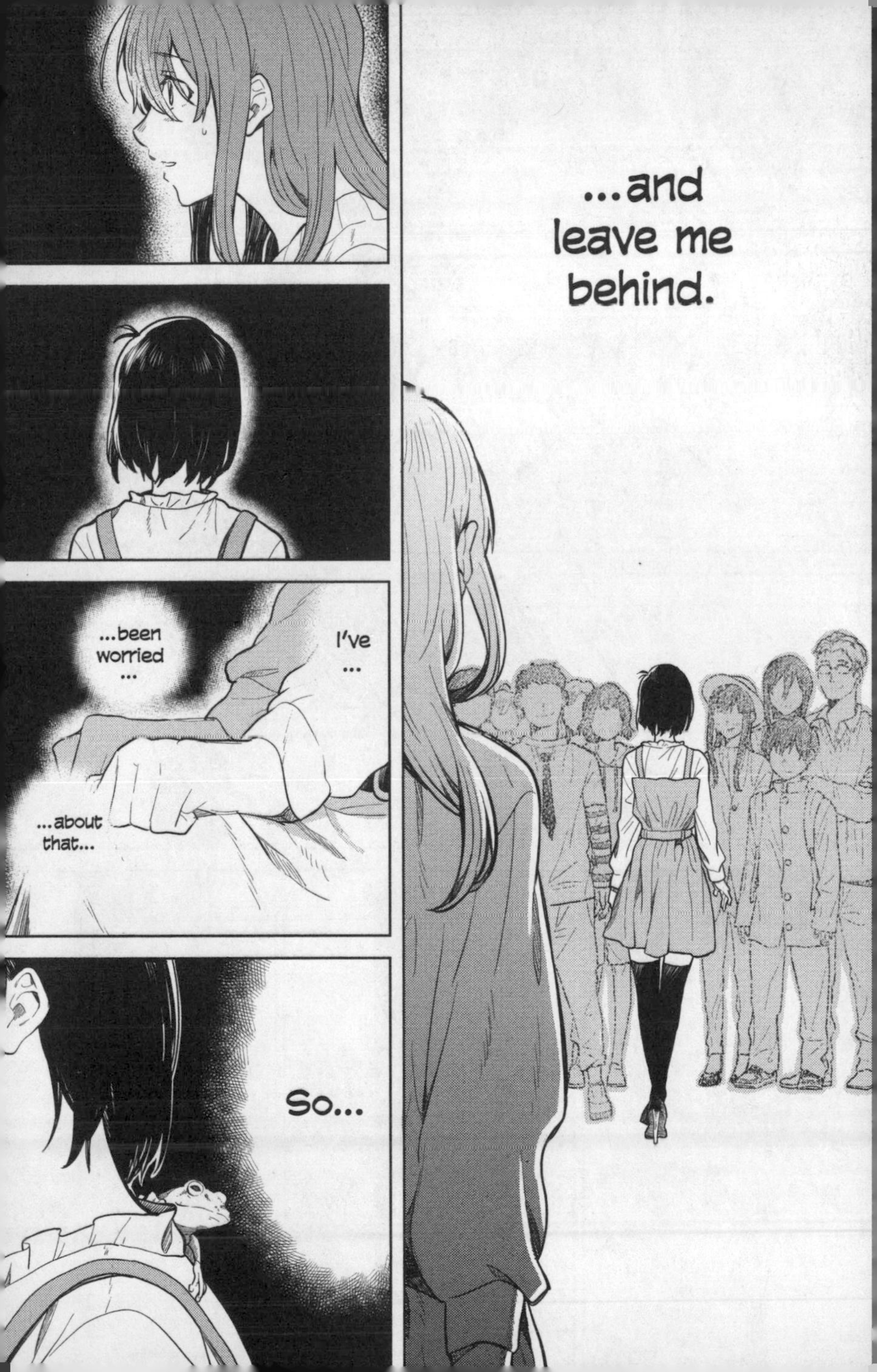
...and leave me behind.
I've ...
...been worried ...
...about that...
So...

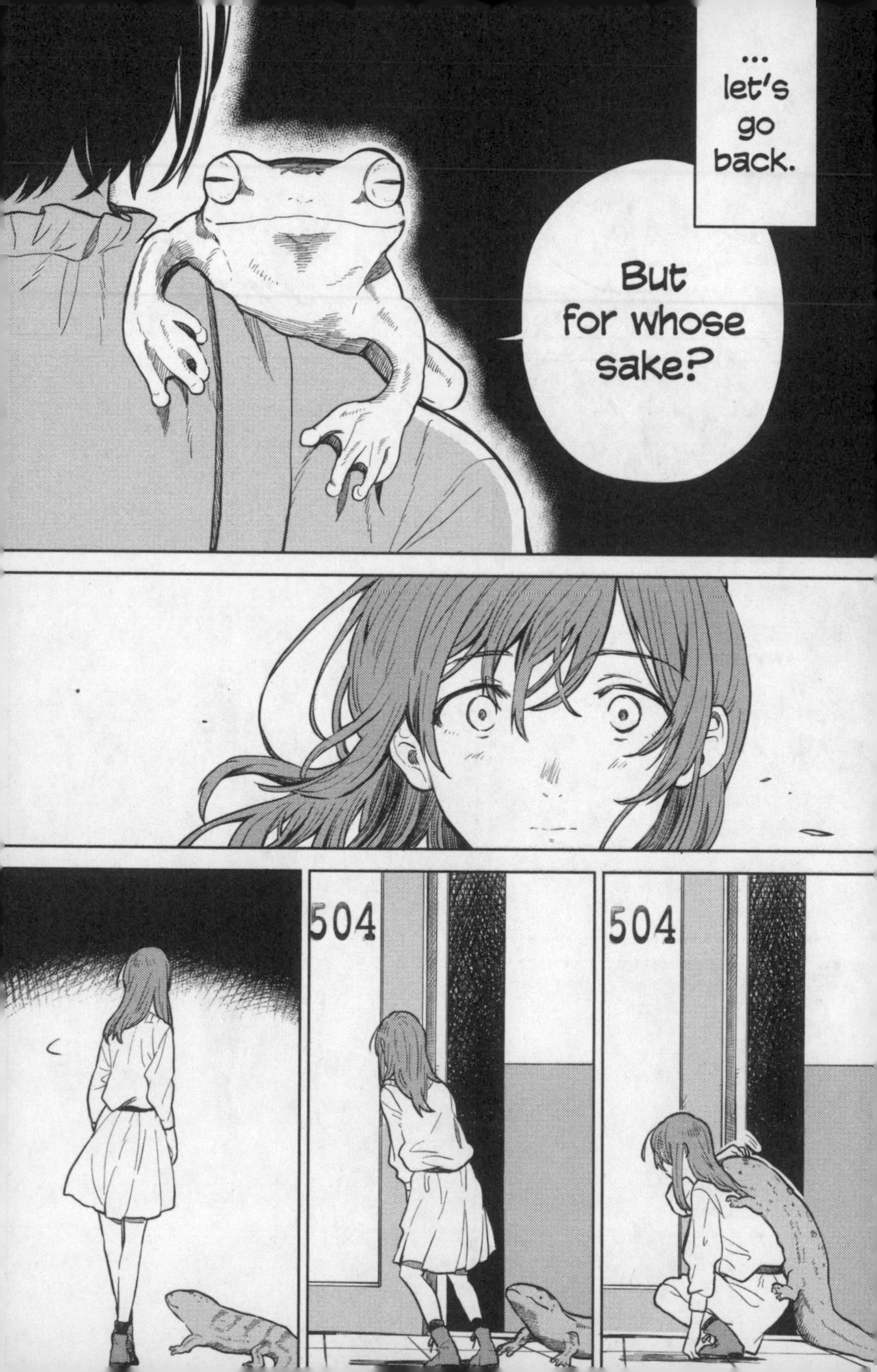
...
let's
go
back.
But
for whose
sake?
504
504

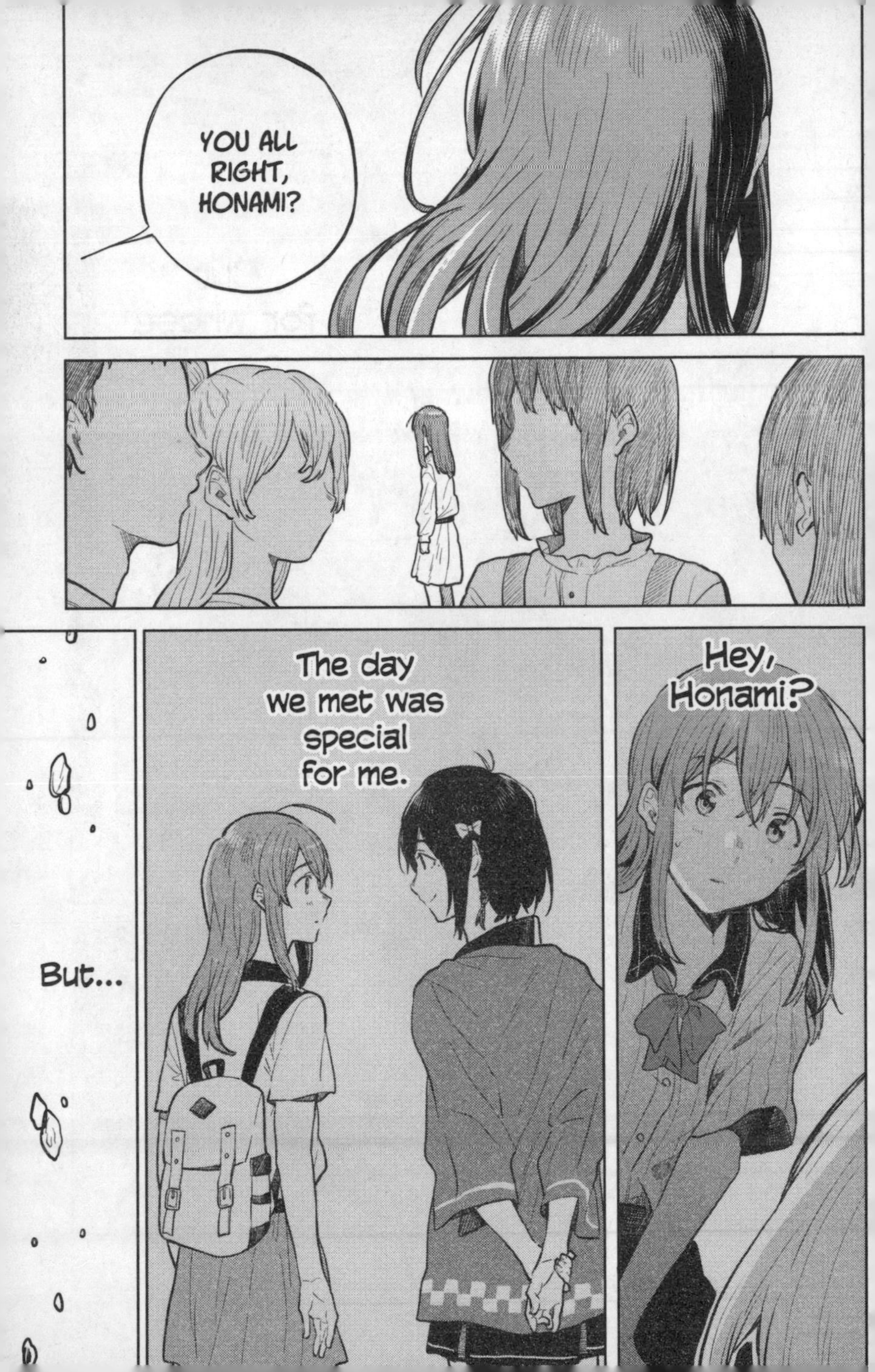
YOU ALL RIGHT, HONAMI?
Hey, Honami?
The day we met was special for me.
But...

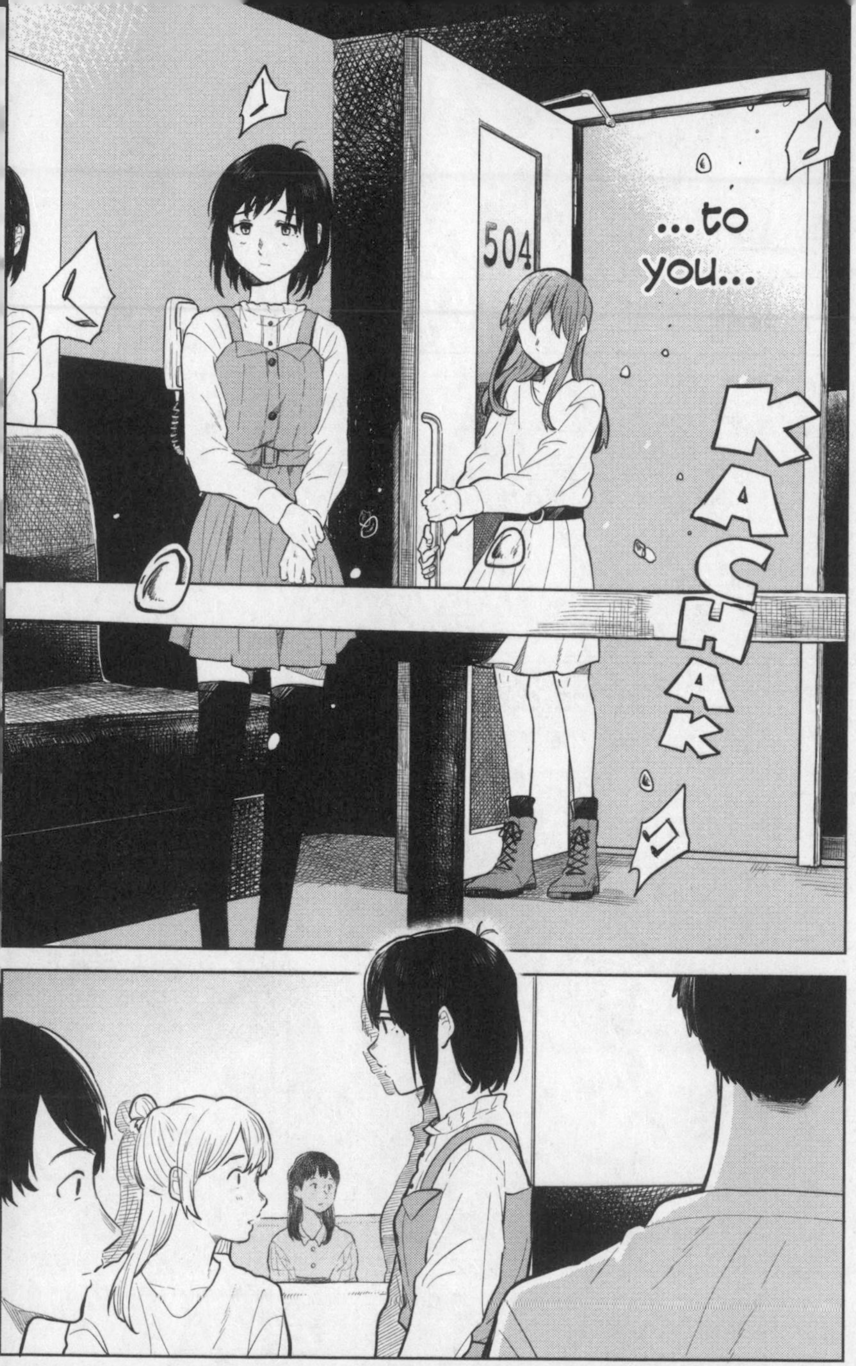
...to you...
504
KACHAK

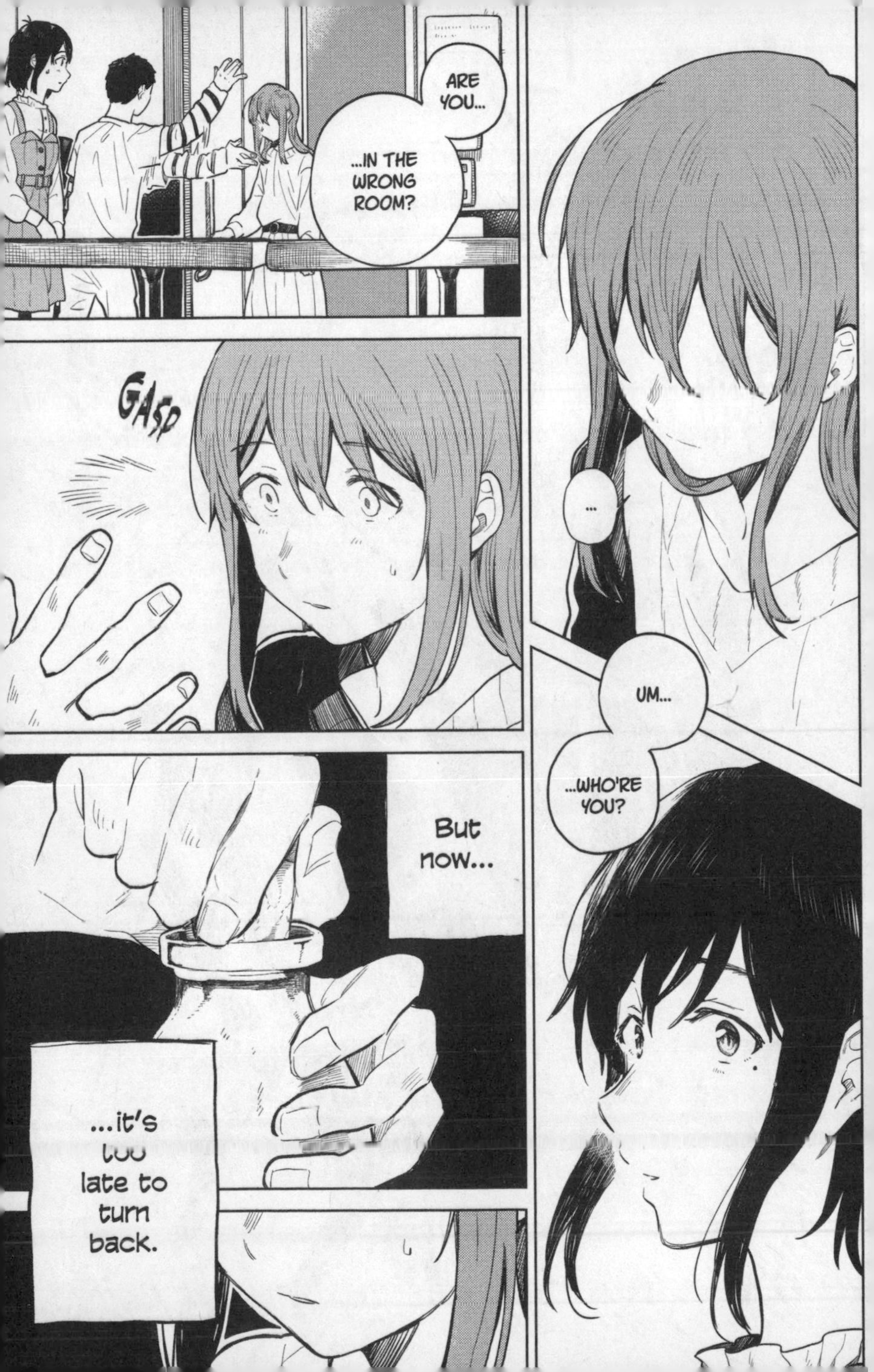
...
ARE YOU...
...IN THE WRONG ROOM?
GASP
UM...
...WHO'RE YOU?
But now...
...it's too late to turn back.

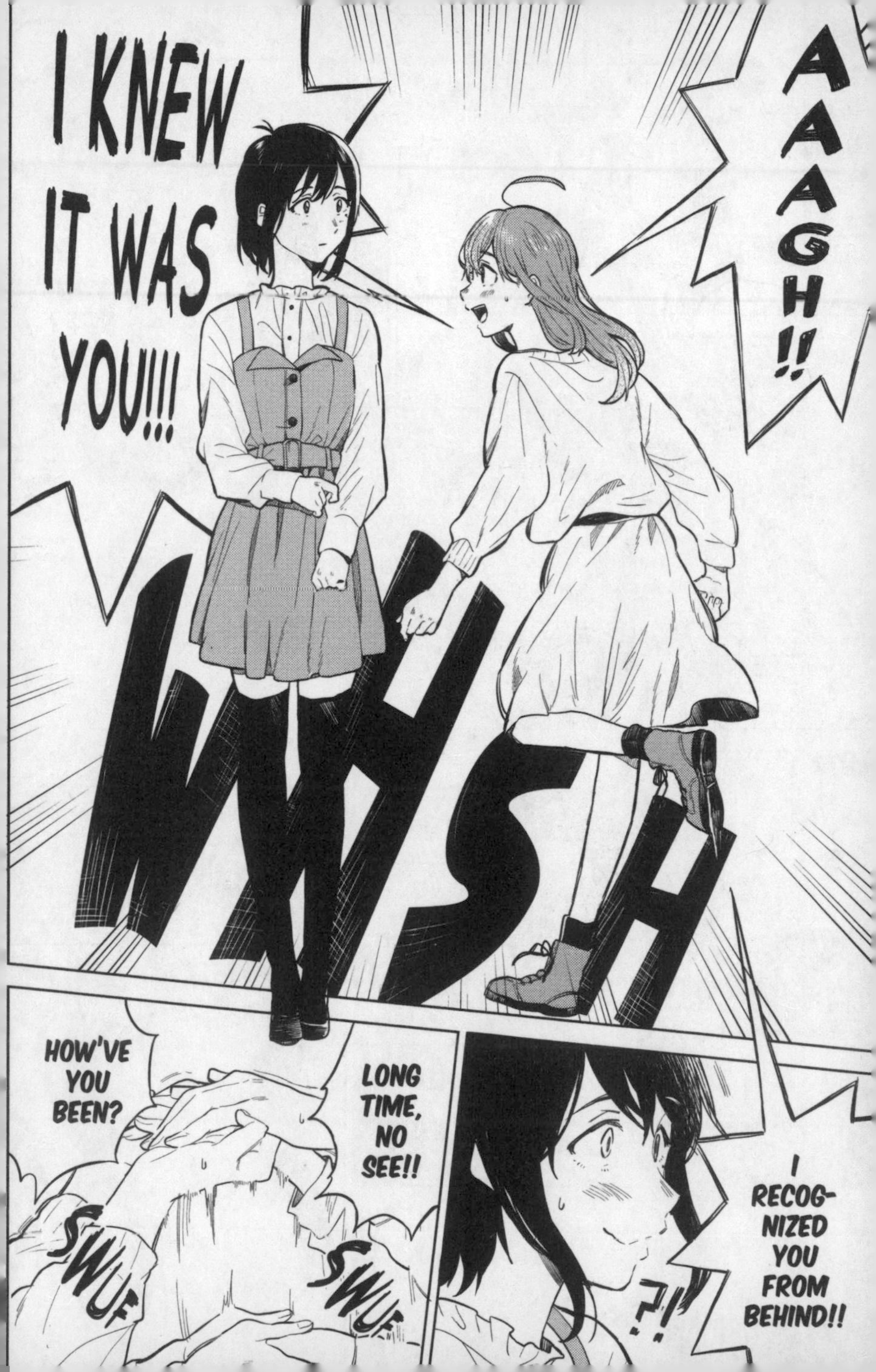
AAAGH!!
I KNEW IT WAS YOU!!!!
WHSH
I RECOG-NIZED YOU FROM BEHIND!!
?!
LONG TIME, NO SEE!!
HOW'VE YOU BEEN?
SWUF
SWUF

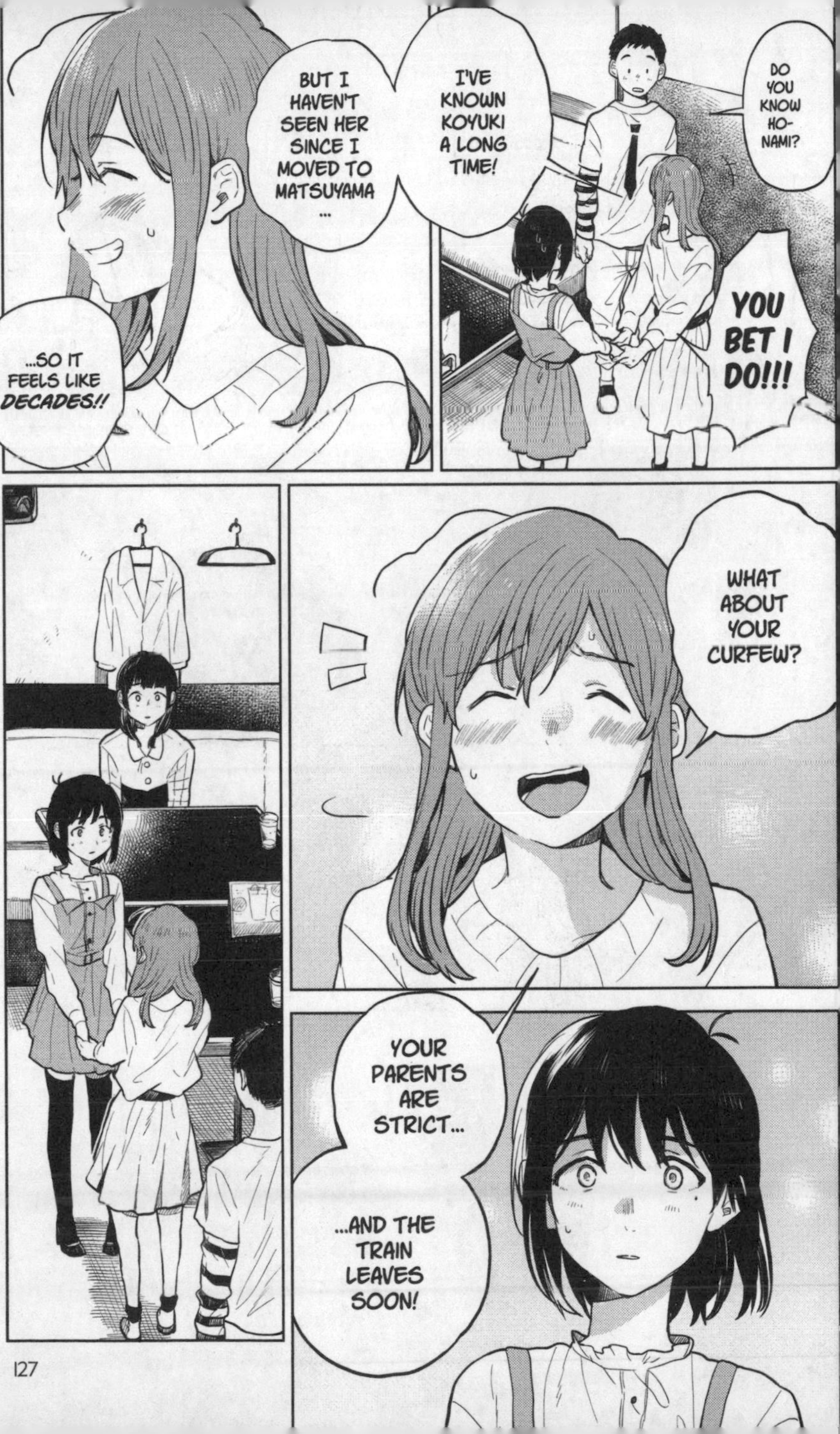

DO YOU KNOW HO-NAMI?
YOU BET I DO!!!
I'VE KNOWN KOYUKI A LONG TIME!
BUT I HAVEN'T SEEN HER SINCE I MOVED TO MATSUYAMA ...
...SO IT FEELS LIKE *DECADES!!*
WHAT ABOUT YOUR CURFEW?
YOUR PARENTS ARE STRICT...
...AND THE TRAIN LEAVES SOON!

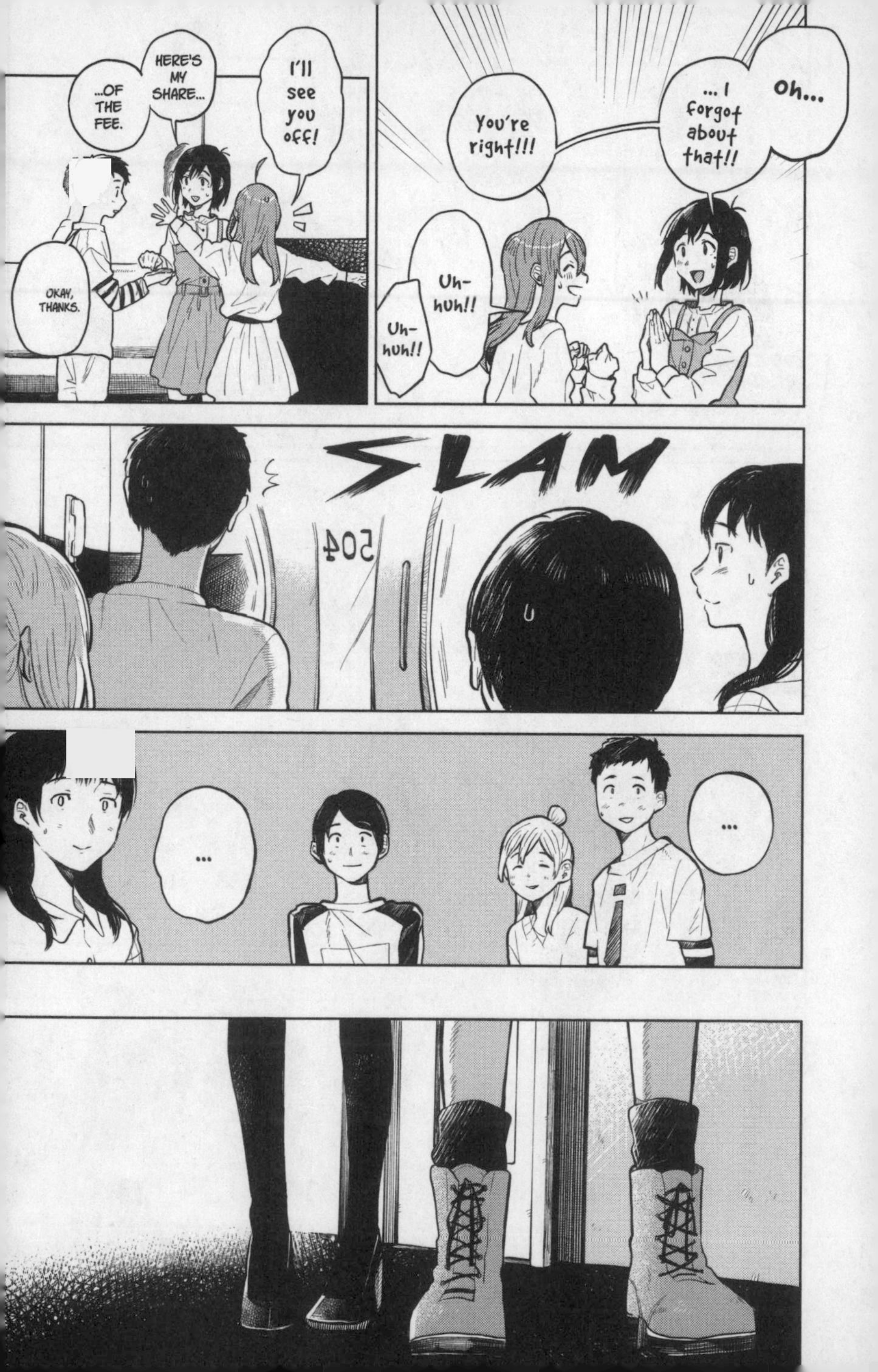
Oh...
...I forgot about that!!
You're right!!!
Uh-huh!!
Uh-huh!!
I'll see you off!
HERE'S MY SHARE...
...OF THE FEE.
OKAY, THANKS.
SLAM
504
...
...

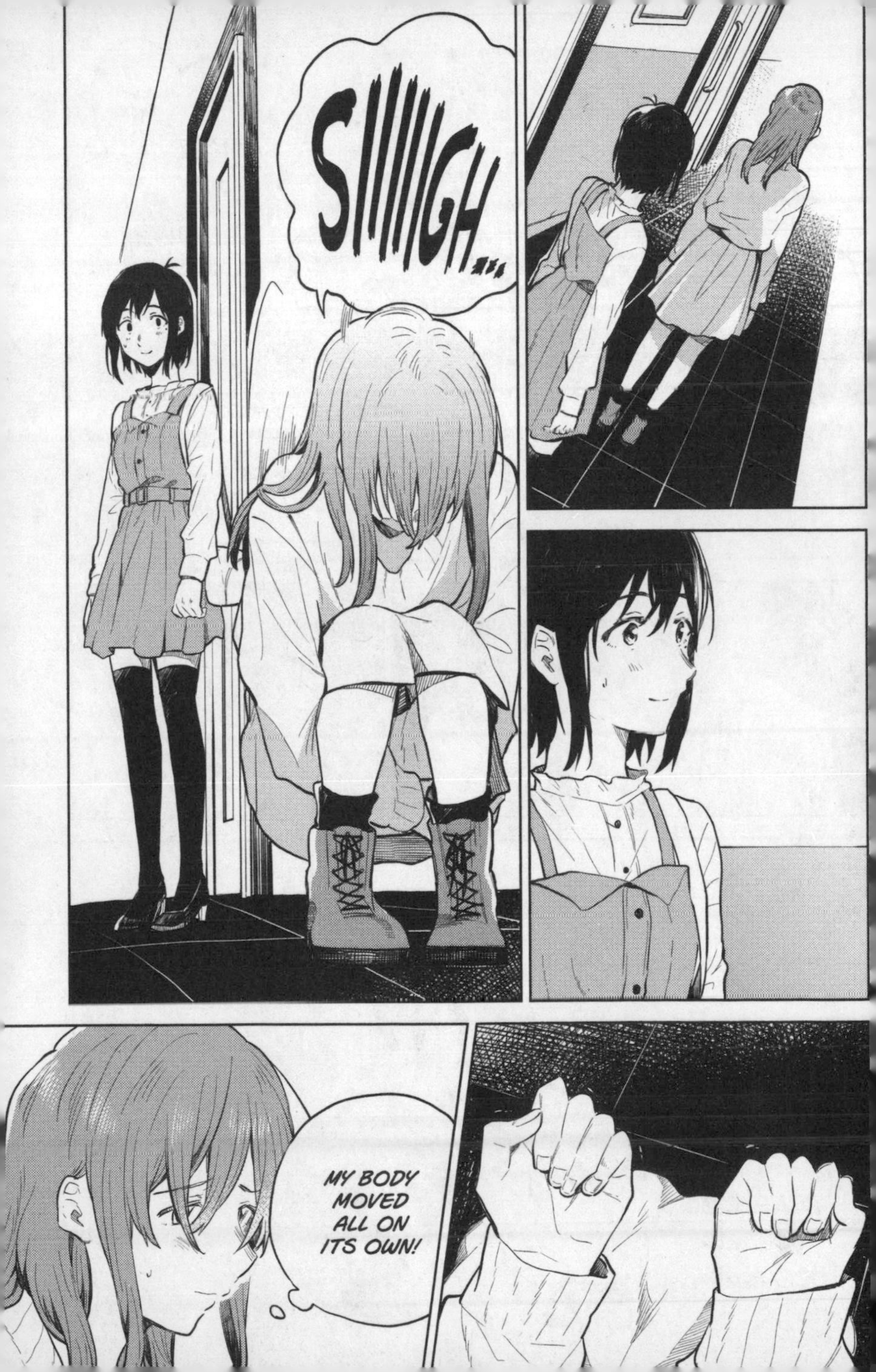
SIIIIGH...
MY BODY MOVED ALL ON ITS OWN!

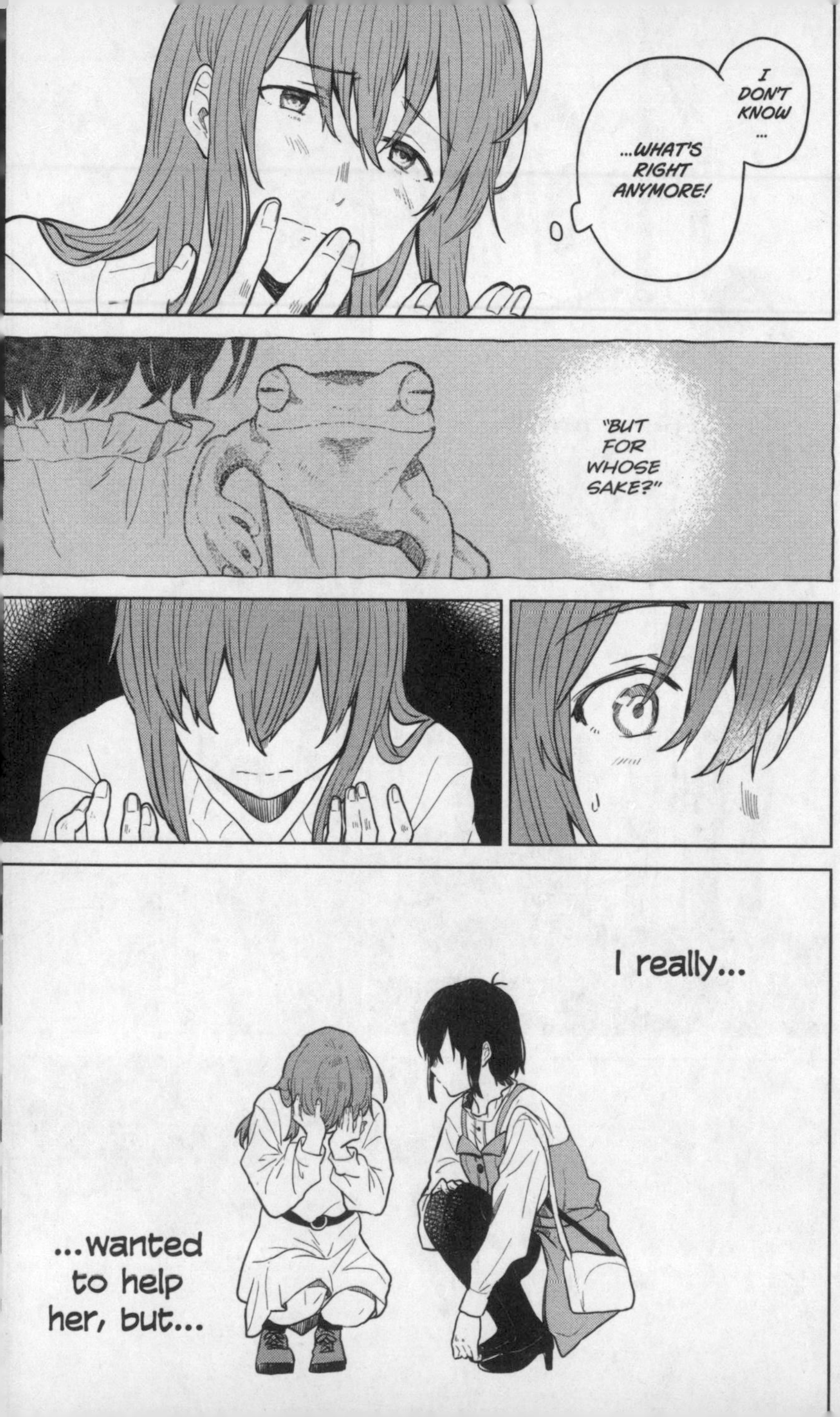
I DON'T KNOW ... ...WHAT'S RIGHT ANYMORE!
"BUT FOR WHOSE SAKE?"
I really...
...wanted to help her, but...

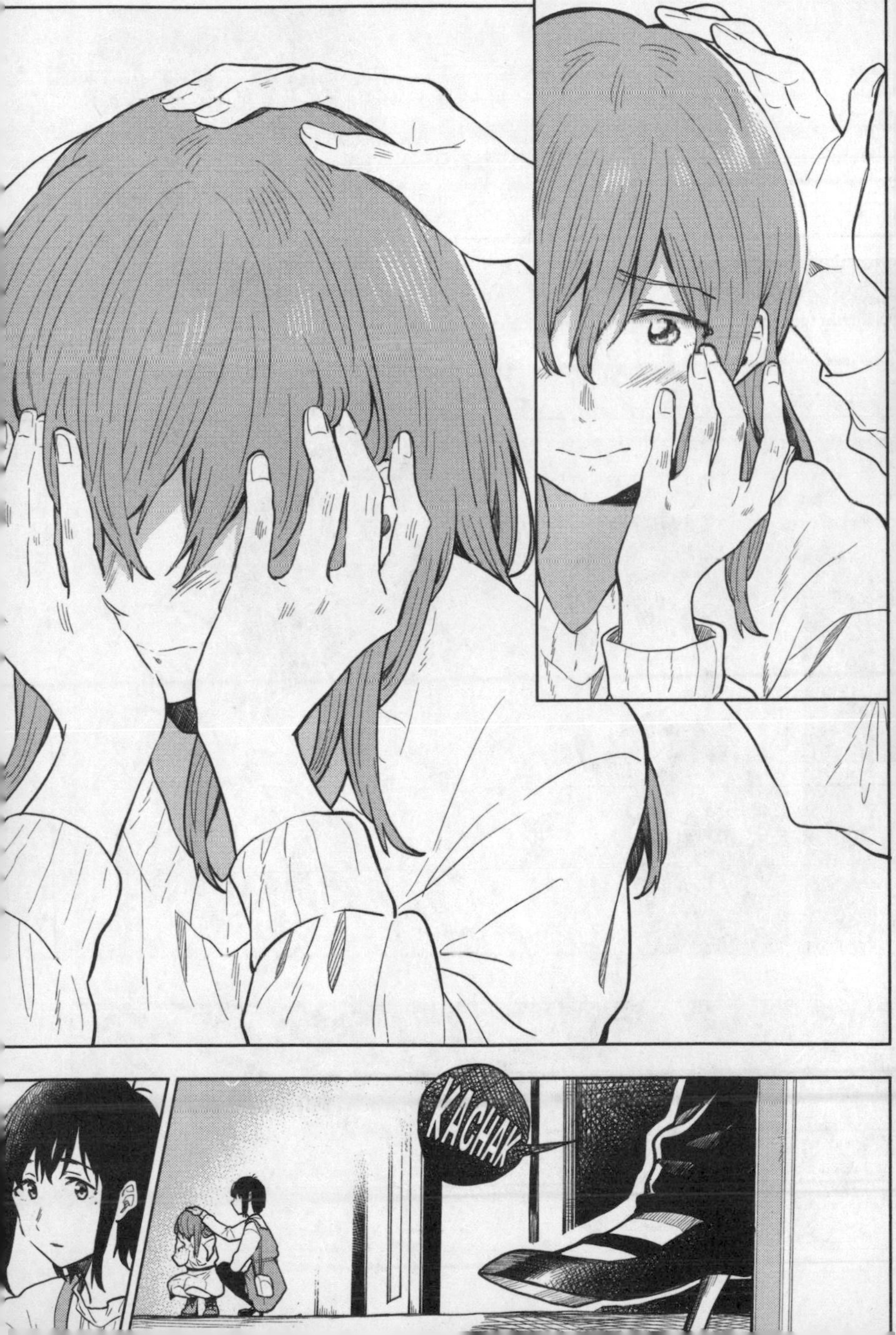
KACHAK

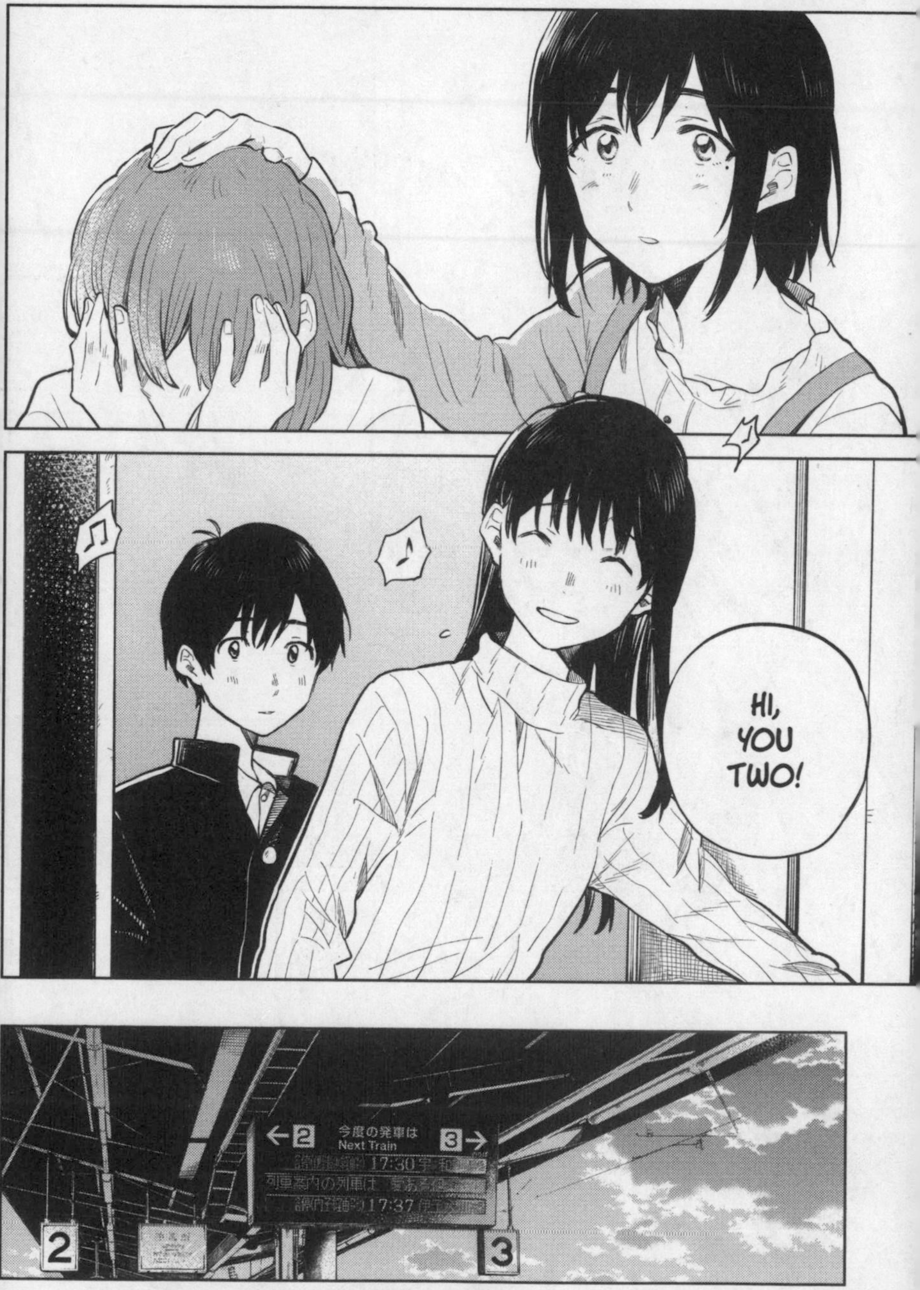
HI, YOU TWO!
← 2 今度の発車は Next Train 3 →
17:30
列車案内の列車は
17:37
2
3

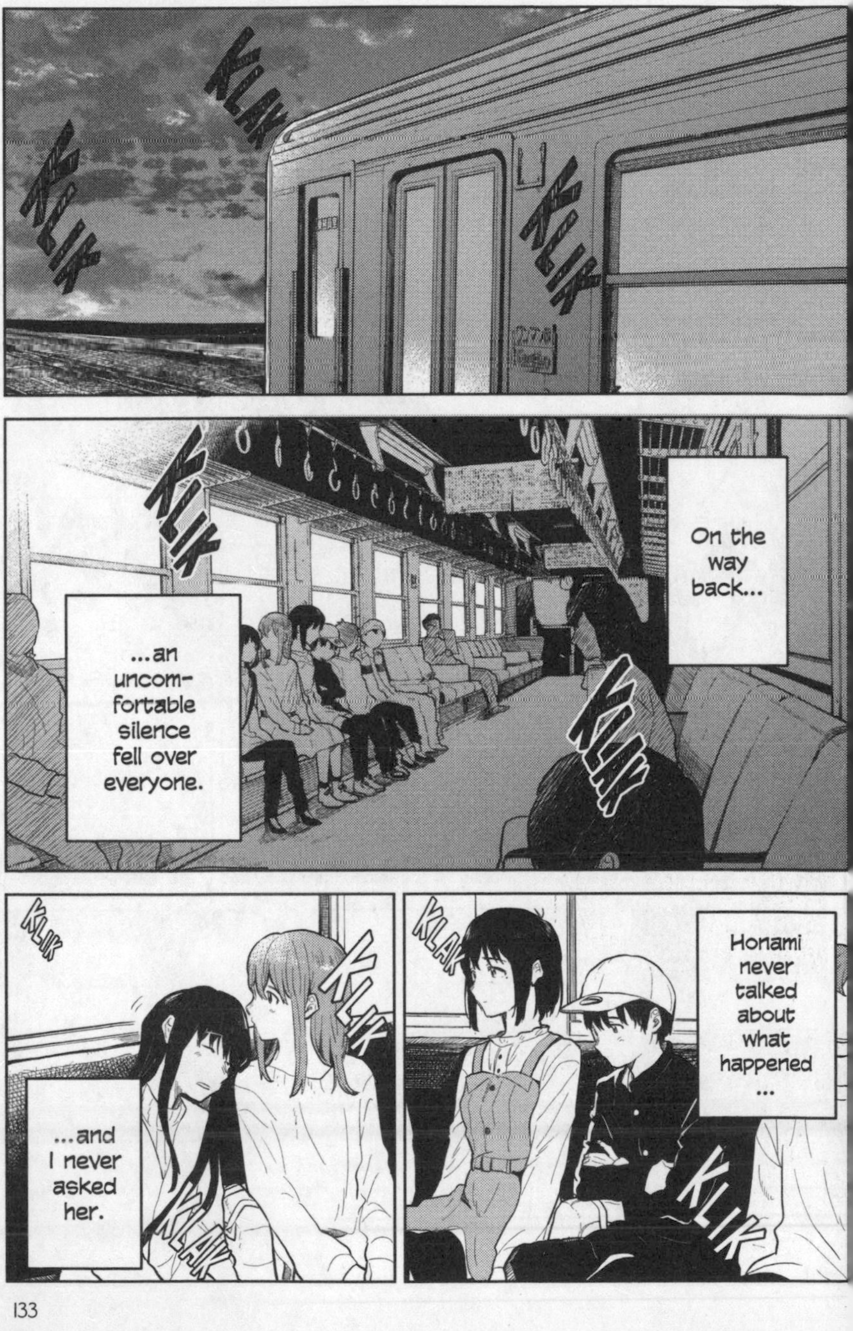
KLIK
KLAK
KLIK
On the way back...
...an uncom-fortable silence fell over everyone.
KLAK
KLIK
Honami never talked about what happened ...
KLAK
KLIK
...and I never asked her.
KLIK
KLAK
KLIK

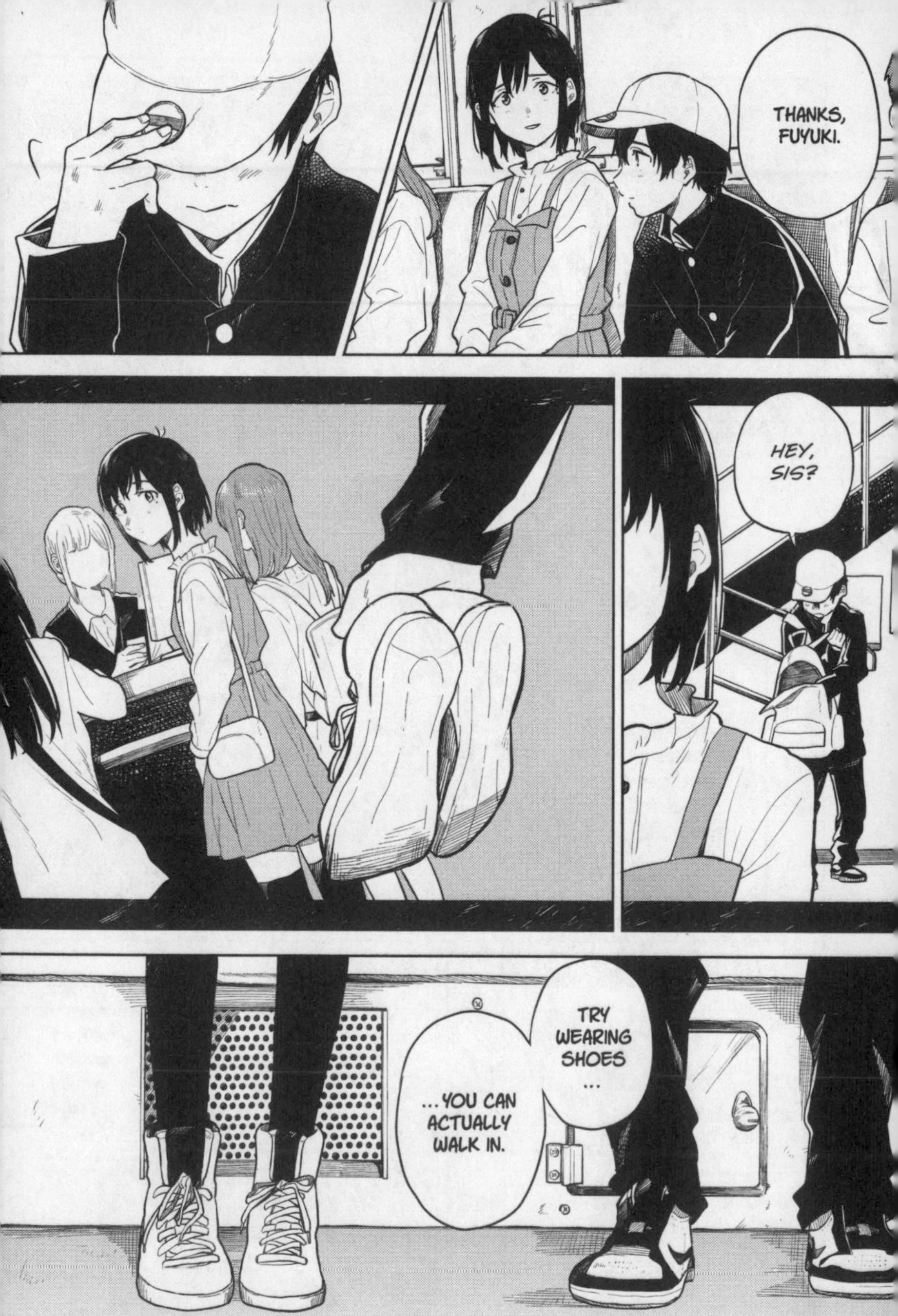
THANKS, FUYUKI.
HEY, SIS?
TRY WEARING SHOES ...
...YOU CAN ACTUALLY WALK IN.

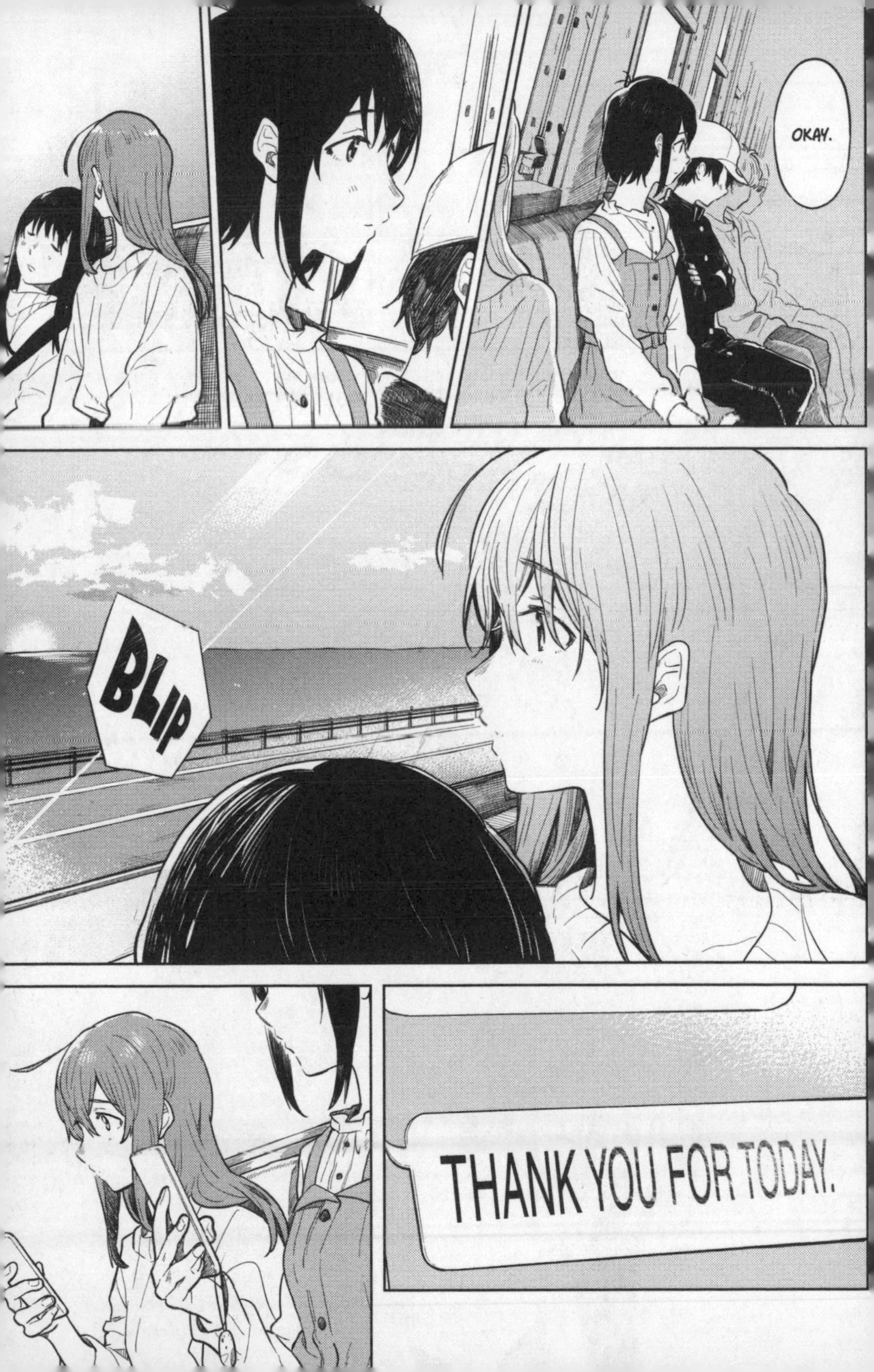
OKAY.
BLIP
THANK YOU FOR TODAY.

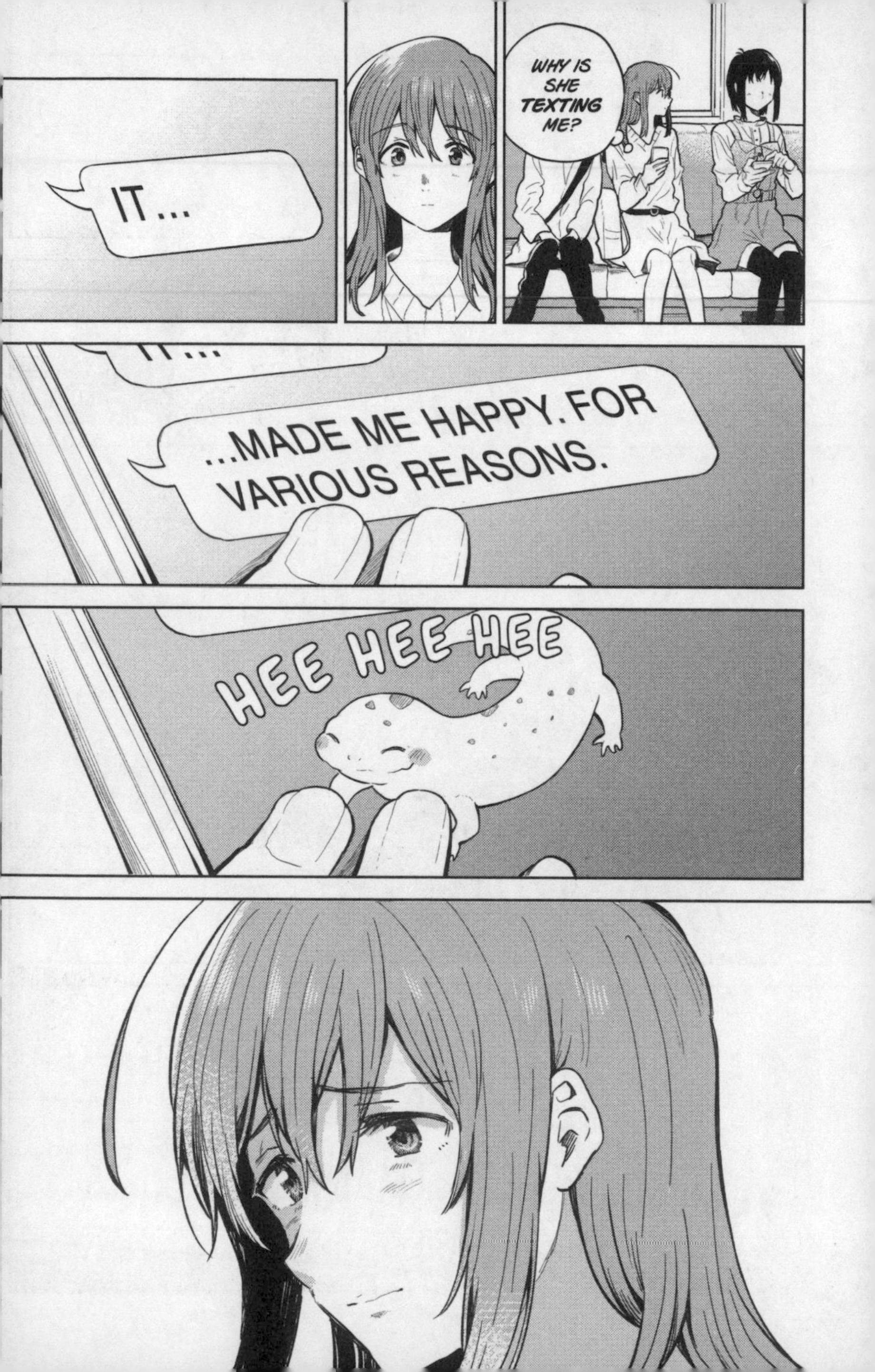
WHY IS SHE TEXTING ME?
IT...
...MADE ME HAPPY. FOR VARIOUS REASONS.
HEE HEE HEE

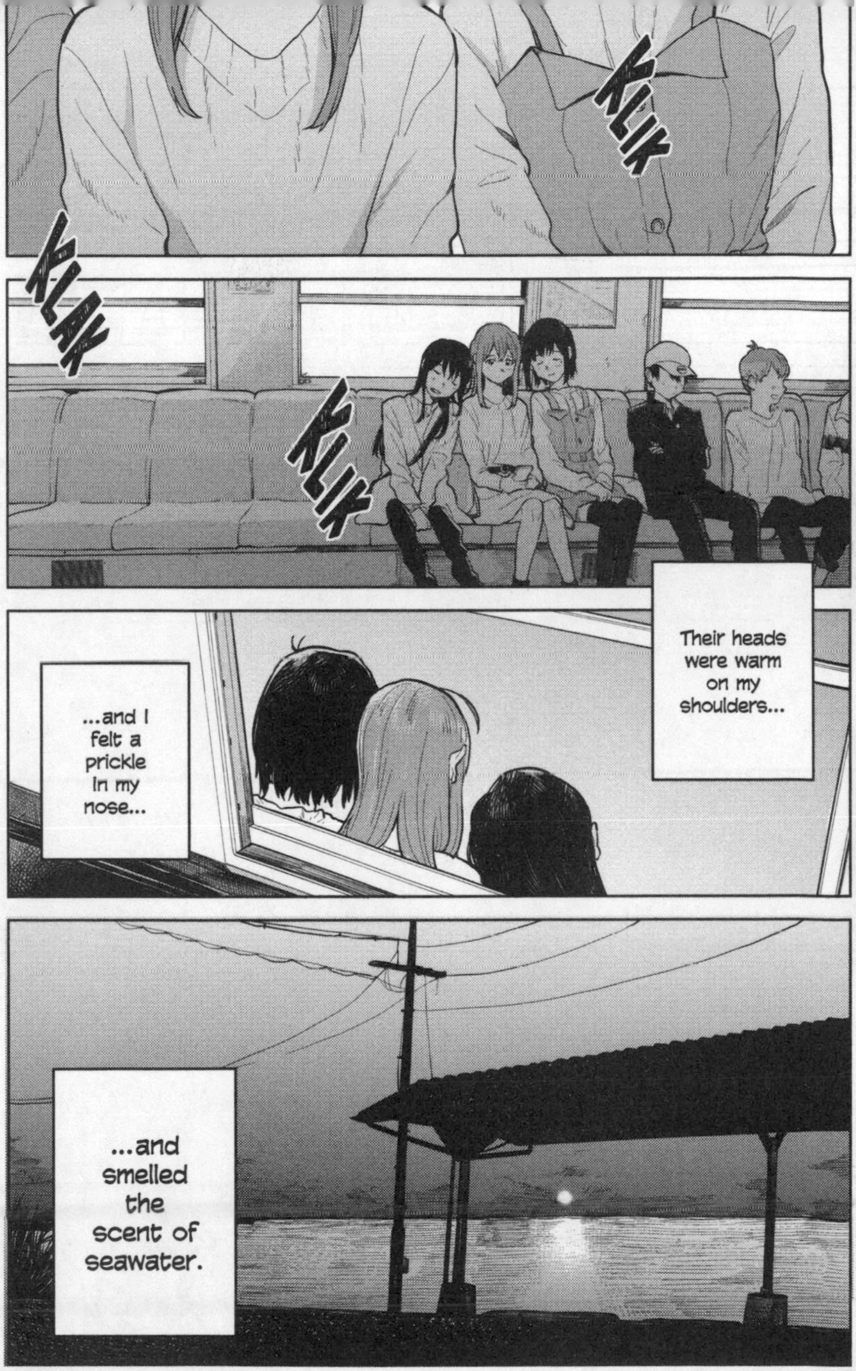
KLIK
KLAK
KLIK
Their heads were warm on my shoulders...
...and I felt a prickle in my nose...
...and smelled the scent of seawater.

A Tropical Fish
Yearns for Snow

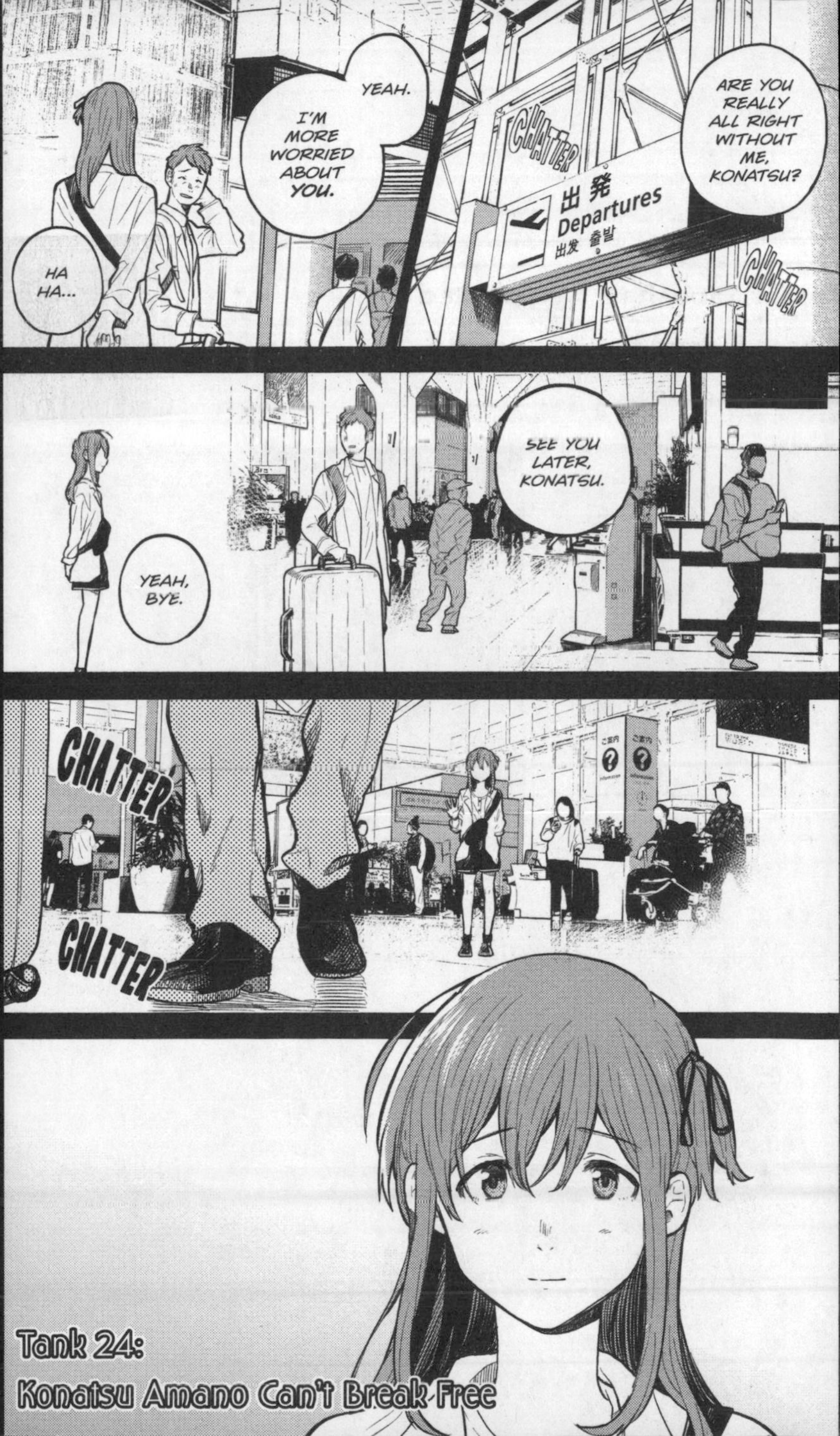
ARE YOU REALLY ALL RIGHT WITHOUT ME, KONATSU?
CHATTER
CHATTER
出発
Departures
出发 출발
YEAH.
I'M MORE WORRIED ABOUT YOU.
HA HA...
SEE YOU LATER, KONATSU.
YEAH, BYE.
CHATTER
CHATTER
Tank 24:
Konatsu Amano Can't Break Free

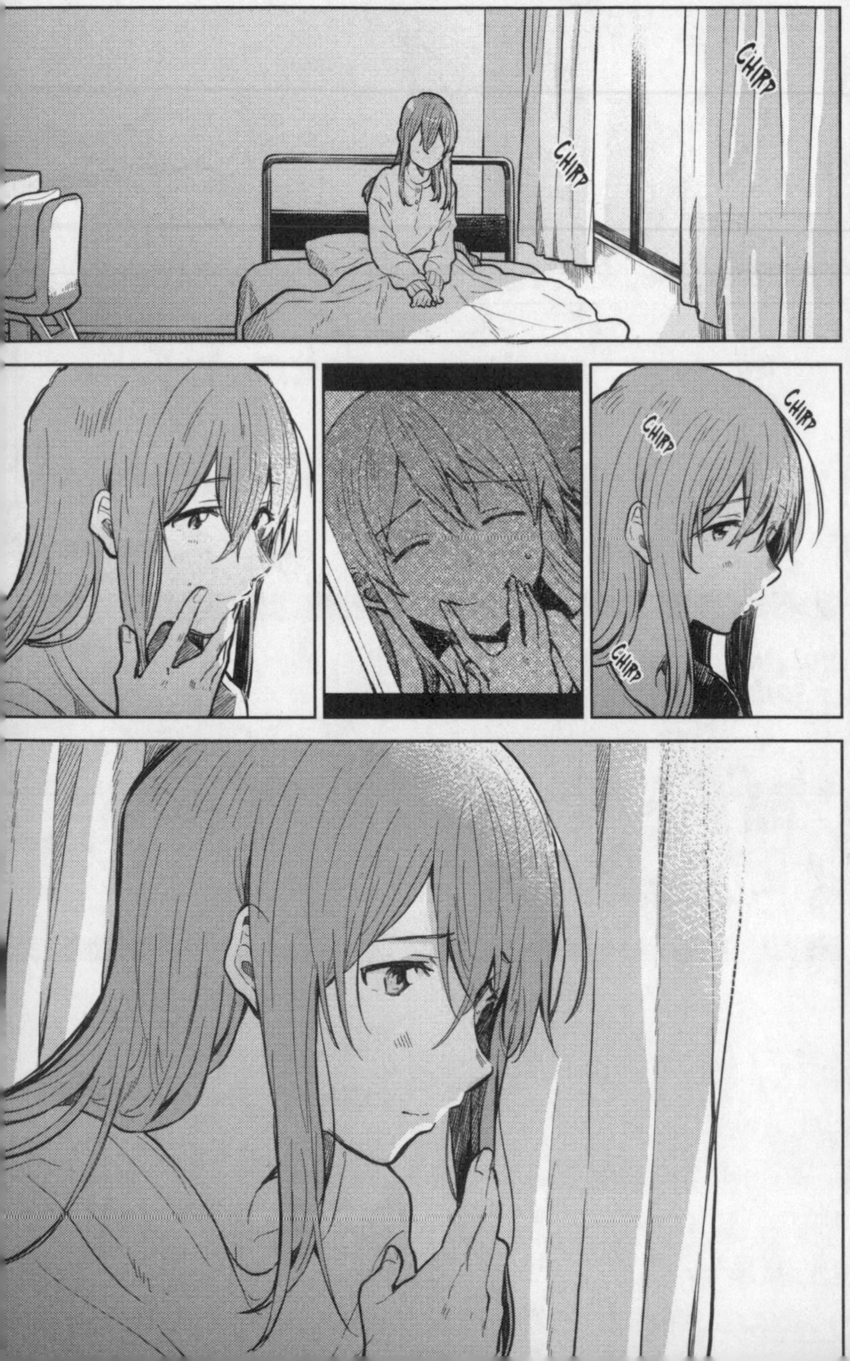
CHIRP
CHIRP
CHIRP
CHIRP
CHIRP

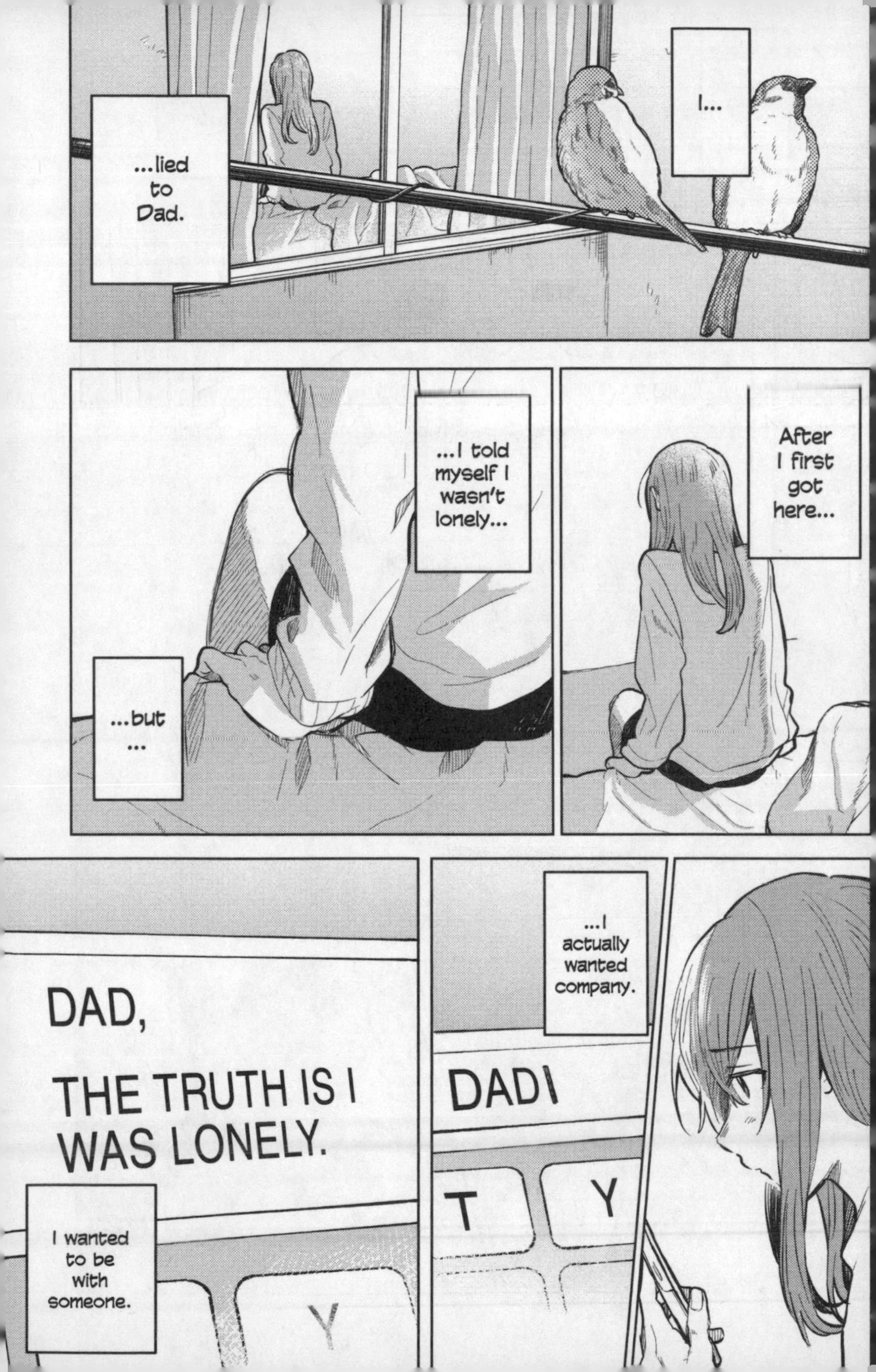
I...
...lied to Dad.
After I first got here...
...I told myself I wasn't lonely...
...but ...
...I actually wanted company.
DADI
T
Y
DAD,
THE TRUTH IS I WAS LONELY.
I wanted to be with someone.
Y

No...

"Some-one"?

Like a frog approaching a lonely salamander...

...I wanted to be by *your* side.

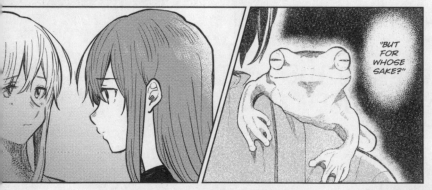

"BUT FOR WHOSE SAKE?"

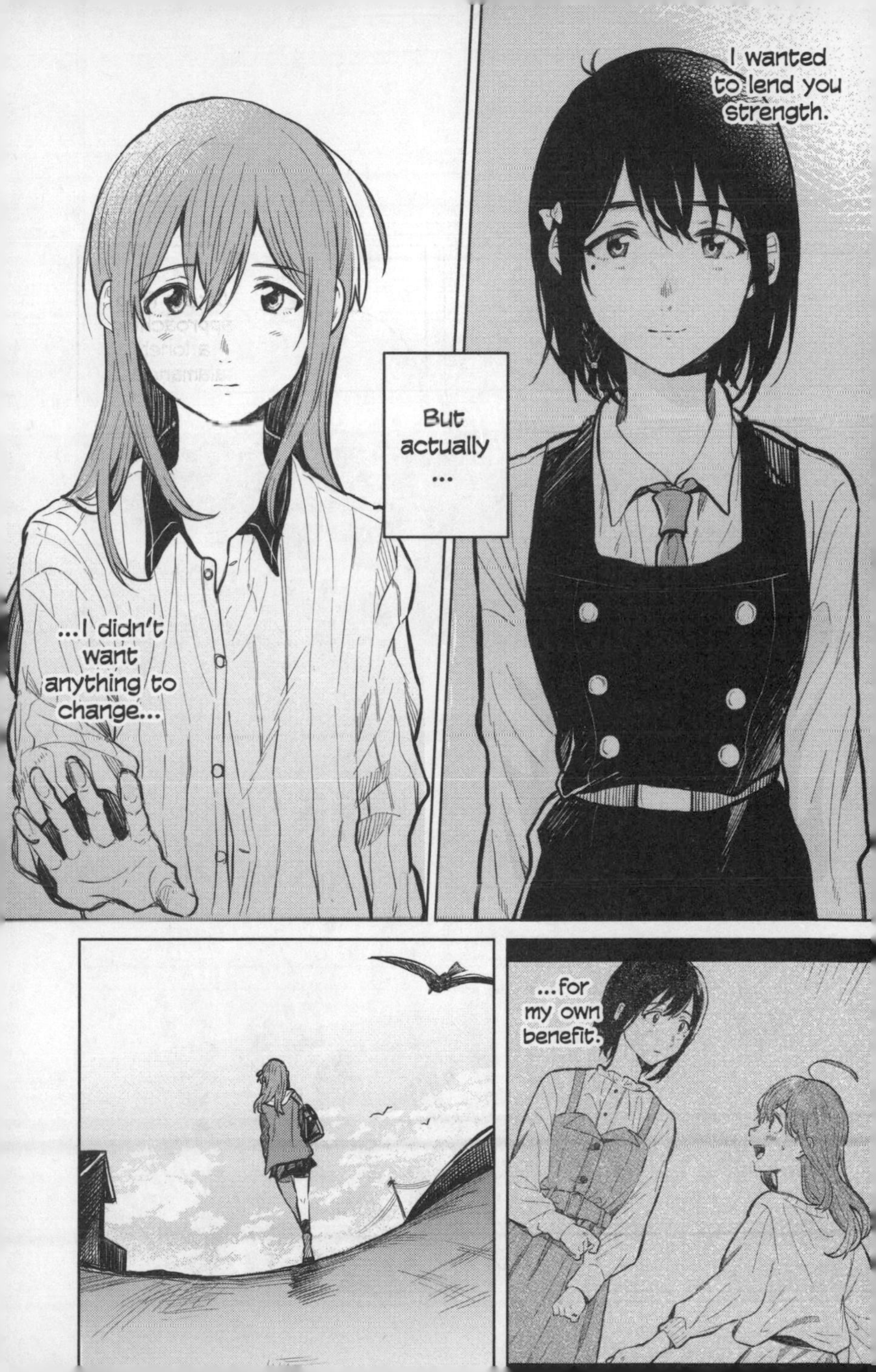
I wanted to lend you strength.
But actually ...
...I didn't want anything to change...
...for my own benefit.

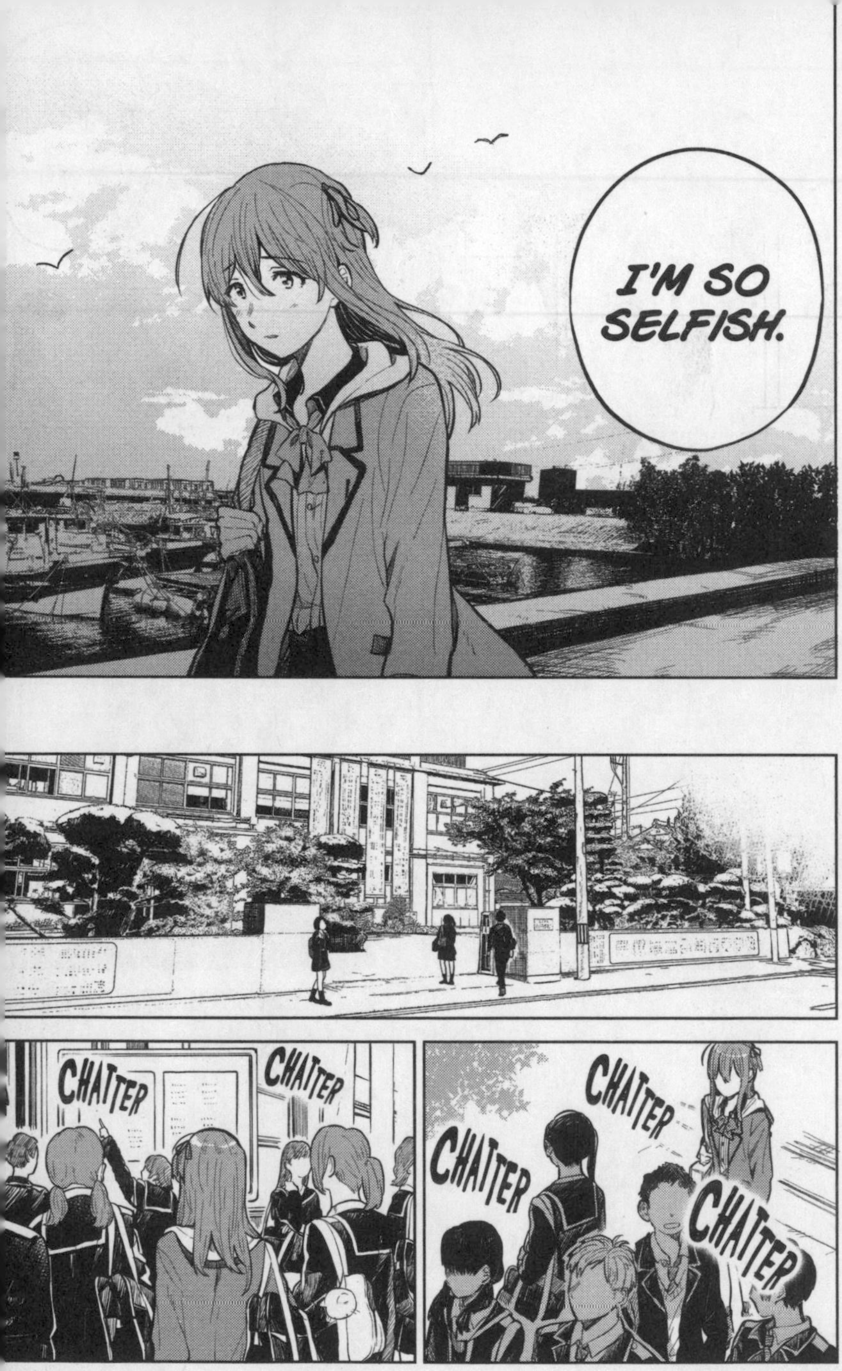
I'M SO SELFISH.
CHATTER
CHATTER
CHATTER
CHATTER
CHATTER

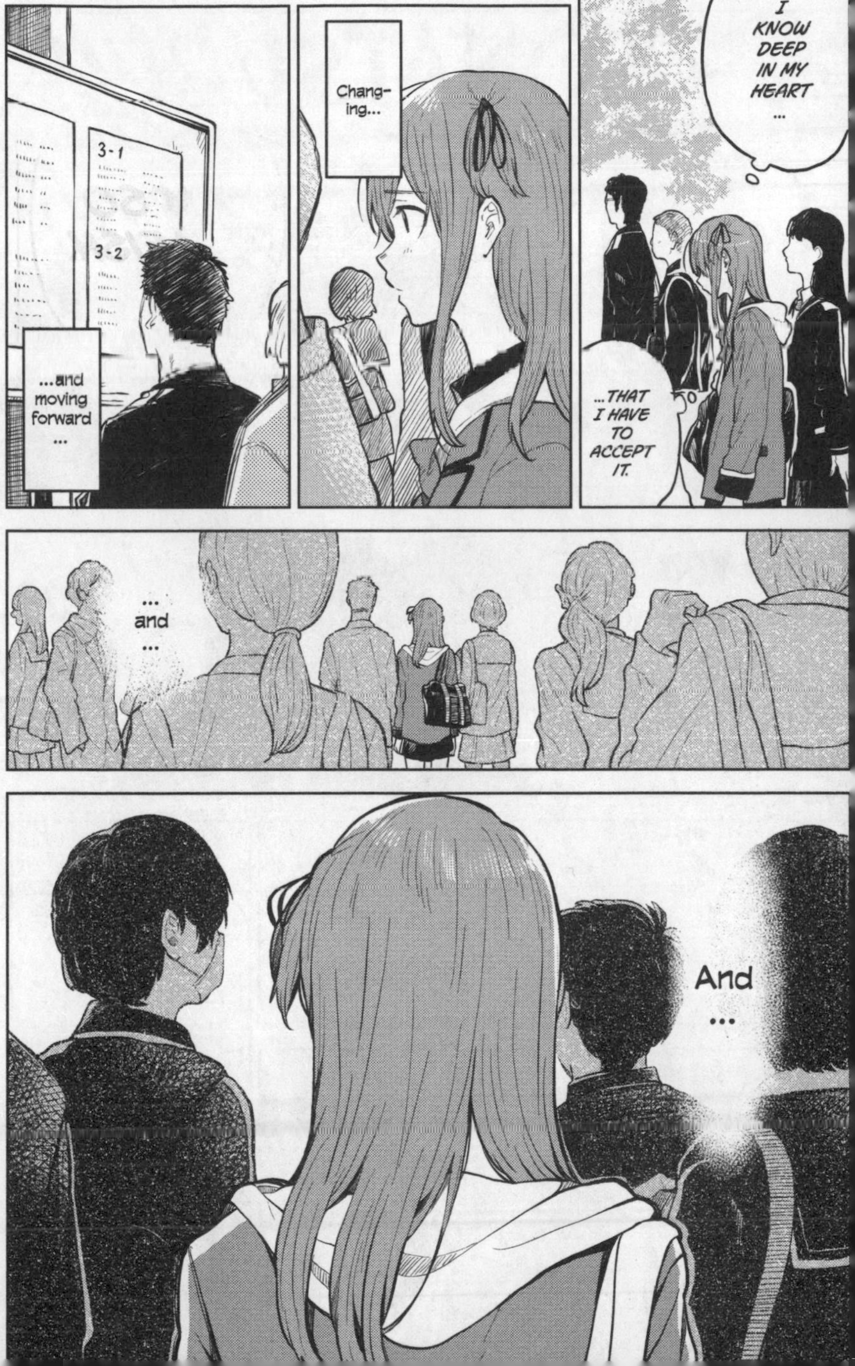
I KNOW DEEP IN MY HEART ...
...THAT I HAVE TO ACCEPT IT.
Chang-ing...
3-1
3-2
...and moving forward ...
... and ...
And ...

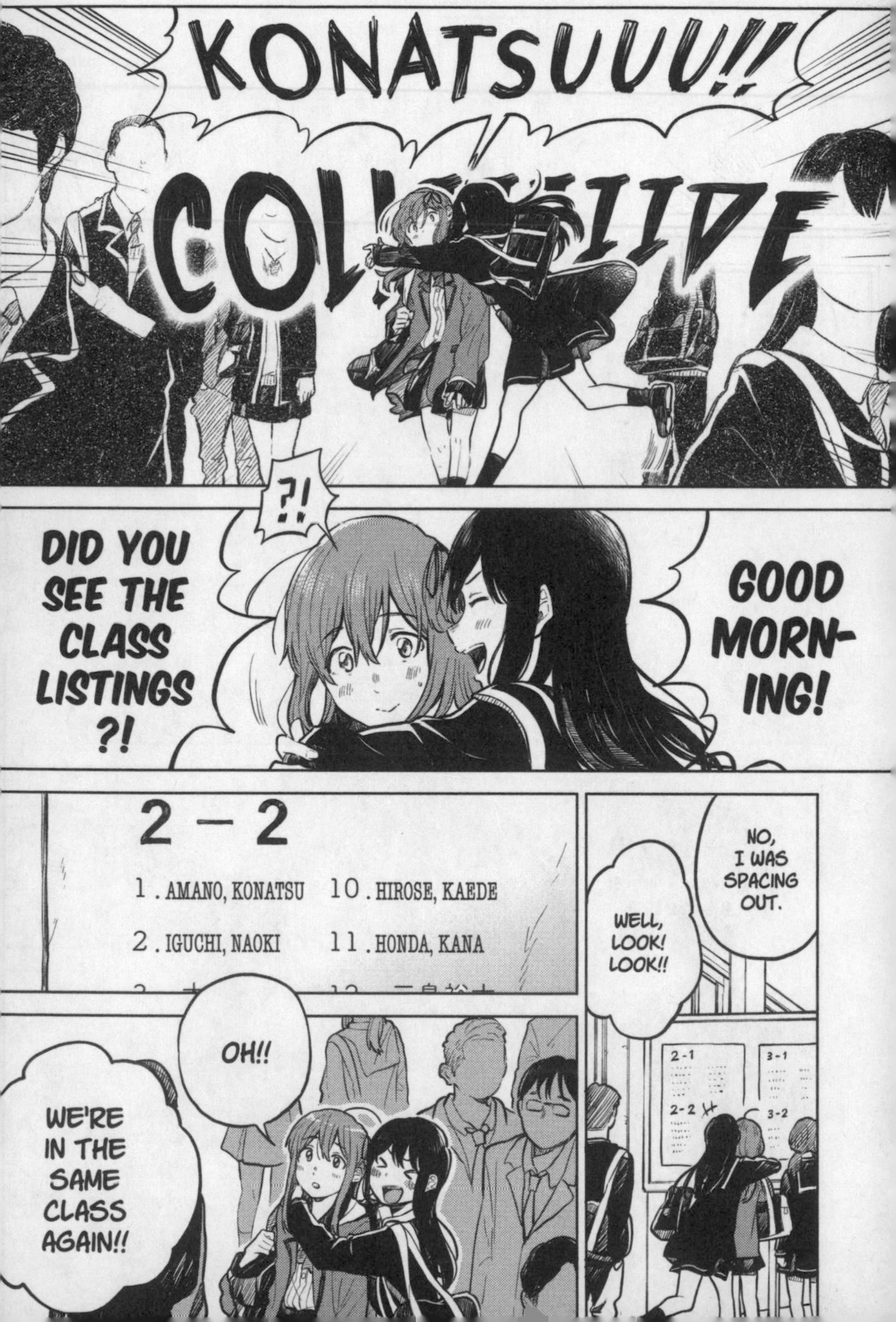
KONATSUUU!!
GOOD MORNING!
?!
DID YOU SEE THE CLASS LISTINGS?!
NO, I WAS SPACING OUT.
WELL, LOOK! LOOK!!
2-1
3-1
2-2
3-2
2 — 2
1. AMANO, KONATSU
10. HIROSE, KAEDE
2. IGUCHI, NAOKI
11. HONDA, KANA
OH!!
WE'RE IN THE SAME CLASS AGAIN!!

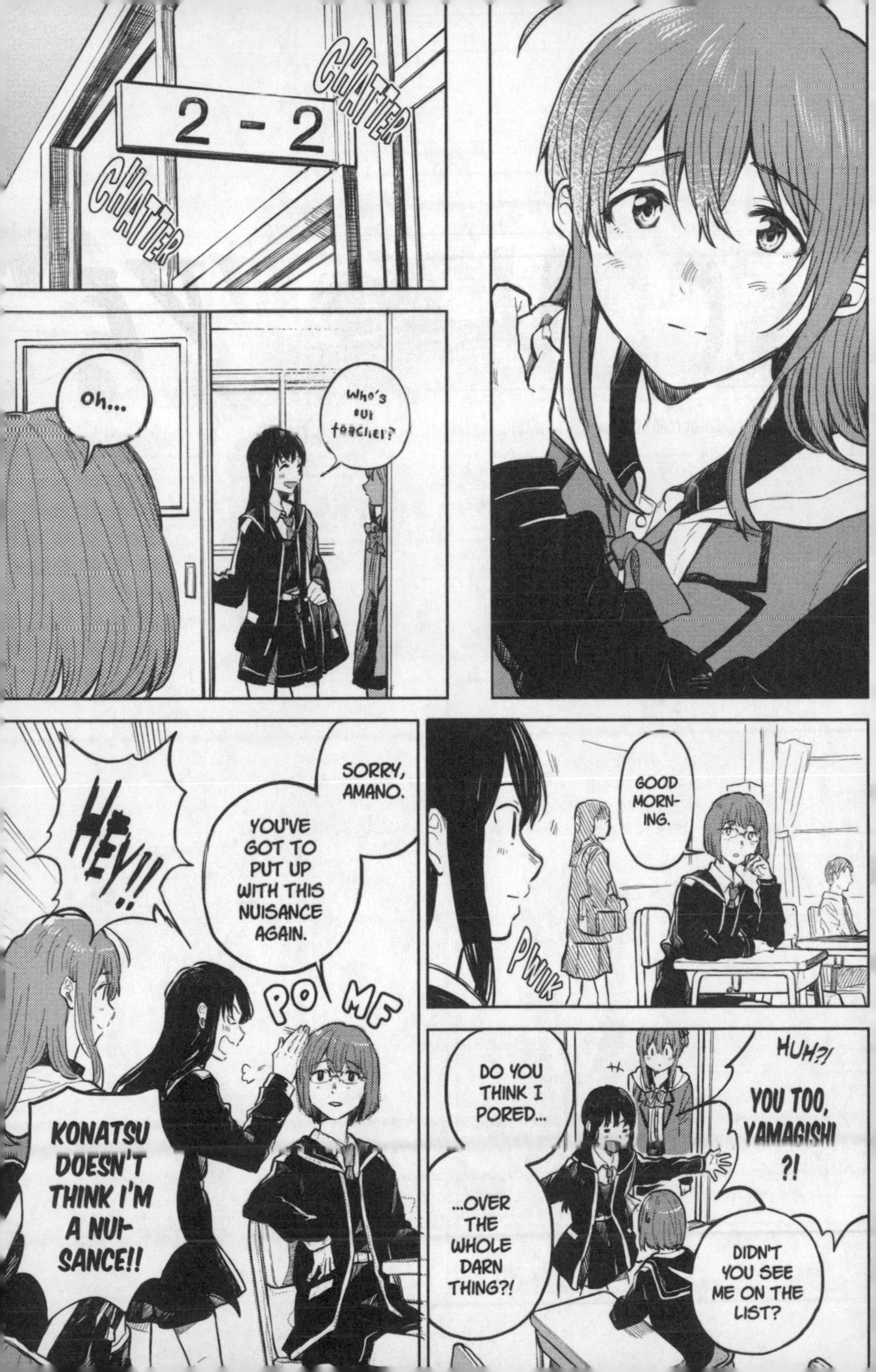
2-2
CHATTER
CHATTER
Who's our teacher?
Oh...
GOOD MORNING.
PWIK
HUH?!
YOU TOO, YAMAGISHI?!
DO YOU THINK I PORED...
DIDN'T YOU SEE ME ON THE LIST?
...OVER THE WHOLE DARN THING?!
SORRY, AMANO.
YOU'VE GOT TO PUT UP WITH THIS NUISANCE AGAIN.
HEY!!
POMF
KONATSU DOESN'T THINK I'M A NUISANCE!!

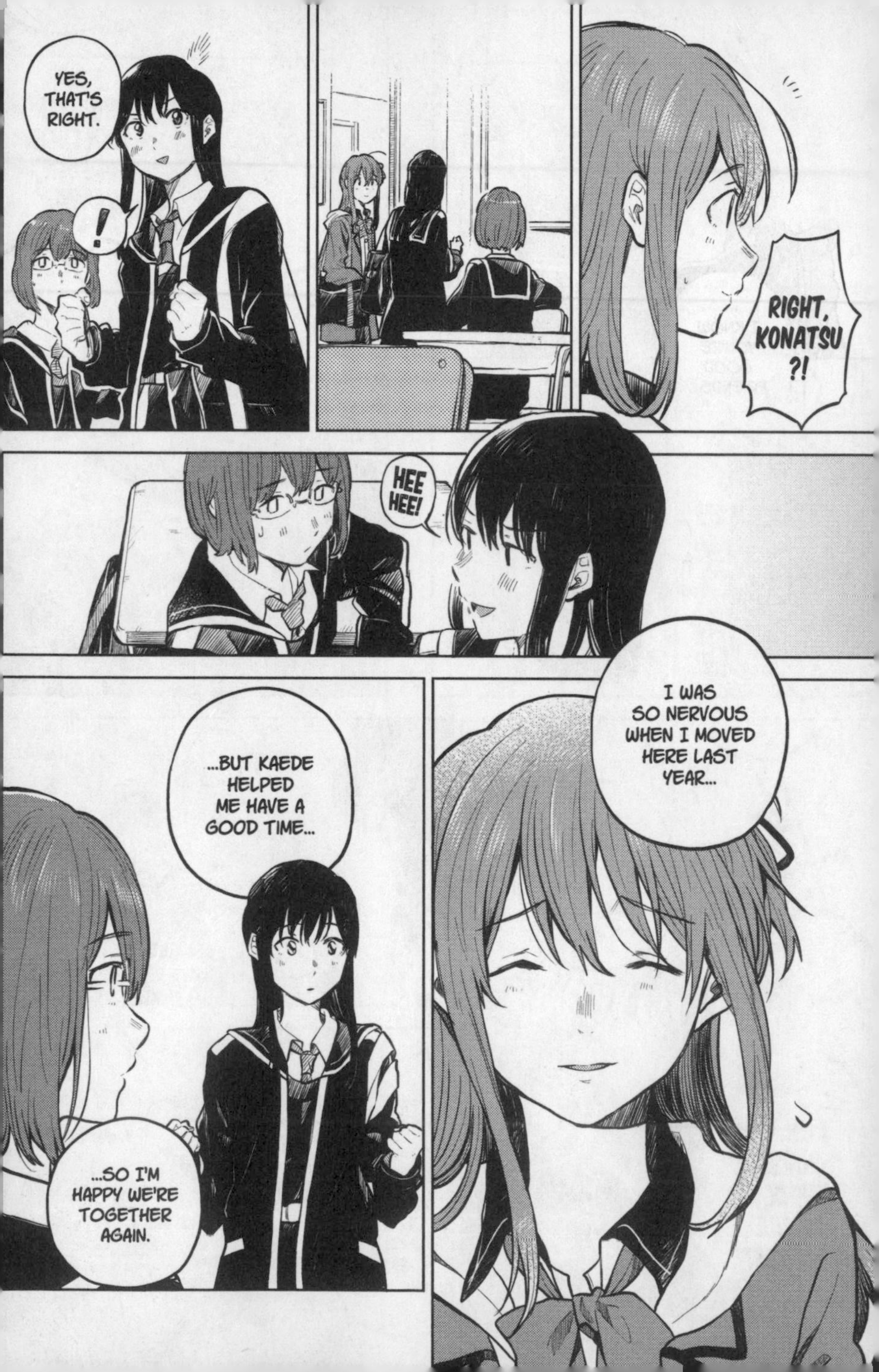
RIGHT, KONATSU?!
YES, THAT'S RIGHT.
!
HEE HEE!
I WAS SO NERVOUS WHEN I MOVED HERE LAST YEAR...
...BUT KAEDE HELPED ME HAVE A GOOD TIME...
...SO I'M HAPPY WE'RE TOGETHER AGAIN.

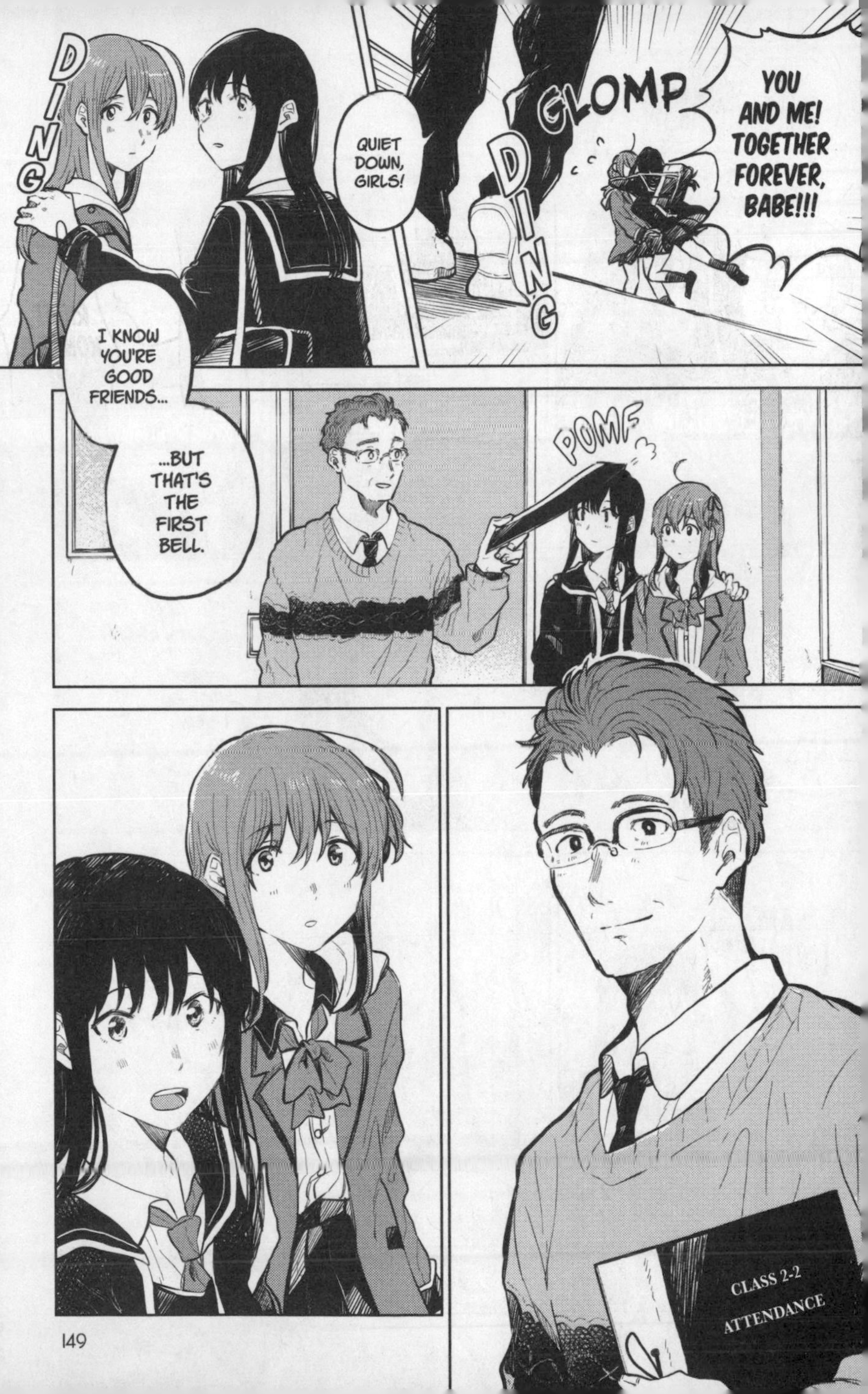
YOU AND ME! TOGETHER FOREVER, BABE!!!
GLOMP
DING
DING
QUIET DOWN, GIRLS!
DING
I KNOW YOU'RE GOOD FRIENDS...
...BUT THAT'S THE FIRST BELL.
POMF
CLASS 2-2
ATTENDANCE

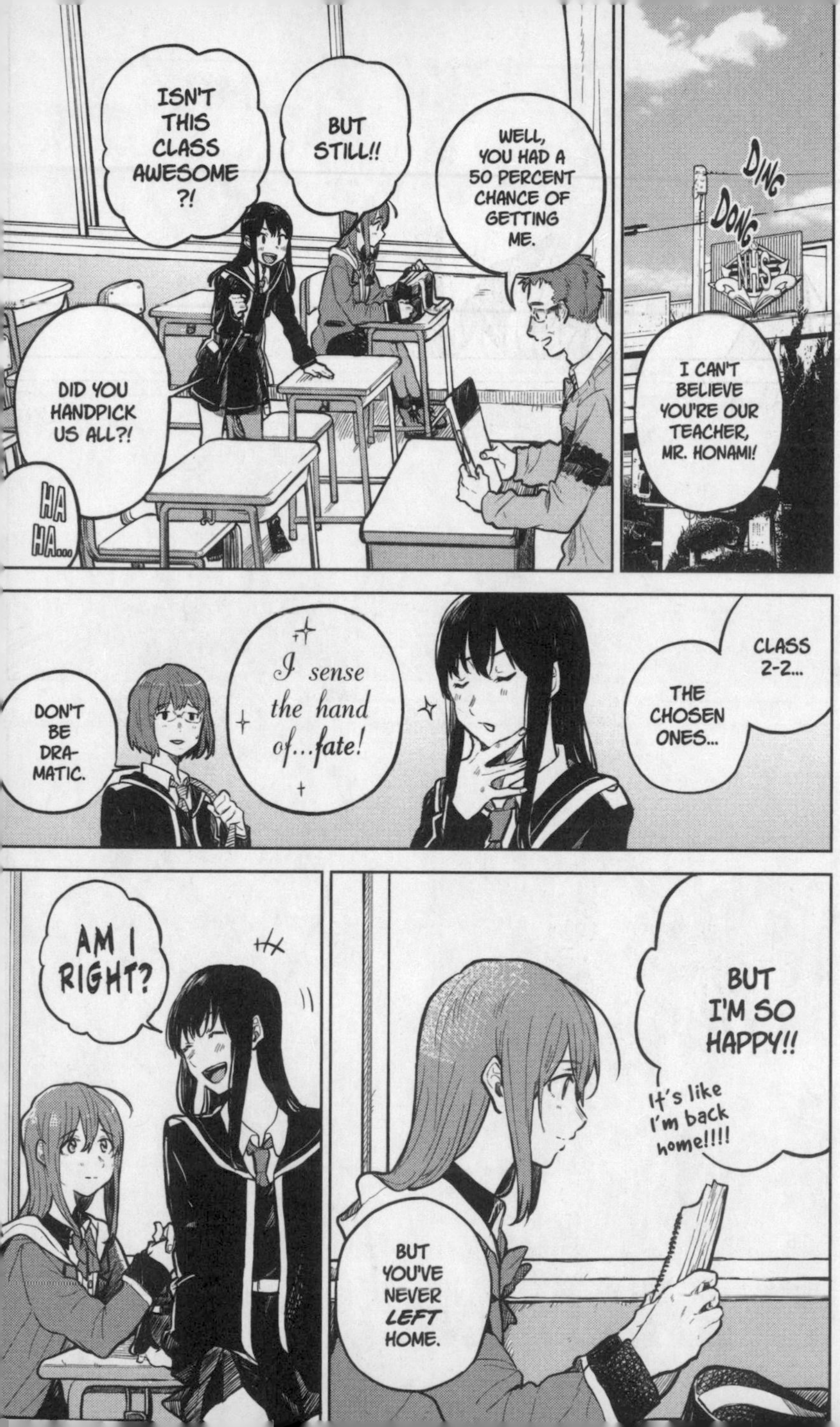
DING
DONG
NHS
I CAN'T BELIEVE YOU'RE OUR TEACHER, MR. HONAMI!
WELL, YOU HAD A 50 PERCENT CHANCE OF GETTING ME.
BUT STILL!!
ISN'T THIS CLASS AWESOME?!
DID YOU HANDPICK US ALL?!
HA HA...
CLASS 2-2...
THE CHOSEN ONES...
I sense the hand of...fate!
DON'T BE DRA-MATIC.
BUT I'M SO HAPPY!!
It's like I'm back home!!!!
BUT YOU'VE NEVER *LEFT* HOME.
AM I RIGHT?

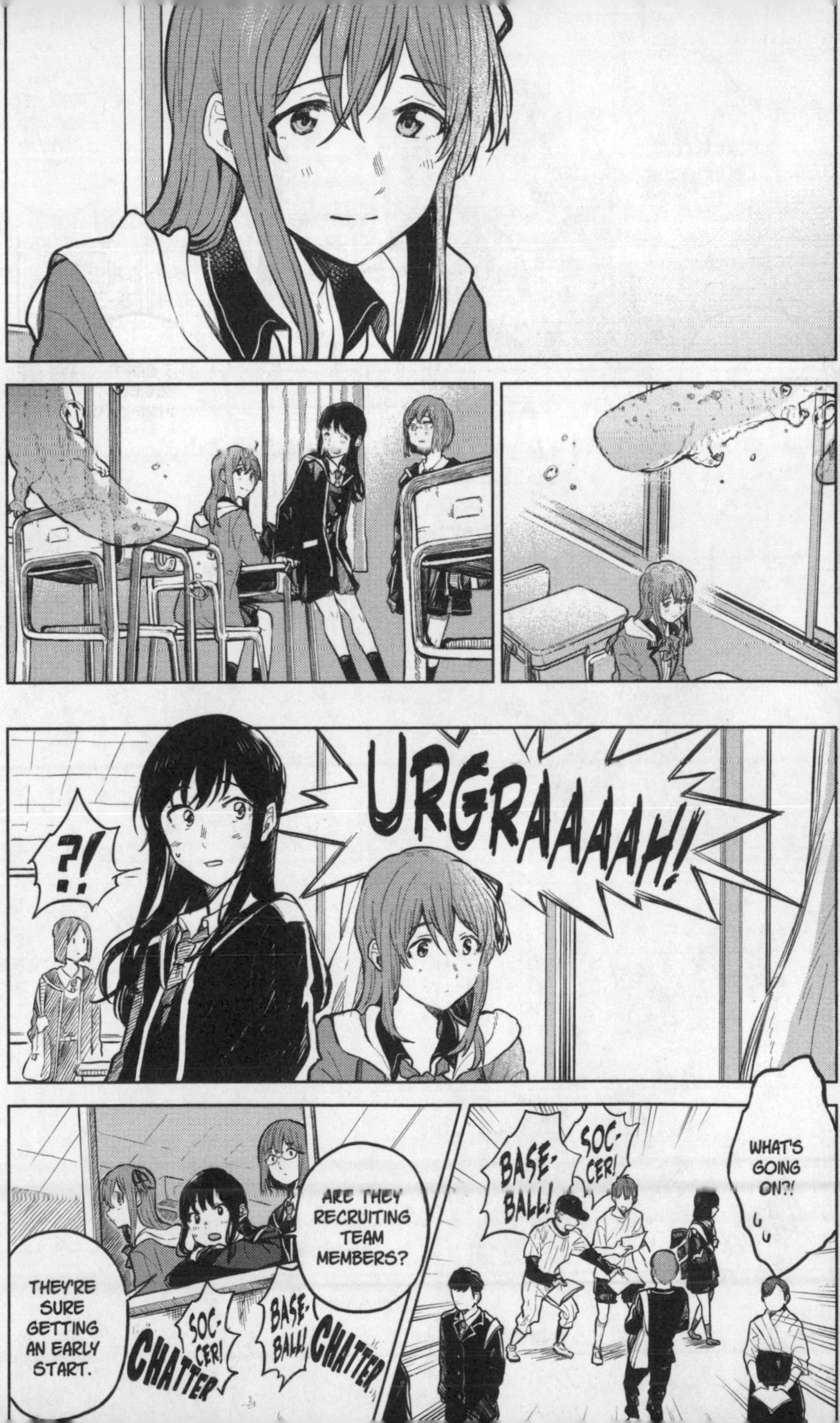
URGRAAAAH!
?!
WHAT'S GOING ON?!
SOC-CER!
BASE-BALL!
ARE THEY RECRUITING TEAM MEMBERS?
BASE-BALL!
CHATTER
SOC-CER!
THEY'RE SURE GETTING AN EARLY START.
CHATTER

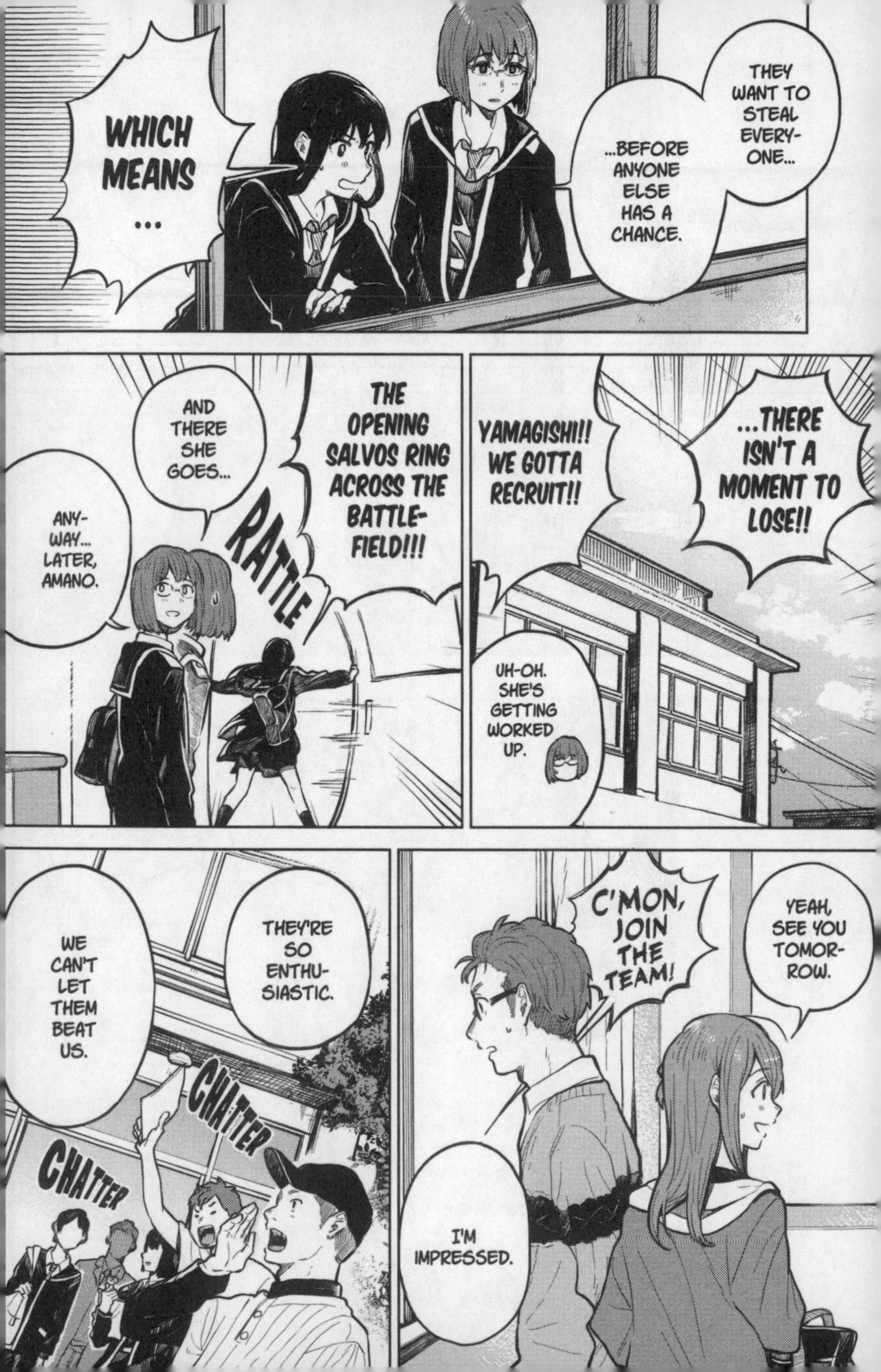
THEY WANT TO STEAL EVERY-ONE...
...BEFORE ANYONE ELSE HAS A CHANCE.
WHICH MEANS ...
...THERE ISN'T A MOMENT TO LOSE!!
YAMAGISHI!! WE GOTTA RECRUIT!!
UH-OH. SHE'S GETTING WORKED UP.
THE OPENING SALVOS RING ACROSS THE BATTLE-FIELD!!!
RATTLE
AND THERE SHE GOES...
ANY-WAY... LATER, AMANO.
YEAH, SEE YOU TOMOR-ROW.
C'MON, JOIN THE TEAM!
I'M IMPRESSED.
THEY'RE SO ENTHU-SIASTIC.
WE CAN'T LET THEM BEAT US.
CHATTER
CHATTER

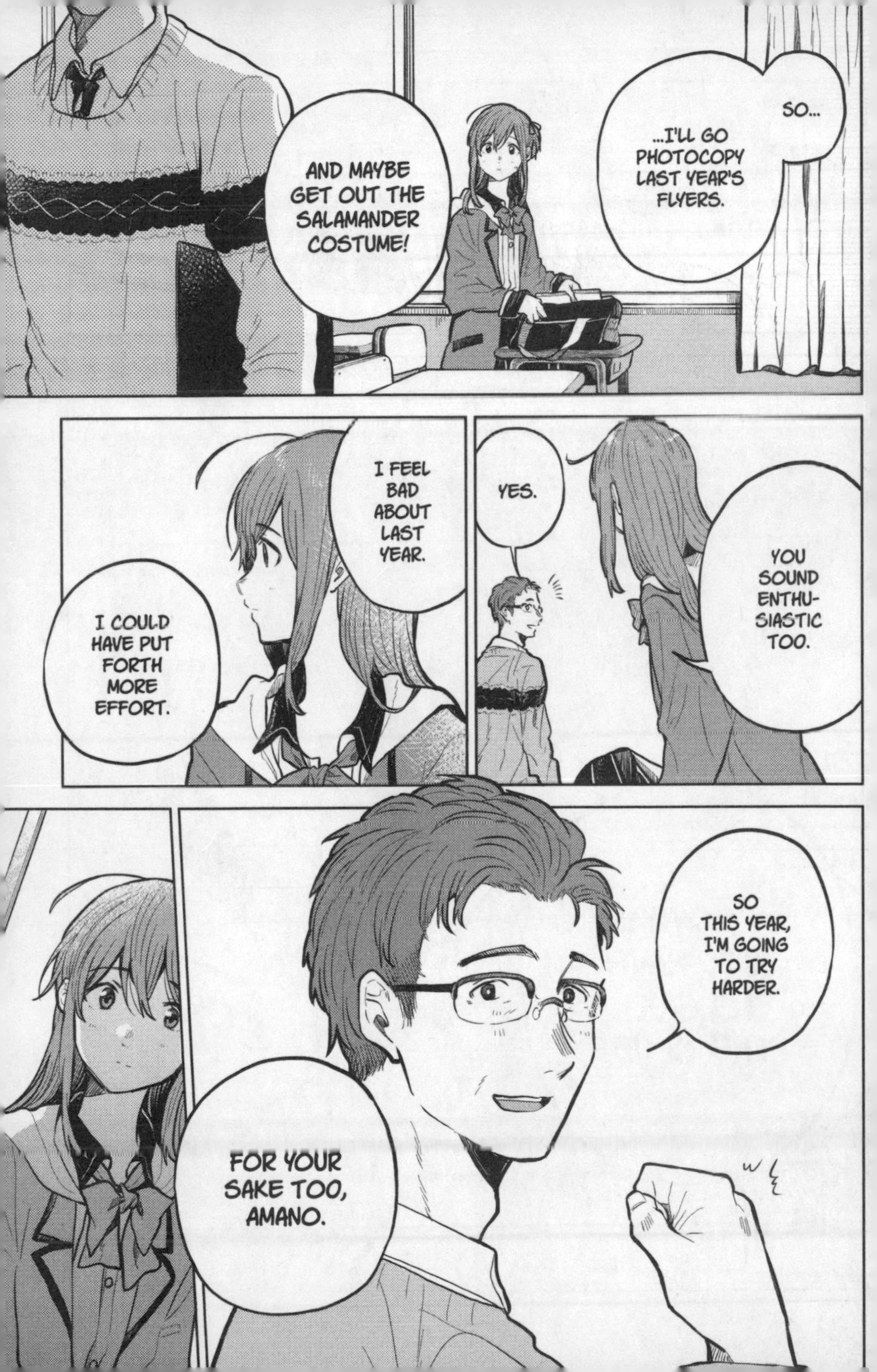
SO...
...I'LL GO PHOTOCOPY LAST YEAR'S FLYERS.
AND MAYBE GET OUT THE SALAMANDER COSTUME!
YOU SOUND ENTHU-SIASTIC TOO.
YES.
I FEEL BAD ABOUT LAST YEAR.
I COULD HAVE PUT FORTH MORE EFFORT.
SO THIS YEAR, I'M GOING TO TRY HARDER.
FOR YOUR SAKE TOO, AMANO.

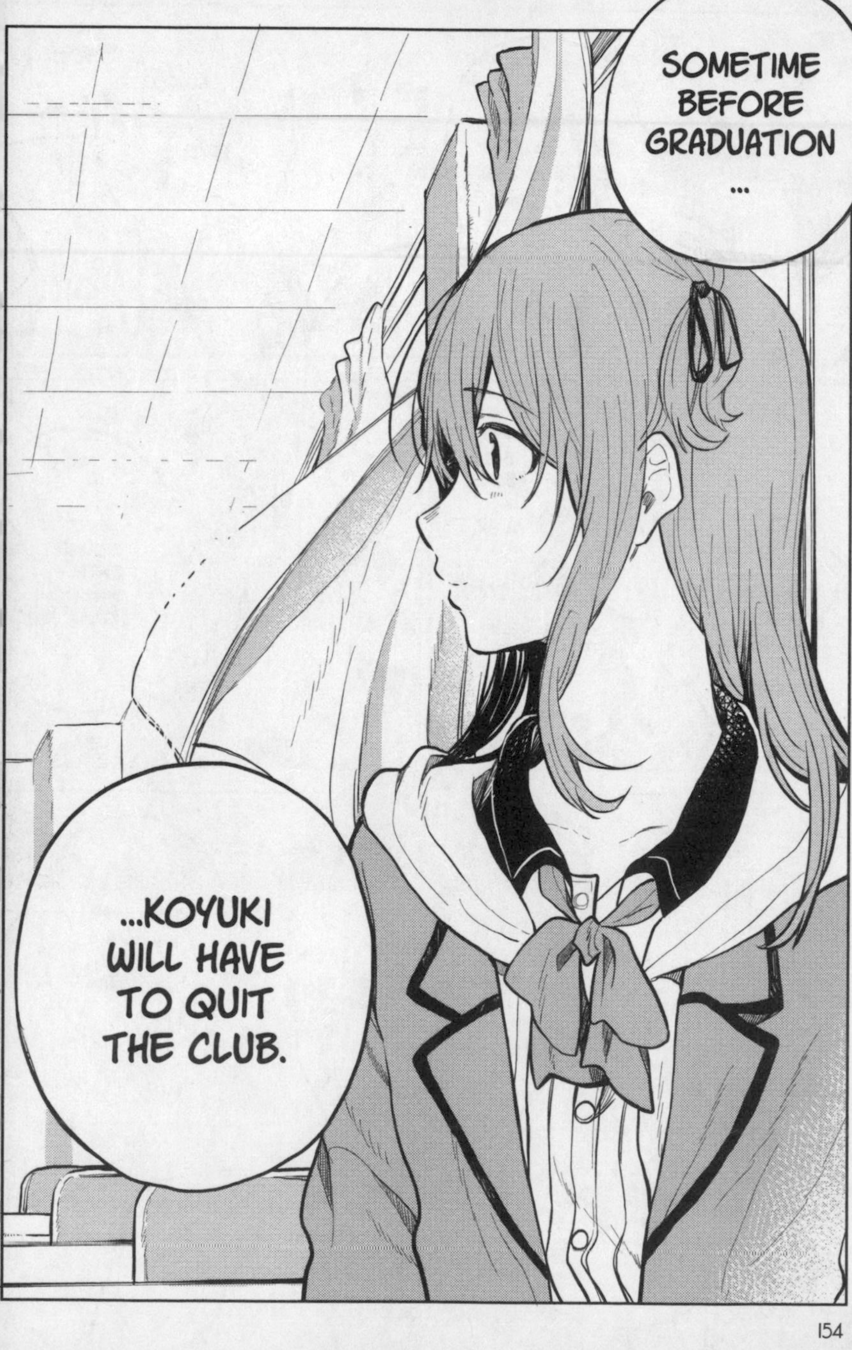
SOMETIME BEFORE GRADUATION ...
...KOYUKI WILL HAVE TO QUIT THE CLUB.

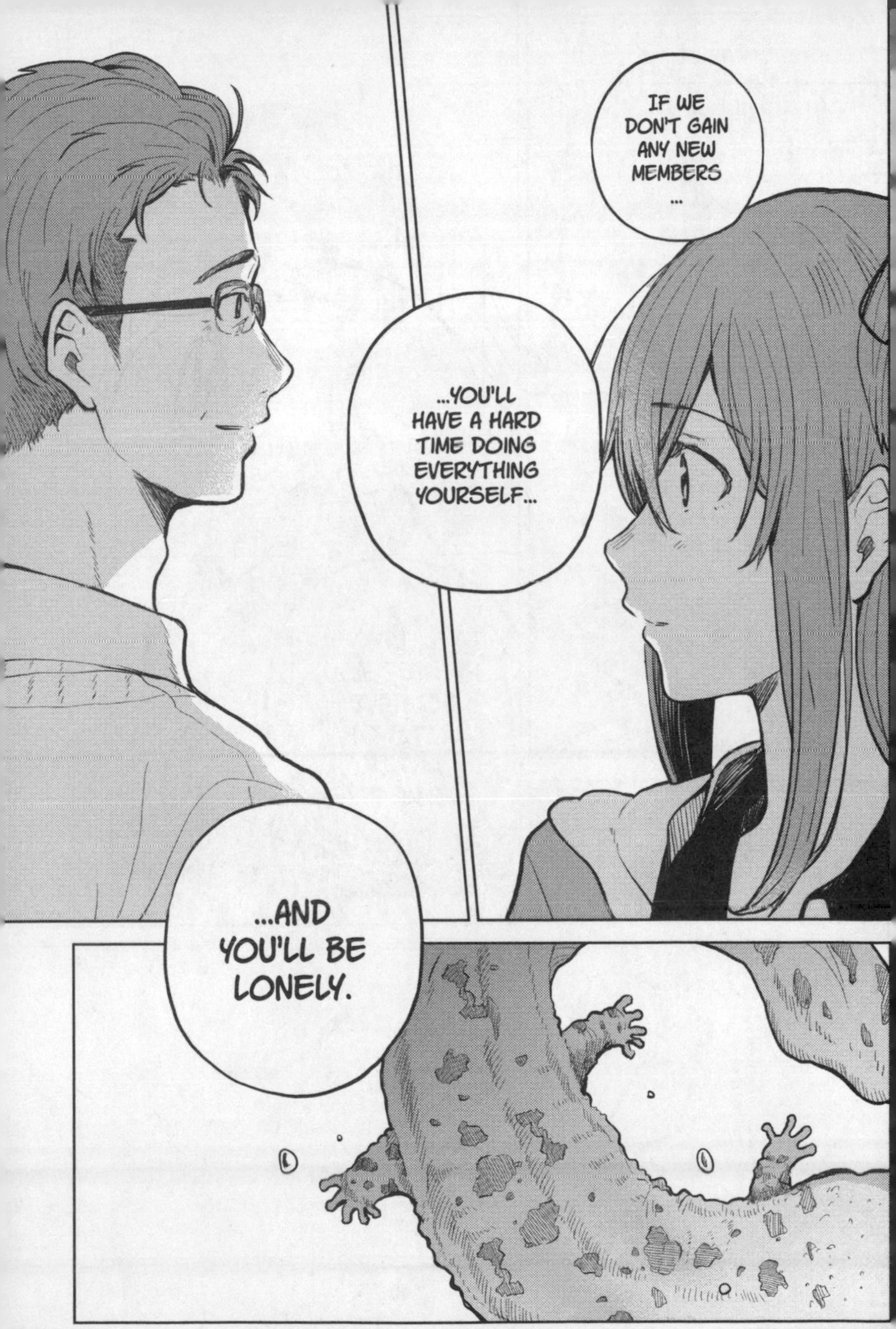
IF WE DON'T GAIN ANY NEW MEMBERS ...
...YOU'LL HAVE A HARD TIME DOING EVERYTHING YOURSELF...
...AND YOU'LL BE LONELY.

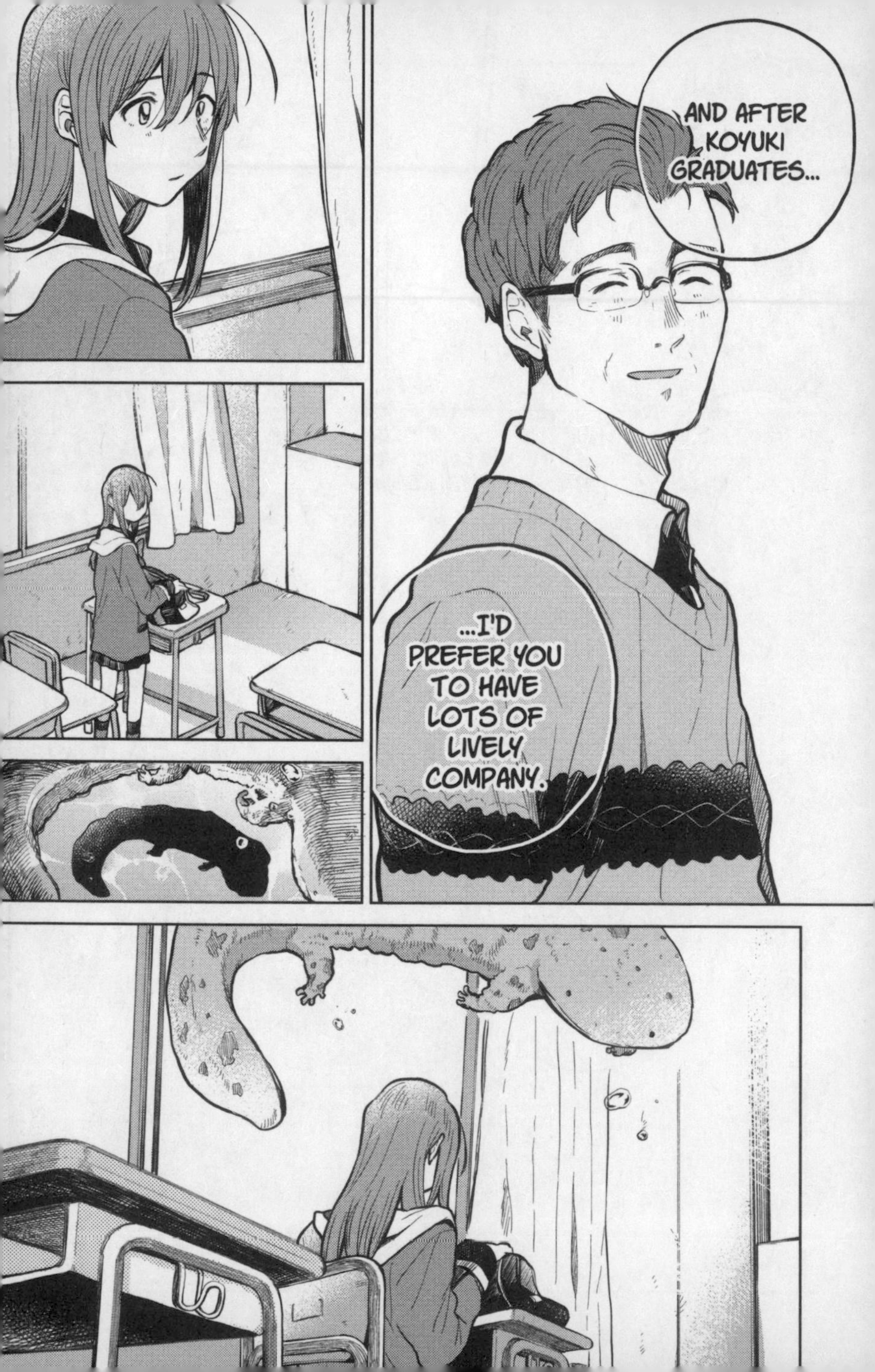
AND AFTER KOYUKI GRADUATES...
...I'D PREFER YOU TO HAVE LOTS OF LIVELY COMPANY.

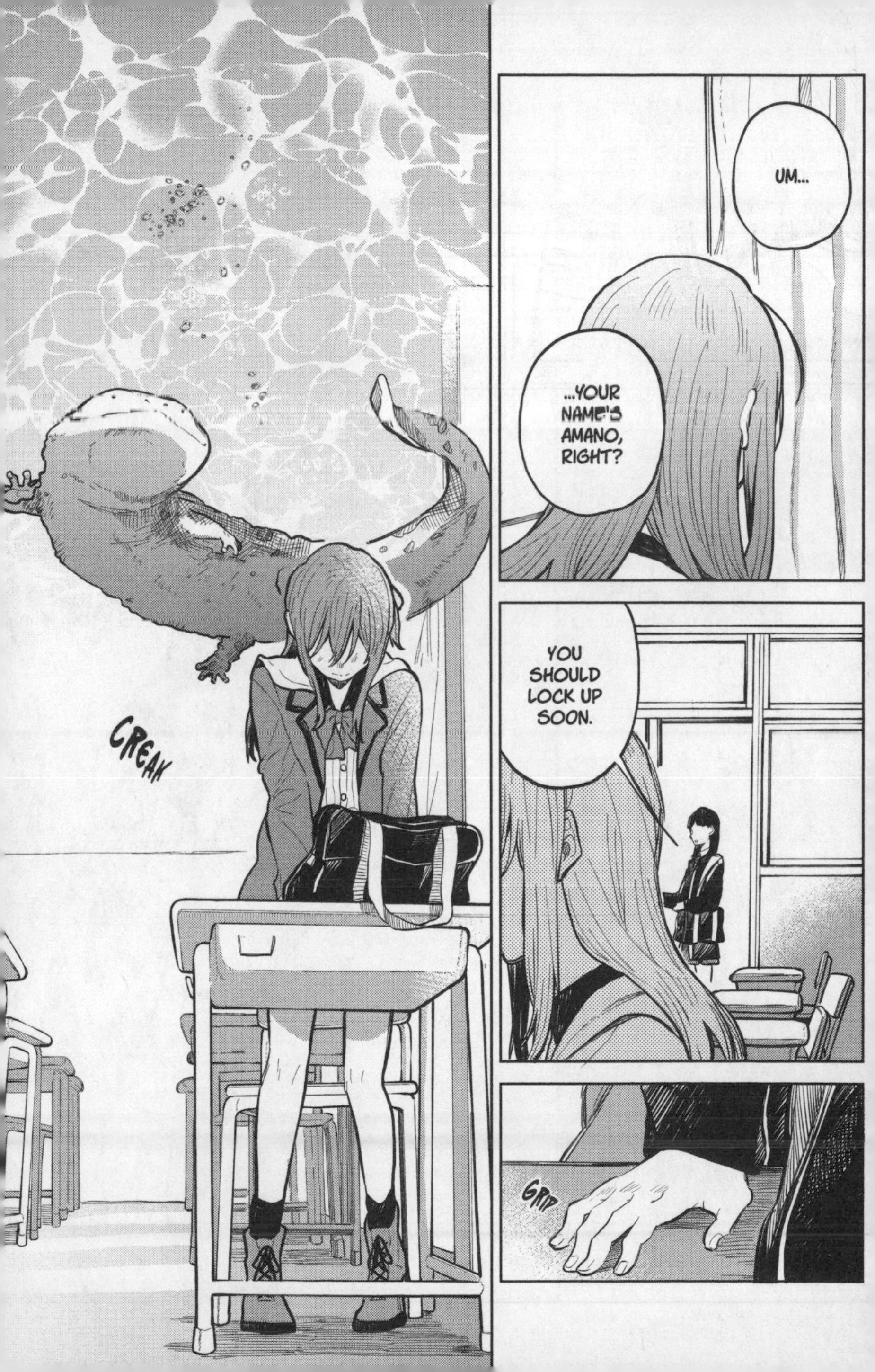
UM...
...YOUR NAME'S AMANO, RIGHT?
YOU SHOULD LOCK UP SOON.
GRIP
CREAK

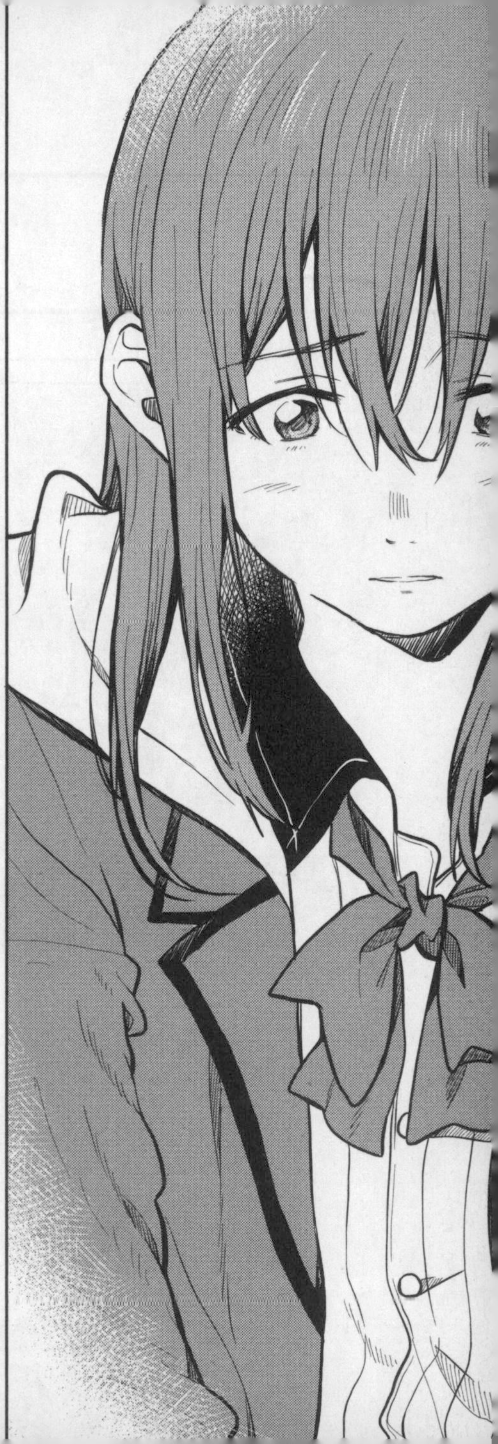
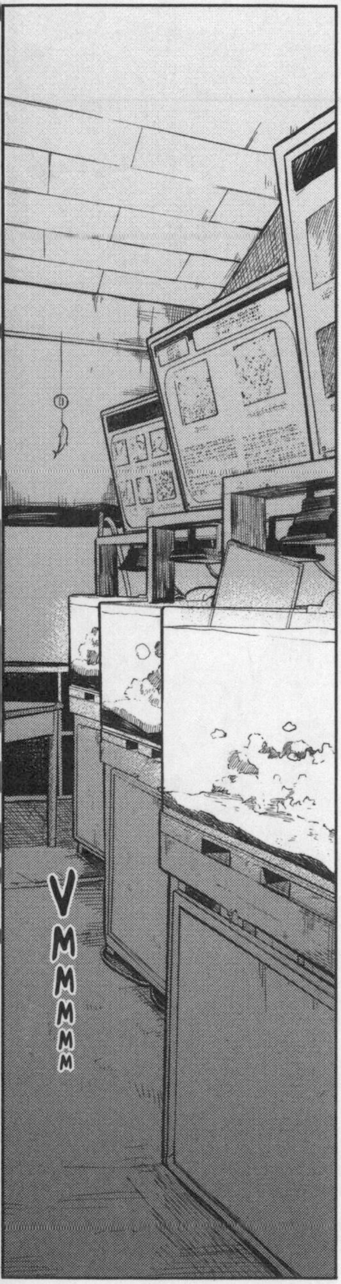
VMMMMM

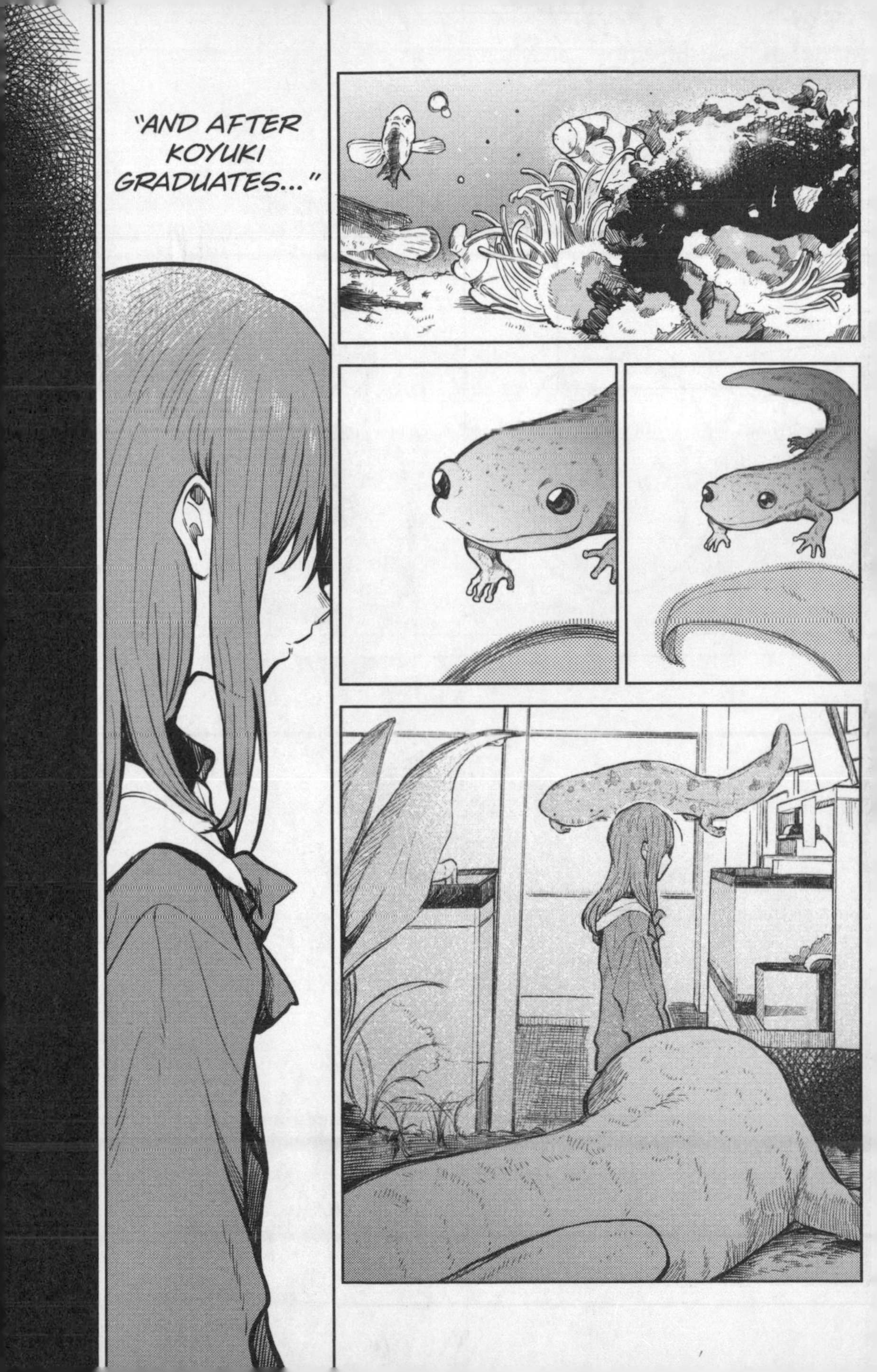
"AND AFTER KOYUKI GRADUATES..."

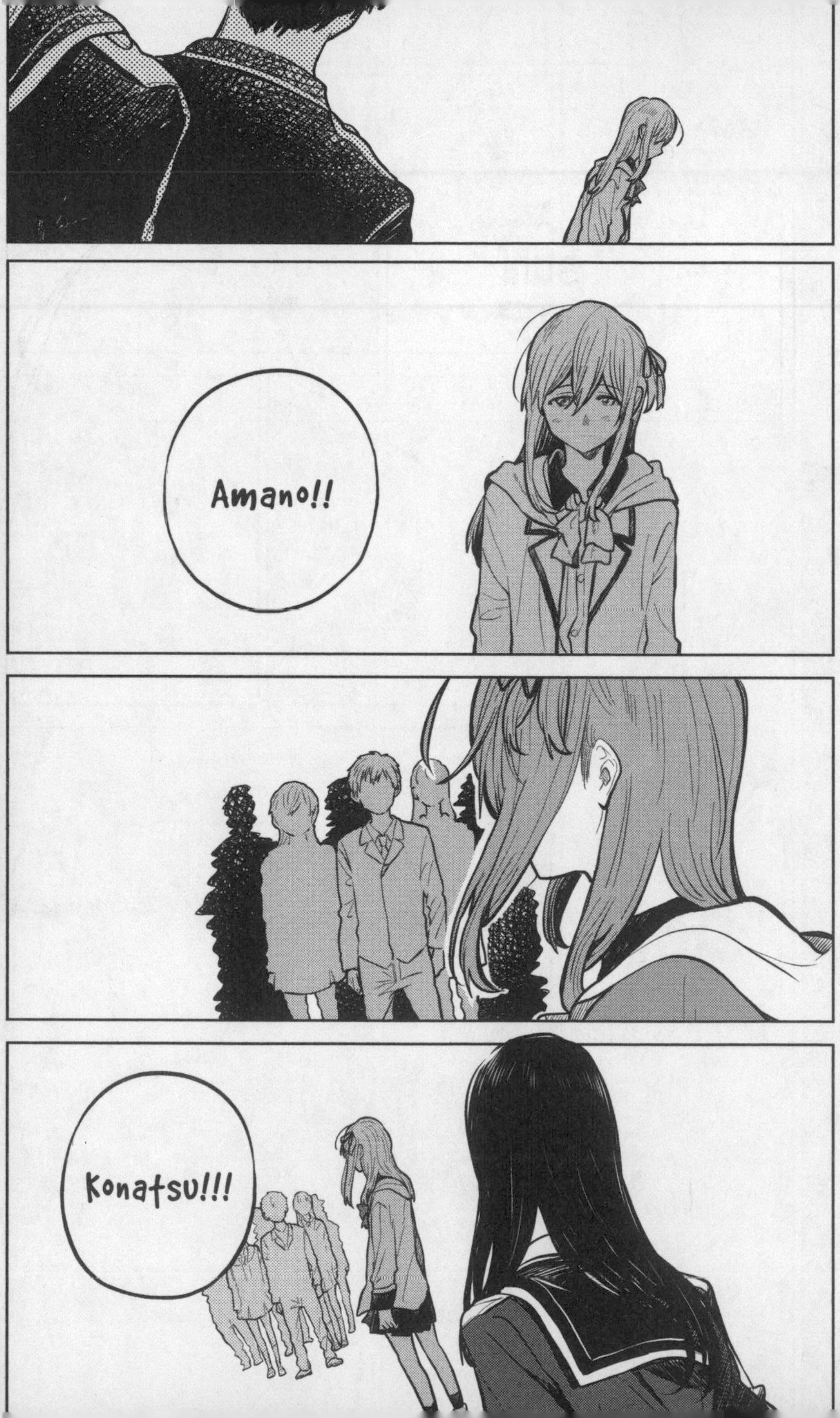
Amano!!
Konatsu!!!

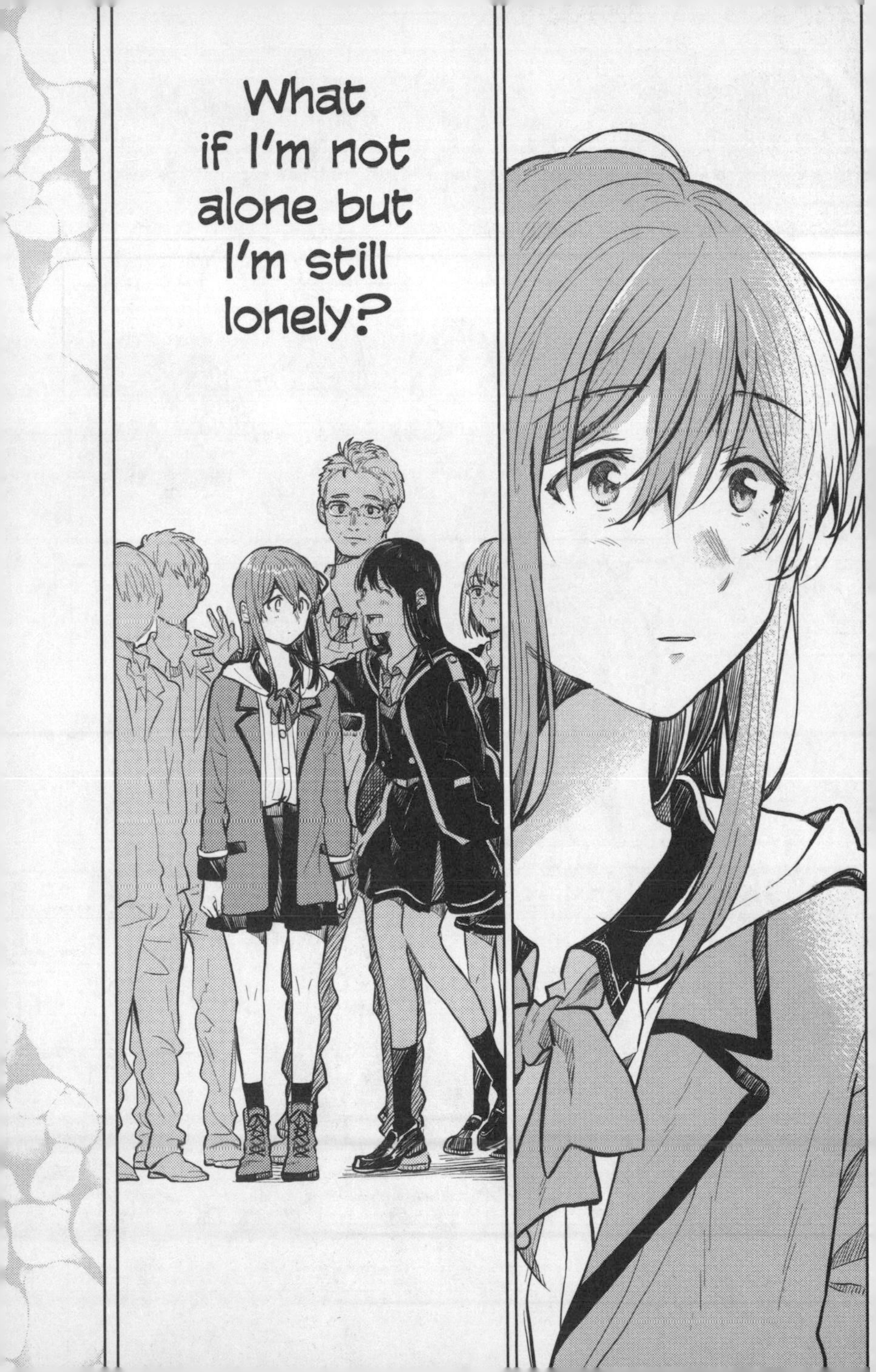
What if I'm not alone but I'm still lonely?

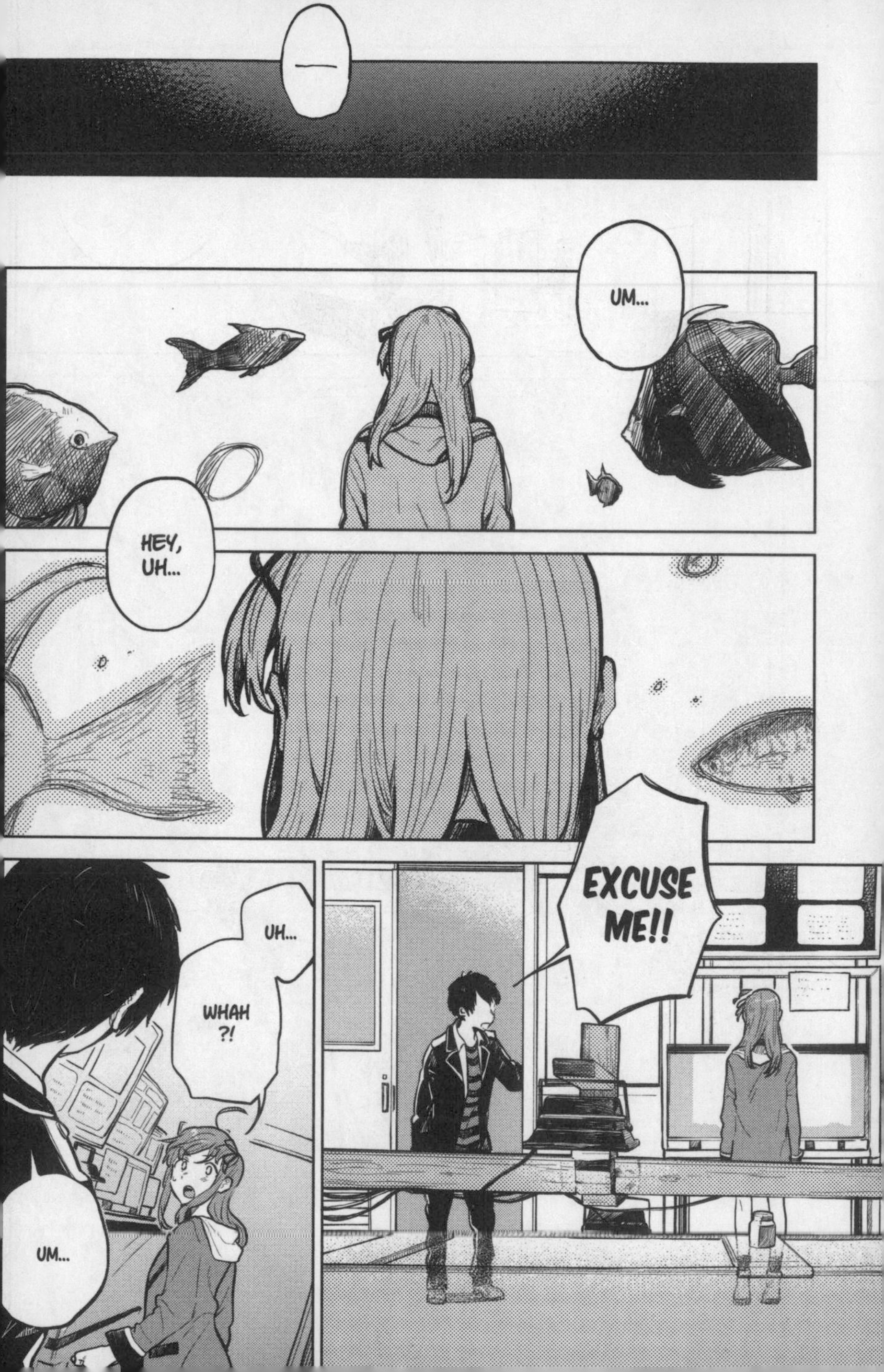
—
UM...
HEY, UH...
EXCUSE ME!!
UH...
WHAH ?!
UM...

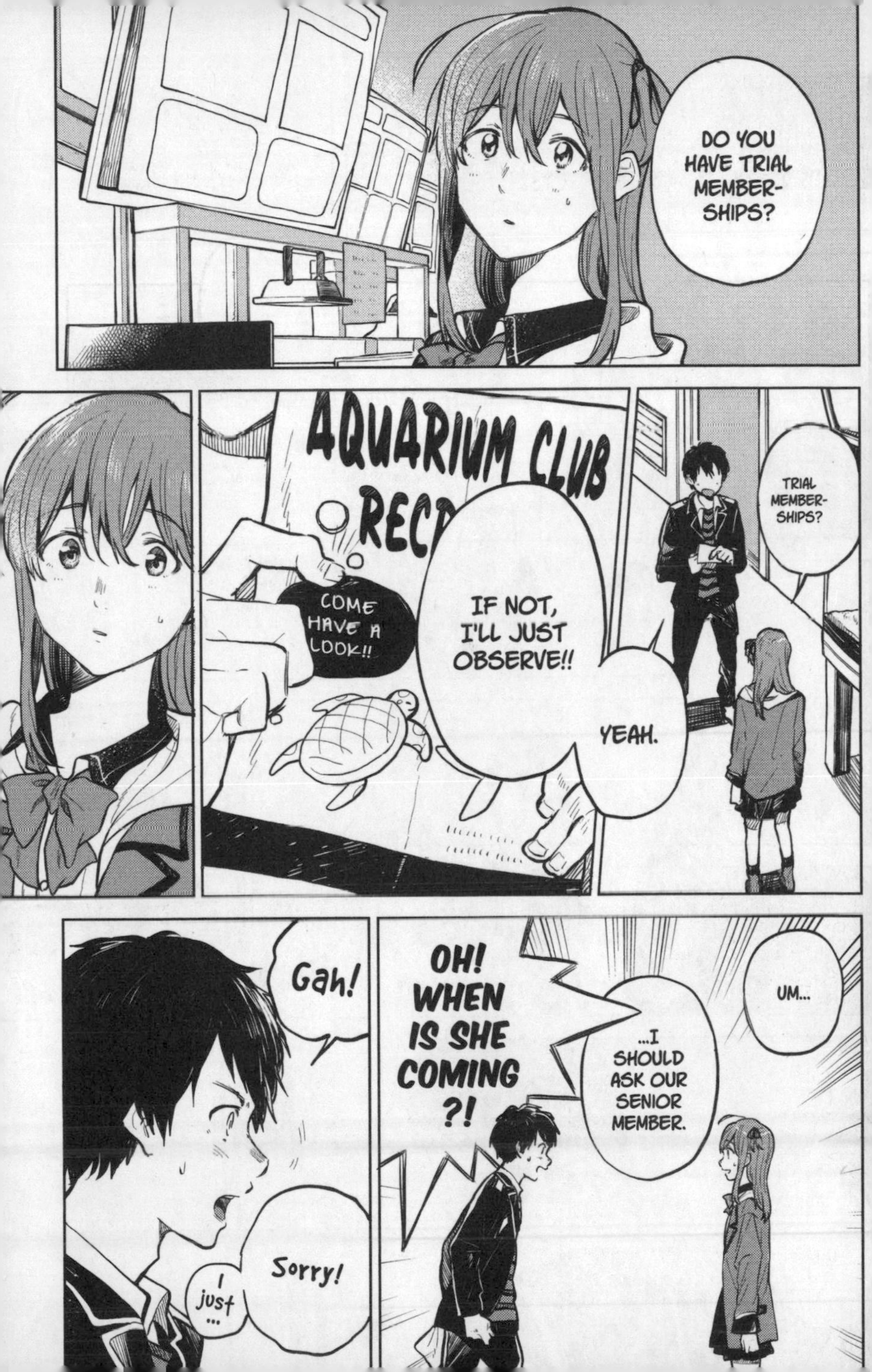
DO YOU HAVE TRIAL MEMBER-SHIPS?
TRIAL MEMBER-SHIPS?
AQUARIUM CLUB RECR
COME HAVE A LOOK!!
IF NOT, I'LL JUST OBSERVE!!
YEAH.
UM...
...I SHOULD ASK OUR SENIOR MEMBER.
OH! WHEN IS SHE COMING?!
Gah!
Sorry!
I just...

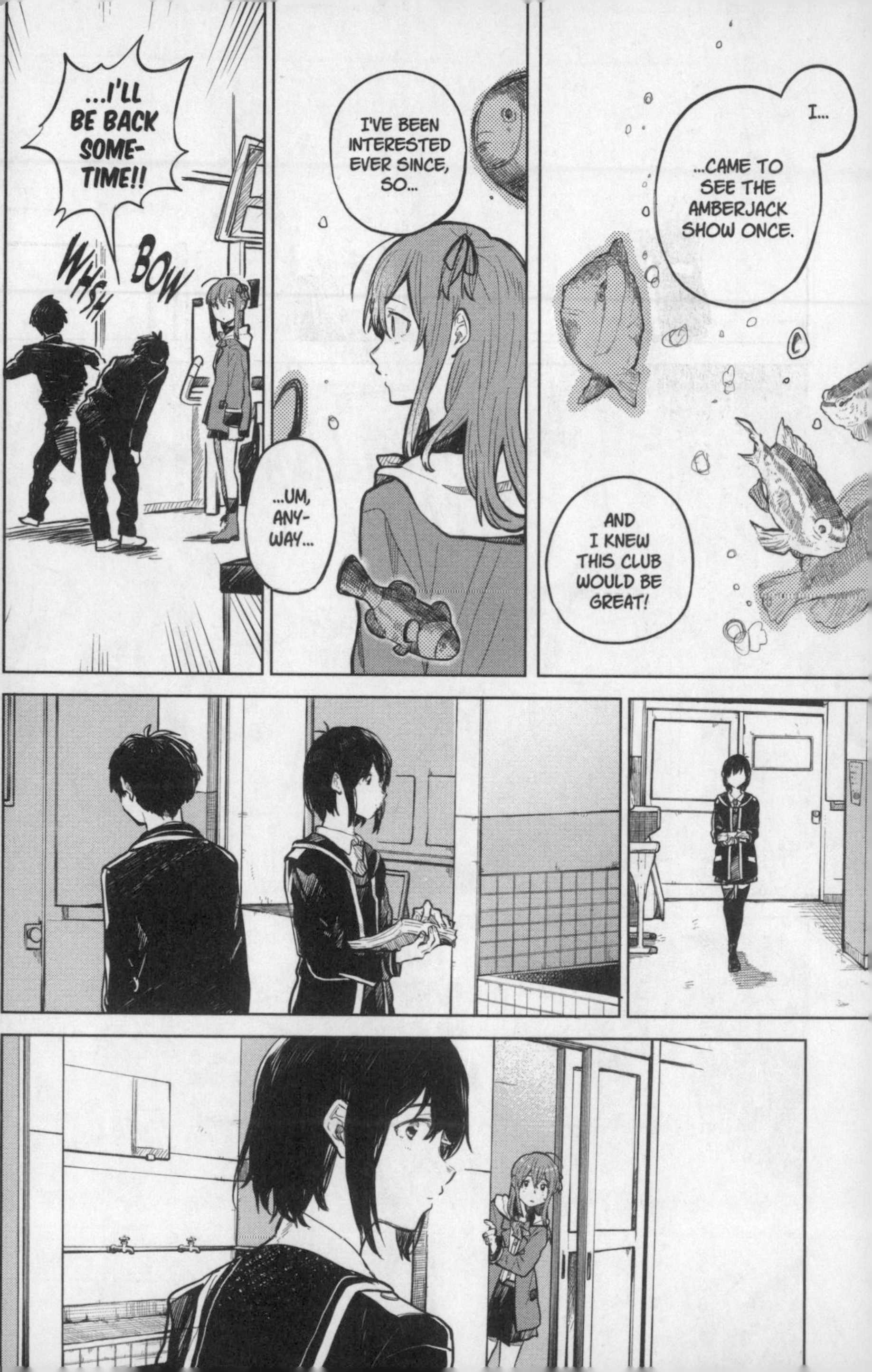
I...
...CAME TO SEE THE AMBERJACK SHOW ONCE.
AND I KNEW THIS CLUB WOULD BE GREAT!
I'VE BEEN INTERESTED EVER SINCE, SO...
...UM, ANY-WAY...
...I'LL BE BACK SOME-TIME!!
BOW
WHSH

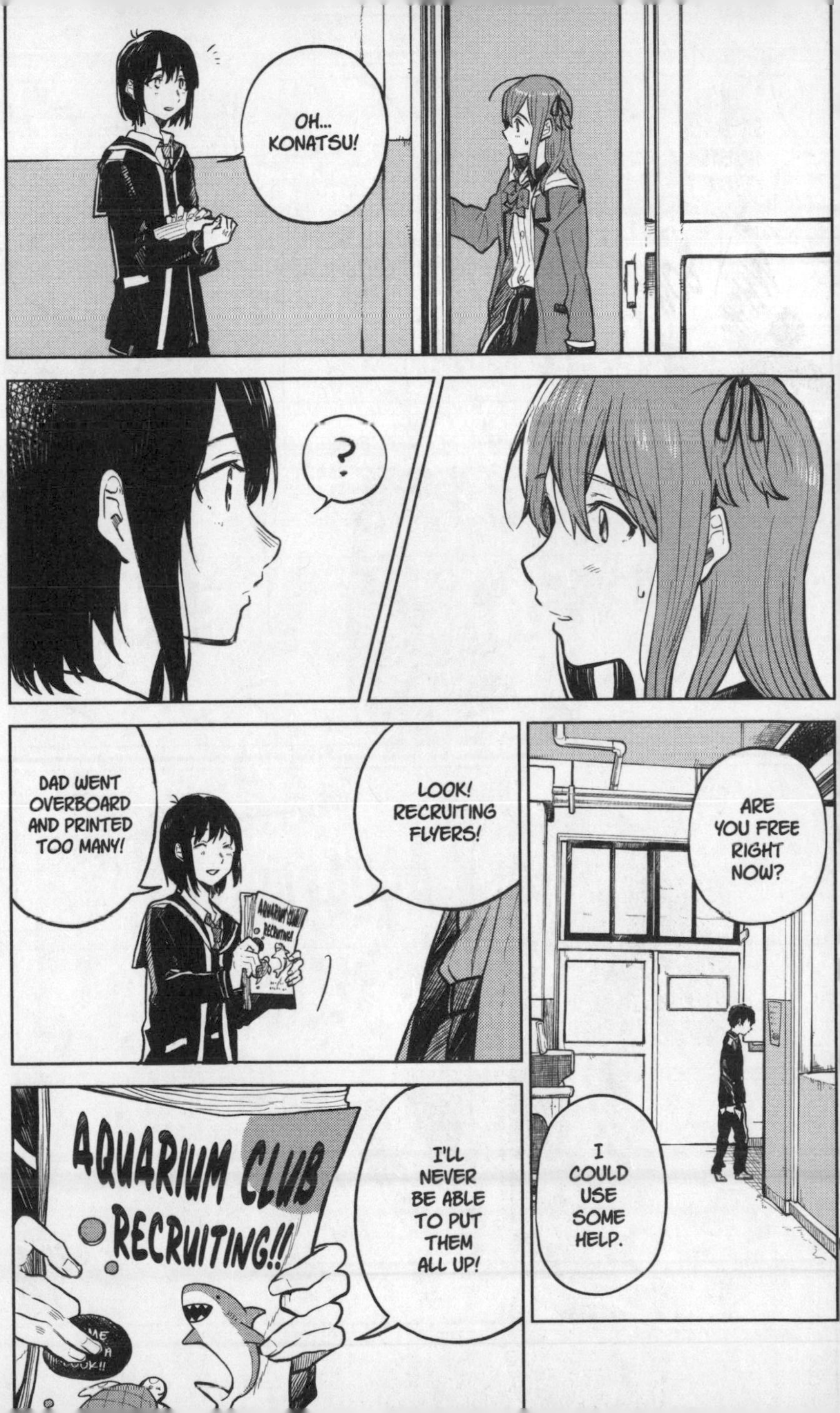
OH... KONATSU!
?
ARE YOU FREE RIGHT NOW?
I COULD USE SOME HELP.
LOOK! RECRUITING FLYERS!
DAD WENT OVERBOARD AND PRINTED TOO MANY!
I'LL NEVER BE ABLE TO PUT THEM ALL UP!
AQUARIUM CLUB RECRUITING!!

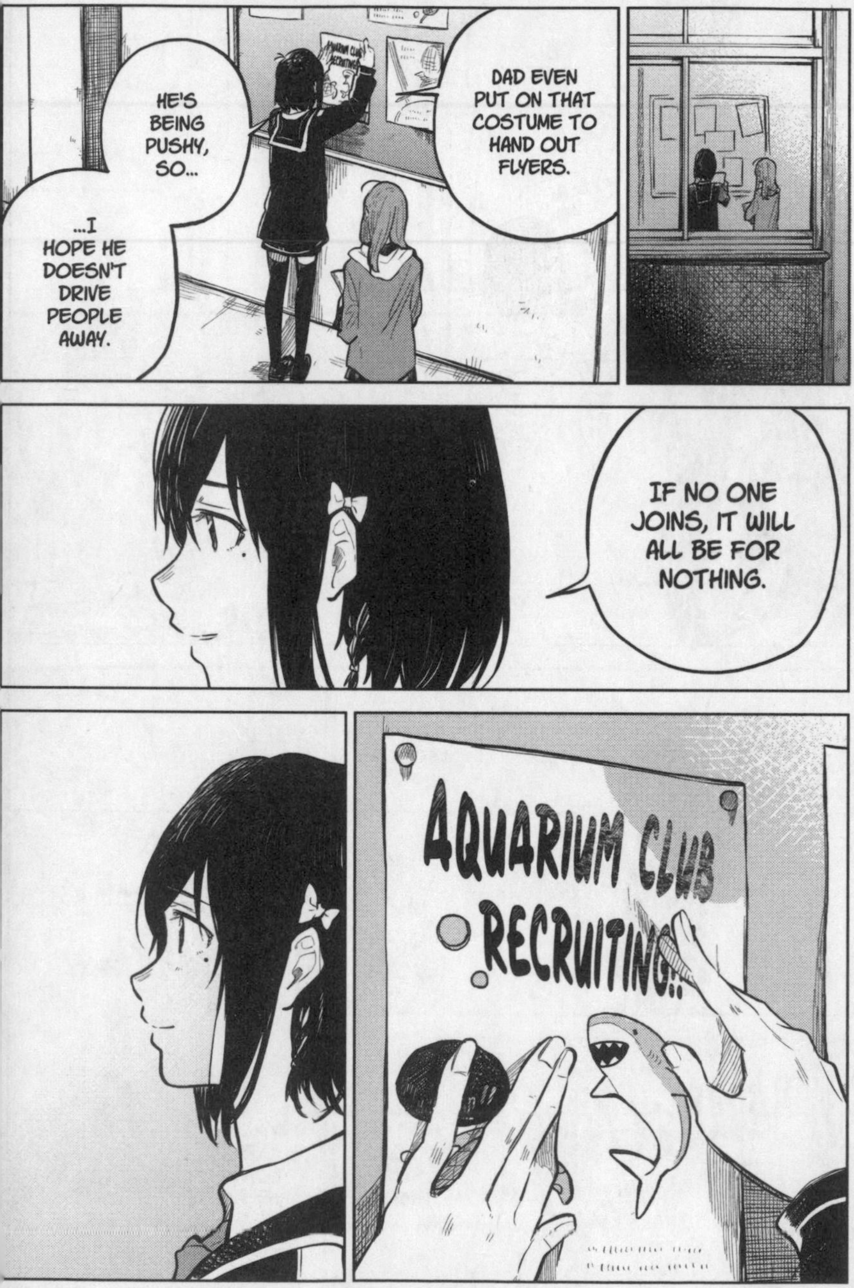
DAD EVEN PUT ON THAT COSTUME TO HAND OUT FLYERS.
HE'S BEING PUSHY, SO...
...I HOPE HE DOESN'T DRIVE PEOPLE AWAY.
IF NO ONE JOINS, IT WILL ALL BE FOR NOTHING.
AQUARIUM CLUB RECRUITING!!

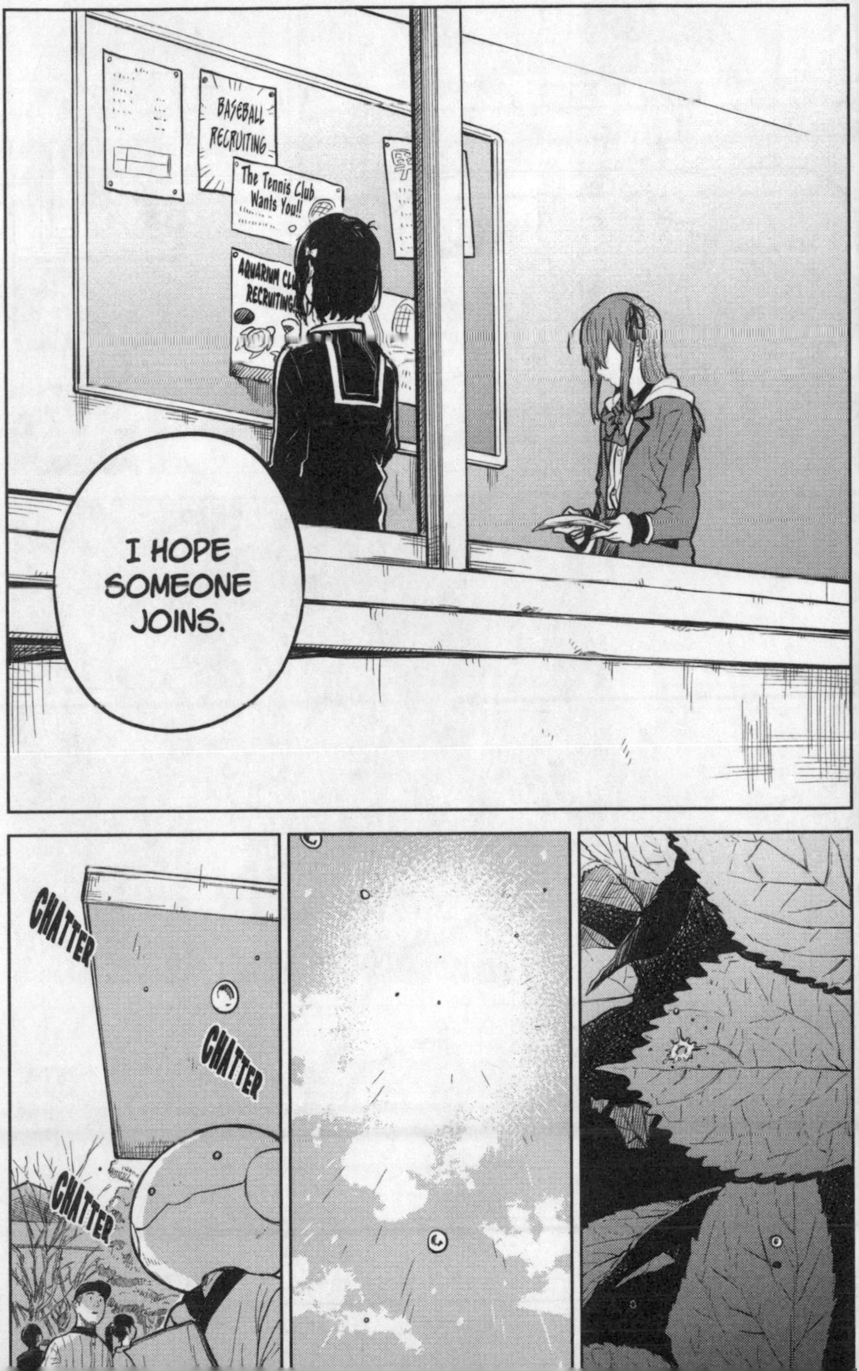
BASEBALL RECRUITING
The Tennis Club Wants You!!
I HOPE SOMEONE JOINS.
CHATTER
CHATTER
CHATTER

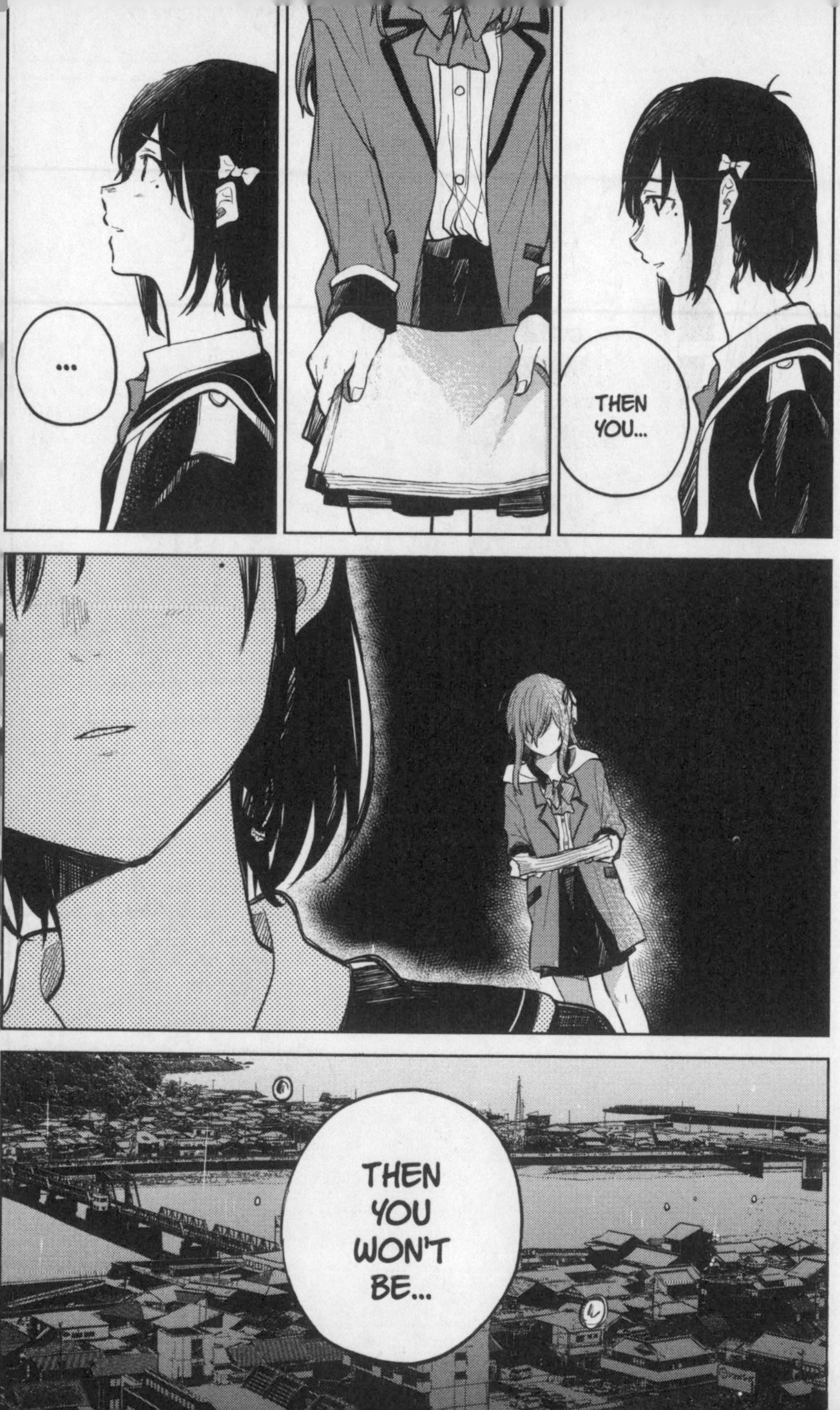
THEN YOU...
...
THEN YOU WON'T BE...

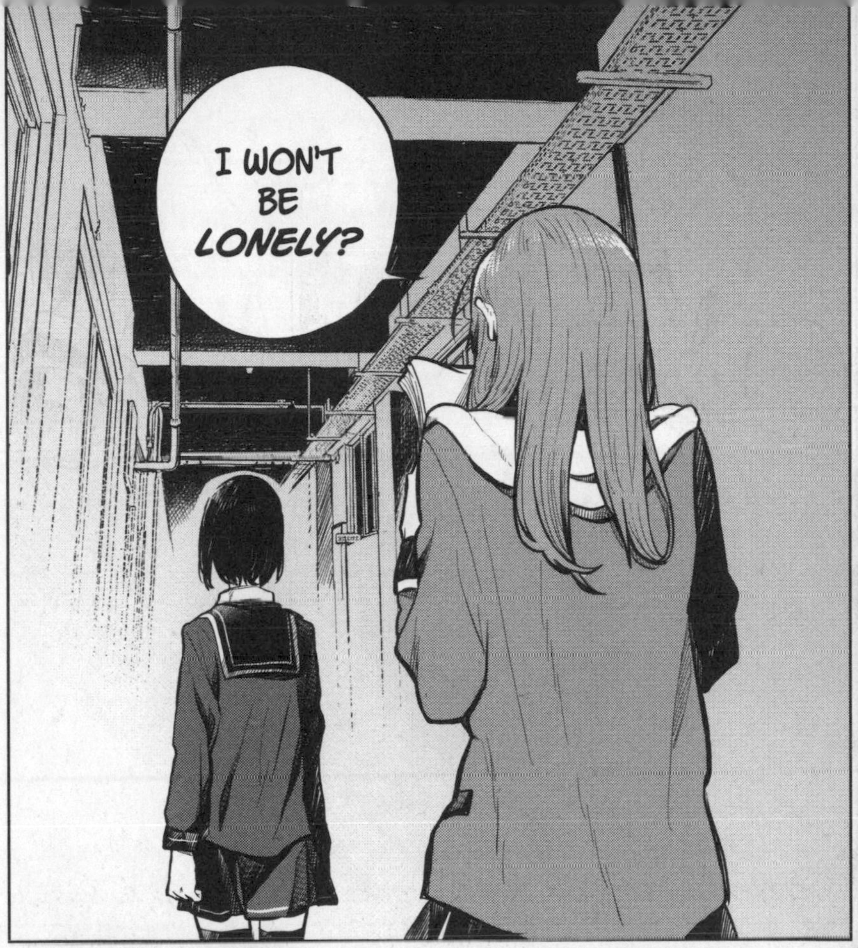
I WON'T BE LONELY?
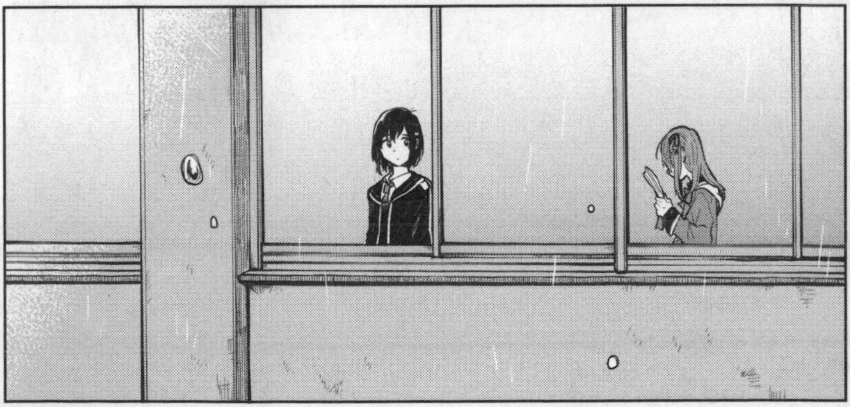

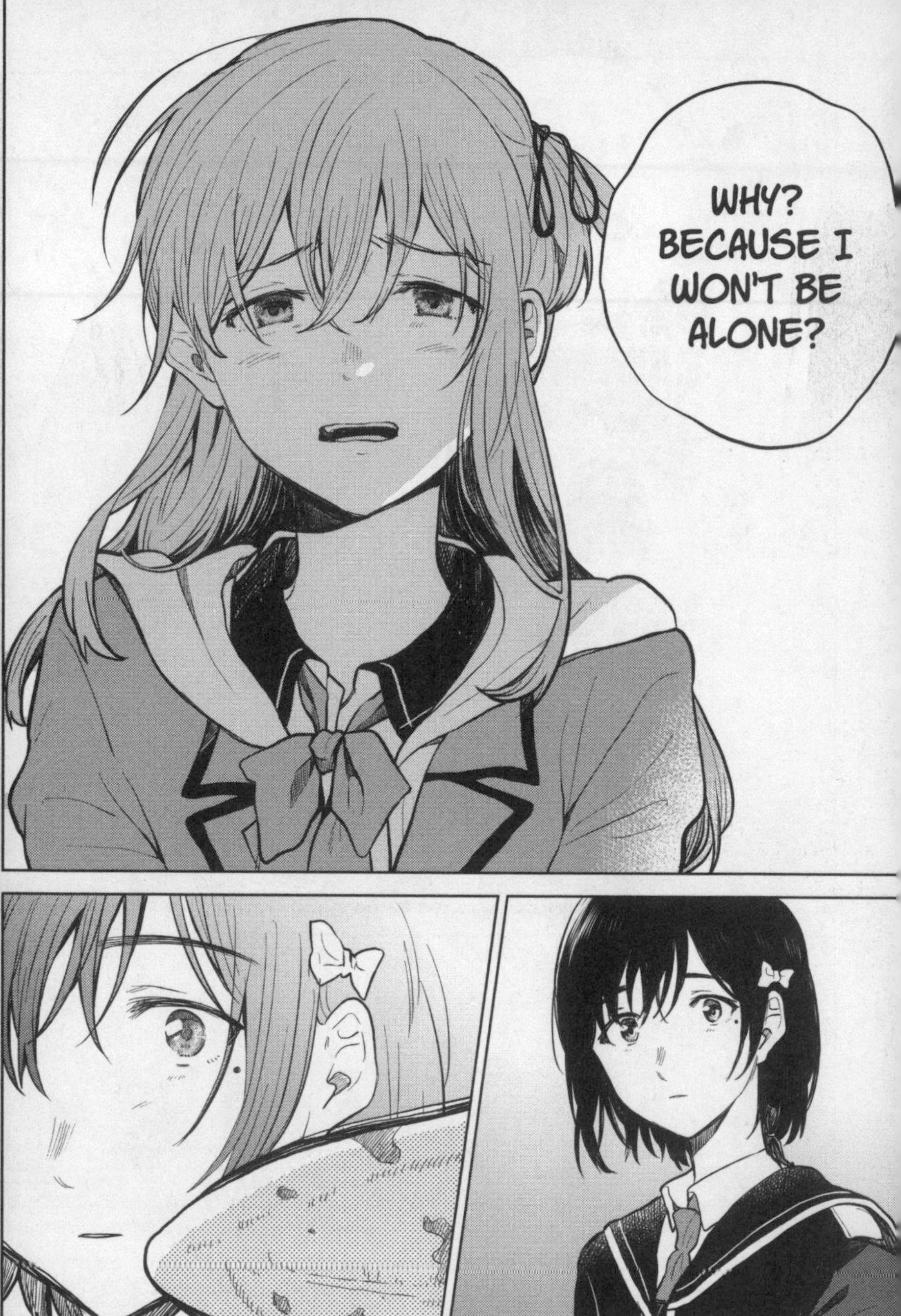
WHY? BECAUSE I WON'T BE ALONE?

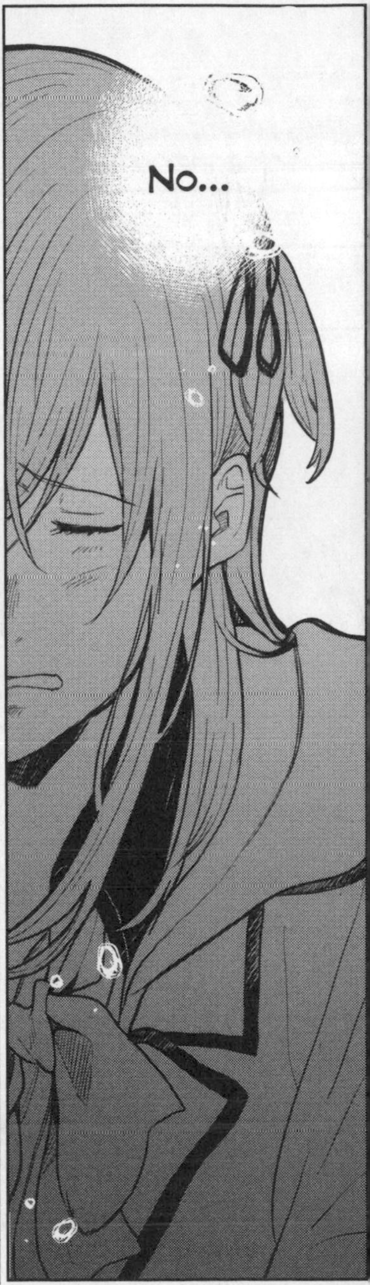
No...

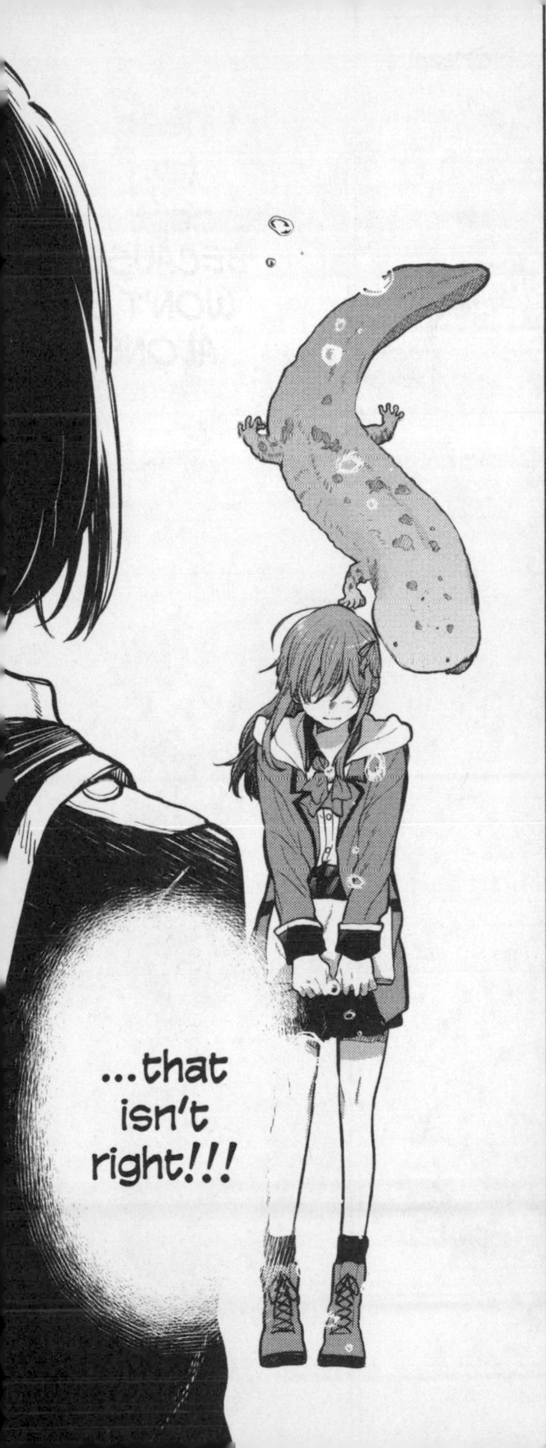
...that isn't right!!!

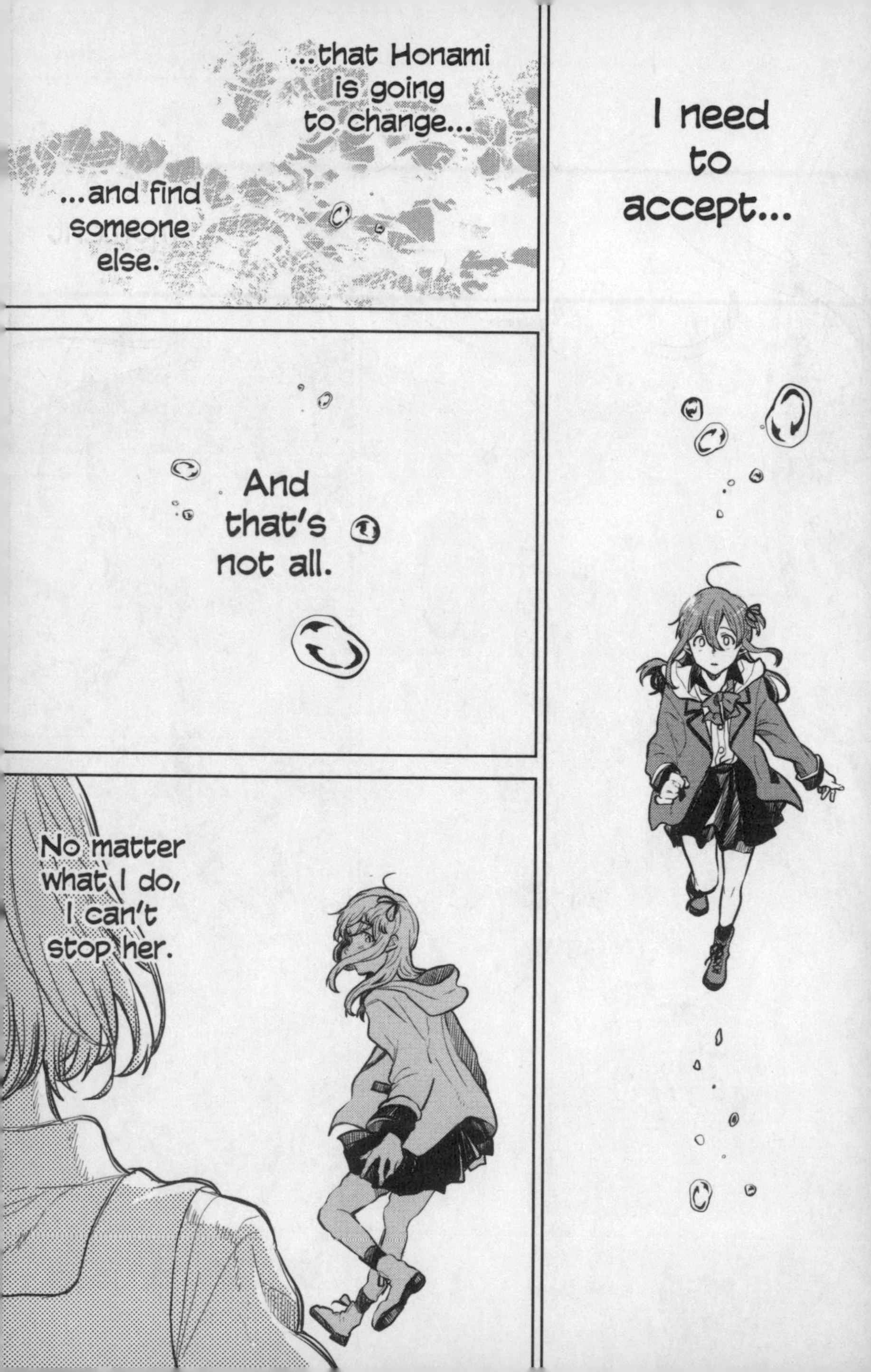
I need to accept...
...that Honami is going to change...
...and find someone else.
And that's not all.
No matter what I do, I can't stop her.

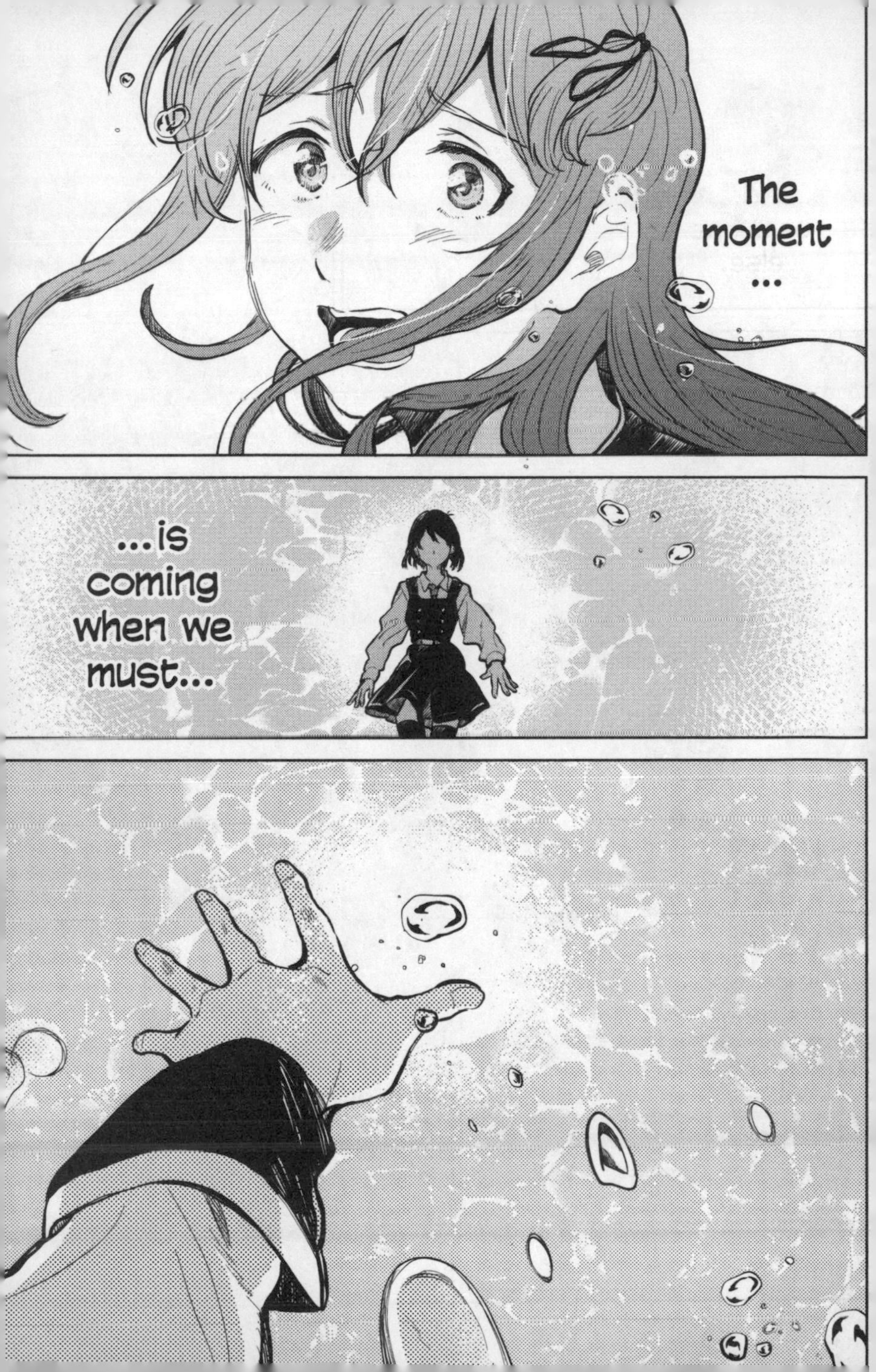
The moment ...
...is coming when we must...

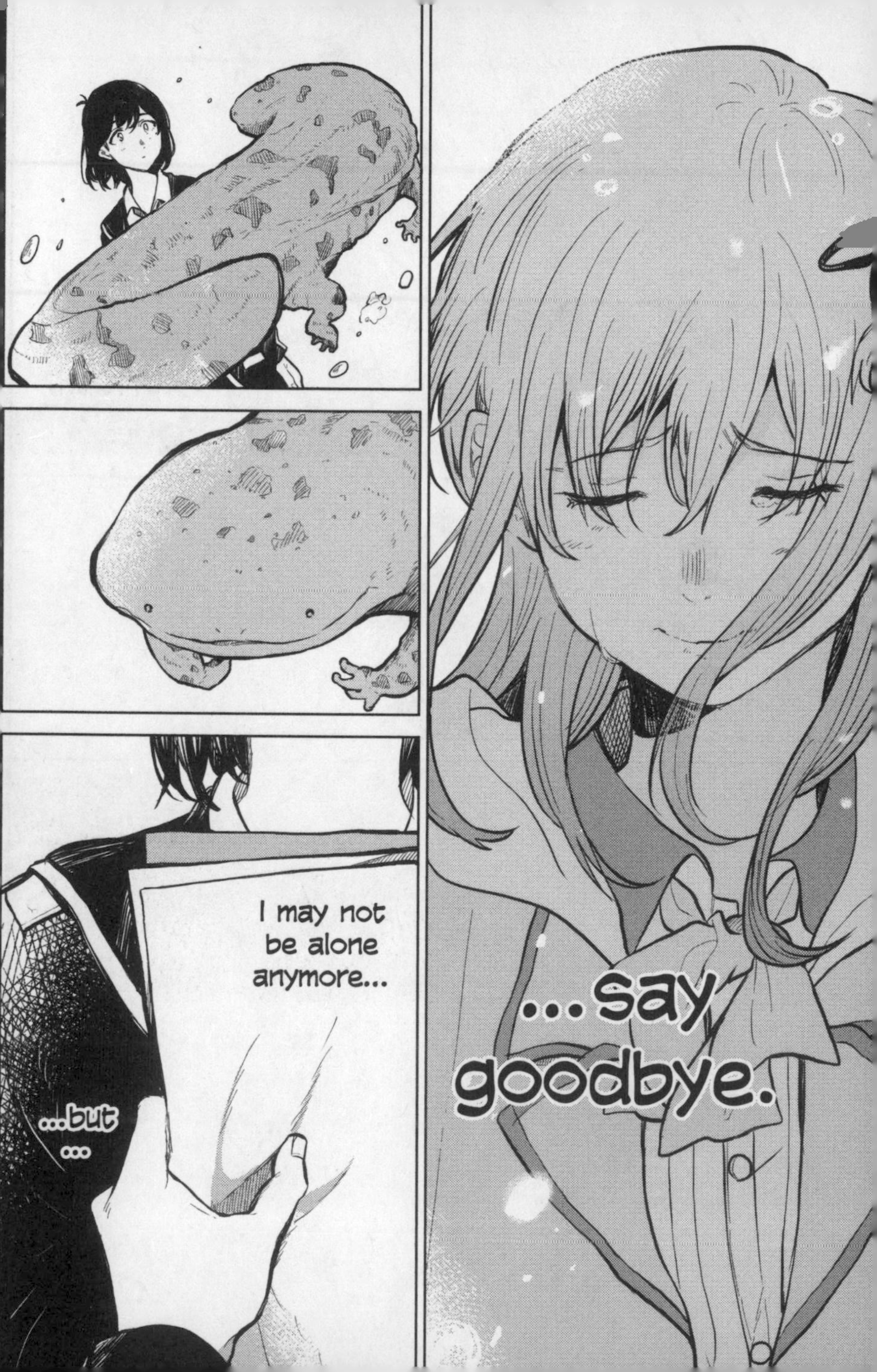
...say goodbye.
I may not be alone anymore...
...but ...

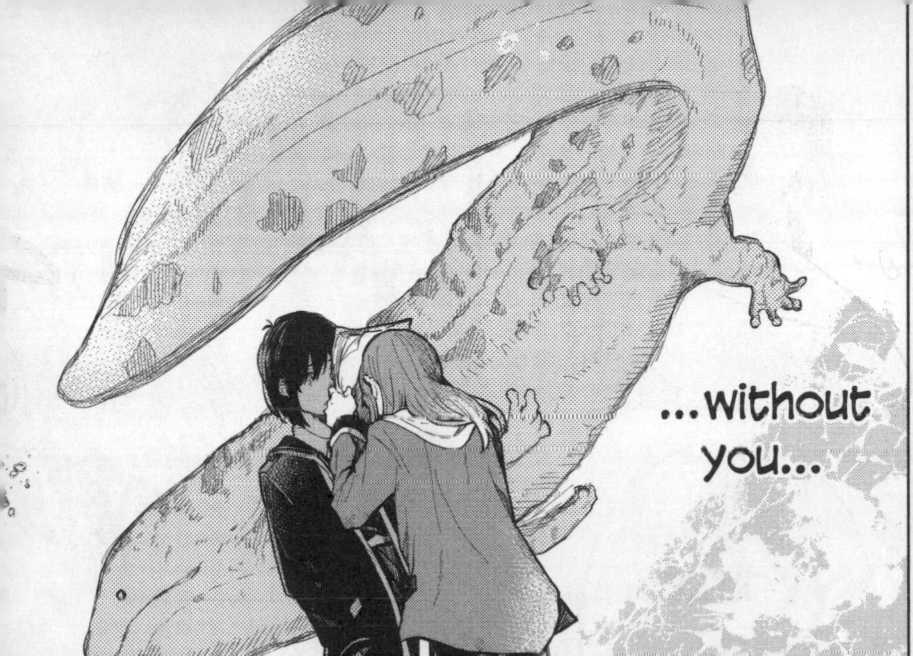
...without you...
...I...
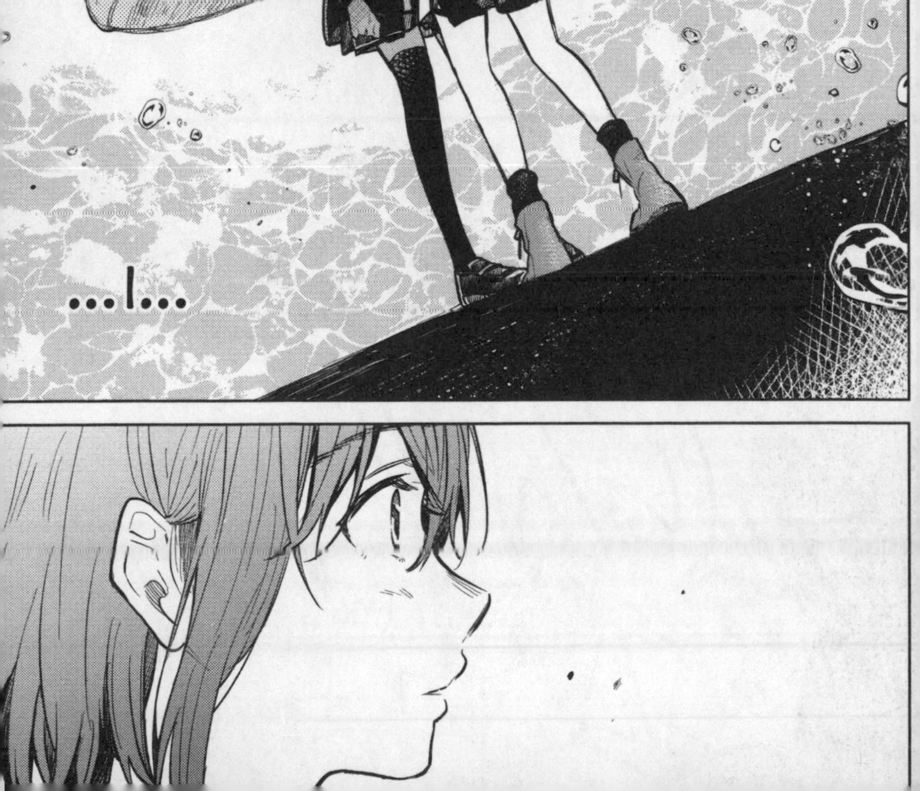

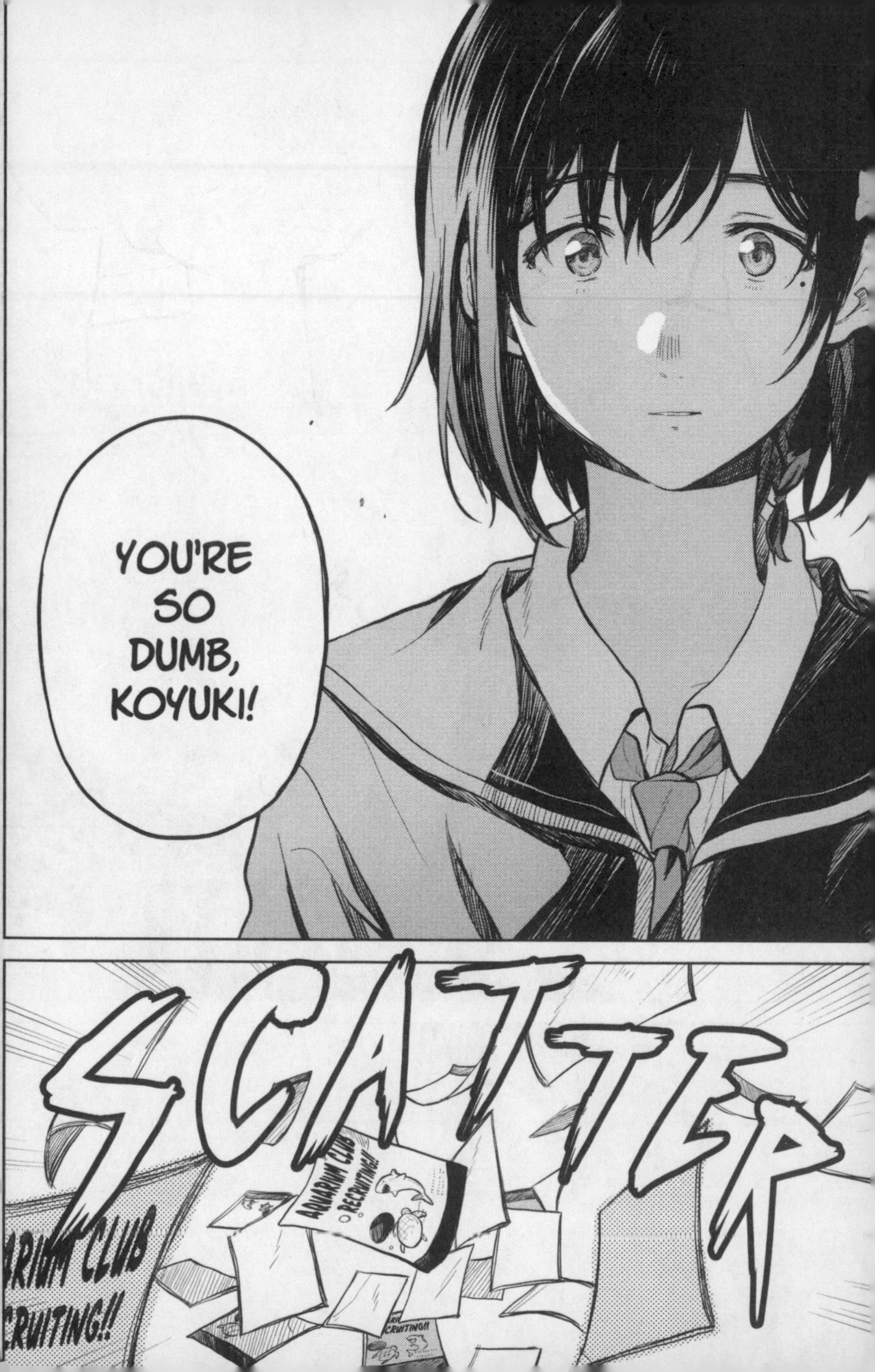
YOU'RE SO DUMB, KOYUKI!
SCATTER
AQUARIUM CLUB RECRUITING!!

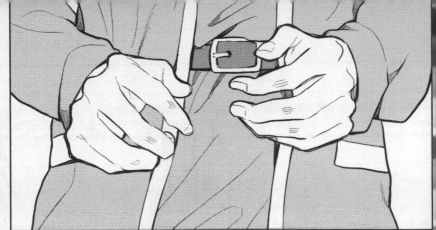

If we lose
what bound us
together...

...what
will be
left?

Continued in Volume 7!

A Tropical fish
Yearns for Snow
Vol. ⑥

Thank you for
reading!!

★ Special Thanks ★

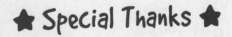

- My editor

Designer
- BALCoLONY: Kato-san

- My family, Hinata, Sakura

- Research cooperation:
Everyone in the Nagahama High School Aquarium club

- All the readers who support me

As always, thank you!!!

A TROPICAL FISH YEARNS FOR SNOW
Vol. 6
VIZ Media Edition

STORY AND ART BY
MAKOTO HAGINO

English Translation & Adaptation/John Werry
Touch-Up Art & Lettering/Eve Grandt
Design/Yukiko Whitley
Editor/Pancha Diaz

NETTAIGYO WA YUKI NI KOGARERU Vol. 6
©Makoto Hagino 2019
First published in Japan in 2019 by KADOKAWA CORPORATION, Tokyo.
English translation rights arranged with KADOKAWA CORPORATION, Tokyo.

Printed in Canada

Published by VIZ Media, LLC
P.O. Box 77010
San Francisco, CA 94107

10 9 8 7 6 5 4 3 2 1
First printing, February 2021

"Bloody" Mary, a vampire with a death wish, has spent the past 400 years chasing down a modern-day exorcist named Maria who is thought to have inherited "The Blood of Maria" and is the only one who can kill Mary. To Mary's dismay, Maria doesn't know how to kill vampires. Desperate to die, Mary agrees to become Maria's bodyguard until Maria can find a way to kill him.

Bloody†Mary

Story and Art by
akaza samamiya

A supernatural romance by the creator of *Kiss of the Rose Princess*!

The DEMON PRINCE of MOMOCHI HOUSE

Story & Art by
Aya Shouoto

On her sixteenth birthday, orphan Himari Momochi inherits her ancestral estate that she's never seen. Momochi House exists on the barrier between the human and spiritual realms, and Himari is meant to act as guardian between the two worlds. But on the day she moves in, she finds three handsome squatters already living in the house, and one seems to have already taken over her role!

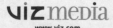

Kiss of the Rose Princess

Story and Art by
Aya Shouoto

Anise Yamamoto has been told that if she ever removes the rose choker given to her by her father, a terrible punishment will befall her. Unfortunately she loses that choker when a bat-like being named Ninufa falls from the sky and hits her. Ninufa gives Anise four cards representing four knights whom she can summon with a kiss. But now that she has these gorgeous men at her beck and call, what exactly is her quest?!

viz media
viz.com

KISS OF ROSE PRINCESS Volume 1 ©Aya SHOUOTO 2009

Queen's Quality

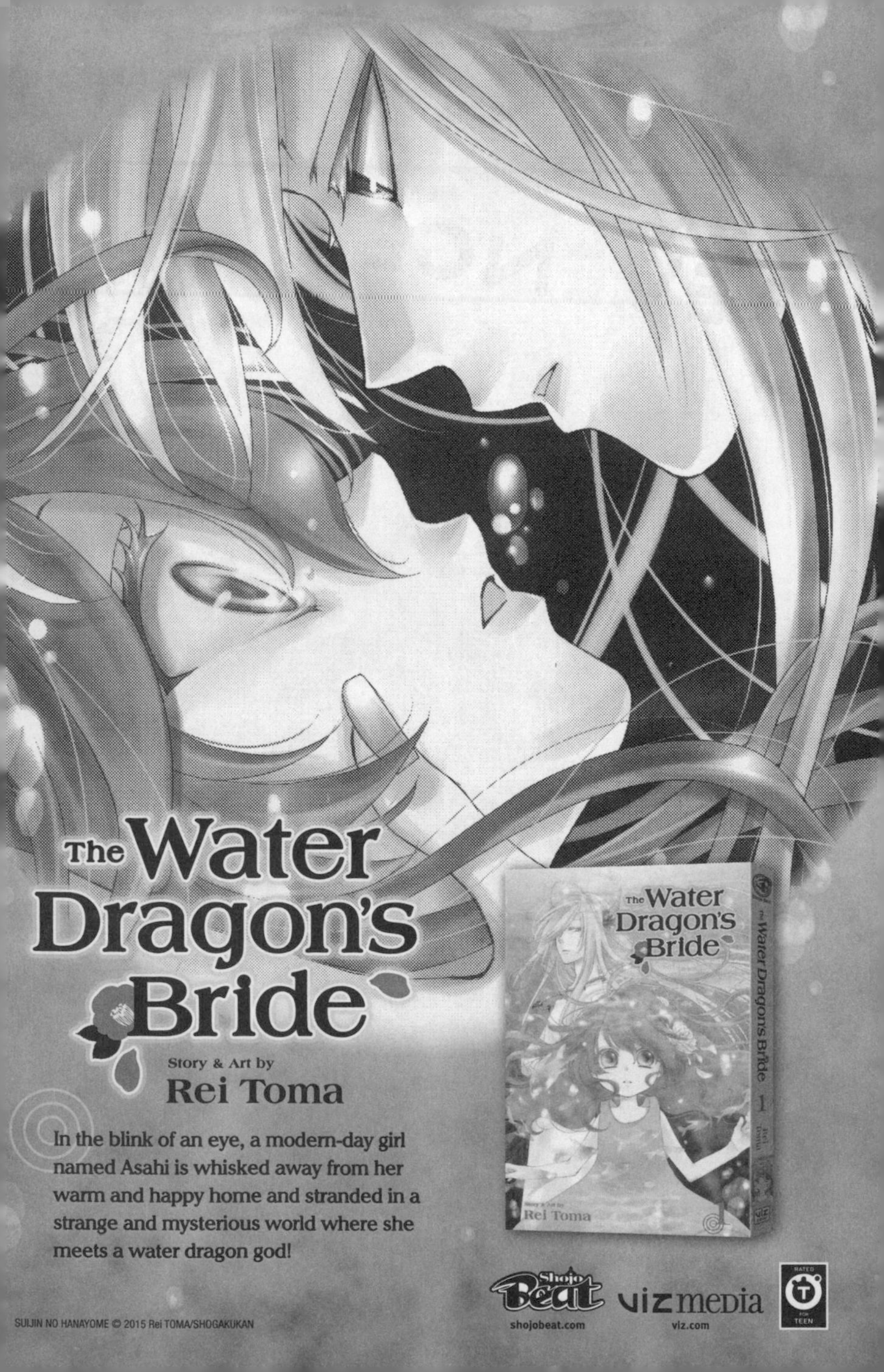
The Water Dragon's Bride
Story & Art by
Rei Toma
In the blink of an eye, a modern-day girl named Asahi is whisked away from her warm and happy home and stranded in a strange and mysterious world where she meets a water dragon god!
The Water Dragon's Bride
The Water Dragon's Bride 1
Rei Toma
Shojo Beat
shojobeat.com
viz media
viz.com
RATED T FOR TEEN
SUIJIN NO HANAYOME © 2015 Rei TOMA/SHOGAKUKAN